Soups

Soups

365 delicious and nutritious recipes

Beverly LeBlanc

METRO BOOKS
NEW YORK

Managing Editor: Grace Cheetham
Editors: Nicole Bator and Victoria Fernandez Salom
Managing Designer: Suzanne Tuhrim
Commissioned photography: William Lingwood
Food Stylist: Bridget Sargeson
Assistant Food Stylist: Jack Sargeson
Prop Stylist: Lucy Harvey
Production: Uzma Taj

Metro Books
122 Fifth Avenue
New York, NY 10011

ISBN: 978-1-4351-3261-0

Printed and bound in China

10 9 8 7 6 5 4 3 2 1

Notes

While every care has been taken in compiling the
recipes for this book, Duncan Baird Publishers, or
any other persons who have been involved in working
on this publication, cannot accept responsibility for
any errors or omissions, inadvertent or not, that may
be found in the recipes or text, nor for any problems
that may arise as a result of preparing one of these
recipes. If you are pregnant or breastfeeding or
have any special dietary requirements or medical
conditions, it is advisable to consult a medical
professional before following any of the recipes
contained in this book.

Notes on the recipes
Unless otherwise stated:
Use medium fruit and vegetables
Use fresh ingredients, including herbs and spices
Do not mix metric and imperial measurements
1 tsp. = 5ml 1 tbsp. = 15ml 1 cup = 240ml

The recipes in this book make 4–6 servings.

To PMOB

Author's Acknowledgments
*I would like to think this book is all my own work.
Many people, however, have contributed much
to the final product. First and foremost, I must thank
my husband Philip Back, who kept up with the
seemingly endless recipe testing and shopping. I also
want to thank my other recipe testers—Philip Clarke,
Henry Johnson, Moya Gibbon, Nicola Placidi, and
Susanna Tee.*

*The team at Duncan Baird have been a pleasure
to work with, especially Nicole Bator with her endless
patience and encouragement. She's an editor's editor.
Thank you also to Grace Cheetham for commissioning
this book, to Victoria Fernandez Salom for her
attentive, careful editing and good suggestions,
and to designer Suzanne Tuhrim and her team for
the attractive, contemporary look of the book.*

*Some of the most enjoyable times while writing
this book were the Masterclasses in Japanese,
Thai, and Italian soups from Shirley Booth, Amara
Nondha-Asa, and Nicola Placidi respectively.
Thank you all.*

*I am also especially appreciative to Paule Caillat
(promenadesgourmandes.com), Niru Gupta
(niruskitchen.com), Amelia Kay, and Susanna Tee
for their general help, and my cousin Kim Wright,
for ideas from her restaurant, Deli in the Rye,
in Jefferson, Ohio.*

*Big thank-yous also go to Rosemary Carr,
Bill Dean, David Healy, Jean Herbert, Victoria Keller,
Maggi McCormack, Norma MacMillan, Lee Rengos
(and her mom), Stefanie Roth, and Floren Shivitz.*

Contents

6 Introduction
10 Basic Recipes
15 Finishing Touches

16 CHAPTER 1
Vegetarian Soups

60 CHAPTER 2
Meat Soups

86 CHAPTER 3
Poultry Soups

112 CHAPTER 4
Seafood Soups

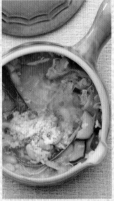

136 CHAPTER 5
Pasta, Legume & Grain
  Soups

170 CHAPTER 6
Big Bowl Soups

192 CHAPTER 7
Chilled Soups

214 Index

Introduction

It can be tempting to think of a book with three-hundred-and-sixty-five recipes as representing a recipe for every day of the year. Instead, I hope you will think of this collection as providing recipes for every occasion.

As I spent several cold, gray winter months totally immersed in reading about, thinking about, writing about, making and eating soups, I came to appreciate that the universal popularity of soups is due not only to their ability to satisfy, warm and comfort but also to their great versatility. The term "soup" embraces many different liquid-based dishes, from thin, clear, delicately flavored broths to big, substantial bowls of noodles, meat, poultry, or vegetables. They can be righteously health conscious or indulgent, filling feasts-in-a-bowl. As you work your way through this book, you will soon appreciate how much soups have going for them. Regardless of how much cooking experience you have or how much time is available, you can make delicious soups.

Supermarkets and fast-food outlets provide plenty of prepared soup options—many of which are very delicious and satisfying. But the case for making your own soups is unbeatable. From a financial perspective, you'll save lots of money. Many of the recipes in this book, for example, make four to six servings for less than the cost of a single pot of soup from my favorite sandwich store. And even today with virtually all ingredients available all year around, the old adage that cooking with the seasons saves you money still holds true. The vegetarian chapter offers plenty of scope for taking advantage of produce when it is most prolific and, therefore, least expensive. Soups can also transform leftovers into a second meal, cutting down on waste as well as your shopping bills. Making soups also gives you the opportunity to experiment with new ingredients. Galangal and hemp oil are two of the ingredients I hadn't used before, and they are now staples in my kitchen.

Somewhat ironically, it is the very versatility of soups that provided me with one of the biggest problems while planning this book: How much soup constitutes a serving? The different-size appetites of adults and children was one obvious factor to consider, let alone the different-size appetites of adults in different countries, as well as whether the soup is intended to be a meal in itself or just a light first course. I had many discussions with my editor about this, and the end result is that the recipes in this book "make 4 to 6 servings." This means you will get four adult-size bowls from a recipe with a little left for "seconds," or six child-size portions. After you've made a few recipes, you'll realize if you need to scale the quantities up or down for your requirements. The recipes in the Big Bowl Soups chapter, however, make soups that are meals in themselves, so when you make one of these recipes you won't have to do much other cooking.

I use the word "satisfying" often when talking about soup. That is because soup-making is a satisfying experience both in the kitchen and at the table. With the majority of recipes in this book, very little effort and very little expense produce a satisfying result that gives more than just the nutrients you need to get through the day. A bowl of soup with a hunk of good bread is an enjoyable meal to share or savor on your own. When I was planning this book I looked North, South, East, and West for inspiration. The result is a mix of international flavors I hope you enjoy exploring and making at home as much as I have enjoyed writing about.

THE TECHNIQUES
PUREEING & STRAINING SOUPS

Soups come in a variety of textures. Pureeing is a basic technique that gives many soups their smooth texture. Almost any soup can be pureed, but it is most suitable for vegetable, seafood, legume, and grain soups.

I've used a hand-held immersion blender for testing the recipes, but an upright blender, a food processor, or a hand-turned food mill, all do the job just as well. I choose the immersion blender for the simple reason it saves on washing up—you just put it in the saucepan and blend until the soup is the texture you desire and then wash the shaft and blade. If you are going to buy an immersion blender, choose a good-quality one with a strong motor. It is a false economy to buy a cheap one. The plus-point of using a food mill, however, is that it both purees and strains at the same time, which can save you time; the down side is that it can require large storage space.

When you use an immersion blender, make sure the pan or bowl you are pureeing in is deep enough that the hot soup doesn't splash out and burn you. These blenders are usually sold with a beaker that is suitable to use when you are pureeing a small quantity but impractical for pureeing a whole soup. And when you are pureeing soups in a blender or food processor, use a folded dish towel to hold the lid in place, otherwise the hot steam can force the lid off and burn you.

Many soups are ready to serve immediately after pureeing, but some are strained to obtain a smoother texture, or to remove small pieces of the ingredients, such as tomato skins and fennel fibers. Sometimes this is a matter of personal preference, but in some recipes it is essential, such as when the soup contains fish bones and scales.

I suggest a standard nonreactive metal strainer. Avoid using one with too fine a mesh; it simply takes too much time and elbow grease to work cooked vegetables through it. Instead, buy a less expensive one with larger holes in the mesh. If you prepare some of the fruit soups in the chilled soups chapter, or use any ingredient with a high acidic content, however, it is best to use a plastic mesh strainer so the acid doesn't react with metal and taint the flavor of your soup.

MAKING STOCK FOR SOUPS

Stock is the liquid that gives extra depth of flavor to many soups. It is perfectly possible to make delicious, satisfying bowls of soup without stock—the Italian Doctor's Bean & Spaghetti Soup and Aegean Red Mullet Soup are two great examples—but most soups rely on stock for their final taste.

The quality of the stock you use determines the quality of your soup, and deciding which stock to use in a recipe is arguably the most important step of the process. You have several options, ranging from homemade stock to prepared fresh stocks from the supermarket, concentrated liquid stocks to be diluted with water, concentrated gelled stocks and powders, and, finally, the ubiquitous bouillon cube. The choice is personal, but least suitable is the bouillon cube, because of its high salt content and metallic taste from the additives and preservatives. Using homemade stock, on the other hand, gives you total control over the quality of all the ingredients that go into your soup, but it is the most time-consuming option. This is why most recipes in this book specify a homemade stock or a ready-made option—the choice is yours.

Homemade stock is easily made by simmering meat, poultry, or seafood bones and trimmings, vegetables, and other flavorings, such as herbs and spices. The process extracts the colors, flavors, and nutrients from the ingredients, all of which are then transferred to your soup. Stock-making can be a very enjoyable time in the kitchen. It is an undemanding task, and the result is satisfying. Once you've made a large pot of stock, you can also use it to flavor sauces and stews.

The stock recipes in this book make larger quantities than specified in most recipes. This is because stock can easily be frozen in useful amounts, and once I've decided to make a homemade stock, I make enough to freeze several portions. If you don't have much freezer space, let the stock simmer, uncovered, for longer until half the quantity is left, which will have a concentrated flavor. Then let this rich, intensely flavored liquid cool completely and freeze it in ice-cube trays. Use each cube straight from the freezer adding enough cold water to complete 1 cup of the stock specified in the recipe.

Skimming soups and stocks—Stocks cook largely unattended, but your attention is most required toward the beginning of the process. As meat, seafood, or poultry bones and trimmings are slowly heated to just below the boil, impurities are released and a gray foam appears on the surface. Use a large metal spoon, a slotted spoon, or a round, perforated skimmer to remove this foam from the surface and discard it before adding the other flavoring ingredients. Take care not to remove too much of the liquid. Skimming can be a slow process, taking up to 30 minutes, but after you've finished this step you can leave the stock to gently simmer on its own. Legumes and vegetables also give off impurities while they simmer, but it isn't necessary to remove these. After you puree legumes, however, the thick layer of foam that rises to the surface should be removed.

- 'Take stock and then make stock' is sage advice. Stock-making is a good way to utilize vegetables past their prime but not yet ready for the trash can. Vegetable trimmings, such as mushrooms trimmings, tomato skins, and onion skins (which give stock a richer, golden brown color) are also excellent additions. Do not, however, include rotten or moldy vegetables.
- Do not include potatoes in stocks because they make the liquid cloudy.
- Always break or chop bones before using them in stock. This gives the finished stock a slightly gelatinous texture that elevates soups made with homemade stock above ready-made versions.
- Trimmings from flat fish, such as flounder or sole, make excellent stock. Ask a fishmonger for these. They will likely be free or very inexpensive. Do not, however, include bones, heads, or trimmings from oily fish in fish stocks.
- If you don't have time to make stock after roasting a chicken or large piece of beef on the bone, freeze the bones. Also freeze fish heads, bones, and trimmings, and shrimp shells.
- Never let a fish, poultry, or meat stock boil, or it will turn cloudy.
- Take care not to overseason stocks or your soup will be too salty. Use only a small amount of salt at the beginning of cooking to draw out the flavor of the other ingredients. Do not season it again. This is especially important if you intend to reduce the stock before freezing.
- Add the flavoring ingredients, such as chopped vegetables, herbs, and spices, after you have finished skimming the surface.

Storing Stocks—Stocks are ready to use immediately after cooking. Alternatively, leave them to cool completely, then cover and refrigerate for up to two days or freeze for up to six months.

COOKING DRIED LEGUMES FOR SOUPS

Legumes cover a broad category of ingredients that includes many dried beans, lentils, and peas. (Peanuts are technically a legume but because they can be eaten raw they are classed as nuts.) Legumes are a good source of vegetarian protein, they are inexpensive and add different textures to soups. Red split lentils and split peas, for example, cook to soft purees; rich lima beans and cannellini beans easily fall apart; chickpeas become soft and creamy but never loose their shape.

Legumes feature prominently in recipes from all over the world, especially the Mediterranean, the Middle East, India, and Southeast Asia. Dried legumes make useful ingredients to have in the cupboard. If you put them in an airtight container they will keep indefinitely; however, the older they are, the tougher their skins become and the longer they take to become tender.

Most legumes are available already cooked in cans, which saves time, but transforming the inedible dried legume into a tender soup ingredient is a simple process. Lentils and split peas can be added straight to the pan to cook with the other ingredients, but most other legumes require overnight soaking in cold water. When you are ready to cook, drain and rinse the legumes, then put them in a saucepan with four times their volume of water, or the amount of liquid specified in a recipe. Cover and bring to a boil, then lower the heat and simmer for the time specified in the recipe.

Dried mung beans, red kidney beans, and soybeans, however, require an initial vigorous boiling for 10 minutes to destroy toxins they contain. Discard the soaking water, cover with fresh water and bring to a boil, then boil, uncovered, 10 minutes. After that follow the simmering time specified in the recipe.

Some recipes cook the soaked and drained legumes as part of the soup-making process, while others specify adding cooked legumes, in which case the canned variety makes a suitable substitute.

Quick Cooking Technique—If you forget to soak dried legumes overnight, put them in a saucepan and cover with plenty of water. Cover and bring to a boil, then boil 10 minutes, set aside, still covered, and let stand 2 hours. Drain and rinse the legumes and continue with the recipe. (Soybeans, mung beans, and red kidney beans do not need additional cooking after this.)

OTHER SIMPLE TECHNIQUES FOR SOUP MAKERS

Adding flavor with cheese rinds and ham hocks—Take a tip from canny Italian cooks and use natural hard cheese rinds to add an intense but subtle flavor to slowly simmered soups. Simply scrub off any markings, wrap the rinds in plastic wrap and freeze them until you're ready to use them. Add a piece of rind to your soup and simmer for anywhere from 10 minutes to several hours—the longer the rind simmers the more likely it is to totally dissolve into the soup. When ready to serve the soup, use a slotted spoon to fish out the soft rind and either discard it or cut it into small pieces to sprinkle over the soup. Parmesan, pecorino, sharp cheddar, and any other hard cheese with a natural rind all work well. Do not use wax-covered rinds.

The end of a prosciutto or Serrano ham also contains lots of flavor, even if not enough meat for cooks to bother slicing. They can be used to add "meatiness" to soups without the expense. You will find these at meat counters and delis, and often you will be given them for free. After gentle simmering, remove the meat from the rind and any bones and finely shred it over the soup.

One word of caution, however: most cheese rinds and ham heels are salty, so don't add extra salt until the end of the cooking process.

Making a bouquet garni—A bouquet garni is a bundle of fresh herbs, and often other ingredients, used to flavor soups. Tying the herbs together in a "bouquet" with a piece of string makes it easier to remove them at the end of cooking. Always lightly crush the herb stems with the back of a knife because they usually have more flavor than the leaves. If you don't have fresh herbs available, put dried herbs in a square of cheesecloth and use a piece of string to secure it closed.

Chargrilling, roasting, and peeling bell peppers—To chargrill bell peppers, heat the broiler to high and lightly grease the broiler rack. Halve the peppers lengthwise and remove the cores and seeds. Put the peppers, cut-sides down, on the broiler rack and broil until lightly charred. Transfer to a bowl, cover with a clean, folded dish towel and let cool, then peel.

To roast bell peppers, heat the oven to 425°F. Prepare the bell peppers as above, put them in a baking dish, and roast 40 to 45 minutes until lightly charred. Remove from the oven and peel as above.

Peeling, seeding, and grating tomatoes—Cut a small cross in the bottom of each tomato, using a sharp knife, put them in a heatproof bowl, and cover with boiling water. Let stand 2 to 3 minutes, then drain. Use a small knife to peel off the skins and discard them. To seed the tomato, cut it in half lengthwise and use a small spoon to scoop out the core and seeds.

A quicker way to peel tomatoes is to grate them on the coarse side of a box grater, pressing firmly, and then discard the skin and core. The disadvantage, however, is that the tomato pulp will also include all the seeds.

Toasting nuts and seeds—Toasting gives nuts and seeds a deeper flavor. Heat a dry skillet over high heat until hot. Arrange the nuts or seeds in a single layer and dry-fry, stirring continuously, about 2 minutes until they start turning golden and you can smell the aroma. Immediately transfer to a plate to prevent them from overbrowning or burning. Toasted nuts and seeds can be stored in airtight containers in a dark cupboard up to 3 months.

Judicious seasoning—You can always add extra seasoning, but it's very difficult to mask the flavor of too much seasoning. Most of the recipes in this book season at an initial stage of cooking to draw out the flavors of the ingredients. Do this very lightly because you will adjust the salt and pepper again before serving. Always cook potatoes and rice in salted water, but season dried legumes after cooking so the salt doesn't draw out the moisture acquired during soaking.

If you accidentally overseason a soup, add a little sugar or, if suitable, boil a peeled and chopped floury potato in the soup. Taste soups before pureeing— you can always discard half the stock and replace it with fresh, unseasoned stock for a less salty taste, if necessary, at that point.

Basic Recipes

Beef Stock

MAKES about 4 quarts   **PREPARATION TIME** 5 minutes, plus overnight chilling (optional)
COOKING TIME 7 hours

5½ pounds beef bones, chopped into
   large pieces (ask the butcher
   to do this)
3 large unpeeled onions, quartered
3 carrots, coarsely chopped
2 celery ribs, coarsely chopped
4 large garlic cloves, lightly crushed

1 bouquet garni made with 1 bay leaf
   and several parsley and thyme
   sprigs tied together
1 tbsp tomato paste
12 black peppercorns, lightly crushed
a small pinch of salt

1   Heat the oven to 450°F. Put the bones in a heavy-bottomed roasting pan and roast
   50 minutes to 1 hour until brown all over.
2   Stir in the onions, carrots, and celery and roast 30 to 40 minutes longer until the
   vegetables are very tender and brown. Watch closely so they do not burn.
3   Transfer the bones and vegetables to a heavy-bottomed stockpot and add
   4½ quarts water. Bring to a boil, uncovered, over high heat, skimming the surface.
   This can take up to 20 minutes. When the foam stops rising, add the remaining
   ingredients, reduce the heat to very low (use a heat diffuser if you have one),
   and simmer, covered, 5 hours. Do not let the liquid boil. Skim the surface
   occasionally, if necessary.
4   Very carefully strain the stock through a cheesecloth-lined colander into a large
   bowl and discard all the flavorings. Skim any fat from the surface and use the stock
   immediately. Alternatively, leave the stock to cool completely, then cover and
   refrigerate overnight. The next day, use a large metal spoon to "scrape" the
   congealed fat off the surface. Once cool, the stock will be lightly gelled.
   See page 8 for storage information.

Rich Chicken Stock

MAKES about 2 quarts   **PREPARATION TIME** 15 minutes, plus overnight chilling (optional)
COOKING TIME 2½ hours

2 celery ribs, with the leaves,
   coarsely chopped
1 large carrot, peeled and chopped
1 large onion, peeled but left whole

1 bouquet garni made with 2 bay
   leaves and several parsley and
   thyme sprigs tied together
1 chicken, about 3½ pounds
6 black peppercorns, lightly crushed
a small pinch of salt

1   Put the celery, carrot, onion, bouquet garni, and 6 cups water in a saucepan.
   Cover and bring to a boil. Skim the surface, then add the remaining ingredients
   and 4½ cups water, or enough to cover the chicken. Bring the liquid to just below
   the boil, skimming the surface as necessary. Do not let the liquid boil.
2   Reduce the heat to very low (use a heat diffuser if you have one), cover,
   and simmer 1¾ to 2¼ hours until the meat almost falls off the bones.
3   Remove the chicken from the pot and set aside for another use. Strain the stock
   into a bowl and discard the flavorings. Skim the fat from the surface and use the
   stock immediately. Alternatively, leave the stock to cool completely, then cover
   and refrigerate overnight. The next day, use a large metal spoon to "scrape" the
   congealed fat off the surface. Once cooled, it will be slightly gelled. See page 8
   for storage information.

Chicken Stock

MAKES about 2 quarts   **PREPARATION TIME** 10 minutes   **COOKING TIME** 3¼ hours

carcass and bones of 1 cooked
   chicken, or 2 pounds chicken
   bones, chopped
1 celery rib, with the leaves, sliced
1 bouquet garni made with 1 bay leaf
   and several parsley and thyme
   sprigs tied together

1 carrot, peeled and chopped
6 whole black peppercorns,
   slightly crushed
a small pinch of salt

1   Put the chicken and 9 cups water in a heavy-bottomed stockpot. Bring to just below
    the boil, skimming the surface as necessary. When the foam stops rising, add the
    remaining ingredients, reduce the heat to low (use a heat diffuser if you have one),
    and simmer, covered, 3 hours. Do not let the liquid boil. Skim the surface
    occasionally, if necessary.
2   Very carefully strain the stock into a bowl and discard the flavorings. Skim any fat
    from the surface and use the stock immediately, or leave it to cool completely.
    Once cool it will be slightly gelled. See page 8 for storage information.

GAME STOCK Prepare and store as Chicken Stock but use the bones from roast
partridge, pheasant, or other game birds, reduce the water to 6 cups and reduce the
simmering time to 1½ hours. Makes about 5 cups.

TURKEY STOCK Prepare and store as Chicken Stock but use broken turkey bones.

Fish Stock

MAKES about 2 quarts   **PREPARATION TIME** 10 minutes   **COOKING TIME** 30 minutes

2¼ pounds fish heads, bones, and
   trimmings from white fish, such
   as sole, halibut, or flounder, rinsed
   to remove any blood and chopped
⅔ cup dry white wine
1 carrot, peeled and thinly sliced
1 large leek, thinly sliced and rinsed
1 onion, thinly sliced

1 bouquet garni made with
   several parsley sprigs and
   1 bay leaf tied together
½ lemon, thinly sliced
1 tsp black peppercorns,
   lightly crushed
a small pinch of salt

1   Put the fish heads, bones, and trimmings in a large saucepan. Add the wine and
    2 quarts water, cover, and bring to just below the boil, skimming the surface
    as necessary. Add the remaining ingredients, reduce the heat to low, and simmer,
    covered, 20 minutes.
2   Very carefully strain the stock into a bowl and discard the flavorings. The stock
    is now ready to use. See page 8 for storage information.

Vegetable Stock

MAKES about 2 quarts   PREPARATION TIME 20 minutes   COOKING TIME 45 minutes

2 tbsp olive, hemp, or sunflower oil
4 celery ribs, with the leaves,
 chopped
2 carrots, coarsely chopped
2 onions, finely chopped
1 leek, sliced and rinsed
6 garlic cloves

1 small tomato, chopped
1 bouquet garni made with 1 bay leaf
 and several parsley and thyme
 sprigs tied together
12 black peppercorns, lightly crushed
½ tsp salt
onion skins (optional)

1 Heat the oil in a saucepan over medium heat. Stir in the celery, carrots, onions, and leek, then reduce the heat to very low and cook, covered, 10 to 15 minutes until very soft. Add the remaining ingredients and 2¼ quarts water, then cover and bring to a boil. Skim the surface, then lower the heat and simmer, partially covered, 20 minutes.
2 Very carefully strain the stock into a bowl and discard all the flavorings. The stock is now ready to use. See page 8 for storage information.

Dashi

MAKES about 5 cups   PREPARATION TIME 5 minutes, plus 30 minutes soaking
COOKING TIME 20 minutes

10-inch piece of dried kombu   ⅔ cup bonito flakes

1 Put the kombu and 6 cups water in a saucepan and let soak 30 minutes.
2 Bring to a boil, uncovered. As soon as it boils, skim the surface, then add the bonito flakes. Skim the surface again, if necessary. Lower the heat and simmer, uncovered, 10 minutes.
3 Strain the dashi into a large bowl and use immediately. Alternatively, let cool, then store in the refrigerator up to 2 days. Freezing isn't recommended for more than 2 weeks as it will lose much of its flavor.

VEGETARIAN DASHI Omit the bonito (fish) flakes in the above recipe. Instead soak 8 dried shiitake mushrooms in 6 cups hot water for at least 30 minutes. Put the mushrooms and the soaking liquid in a saucepan. Add the kombu and let soak 30 minutes. Slowly bring to a boil, uncovered. As soon as it boils, skim the surface, then lower the heat and simmer, uncovered, 10 minutes. Strain through a cheesecloth-lined strainer, and use the dashi as above.

INSTANT DASHI Many good-quality powdered dashi mixes are sold in Japanese food stores, whole food stores, and on the internet. Follow the instructions on the package, which is usually to dissolve 2 teaspoons powder in 5½ cups water. If you are a vegetarian, check the labeling closely, or ask an assistant (it will be written in Japanese), because instant dashi is made with and without bonito (fish flakes).

Beef Consommé

MAKES 5½ cups   PREPARATION TIME 15 minutes, plus 30 minutes chilling
and slow straining   COOKING TIME 50 minutes

10 ounces ground shin of beef
1 carrot, peeled and diced
1 celery rib, finely chopped
1 leek, thinly sliced and rinsed
3 egg whites

1 tbsp tomato paste
6½ cups Beef Stock (see page 10)
    or ready-made stock
salt and freshly ground black pepper

1   Mix the ground beef, carrot, celery, and leek together in a large bowl. Beat the egg
    whites in another bowl until frothy, then add the tomato paste and mix together.
    Add this mixture to the ground beef and stir until well combined. Cover and chill
    30 minutes.
2   Pour the stock into a saucepan, add the chilled egg-white mixture, and season with
    salt and pepper. Slowly bring to a boil, stirring. As soon as the liquid is frothy, stop
    stirring. When the liquid comes to a boil, immediately reduce the heat to very low
    (use a heat diffuser if you have one) and simmer, without stirring, 30 to 40 minutes
    until a solid crust forms.
3   Meanwhile, line a strainer with cheesecloth and set it over a large bowl. Gently
    poke a hole in the middle of the crust to see if the stock is sparkling clear. When
    the stock is clear, increase the hole in the crust and use a ladle to transfer the stock
    to the cheesecloth-lined strainer: do not push it through or squeeze the cloth. Once
    strained, the consommé is ready to use. Alternatively, let cool completely, cover
    and refrigerate up to 2 days or freeze up to 6 months.

CHICKEN CONSOMMÉ Make as above but replace the stock with Chicken Stock
(see page 11) and the meat with very finely chopped or ground boneless, skinless
chicken legs.

Parsley Dumplings

MAKES 12 or 24 dumplings   PREPARATION TIME 15 minutes
COOKING TIME 15 minutes

2 cups panko (Japanese
    breadcrumbs), crushed, or fine
    dried breadcrumbs
½ cup self-rising flour, plus extra
    for shaping
½ teaspoon baking powder
3 tablespoons finely chopped parsley
    or dill

¼ teaspoon salt
1 egg, beaten
3 tablespoons milk
1 tablespoons olive or hemp oil,
    plus extra if making the dumplings
    in advance

1   These can be shaped and cooked up to a day in advance. Mix the panko, flour,
    baking powder, parsley, and salt in a bowl. Make a well in the middle, add the egg,
    milk, and oil, then gradually beat together until a thick, crumbly dough forms. Lightly
    flour your hands and divide the mixture into 12 or 24 equal pieces. Roll into balls,
    taking care to smooth over all cracks and openings or the dumplings will become
    soggy. Meanwhile, bring a large saucepan of water to a boil.
2   Lower the heat so the water is just boiling. Add the dumplings and cook until they
    rise to the surface, then cook 10 minutes longer.
3   Use a slotted spoon to transfer the dumplings to the soup and finish as instructed
    in the recipe. If not using at once, transfer the dumplings to a plate and pour off any
    excess water. Let cool, then very lightly coat with oil to prevent them from sticking
    together, cover with plastic wrap, and refrigerate up to 1 day. Reheat in gently
    simmering soup.

POLENTA DUMPLINGS Make as above, but replace the panko or breadcrumbs with
2 cups medium polenta.

Croutes

MAKES 4 to 6   PREPARATION TIME 5 minutes   COOKING TIME 6 minutes

4 to 6 slices of French bread, sliced
   on the diagonal

olive or hemp oil (optional)

1   Heat the broiler to high and position the broiler rack 4 inches from the heat. Put the
    bread slices on the rack and toast 2 to 3 minutes on each side until golden brown
    and crisp. Brush with oil, if desired, and serve warm or at room temperature.
    The croutes can be stored in an airtight container up to 3 days.

    GRUYÈRE OR CHEDDAR CROUTES Follow the recipe as above. Brush with oil, then
    sprinkle with grated cheese and broil until the cheese melts and is very lightly tinged.
    Serve warm.

    GOAT CHEESE CROUTES Follow the recipe as above, but use a basil- or herb-flavored
    olive oil, if you like. After brushing with oil, sprinkle with crumbled or chopped rindless
    goat cheese and broil until the cheese melts. Serve warm.

Croutons

MAKES 4 to 6 servings   PREPARATION TIME 5 minutes   COOKING TIME 4 to 6 minutes

1 tablespoon butter
olive or hemp oil

2 slices of day-old sliced white or
   wholewheat bread, cut into ¼- to
   ½-inch cubes, with crusts removed

1   Croutons are best made just before serving, so they are added to the soup hot,
    however, they can be made up to two days in advance and stored in an airtight
    container. Line a plate with several layers of paper towels and set aside. Melt the
    butter with the oil in a large skillet over medium-high heat. Working in batches,
    if necessary, add the bread cubes and fry, stirring, 2 to 3 minutes until golden
    brown and crisp.
2   Remove the croutons from the pan and drain on the paper. If not using
    immediately, let cool completely, then store in an airtight container and reheat
    in a low oven before serving.

    DILL CROUTONS Prepare as above but toss with 2 tablespoons chopped dill
    while draining.

    GARLIC CROUTONS Use garlic-flavored olive or sunflower oil in the recipe above.

Rouille

MAKES about ¾ cup; enough for 4 to 6 servings   PREPARATION TIME 10 minutes,
plus chargrilling the pepper

1 cup fresh breadcrumbs
2 large garlic cloves, chopped
1 large red bell pepper, chargrilled
   (see page 9), peeled, seeded, and
   chopped, or 1 roasted red pepper
   in oil, drained and chopped

½ cup extra-virgin olive oil, plus
   extra as needed
salt and cayenne pepper

1   Put the breadcrumbs, garlic, and red pepper in a beaker or deep bowl and blend until
    a thick paste forms. Add half the olive oil, season with salt and cayenne pepper,
    and blend again. Slowly add the remaining oil, while blending, until a thick sauce
    forms. Cover and refrigerate until required. Store in the refrigerator up to 2 days.

Finishing Touches

Spiced Seeds—Heat a dry skillet over high heat. Add ¼ cup each pumpkin and sunflower seeds, 3 tablespoons sesame seeds, and 1 teaspoon fennel seeds, if desired, and cook, stirring, 2 to 3 minutes until the seeds pop and start to color. Immediately sprinkle 1 tablespoon light soy sauce or tamari soy sauce over and stir until it evaporates. Transfer the seeds to a bowl and stir in ½ teaspoon celery seed. Store in an airtight container.

Dukkah—Heat a dry skillet over high heat until hot. Add 4 tablespoons blanched hazelnuts or shelled pistachios and dry-fry, stirring, 2 to 3 minutes until golden brown. Immediately transfer to a mortar or mini food processor. Lightly crush the nuts, then put them in a bowl. Reheat the pan. One at a time dry-fry 2 teaspoons crushed coriander seeds, 2 teaspoons sesame seeds, and 1 teaspoon cumin seeds, then add them to the nuts. Add ½ teaspoon dried thyme, season with salt, and stir. Store in an airtight container for up to 1 week.

Roasted Pumpkin Seeds—Heat the oven to 350°F. Dissolve ½ tablespoon salt in 2 cups water in a saucepan over high heat. Add ½ cup pumpkin seeds and bring to a boil. Immediately lower the heat and simmer 10 minutes. Drain and pat dry. Toss the seeds with 1 teaspoon olive or hemp oil and spread out on a baking sheet. Roast 10 to 20 minutes, stirring frequently, until golden brown. Meanwhile, line a plate with several layers of paper towels. Transfer the seeds onto the paper and let cool. Store in a sealed container in the refrigerator up to 2 weeks.

Chili Bon-Bon—This piquant sherry is great for adding to curried soups as an alternative to hot pepper sauce. Fill a jar with medium or dry sherry and add 2 or 3 slit and seeded bird's-eye chilies. Seal the jar, shake, and set aside at least 5 days before using. This keeps indefinitely in the refrigerator or a cupboard.

Crushed Herb Oils—Make this with basil, cilantro, or parsley leaves. Put a handful of leaves in a mortar with a pinch of salt and use a pestle to pound them to a paste. Slowly add olive or hemp oil, 1 tablespoon at a time, pounding until the oil is thick and fragrant. Adjust the salt and add pepper, if necessary. These are best freshly made; they will keep in a covered container in the refrigerator 1 day, but they loose their vibrant flavor and the color dulls.

Chilies in Vinegar—This traditional accompaniment to Thai soups is usually made just before you start cooking the soup. Thickly slice long red chillies (not bird's-eye chilies unless you like very hot food), seed if desired, and put them in a small bowl. Cover with distilled white vinegar and set aside until required.

Crisp-Fried Garlic—This is a traditional accompaniment to Thai soups that is usually prepared just before you start cooking the soup. Put 5 coarsely chopped garlic cloves in 2 inches olive, hemp, or sunflower oil in a small saucepan over a high heat. Heat just until the garlic is golden brown and small bubbles appear around the edge, then immediately pour into a heatproof bowl and set aside to cool. Serve in little bowls for diners to add to their soup at the table, if they like.

Crisp-Fried Shallots—Cut 2 or 3 shallots in half lengthwise, then thinly slice. Heat the oil and cook as above. If you remove the shallots and oil from the heat before they turn brown they will not overcook in the residual heat and burn. When cool, use a slotted spoon to remove the shallots from the oil and drain on paper towels. Store in an airtight container up to 2 days and use to sprinkle over soups.

Crunchy Mixed Seeds—Mix together 4 tablespoons each sunflower and pumpkin seeds, 2 tablespoons white sesame seeds, 1 tablespoon hemp seeds, and 1 tablespoon lightly cracked flaxseed. Cover and refrigerate up to 1 month.

Goji Berry & Seed Mix—Mix together 4 tablespoons goji berries, 2 tablespoons sunflower seeds, 1 tablespoon hemp seeds, 1 tablespoon sesame seeds, and ½ teaspoon celery seeds. Cover and refrigerate up to 2 weeks.

CHAPTER 1

VEGETARIAN SOUPS

This chapter is a cornucopia of recipes that celebrate the seasons. Brighten up the bleak winter months with hearty, colorful soups such as Golden Carrot & Sesame Soup and Thai-Style Pumpkin Soup. Usher in spring with Sorrel & Spinach Soup, which has an intense green color and fresh flavor to help shake off the winter blues. Then, when warmer temperatures make you long for lighter choices, enjoy Summer Tomato Soup with Noodles and Rich Pepper & Orange Soup. You'll also find four seasonal farmers' market soups here, one for each season, designed to make the most of the produce that is at its best then.

Obviously, none of the soups in this chapter contain meat or meat stock, but many do contain dairy products. If you are following a vegan diet, though, you'll still find plenty of choices. Arame & Tofu Soup, Mushroom Miso Soup, and Vegetable "Spaghetti" Soup are just a few of the tempting options. See also the Pasta, Legume & Grain and Chilled Soups chapters for more vegetarian and vegan recipes.

001 Artichoke Soup with Red Pepper Swirl

PREPARATION TIME 25 minutes, plus making the stock   COOKING TIME 1 hour

3 large globe artichokes, about
  1½ pounds, well rinsed between
  the leaves and stems trimmed off
2 onions, coarsely chopped
4 large garlic cloves, halved
1 lemon, sliced
5½ cups Vegetable Stock
  (see page 12) or ready-made stock
¼ cup sour cream
salt and ground white pepper
chopped dill, to serve (optional)

RED PEPPER SWIRL
1 roasted red pepper in olive oil,
  drained and chopped
a pinch of salt
1 tablespoon extra-virgin olive oil
  or hemp oil, or the oil from the
  jarred pepper, plus extra
  as needed
½ teaspoon balsamic vinegar

1   Put the artichokes, onions, garlic, lemon, and stock in a large saucepan. Top up
    with enough water to cover the artichokes, if necessary. Cover and bring to a boil,
    then lower the heat and simmer, partially covered, 40 to 45 minutes until the
    artichokes are tender and a leaf pulls out easily. Strain the artichokes, reserving
    the cooking liquid, onions and garlic, and set aside until cool enough to handle.
2   Meanwhile, make the red pepper swirl. Blend the red pepper and salt until smooth.
    Blend in the oil, then the vinegar and adjust the salt. Add extra oil for a smoother
    puree, if you like, then set aside until required.
3   Pull away the leaves from the artichokes and set aside. Use a small spoon to scoop
    out the hairy chokes from the bottom of the artichokes and discard, taking care not
    to scoop into the heart. Chop the artichoke hearts and put them in a deep bowl
    or blender. Scrape the flesh away from the leaves and add it to the bowl. Add the
    onions, garlic and 2 cups cooking liquid and blend until smooth.
4   Return the soup to the rinsed-out pan and slowly stir in enough of the remaining
    cooking liquid to achieve the preferred consistency. (Any leftover cooking liquid
    can be used in other recipes or frozen for up to 6 months.)
5   Season with salt and white pepper and reheat. Stir in the sour cream and adjust
    the salt and pepper, if necessary. Heat the red pepper swirl in a separate pan over
    low heat. Serve immediately, drizzled with the red pepper swirl and sprinkled with
    dill, if using.

002 Annie's Herbed Peas-in-a-Pod Soup

PREPARATION TIME 15 minutes, plus making the stock   COOKING TIME 20 minutes

5½ cups Vegetable Stock
  (see page 12) or ready-made stock
6½ cups shelled fresh peas, with the
  pods reserved
1 tablespoon butter
1½ tablespoons olive or hemp oil
2 hearts of lettuces, cored and
  leaves shredded

2 tablespoons snipped chives
1 tablespoon chopped mint leaves,
  plus extra, very finely chopped,
  to serve
½ cup crème fraîche or sour cream
salt and ground white pepper
borage or marigold petals, to serve
  (optional)

1   Put the stock and pea pods in a saucepan. Cover and bring to a boil, then lower the
    heat and simmer 10 minutes, or until the pods are very tender. Blend until smooth,
    then strain into a large bowl and work the pods through the strainer into the bowl,
    rubbing back and forth with a spoon and scraping the bottom of the strainer.
    Set the stock aside.
2   Wash and dry the pan, then melt the butter with the oil over medium heat.
    Add the peas, lettuce, chives, and mint and reduce the heat to low. Cook, covered,
    5 minutes. Slowly stir in the stock and season with salt and white pepper. Bring
    to a boil, uncovered, then turn off the heat and blend until smooth. Stir in the crème
    fraîche and adjust the salt and pepper, if necessary, then serve sprinkled with extra
    mint and flower petals, if using.

003 Two-Bean Soup

PREPARATION TIME 15 minutes, plus soaking the beans overnight
COOKING TIME 1¾ hours

1 cup dried flageolet beans
1 garlic clove, chopped
1 bouquet garni made with the
  leaves from the celery, 1 bay leaf,
  1 parsley sprig, and 1 thyme sprig,
  tied together
½ onion, chopped

½ celery rib, left whole
4½ cups chopped green beans
salt and freshly ground black pepper
finely grated zest of 1 lemon,
  to serve
chopped dill, to serve

1 Put the dried beans in a bowl, cover with water, and let soak overnight, then drain. Transfer to a saucepan, add 6 cups water, cover, and bring to a boil. Add the garlic and bouquet garni, lower the heat and simmer, covered, 1¼ hours.

2 Add the green beans and season with salt and pepper. Return the water to a boil, then lower the heat and simmer, uncovered, 15 to 20 minutes longer until both beans are very tender. Strain the cooking liquid into a large bowl and reserve. Discard the bouquet garni, and blend the beans until smooth.

3 Work the bean mixture through a strainer into the pan, rubbing back and forth with a spoon. Stir in 5 cups of the reserved cooking liquid, or enough to achieve the preferred consistency, then reheat. (Any leftover stock can be used in other recipes or frozen for up to 6 months.) Adjust the salt and pepper, if necessary, and serve sprinkled with lemon zest and dill.

004 Eggplant & Mushroom Soup

PREPARATION TIME 20 minutes, plus 30 minutes resting and making the stock
and croutes (optional) COOKING TIME 1¾ hours

1 eggplant, about 12 ounces, pricked
  all over with a fork
1 ounce dried porcini mushrooms
3 tablespoons olive oil
1 leek, halved lengthwise, thinly
  sliced and rinsed
2 large garlic cloves, very finely
  chopped
9 ounces portobello or cremini
  mushrooms, trimmed and sliced

2½ cups Vegetable Stock
  (see page 12) or ready-made stock
1¾ cups peeled and chopped
  sweet potatoes
1 rosemary sprig
salt and freshly ground black pepper
snipped chives, to serve
1 recipe quantity Goat Cheese
  Croutes (see page 14), to serve
  (optional)

1 Heat the oven to 425°F. Put the eggplant in a roasting pan and roast 1 to 1¼ hours until very softened. Remove the pan from the oven, cover with a clean, thick towel or two clean dish towels and set aside 30 minutes, then cut the eggplant in half and scoop the flesh into a bowl.

2 Meanwhile, put the dried mushrooms in a heatproof bowl and cover with 3 cups hot water. Let soak at least 30 minutes until tender, then strain the soaking liquid through a cheesecloth-lined strainer and set aside. Squeeze the mushrooms dry, trim off the bottom of each stem and thinly slice the caps and stems, then set aside.

3 Heat the oil in a saucepan over medium heat. Add the leek and garlic and fry, stirring occasionally, 2 minutes. Add the portobello mushrooms, season with salt, and fry, stirring occasionally, 5 to 8 minutes until the mushrooms give off their liquid. Stir in the stock and 2½ cups of the reserved mushroom soaking liquid, then add the porcini mushrooms, sweet potatoes, and rosemary. Cover and bring to a boil, then lower the heat and simmer 10 minutes. Stir in the eggplant flesh, simmer 10 minutes longer. Discard the rosemary and then beat to blend the ingredients.

4 Adjust the salt and pepper, if necessary, then serve sprinkled with chives and with cheese croutes on the side, if you like.

005 Egyptian Eggplant & Tomato Soup

PREPARATION TIME 20 minutes, plus making the stock and croutons (optional)
COOKING TIME 35 minutes

½ cup olive oil, plus extra as needed
2 eggplants, about 1½ pounds total
   weight, peeled, cut into 1-inch
   slices, and patted dry
1 large onion, very finely chopped
2 garlic cloves, very finely chopped
½ teaspoon ground coriander
½ teaspoon ground cumin

2½ cups tomato and vegetable juice
2 cups Vegetable Stock (see page 12)
6 tablespoons Greek yogurt
salt and freshly ground black pepper
chopped mint leaves, to serve
1 recipe quantity Garlic Croutons
   (see page 14), to serve

1   Heat two large skillets over high heat until a splash of water "dances" on the surface. Lower the heat to medium and add a thin layer of oil to each. Add as many eggplant slices as will fit in a single layer and fry 3 to 3½ minutes on each side until just beginning to brown. Do not overbrown or the soup will taste bitter. Transfer the slices to a large bowl or blender. Add extra oil to the pans between batches, if necessary.

2   Blend the eggplants until smooth, then set aside.

3   Heat 2 tablespoons of the oil in a saucepan over medium heat. Add the onion and fry, stirring occasionally, 10 to 12 minutes until golden brown. Stir in the garlic, coriander, and cumin and fry, stirring continuously, 30 seconds, or until aromatic. Add the tomato and vegetable juice and stock, stir in the eggplant puree, and season with salt and pepper. Cover and bring to a boil, then lower the heat and simmer, uncovered, 5 minutes, stirring occasionally.

4   Stir in the yogurt and adjust the salt and pepper, if necessary. Serve sprinkled with mint and with the croutons for adding at the table.

006 Asparagus & Pea Soup

PREPARATION TIME 15 minutes, plus making the stock   COOKING TIME 30 minutes

1 tablespoon butter
1 tablespoon olive or hemp oil
1 shallot, sliced
4½ cups chopped asparagus
1 russet potato, peeled and chopped

4½ cups Vegetable Stock
  (see page 12) or ready-made stock
¼ cup frozen peas
¼ cup crème fraîche or sour cream
salt and freshly ground black pepper

1 Melt the butter with the oil in a saucepan over medium heat. Add the shallot and fry, stirring, 3 to 5 minutes until softened. Stir in the asparagus, potato, and stock and season with salt and pepper.

2 Cover and bring to a boil, then lower the heat and simmer, partially covered, 10 minutes. Add the peas and simmer 5 to 8 minutes until the potato is tender. Blend the soup until smooth. Stir in the crème fraîche, adjust the salt and pepper, if necessary, and serve.

007 Vegetarian Borscht

PREPARATION TIME 20 minutes, plus making the stock   COOKING TIME 40 minutes

1½ tablespoons olive or hemp oil
1 onion, finely chopped
1 teaspoon caraway seeds
¼ teaspoon hot paprika, or to taste
5½ cups Vegetable Stock (see
  page 12) or ready-made stock
2½ cups peeled and grated beets
1 bay leaf

1 waxy potato, peeled and diced
1 cup shredded white cabbage
½ cup peeled and diced turnip
2 tablespoons red wine or apple
  cider vinegar
2 tablespoons orange juice
salt and freshly ground black pepper
sour cream or smetana, to serve

1 Heat the oil in a saucepan over medium heat. Add the onion and fry, stirring, 3 to 5 minutes until softened. Add the caraway seeds and paprika and stir 30 seconds, or until aromatic. Watch closely so the spices do not burn.

2 Immediately add the stock, beets, bay leaf, potato, cabbage, turnip, vinegar, and orange juice. Season with salt and pepper, cover, and bring to a boil. Lower the heat and simmer 25 minutes, or until the vegetables are tender.

3 Discard the bay leaf. Transfer about one-third of the vegetables to a deep bowl or blender and blend until smooth. Return this mixture to the pan and adjust the salt and pepper, if necessary. Serve sprinkled with dill and topped with sour cream.

008 Beet & Apple Soup

PREPARATION TIME 15 minutes, plus making the stock   COOKING TIME 55 minutes

1 large cooking apple, peeled
  and chopped
1 tablespoon lemon juice
1½ tablespoons olive or hemp oil
1 onion, chopped
½ tablespoon caraway seeds
3½ cups Vegetable Stock
  (see page 12)

3½ cups peeled and diced beets
salt and freshly ground black pepper

HORSERADISH & DILL CREAM
5 tablespoons sour cream
1 tablespoon grated horseradish
½ tablespoon chopped dill
a pinch of salt

1 Toss the apple and lemon juice together in a bowl and set aside. Heat the oil in a saucepan over medium heat. Add the onion and fry, stirring, 3 to 5 minutes until softened. Add the caraway seeds and stir 30 seconds, or until aromatic. Watch closely so they do not burn. Add the stock and beets, cover, and bring to a boil. Lower the heat and simmer 30 minutes.

2 Meanwhile, make the horseradish and dill cream. Put all the ingredients in a bowl and stir, then cover and chill.

3 Add the apple and any remaining lemon juice to the pan and simmer 10 minutes, or until the beets are tender. Blend the soup until smooth, then season with salt and pepper. Serve topped with the horseradish cream.

009   Broccoli & Parsley Soup

PREPARATION TIME 15 minutes, plus making the stock and pumpkin seeds
COOKING TIME 30 minutes

1 tablespoon sunflower oil
2 shallots, chopped
2 large garlic cloves, finely chopped
4 cups Vegetable Stock (see page 12)
   or ready-made stock
12 ounces broccoli, cut into florets
   and the stems sliced
1 bunch of curly parsley,
   about 1 ounce, leaves and
   stems chopped

a pinch of chili flakes, or to taste
1 Parmesan or other cheese rind,
   about 3 x 2 inches (see page 9;
   optional)
salt and freshly ground black pepper
Roasted Pumpkin Seeds
   (see page 15), to serve
snipped chives, to serve (optional)

1   Heat the oil in a saucepan over medium heat. Add the shallots and fry, stirring
    occasionally, 2 minutes. Stir in the garlic and fry 1 to 3 minutes longer until the
    shallots are softened but not colored.
2   Add the stock, broccoli, parsley, chili flakes, and cheese rind, if using, and season
    with salt and pepper, but remember the rind is salty, if you are using it. Cover and
    bring to a boil, then lower the heat and simmer 15 to 20 minutes until the broccoli
    stems are very tender.
3   Discard the cheese rind, if used. Blend the soup, then adjust the salt and pepper,
    if necessary. Serve sprinkled with the seeds and chives, if you like.

010 Broccoli & Spinach Soup

PREPARATION TIME 15 minutes, plus making the stock   COOKING TIME 35 minutes

2 tablespoons butter
1 tablespoon olive or hemp oil
1 heaping cup thinly sliced and
    rinsed leek
1 large garlic clove, crushed
5½ cups Vegetable Stock
    (see page 12) or ready-made stock

1 russet potato, peeled and diced
2½ cups chopped broccoli
3 ounces baby spinach leaves
freshly grated nutmeg, to taste
salt and freshly ground black pepper
2 to 3 ounces blue cheese, such
    as Roquefort, crumbled, to serve

1   Melt the butter with the olive oil in a saucepan over medium heat. Stir in the leek
    and garlic, reduce the heat to low, and cook, covered, 10 to 12 minutes, stirring
    occasionally, until the leeks are softened. Add the stock, potato, and broccoli.
2   Season with salt and pepper. Cover and bring to a boil, then lower the heat and
    simmer, covered, 15 to 20 minutes until the broccoli and potatoes are very tender.
    Add the spinach and stir until it wilts, then strain the soup into a large bowl.
3   Return the vegetables to the pan and blend until smooth. Stir in enough of the
    stock to achieve the preferred consistency. Reheat the soup and add the nutmeg.
    Adjust the salt and pepper, if necessary, then serve topped with the cheese.

011 Creamy Brussels Sprout Soup

PREPARATION TIME 15 minutes, plus making the stock   COOKING TIME 30 minutes

1½ tablespoons garlic-flavored
    olive oil
1 onion, chopped
6½ cups chopped Brussels sprouts
12 ounces soft tofu, drained

4½ cups Vegetable Stock (see
    page 12) or ready-made stock
¼ cup orange juice
salt and freshly ground black pepper
chopped parsley leaves, to serve

1   Heat the oil in a saucepan over medium heat. Add the onion and fry, stirring
    occasionally, 8 to 10 minutes until light golden brown. Add the Brussels sprouts
    and stir 5 to 8 minutes until they wilt. Add the tofu and 2¼ cups of the stock and
    season with salt and pepper. Bring to a boil, stirring occasionally, then lower the
    heat and simmer, covered, 5 minutes.
2   Blend the soup until smooth, then stir in enough of the remaining stock to achieve
    the preferred consistency. (Any leftover stock can be used in other recipes
    or frozen for up to 6 months.)
3   Stir in the juice and reheat. Adjust the salt and pepper, if necessary, and serve
    sprinkled with parsley.

012 Basque-Style Cabbage & Bean Soup

PREPARATION TIME 10 minutes, plus making the stock   COOKING TIME 45 minutes

5½ cups Vegetable Stock
    (see page 12) or ready-made stock
2 onions, sliced, skins reserved
3 tablespoons olive oil
4 large garlic cloves, chopped

5¾ cups shredded white cabbage
1 can (15-oz.) pinto beans, rinsed
salt and freshly ground black pepper
sherry or red wine vinegar, to serve
smoked paprika, to serve

1   Put the stock and onion skins in a saucepan. Cover and bring to a boil over high
    heat, then lower the heat and simmer 10 minutes.
2   Meanwhile, heat the oil in another saucepan over medium heat. Add the onions
    and fry, stirring, 7 minutes. Stir in the garlic and fry 1 to 3 minutes until the onions
    are light brown. Stir in the cabbage. Strain the stock into the pan, discarding the
    onion skins. Season with salt and pepper, cover and bring to a boil. Lower the heat
    and simmer 10 minutes. Add the beans and simmer 5 minutes to warm through.
    Adjust the salt and pepper, if necessary.
3   Put 1 tablespoon sherry in each bowl and sprinkle with a little paprika. Ladle the
    soup into the bowls and serve.

013 Cabbage & Sauerkraut Soup

PREPARATION TIME 15 minutes, plus making the stock   COOKING TIME 45 minutes

1½ tablespoons garlic-flavored
   olive oil
1 large onion, chopped
1 teaspoon caraway seeds
4¼ cups Vegetable Stock
   (see page 12) or ready-made stock
1 can (15-oz.) crushed tomatoes
1 tablespoon tomato paste
½ teaspoon light brown sugar

1 bay leaf
3 cups scrubbed new potatoes cut
   into bite-size pieces
3 cups cored and thinly sliced savoy
   cabbage
1 cup sauerkraut, drained
salt and freshly ground black pepper
chopped parsley leaves, to serve
sour cream (optional), to serve

1 Heat the oil in a large saucepan over medium heat. Add the onion and fry, stirring
   occasionally, 3 to 5 minutes until softened but not colored. Add the caraway seeds
   and fry 30 seconds, or until aromatic. Watch closely so they do not burn.
2 Stir in the stock, tomatoes, tomato paste, sugar, and bay leaf and season with
   salt and pepper. Cover and bring to a boil, then lower the heat and simmer
   10 minutes.
3 Stir in the potatoes and cabbage and simmer, covered, 10 minutes. Stir in the
   sauerkraut and simmer, covered, 10 minutes longer, or until the potatoes and
   cabbage are tender. Discard the bay leaf. Adjust the salt and pepper, if necessary,
   then serve sprinkled with parsley and topped with sour cream, if you like.

014 Thick Cabbage & Bread Soup

PREPARATION TIME 20 minutes, plus overnight soaking and cooking the beans (optional)
and making the stock   COOKING TIME 1½ hours

½ cup dried borlotti beans or 1 cup
   canned borlotti beans, rinsed
2 tablespoons garlic-flavored olive oil
2 celery ribs, finely chopped
2 carrots, peeled and finely chopped
1 onion, finely chopped
1 teaspoon celery seeds
5½ cups Vegetable Stock
   (see page 12) or ready-made stock,
   plus extra as needed
3 cups shredded white cabbage
1 tablespoon tomato paste
1 small handful of parsley, tied
   together with the stalks crushed

1 cup day-old country-style bread
   with crusts removed and the
   crumb torn into pieces
celery salt
freshly ground black pepper

PAPRIKA & LEMON OIL
3 tablespoons olive or hemp oil
1½ teaspoons sweet, smoked
   or hot paprika
finely grated zest of 1 lemon

1 If using dried beans, put them in a bowl, cover with water, and let soak overnight,
   then drain. Transfer to a saucepan, add 6 cups water, cover, and bring to a boil.
   Lower the heat and simmer, covered, 1 hour, then drain.
2 To make the paprika oil, put the oil and paprika in a small saucepan over medium-
   high heat and heat just until bubbles appear around the edge. Do not boil.
   Immediately pour the oil into a heatproof bowl, add the lemon zest and set aside.
3 Heat the garlic oil in a saucepan over medium heat. Add the celery, carrots,
   and onion, reduce the heat to low, and cook, covered, 8 to 10 minutes, stirring
   occasionally, until the onion is softened and just beginning to color. Add the garlic
   and stir 1 minute, then add the celery seeds and stir 30 seconds. Watch closely
   so they do not burn.
4 Add the stock, cabbage, tomato paste, and parsley and season with celery salt and
   pepper. Cover and bring to a boil, then lower the heat and simmer 3 to 5 minutes
   until the cabbage is tender. Add the beans and simmer 3 to 5 minutes longer
   to warm through.
5 Discard the parsley and stir in the bread. Let stand, covered, 5 minutes to thicken.
   If it becomes too thick, stir in a little extra stock and reheat. Adjust the celery salt
   and pepper, if necessary, then serve drizzled with the paprika oil.

015 Carrot & Roasted Pepper Broth

PREPARATION TIME 15 minutes, plus making the stock and pesto (optional)
COOKING TIME 35 minutes

1 tablespoon olive or hemp oil
1 large leek, halved lengthwise,
   sliced and rinsed
2 garlic cloves
5½ cups Vegetable Stock
   (see page 12) or ready-made stock
2 carrots, peeled and thinly sliced
1 bay leaf

2 roasted red peppers in olive oil,
   drained and chopped
2 tablespoons chopped
   parsley leaves
salt and freshly ground black pepper
1 recipe quantity Pumpkin Seed
   Pesto (see page 33), to serve
   (optional)

1 Heat the oil in a saucepan over medium heat. Add the leek and fry, stirring,
   2 minutes. Add the garlic and fry 1 to 3 minutes until the leek is softened but not
   colored. Add the stock, carrots, and bay leaf and season with salt and pepper.
2 Cover and bring to a boil, then lower the heat and simmer 15 to 20 minutes until
   the carrot is very tender. Add the roasted peppers and parsley and warm through.
   Discard the bay leaf and adjust the salt and pepper, if necessary, then serve topped
   with the pesto, if you like.

016 Carrot & Parsnip Soup

PREPARATION TIME 15 minutes, plus making the stock   COOKING TIME 30 minutes

1 tablespoon butter
1 tablespoon sunflower or olive oil
2 cups peeled and chopped carrots
1 heaping cup peeled and chopped
   parsnips
1 onion, chopped
1 large garlic clove, finely chopped

3½ cups Vegetable Stock
   (see page 12) or ready-made stock
salt and freshly ground black pepper
2 to 3 tablespoons red wine vinegar,
   to serve
chopped parsley leaves, to serve

1 Melt the butter with the oil in a large saucepan over medium heat. Add the carrots,
   parsnips, and onion and cook, covered, 7 minutes, stirring occasionally. Add the
   garlic and cook, stirring occasionally, 1 to 3 minutes longer until the vegetables are
   softened but not colored.
2 Stir in the stock and season with salt and pepper. Cover and bring to a boil over
   high heat, then lower the heat and simmer 10 to 15 minutes until the vegetables
   are very tender. Blend the soup until smooth, then adjust the salt and pepper,
   if necessary. Drizzle each portion with ½ tablespoon vinegar and serve sprinkled
   with parsley.

017 Parmesan Broth with Peas & Carrots

PREPARATION TIME 15 minutes, plus making the stock   COOKING TIME 35 minutes

5½ cups Vegetable Stock
   (see page 12) or ready-made stock
1 onion, peeled and quartered
1 Parmesan cheese rind, 3 x 2 inches
   (see page 9)
⅔ cup frozen peas

1 cup diced carrot, the same size
   as the peas
2 romaine lettuce leaves, shredded
salt and freshly ground black pepper
extra-virgin olive oil, to serve
freshly grated Parmesan cheese,
   to serve

1 Put the stock, onion, and cheese rind in a saucepan, cover, and bring to a boil,
   then lower the heat and simmer 20 minutes.
2 Discard the onion. Return the stock to a boil, add the peas and carrots, and boil,
   uncovered, 3 to 5 minutes until they are tender. Stir in the lettuce and simmer
   30 seconds, or until it wilts. Season with salt and pepper, but remember the
   cheese rind was salty. Discard the rind. Serve drizzled with oil and with Parmesan
   cheese for adding at the table.

Golden Carrot & Sesame Soup

PREPARATION TIME 15 minutes, plus making the stock and toasted seeds
COOKING TIME 30 minutes

1½ tablespoons olive or hemp oil,
  plus extra to serve
1 onion, chopped
2 large garlic cloves, chopped
½ teaspoon ground coriander
¼ teaspoon turmeric
a pinch of cayenne pepper,
  or to taste
4 cups Vegetable Stock (see page 12)
  or ready-made stock

2½ cups peeled and thinly
  sliced carrots
2 tablespoons tahini
lemon juice, to taste
salt and freshly ground black pepper
toasted white sesame seeds
  (see page 9), to serve
black sesame seeds, to serve
chopped cilantro leaves, to serve

1 Heat the oil in a saucepan over medium heat. Add the onion and fry, stirring occasionally, 2 minutes. Add the garlic and fry 1 to 3 minutes until the onion is softened but not colored. Add the coriander, turmeric, and cayenne pepper and stir 30 seconds. Watch closely so the spices do not burn.

2 Add the stock and carrots and season with salt and pepper. Cover and bring to a boil, then lower the heat and simmer 12 to 15 minutes until the carrots are very tender. Add the tahini and stir until it dissolves.

3 Blend the soup to the preferred consistency, then add the lemon juice and adjust the salt and pepper, if necessary. Serve sprinkled with sesame seeds and cilantro leaves and drizzled with oil.

019 Carrot & Cilantro Soup

PREPARATION TIME 10 minutes, plus making the stock and dukkah
COOKING TIME 35 minutes

1 tbsp butter
1 tablespoon olive or hemp oil
2½ cups peeled and sliced carrots
1 onion, sliced
½ teaspoon ground coriander
1 bunch of cilantro, about 1 ounce,
   stems and leaves chopped

4 cups Vegetable Stock (see page 12)
   or ready-made stock
½ teaspoon sugar
salt and freshly ground black pepper
plain yogurt, to serve (optional)
Dukkah (see page 15), to serve

1   Melt the butter with the oil in a saucepan over medium heat. Add the carrots and
    onion and fry, stirring occasionally, 3 to 5 minutes until the onion is softened but
    not colored. Add the coriander and stir 30 seconds. Watch closely so it does not
    burn. Add the cilantro, stock, and sugar and season with salt and pepper. Cover and
    bring to a boil, then lower the heat and simmer 15 to 20 minutes until the carrots
    are very tender. Blend the soup until smooth.
2   Adjust the salt and pepper, if necessary. Swirl a little yogurt over each portion,
    if you like, sprinkle with the dukkah, and serve.

020 Vegetable "Spaghetti" Soup

PREPARATION TIME 15 minutes, plus making the stock   **COOKING TIME** 10 minutes

4 cups Vegetable Stock (see page 12)
   or ready-made stock
1¾ cups tomato puree
6 garlic cloves, chopped
1 leek, sliced and rinsed

1 carrot, peeled
1 zucchini
salt and freshly ground black pepper
basil leaves, torn, to serve

1   Put the stock, tomato puree, garlic, and leek in a saucepan. Cover and bring to a
    boil, then lower the heat and simmer while you prepare the vegetables in step 2.
2   Use a julienne tool to cut the carrot and zucchini into long, thin "spaghetti" strands.
    Alternatively, use a vegetable peeler to cut wide, thin strips of the vegetables, then
    stack the strips and cut into long, thin strips. Strain the stock.
3   Discard the garlic and leek. Return the stock to the pan, cover, and bring to a boil.
    Add the carrot and boil 30 seconds, then add the zucchini and boil 30 seconds
    to 1 minute longer until tender. Season with salt and pepper, then transfer the
    vegetables to bowls. Ladle the soup over them and serve sprinkled with basil.

021 Cauliflower & Cheese Soup

PREPARATION TIME 10 minutes, plus making the stock and croutons
COOKING TIME 15 minutes

5½ cups small cauliflower florets
1 leek, sliced and rinsed
1 tablespoon lemon juice
2½ cups milk
2 teaspoons powdered mustard

1¼ cups grated cheddar cheese
freshly grated nutmeg
salt and freshly ground black pepper
1 recipe quantity Garlic Croutons
   (see page 14), hot, to serve

1   Put the cauliflower, leek, lemon juice, and 6 cups water in a saucepan, adding more
    water, if necessary, so the vegetables are covered. Season lightly with salt, then
    cover and bring to a boil. Lower the heat and simmer 5 to 8 minutes until the
    cauliflower is very tender. Drain and set aside.
2   Return the cauliflower and leek to the pan. Add the milk and powdered mustard
    and simmer over low heat 5 minutes. Do not boil. Blend the soup until smooth,
    then stir in enough of the reserved stock to achieve the preferred consistency.
    Add the cheese and stir until it melts. Season with nutmeg and adjust the salt
    and pepper, if necessary. Serve sprinkled with the croutons.

022 Celery Root & Pear Soup

PREPARATION TIME 20 minutes, plus making the stock and croutes (optional)
COOKING TIME 25 minutes

2½ cups peeled and chopped
  celery root
2 tablespoons lemon juice
1 large pear, peeled and chopped
1 tablespoon olive or hemp oil
1 onion, finely chopped
2 garlic cloves, finely chopped

1 russet potato, peeled and chopped
4 cups Vegetable Stock (see page 12)
  or ready-made stock
salt and ground white pepper
Goat Cheese Croutes (see page 14),
  to serve (optional)

1 Toss the celery root with half the lemon juice in a bowl. Toss the pear with the remaining lemon juice in another bowl and set both bowls aside.
2 Heat the oil in a saucepan over medium heat. Add the onion and fry, stirring, 2 minutes. Add the garlic and fry 1 to 3 minutes until softened. Add the stock, celery root, and potato and season with salt and white pepper. Cover and bring to a boil, then lower the heat and simmer 10 to 15 minutes until the vegetables are tender. Add the pear and any remaining lemon juice. Blend the soup.
3 Adjust the salt and pepper, if necessary. Serve with croutes on the side, if you like.

023 Curried Cauliflower & Potato Soup

PREPARATION TIME 15 minutes, plus making the stock   COOKING TIME 30 minutes

1½ tablespoons sunflower
  or peanut oil
2 large garlic cloves, crushed
1 green chili, seeded and chopped
1 teaspoon cumin seeds
1 teaspoon turmeric
1 large waxy potato, diced

5½ cups Vegetable Stock
  (see page 12) or ready-made stock
½ teaspoon salt, plus extra to season
6¾ cups cauliflower florets
2 handfuls of baby spinach leaves
a large pinch of garam masala
freshly ground black pepper

1 Heat the oil in a saucepan over medium heat. Add the garlic, chili, cumin seeds, and turmeric and stir 30 seconds. Watch closely so they do not burn. Add the potato and stir well. Add the stock and salt and season with pepper. Cover and bring to a boil, then lower the heat and simmer 5 minutes.
2 Add the cauliflower and simmer 10 to 15 minutes until tender. Add the spinach and stir until it wilts. Adjust the salt and pepper, if necessary, and stir in the garam masala, then serve.

024 Roasted Cauliflower & Pepper Soup

PREPARATION TIME 15 minutes, plus making the stock   COOKING TIME 35 minutes

6¾ cups cauliflower florets
1 red bell pepper, halved and seeded
1½ tablespoons olive or hemp oil
1 large onion, finely chopped
2 large garlic cloves, chopped

1 tablespoon all-purpose
  or wholewheat flour
1¾ cups Vegetable Stock
  (see page 12) or ready-made stock
salt and freshly ground black pepper

1 Heat the oven to 400°F. Roast the cauliflower and pepper in a baking tray 25 to 30 minutes, stirring twice, until softened but not charred.
2 Meanwhile, heat the oil in a saucepan over medium heat. Add the onion and fry, stirring, 2 minutes. Add the garlic and stir 1 to 3 minutes until the onion is softened. Sprinkle in the flour and stir 2 minutes. Slowly add the stock, stirring to prevent lumps from forming. Bring to a boil, then lower the heat and simmer, partially covered, until the roasted vegetables are ready.
3 Remove the vegetables from the oven and coarsely chop. Add to the soup, season with salt and pepper, and simmer 5 minutes, then blend until smooth. Work the soup through a strainer into a large bowl, rubbing back and forth with a spoon and scraping the bottom of the strainer. Return the soup to the pan and reheat it. Adjust the salt and pepper, if necessary, and serve.

025 Mediterranean Fennel Soup

PREPARATION TIME 15 minutes, plus making the stock   **COOKING TIME** 45 minutes

2 tablespoons garlic-flavored olive oil
2 large fennel bulbs, sliced, with the
  fronds reserved
2 shallots, sliced
1 teaspoon fennel seeds
½ cup dry white wine
4 cups chopped tomatoes

1 tablespoon tomato paste
4½ cups Vegetable Stock
  (see page 12) or ready-made stock
⅔ cup large pitted black olives, sliced
salt and freshly ground black pepper
French bread, to serve

1   Heat the oil in a large saucepan over medium heat. Add the fennel and shallots
    and fry, stirring occasionally, 3 to 5 minutes until the shallots are softened but not
    colored. Add the fennel seeds and stir 30 seconds. Stir in the wine, increase the
    heat to high, and cook 5 to 6 minutes until almost evaporated.
2   Add the tomatoes, tomato paste, stock, and olives and season with pepper.
    Do not add salt at this point because the olives are salty. Cover and bring to a boil,
    then lower the heat and simmer 20 to 25 minutes. Adjust the salt and pepper,
    but remember salt might not be necessary. Serve sprinkled with the fennel
    fronds and with French bread on the side.

026　Fennel & Celery Root Soup

PREPARATION TIME 20 minutes, plus making the stock and seeds
COOKING TIME 35 minutes

1½ cups peeled and chopped
　celery root
½ tablespoon lemon juice
3 tablespoons olive or hemp oil
2 fennel bulbs, with the fronds, sliced
1 shallot, sliced
1 small russet potato, peeled and
　chopped
2 tablespoons aniseed-flavored spirit,
　such as Pernod

3½ cups Vegetable Stock
　(see page 12) or ready-made stock
1 bouquet garni made with 1 celery
　rib, 1 bay leaf, 1 parsley sprig, and
　1 thyme sprig tied together
1¾ cups whole milk
celery salt
ground white pepper
Spiced Seeds (see page 15),
　to serve

1　Toss the celery root with the lemon juice and set aside. Heat the oil in a saucepan
　over medium heat. Stir in the celery root, fennel, shallot, and potato, then lower
　the heat to low and cook, covered, 10 to 12 minutes until softened but not colored.
　Add the spirit and cook 1 to 2 minutes until it evaporates. Add the stock and
　bouquet garni and season with celery salt and white pepper.
2　Cover and bring to a boil, then reduce the heat to low. Simmer 12 to 15 minutes
　until all the vegetables are very tender. Discard the bouquet garni and blend the
　soup until smooth.
3　Work the soup through a strainer into a large bowl, rubbing back and forth with
　a spoon and scraping the bottom of the strainer. Return the soup to the pan,
　add the milk and reheat. Do not boil.
4　Adjust the salt and pepper, if necessary, then serve sprinkled with seeds. If you
　reheat the soup, do not boil it. You can also serve this soup chilled, adding a little
　extra stock to thin it and seasoning again with salt and pepper after chilling,
　if necessary.

027　Roasted Mediterranean Vegetable Soup

PREPARATION TIME 15 minutes, plus 20 minutes resting and making the stock
and flavored oil　COOKING TIME 1¾ hours

1 eggplant, about 12 ounces, pricked
　all over with a fork
2 red bell peppers, left whole
2 garlic cloves, whole and unpeeled
2 red onions, halved and unpeeled
3 tablespoons olive or hemp oil,
　plus extra to serve

2 large tomatoes, halved
2 oregano or marjoram sprigs
4¼ cups Vegetable Stock
　(see page 12) or ready-made stock
salt and freshly ground black pepper
1 recipe quantity Crushed Basil Oil
　(see page 15), to serve

1　Heat the oven to 425°F. Put the eggplant, red peppers, garlic, and onions in a large
　roasting pan. Drizzle with half the oil and toss to coat. Roast 55 minutes, then add
　the tomatoes, cut-sides down, and roast 20 to 30 minutes longer until the
　vegetables are very tender and the tomato skins burst. Remove the pan from
　the oven, cover with two clean dish towels, and let rest 20 minutes.
2　Cut the eggplant in half and scoop the flesh into a bowl. Working on a plate
　to collect the juices, peel off the pepper skins and discard the stems, cores,
　and seeds. Add the flesh and any juices to the bowl. Squeeze the garlic flesh into
　the bowl. Peel the onions and coarsely chop, then add them to the bowl. Peel,
　halve, and seed the tomatoes, then chop and add them to the bowl.
3　Heat the remaining oil in a saucepan over medium heat. Add the vegetables and
　their juices to the pan along with the stock and oregano. Season with salt and
　pepper, cover, and bring to a boil. Lower the heat and simmer 10 minutes. Discard
　the oregano sprigs and blend the soup until smooth. Adjust the salt and pepper,
　if necessary, then serve drizzled with basil oil.

028 Zucchini & Dolcelatte Soup

PREPARATION TIME 15 minutes, plus making the stock and croutes
COOKING TIME 30 minutes

1 tablespoon olive or hemp oil, plus
  extra to serve
1 celery rib
1 leek, sliced and rinsed
3¼ cups chopped zucchini
5½ cups Vegetable Stock
  (see page 12) or ready-made stock
1 bay leaf

3½ ounces dolcelatte cheese,
  chopped, with rind removed
salt and freshly ground black pepper
1 recipe quantity Garlic Croutes
  (see page 14), to serve
snipped chives, to serve
flaxseed, lightly crushed, to serve

1 Heat the oil in a saucepan over medium heat. Add the celery and leek and fry,
  stirring occasionally, 8 to 10 minutes until light golden brown. Add the zucchini
  and fry 2 to 3 minutes until the skins turn bright green.
2 Add the stock and bay leaf and season with salt and pepper, but remember the
  cheese added later will be salty. Cover and bring to a boil. Lower the heat and
  simmer, covered, 5 to 8 minutes until the zucchini are tender. Discard the bay leaf,
  then blend the soup to the preferred consistency. Add the cheese, stir until it melts
  and adjust the salt and pepper, if necessary.
3 Divide the croutes into bowls and drizzle with oil. Ladle the soup over them,
  sprinkle with chives and seeds and serve. You can also serve this soup chilled,
  adding a little extra stock to thin it and seasoning again with salt and pepper
  after chilling, if necessary.

029 Vegetable Chowder

PREPARATION TIME 20 minutes, plus making the stock and seeds
COOKING TIME 35 minutes

2 tablespoons canola or sunflower oil
1 carrot, peeled and diced
1 celery rib, thinly sliced
1 onion, finely chopped
1 red bell pepper, seeded and
  finely chopped
2½ cups Vegetable Stock
  (see page 12) or ready-made stock
4 new potatoes, diced
1⅓ cups frozen corn kernels

5 tablespoons all-purpose
  or wholewheat flour
a pinch of cayenne pepper
2½ cups whole milk
1 heaping cup grated sharp cheddar
  or Gruyère cheese
salt and freshly ground black pepper
Roasted Pumpkin Seeds
  (see page 15), to serve
chopped parsley leaves, to serve

1 Heat the oil in a saucepan over medium heat. Stir in the carrot, celery, onion,
  and red pepper. Reduce the heat to low and cook, covered, 10 to 12 minutes,
  stirring occasionally, until the vegetables are softened but not colored. Add the
  stock, potatoes, and corn and season with salt and pepper. Cover and bring
  to a boil. Lower the heat and simmer 10 to 12 minutes until the potatoes and
  carrots are tender.
2 Meanwhile, put the flour and cayenne pepper in a large bowl and make a well
  in the middle. Heat the milk in a small pan until simmering but not boiling, then
  slowly pour it into the flour, stirring continuously to prevent lumps from forming.
3 When the vegetables are tender, increase the heat to medium but do not let the
  soup boil. Add a ladleful of the hot soup to the milk mixture and stir together, then
  whisk the mixture into the soup. Add the cheese and simmer 2 minutes, stirring
  continuously. Do not boil. Adjust the salt and pepper, if necessary, then serve
  sprinkled with the seeds and parsley. If you reheat the soup, do not boil it.

030 Scandinavian Vegetable Soup

PREPARATION TIME 15 minutes, plus making the stock   COOKING TIME 40 minutes

5½ cups Vegetable Stock
  (see page 12) or ready-made stock
1½ cups chopped green beans
3 red potatoes, thinly sliced
1 carrot, peeled and diced
2½ cups small cauliflower florets
1 bay leaf
1 teaspoon ground coriander
a pinch of cayenne pepper,
  or to taste

1¼ cups frozen peas
2 tablespoons butter
1½ teaspoons all-purpose flour
scant 1 cup whole milk
1 extra-large egg yolk
2 tablespoons crème fraîche
  or sour cream
3 radishes, grated
salt and ground white pepper
finely chopped dill, to serve

1   Put the stock, green beans, potatoes, carrot, cauliflower, bay leaf, coriander, and cayenne in a large saucepan. Season with salt and white pepper, then cover and bring to a boil. Lower the heat and simmer 12 minutes, then add the peas and simmer 2 to 3 minutes longer until all the vegetables are tender.

2   Strain the stock into a bowl and reserve. Discard the bay leaf, set the vegetables aside, and keep warm. Return the pan to a low heat and melt the butter. Sprinkle in the flour and stir 2 minutes, then slowly stir in the reserved stock, stirring continuously to prevent lumps from forming. Cover and bring to a boil, then reduce the heat to low. Simmer, covered, 5 minutes, then stir in the milk.

3   Beat the egg yolk and crème fraîche together in a bowl, then whisk in a ladleful of the hot soup. Remove the pan from the heat and whisk the egg mixture into the soup. Return the vegetables to the pan, add the radishes, and reheat gently but do not boil. Adjust the salt and pepper, if necessary. Serve sprinkled with dill. If you reheat the soup, do not boil it.

031 Italian Bread & Tomato Soup

PREPARATION TIME 15 minutes, plus making the stock and 30 minutes standing
COOKING TIME 20 minutes

5 tablespoons fruity extra-virgin olive
  oil, plus extra to serve
1 red onion, finely chopped
4 large garlic cloves, crushed
3½ cups chopped plum tomatoes
1 tablespoon tomato paste
a small handful of basil leaves, plus
  extra to serve
½ teaspoon sugar

a pinch of dried chili flakes,
  or to taste
6 cups Vegetable Stock (see page 12)
  or ready-made stock
4 thick slices of day-old ciabatta
  or other country-style bread, torn
  into pieces
salt and freshly ground black pepper

1   Heat the oil in a large saucepan over medium heat. Add the onion and fry, stirring occasionally, 2 minutes. Add the garlic and fry 1 to 2 minutes until the onion is softened but not colored. Stir in the tomatoes, tomato paste, basil, sugar, and chili flakes and cook, stirring 5 to 10 minutes until the tomatoes are softened and breaking down. Season with salt and pepper.

2   Add the stock, cover, and bring to a boil, then stir in the bread and remove the pan from the heat. Let stand, covered, at least 30 minutes.

3   Reheat the soup and adjust the salt and pepper, if necessary. Serve sprinkled with the basil and drizzled with extra oil.

032 Celery & Celery Root Soup

PREPARATION TIME 15 minutes, plus making the stock and seeds
COOKING TIME 30 minutes

1 tablespoon butter
1 tablespoon sunflower oil
½ onion, finely chopped
4½ cups chopped celery ribs
    and leaves
1¼ cups peeled and chopped
    celery root

3½ cups Vegetable Stock
    (see page 12) or ready-made stock,
    plus extra as needed
celery salt
freshly ground black pepper
Spiced Seeds (see page 15), to serve

1   Melt the butter with the oil in a saucepan over medium heat. Add the onion and
    fry, stirring, 3 to 5 minutes until softened but not colored. Stir in the celery, celery
    root, and stock. Season with celery salt and pepper, cover, and bring to a boil.
    Lower the heat and simmer, uncovered, 10 to 15 minutes until the vegetables
    are very tender.

2   Blend the soup, then, working in batches, strain it into a large bowl and work
    it through the strainer, rubbing back and forth with a spoon and scraping the bottom
    of the strainer. Return the soup to the pan, reheat, and adjust the salt and pepper,
    if necessary. Serve sprinkled with the seeds. You can also serve this soup chilled,
    adding a little extra stock to thin it, if necessary.

033 Winter Potage

PREPARATION TIME 20 minutes, plus making the stock   COOKING TIME 45 minutes

2 tablespoons butter
1 tablespoon olive or hemp oil
4 large garlic cloves, chopped
1½ cups peeled and diced carrots
1¼ cups peeled and diced
    celery roots
1 parsnip, peeled and chopped
1 russet potato, peeled and diced
3¾ cups Vegetable Stock
    (see page 12) or ready-made stock
1 Parmesan cheese rind, about
    3 x 2 inches (see page 9)
salt and freshly ground black pepper

PUMPKIN SEED PESTO
5 tablespoons garlic-flavored
    olive oil
⅓ cup unsalted hulled
    pumpkin seeds
3 tablespoons flat-leaf
    parsley leaves
1 scallion, finely chopped
1½ teaspoons lemon juice,
    or to taste

1   Melt the butter with the oil in a saucepan over medium heat. Stir in the garlic,
    carrot, celery root, parsnip, and potato, then add 4 tablespoons of the stock and
    season very lightly with salt and pepper. Reduce the heat to low (use a heat
    diffuser if you have one) and cook, covered, 20 to 25 minutes, stirring occasionally
    and adding extra stock, if necessary, until the vegetables are tender. (The longer
    the vegetables cook, the sweeter they will taste.)

2   Meanwhile, make the pesto. Line a plate with several layers of paper towels and
    set aside. Heat half the oil in a skillet over high heat until it shimmers. Add the
    seeds and fry 30 seconds to 1 minute until they start to pop and turn golden brown.
    Watch closely so they do not overbrown or burn. Immediately turn them out onto
    the paper and set aside to cool, then transfer to a mini food processor or blender.
    Add the parsley, scallion, and remaining oil and season with salt and pepper. Cover
    and blend until a thick paste forms, then add the lemon juice. Adjust the salt and
    pepper and add extra lemon juice, if necessary.

3   Stir the remaining stock into the soup, add the cheese rind and simmer, covered,
    15 minutes. Discard the cheese rind, then blend the soup until smooth. Adjust the
    salt and pepper, if necessary, but remember the cheese rind was salty. Serve
    topped with a dollop of the pesto. Any leftover pesto can be stored in a covered
    container in the refrigerator up to 2 days with an extra layer of olive oil on top,
    although the flavor does become a little bitter.

034 Sunshine Winter Soup

PREPARATION TIME 15 minutes, plus making the stock and seeds
COOKING TIME 30 minutes

1½ tablespoons olive or hemp oil
3 celery ribs, finely chopped,
   with the leaves reserved
2 large carrots, peeled and diced
2 shallots, finely chopped
1 teaspoon fennel seeds
a large pinch of saffron threads
6 cups Vegetable Stock (see page 12)
   or ready-made stock

3¼ cups peeled, seeded,
   and diced pumpkin
1 bouquet garni made with the
   reserved celery leaves, 2 parsley
   sprigs, 1 bay leaf, and 1 thyme
   sprig tied together
salt and freshly ground black pepper
toasted sunflower seeds
   (see page 9), to serve
snipped chives, to serve

1 Heat the oil in a saucepan over medium heat. Add the celery, carrots, and shallots
and stir 3 to 5 minutes until the shallots are softened but not colored. Add the
fennel seeds and saffron and stir 30 seconds, or until aromatic. Watch closely
so they do not burn.

2 Add the stock, pumpkin, and bouquet garni and season with salt and pepper.
Cover and bring to a boil, then lower the heat and simmer, partially covered,
12 to 15 minutes until the vegetables are tender. Discard the bouquet garni and
adjust the salt and pepper, if necessary. Serve sprinkled with the seeds and chives.

035 Summer Farmers' Market Soup

PREPARATION TIME 15 minutes, plus making the stock and preparing the tomatoes
COOKING TIME 30 minutes

6 cups Vegetable Stock (see page 12)
    or ready-made stock
freshly cut kernels from 2 corn
    cobs, with the cobs reserved
    and halved
1½ tablespoons sunflower oil
1 onion, finely chopped
1 large garlic clove, finely chopped

3 large tomatoes, peeled
    (see page 9), seeded, and chopped
2 zucchini, diced
1½ teaspoons marjoram leaves,
    chopped
salt and freshly ground black pepper
basil leaves, torn, to serve

1 Put the stock and corn cobs in a saucepan and season with salt. Cover and bring
   to a boil. Lower the heat and simmer 10 minutes, then discard the corn cobs.
2 Meanwhile, heat the oil in another saucepan over medium heat. Add the onion and
   garlic and fry, stirring occasionally, 3 to 5 minutes until softened but not colored.
   Add the tomatoes and zucchini and stir 2 minutes.
3 Add the stock and marjoram to the vegetables, cover, and bring to a boil. Lower the
   heat and simmer 3 minutes, then add the corn kernels and simmer 3 to 5 minutes
   longer until the kernels are tender. Adjust the salt and pepper, if necessary,
   and serve sprinkled with basil.

036 Fall Farmers' Market Soup

PREPARATION TIME 15 minutes, plus making the stock and croutes
COOKING TIME 40 minutes

1½ tablespoons olive or hemp oil
1½ cups seeded, peeled, and diced
    butternut squash
1 carrot, peeled and diced
2 garlic cloves, finely chopped
1 leek, halved lengthwise, thinly
    sliced, and rinsed
1 cup sweet apple or dry hard cider,
    to taste

4½ cups Vegetable Stock
    (see page 12) or ready-made stock
2 sage sprigs
2 tablespoons crème fraîche
    or sour cream (optional)
salt and freshly ground black pepper
chopped parsley leaves, to serve
1 recipe quantity Cheddar Croutes
    (see page 14), to serve

1 Heat the oil in a saucepan over medium heat. Stir in the squash, carrot, garlic,
   and leek, then cover and reduce the heat to low. Cook 10 to 12 minutes, stirring
   occasionally, until the vegetables begin to soften. Stir in the cider, stock, and sage
   and season with salt and pepper, then cover again and bring to a boil.
2 Lower the heat and simmer 15 to 20 minutes until the vegetables are tender.
   Discard the sage sprigs, then stir in the crème fraîche, if using. Adjust the salt and
   pepper, if necessary, and serve sprinkled with parsley and with croutes on the side.

037 Winter Farmers' Market Soup

PREPARATION TIME 20 minutes, plus making the stock and seeds
COOKING TIME 30 minutes

1 tablespoon butter
1 tablespoon olive or hemp oil
1 large carrot, peeled and diced
1 head of Belgian endive, halved
   lengthwise and sliced
1 small red potato, peeled and diced
1 large onion, finely chopped
1 shallot, finely chopped
1¼ cups peeled and diced celery root
5½ cups Vegetable Stock
   (see page 12) or ready-made stock

1 bouquet garni made with 1 piece
   of celery rib, 1 bay leaf, and
   several parsley and thyme sprigs
   tied together
¼ cup sour cream
2 tablespoons snipped chives
2 scallions, thinly sliced
salt and freshly ground black pepper
Spiced Seeds (see page 15)
1 roasted red pepper in olive oil,
   drained and diced, to serve

1 Melt the butter with the oil in a saucepan over medium heat. Add the carrot, endive, potato, onion, shallot, and celery root and fry, stirring, 3 to 5 minutes until the onion is softened but not colored. Add the stock and bouquet garni and season with salt and pepper. Cover and bring to a boil, then lower the heat and simmer 10 to 15 minutes until the vegetables are tender. Discard the bouquet garni.

2 Blend one-third of the soup until smooth, then return it to the pan. Add the sour cream, chives and scallions and reheat, then adjust the salt and pepper. Serve sprinkled with the seeds and the pepper.

038 Spring Farmers' Market Soup

PREPARATION TIME 15 minutes, plus making the stock   COOKING TIME 35 minutes

5½ cups Vegetable Stock
   (see page 12) or ready-made stock
4 large tomatoes, chopped
1 large shallot, sliced
2 large garlic cloves, chopped
1 bouquet garni made with 1 piece
   of celery rib with leaves, 1 bay leaf,
   and several basil sprigs
   tied together

1 teaspoon sugar
1 teaspoon dried mint
6 baby carrots, halved lengthwise
4 new potatoes, halved or quartered
1⅓ cups shelled peas
12 asparagus tips
salt and freshly ground black pepper
freshly grated Parmesan cheese,
   to serve

1 Put the stock, tomatoes, shallot, garlic, bouquet garni, and sugar in a saucepan over high heat. Cover and bring to a boil, then uncover and boil gently 10 minutes to reduce slightly. Strain the stock into a bowl, pressing down to extract as much flavor as possible.

2 Return the stock to the pan, add the mint and return to a boil. Add the carrots and potatoes and season with salt and pepper. Lower the heat and simmer, covered, 8 minutes. Add the peas and simmer 3 to 5 minutes longer, if frozen, or 5 to 8 minutes, if fresh. Add the asparagus for the final 3 minutes and simmer until all the vegetables are tender but still retain a little crispness. Adjust the salt and pepper, if necessary, and serve with Parmesan cheese on the side.

039 Twice-Cooked Sweet Potato Soup

PREPARATION TIME 15 minutes, plus making the stock and berry and seed mix
COOKING TIME 50 minutes

2 sweet potatoes, about 12 ounces,
  pricked all over with a fork
1 tablespoon butter
1 tablespoon sunflower oil
1 shallot, finely chopped
1 large garlic clove, chopped
3 to 4 cups Vegetable Stock
  (see page 12) or ready-made stock

¼ cup crème fraîche or sour cream,
  plus extra to serve (optional)
freshly grated nutmeg, to taste
salt and freshly ground black pepper
Goji Berry & Seed Mix (see page 15),
  to serve
snipped chives, to serve

1   Heat the oven to 425°F. Put the sweet potatoes on the oven rack and roast
    30 to 40 minutes until very tender when pierced with a knife. Transfer them
    to a heatproof bowl, cover with a clean dish towel, and set aside until cool enough
    to handle, then pull away and discard the skins. Set aside the potato flesh.
2   Melt the butter with the oil in a saucepan over medium heat. Add the shallot and
    fry, stirring occasionally, 2 minutes. Stir in the garlic and fry 1 to 3 minutes until the
    shallot is softened but not colored.
3   Stir in the sweet potatoes, mashing them up with a wooden spoon. Slowly stir in
    1½ cups of the stock, then season with salt and pepper and bring to a boil, stirring.
    Remove the pan from the heat.
4   Slowly stir in enough of the remaining stock to achieve the preferred consistency.
    (Any leftover stock can be used in other recipes or frozen for up to 6 months.)
    Return the pan to the heat and reheat, then stir in the crème fraîche and nutmeg.
    Adjust the salt and pepper, if necessary, and serve topped with crème fraîche,
    if you like, and sprinkled with berry and seed mix and chives.

040 Gujarati Yogurt Soup

PREPARATION TIME 15 minutes   **COOKING TIME** 10 minutes

8 fresh curry leaves
1 green chili, seeded (optional)
  and chopped, or to taste
½-inch piece of gingerroot,
  peeled and grated, or to taste
¼-inch piece of white turmeric
  (optional; look for it in Asian
  food stores)
1-inch piece cucumber, seeded
  and chopped

2 tablespoons chickpea flour
½ teaspoon ground coriander
2½ cups plain yogurt
2 tablespoons ghee or sunflower oil
1 teaspoon cumin seeds
1 teaspoon black mustard seeds
½ teaspoon fenugreek seeds
a pinch of ground asafetida
salt
2 handfuls of cilantro leaves, torn

1   Put half the curry leaves, the chili, ginger, and white turmeric, if using, in a small
    food processor and blend until very finely chopped (or use a mortar and pestle).
    Add the cucumber and blend again until the mixture forms a paste.
2   Put the chickpea flour and coriander in a bowl and season with salt, then add the
    yogurt and 2½ cups water and stir until smooth. Adjust the salt, if necessary,
    adding more chili and ginger, if you like.
3   Melt the ghee in a saucepan over medium heat. Add the cumin, mustard,
    and fenugreek seeds and stir 30 seconds, or until they crackle and pop. Watch
    closely so they do not burn. Stir in the asafetida and remaining curry leaves and stir
    just until the leaves sizzle.
4   Reduce the heat to very low (use a heat diffuser if you have one) and add the
    yogurt mixture, stirring continuously to prevent it from separating. Watch closely
    because the mixture will splutter. Stir 8 to 10 minutes until the soup thickens.
    Serve sprinkled with the cilantro leaves.

041 Leek & Sweet Potato Herb Soup

PREPARATION TIME 15 minutes, plus making the stock **COOKING TIME** 15 minutes

1 small handful of chervil
1 small handful of thyme
2 tarragon sprigs
1 large handful of curly-leaf parsley,
  leaves finely chopped and stems
  reserved and lightly crushed
1 small handful of chives, half of
  them chopped and kept separate
6 cups Vegetable Stock (see page 12)
  or ready-made stock

2 leeks, sliced in half lengthwise,
  thinly sliced, and rinsed
1 tablespoon butter
1 tablespoon sunflower, olive,
  or hemp oil
2 cups peeled and diced sweet
  potatoes
salt and freshly ground black pepper

1 Strip the leaves from half the chervil, thyme, and tarragon sprigs and mix them
   together with the chopped parsley and snipped chives, then set aside.
2 Put the parsley stems, whole chives and whole chervil, thyme, and tarragon sprigs
   in a saucepan. Add the stock and half the leeks and season lightly with salt. Cover
   and bring to a boil, then boil, uncovered, 10 minutes.
3 Meanwhile, melt the butter with the oil in a saucepan over medium heat. Stir in
   the sweet potatoes and remaining leek and reduce the heat to low. Cook, covered,
   8 to 10 minutes, stirring occasionally, until the leek is softened but not colored.
4 Strain the stock into the pan with the sweet potatoes, pressing down to extract
   as much flavor as possible. Bring to a boil, uncovered, then lower the heat and
   simmer 2 to 3 minutes until the potatoes are tender. Adjust the salt and pepper,
   if necessary. Just before serving, stir in the chopped herbs and simmer no longer
   than 30 seconds, then serve.

042 Potato & Mixed Vegetable Soup

PREPARATION TIME 15 minutes, plus making the stock   COOKING TIME 35 minutes

1 tablespoon butter
1 tablespoon olive or hemp oil
1 carrot, peeled and diced
1 onion, finely chopped
1 red bell pepper, chopped
5½ cups Vegetable Stock
  (see page 12) or ready-made stock

1 russet potato, peeled and cut into
  bite-size pieces
1 bay leaf
¼ cup chopped parsley leaves, plus
  extra to serve
salt and freshly ground black pepper
ground sumac, to serve

1   Melt the butter with the oil in a saucepan over medium heat. Stir in the carrot, onion, and pepper, reduce the heat to low and cook, covered, 10 to 12 minutes, stirring occasionally, until softened but not colored.

2   Add the stock, potato, and bay leaf and season with salt and pepper. Cover and bring to a boil, then reduce the heat to low. Simmer 10 to 12 minutes until the potato is tender. Discard the bay leaf, stir in the parsley and adjust the salt and pepper, if necessary. Serve sprinkled with parsley and sumac.

043 Curried Potato & Kale Soup

PREPARATION TIME 15 minutes, plus making the stock   COOKING TIME 30 minutes

1½ tablespoons sunflower
  or peanut oil
1 large onion, finely chopped
2 large garlic cloves, crushed
1 teaspoon ground coriander
1 teaspoon ground cumin
½ teaspoon cayenne pepper
½ teaspoon fenugreek seeds

½ teaspoon turmeric
4½ cups Vegetable Stock
  (see page 12) or ready-made stock
2 cups chopped kale leaves, rinsed
1 large russet potato, peeled
  and chopped
salt and freshly ground black pepper

1   Heat the oil in a saucepan over medium heat. Add the onion and fry, stirring occasionally, 2 minutes. Add the garlic and fry 1 to 3 minutes longer until the onion is softened. Stir in the coriander, cumin, cayenne pepper, fenugreek, and turmeric and stir 30 seconds. Watch closely so the spices do not burn.

2   Add the stock, kale, and potato and season with salt and pepper. Cover and bring to a boil. Lower the heat and simmer 12 to 15 minutes until the potato is tender but still holding its shape.

3   Blend about one-third of the soup until smooth, then stir this mixture back into the pan. Adjust the salt and pepper, if necessary, and serve.

044 No-Fat Vegetable Pot

PREPARATION TIME 20 minutes, plus making the stock   COOKING TIME 40 minutes

6 cups Vegetable Stock (see page 12)
  or ready-made stock
2 cups tomato puree
4 garlic cloves, very finely chopped
1 bouquet garni made with the
  leaves of 1 celery rib, 1 bay leaf,
  and a few parsley sprigs tied
  together

2¾ cups peeled, seeded, and
  chopped butternut squash
1 onion, chopped
1 carrot, peeled and sliced
1 celery rib, thinly sliced
1 leek, sliced and rinsed
1 parsnip, peeled and sliced
a pinch of dried chili flakes (optional)
salt and freshly ground black pepper

1   Put the stock, tomato puree, garlic, and bouquet garni in a saucepan and season with salt and pepper. Cover and bring to a boil, then uncover and boil 10 minutes to reduce slightly. Add the squash, onion, carrot, celery, leek, parsnip, and chili flakes and return to a boil.

2   Lower the heat and simmer, covered, 15 to 20 minutes until all the vegetables are tender. Discard the bouquet garni and adjust the salt and pepper, if necessary, then serve. Any leftover soup can be blended and used as a pasta sauce.

045 Roasted Garlic & Tomato Soup

PREPARATION TIME 15 minutes, plus making the stock
COOKING TIME 30 minutes

1 large garlic bulb,
  whole and unpeeled
2 tablespoons fruity extra-virgin olive
  oil, plus extra for roasting the
  garlic and to serve
2 onions, finely chopped
2 large garlic cloves, finely chopped
2⅔ cups tomato puree

2 cups Vegetable Stock (see page 12)
  or ready-made stock
1 Parmesan cheese rind, about
  3 x 2 inches (see page 9; optional)
a pinch of chili flakes (optional)
salt and freshly ground black pepper
a small handful of basil leaves,
  to serve

1   Heat the oven to 400°F. Rub the whole garlic with oil, put it directly on the oven
    rack, and roast 25 to 30 minutes until very soft.
2   Meanwhile, heat the oil in a saucepan over medium heat. Add the onion and fry,
    stirring occasionally, 2 minutes. Stir in the chopped garlic and fry 1 to 3 minutes
    longer until the onion is softened but not colored. Stir in the tomato puree
    and stock and add the cheese rind and chili flakes, if using. Season with salt
    and pepper, but remember if you have used the cheese rind, it was salty.
    Cover and bring to a boil, then lower the heat and leave to simmer until the
    garlic finishes roasting.
3   When the roasted garlic is tender, transfer it to a work surface, using a clean dish
    towel to protect your fingers. Set aside until cool enough to handle, then separate
    it into cloves and squeeze the softened flesh directly into the soup. Use a wooden
    spoon to mash the garlic against the side of the pan and stir until it "dissolves."
    Discard the cheese rind. Adjust the salt and pepper, if necessary, then serve
    topped with basil leaves and drizzled with olive oil.

046 Slow-Cooked Tomato & Orange Soup

PREPARATION TIME 15 minutes, plus making the stock and croutes (optional)
COOKING TIME 1¼ hours

2 tablespoons butter
1 tablespoon olive or hemp oil
2 celery ribs, finely chopped
2 shallots, finely chopped
2 large garlic cloves, finely chopped
4¼ cups chopped juicy tomatoes
4½ cups Vegetable Stock (see
  page 12) or ready-made stock
a pinch of sugar

a pinch of cayenne pepper
finely grated zest of 1 orange
2 to 4 tablespoons orange juice
salt and freshly ground black pepper
1 recipe quantity Goat Cheese
  Croutes (see page 14),
  to serve (optional)

1   Melt the butter with the oil in a saucepan over medium heat. Add the celery
    and shallots and fry, stirring occasionally, 2 minutes. Stir in the garlic and fry
    1 to 3 minutes longer until the shallots are softened but not colored. Add the
    tomatoes and stir 2 minutes, then stir in the stock, sugar, and cayenne pepper,
    and season with salt and pepper. Cover and bring to a boil, then reduce the heat
    to low (use a heat diffuser if you have one) and simmer 1 hour.
2   Strain the soup to remove the tomato seeds and skins, rubbing back and forth with
    a spoon and scraping the bottom of the strainer. Return the soup to the pan and
    blot with folded paper towel to remove the excess fat from the surface. Stir in the
    orange zest and 2 tablespoons of the orange juice and reheat. Adjust the salt and
    pepper, and add more orange juice, if you like. Serve with croutes, if you like.

047 Tomato & Thyme Soup with Polenta Dumplings

PREPARATION TIME 15 minutes, plus making the stock and dumplings
COOKING TIME 45 minutes

2 tablespoons butter
1 tablespoon sunflower oil
1 large onion, thinly sliced
1 garlic clove, crushed
¾ cup dry white wine
3 tablespoons all-purpose
   or wholewheat flour
a pinch of powdered mustard
2½ cups Vegetable Stock
   (see page 12) or ready-made stock

2 cans (15 oz.) crushed tomatoes
½ bunch of lemon thyme, about
   ½ ounce, tied together, plus extra
   leaves to serve
¼ cup tomato paste
2 teaspoons sugar
1 cup light cream
1 recipe quantity Polenta Dumplings
   (see page 13)
salt and freshly ground black pepper

1 Melt the butter with the oil in a saucepan over medium heat. Add the onion and fry, stirring occasionally, 2 minutes. Add the garlic and fry 1 to 3 minutes until the onion is softened but not colored. Stir in the wine, increase the heat to high, and cook 6 to 8 minutes until it almost evaporates, then reduce the heat to low.

2 Sprinkle in the flour and powdered mustard and stir 2 minutes. Slowly add the stock, stirring to prevent lumps from forming, then stir in the tomatoes, thyme, tomato paste, and sugar and season with salt and pepper. Cover and bring to a boil, then lower the heat and simmer 15 minutes.

3 Discard the thyme sprigs and blend the soup. Strain the soup into a large bowl and work it through the strainer, rubbing back and forth with a spoon and scraping the bottom of the strainer. Return the soup to the pan, stir in the cream, and reheat without boiling. Add the dumplings and simmer to reheat. Adjust the salt and pepper, if necessary, then serve sprinkled with extra thyme leaves. If you reheat the soup, do not boil it.

048 Chargrilled Pepper & Sun-Dried Tomato Soup

PREPARATION TIME 10 minutes, plus making the chargrilled peppers and stock
COOKING TIME 35 minutes

8 sun-dried tomatoes in oil,
  drained, with 1½ tablespoons
  of the oil reserved
1 large shallot, sliced
2 large garlic cloves, crushed
3 large red bell peppers,
  chargrilled (see page 9),
  peeled, seeded, and sliced

4¼ cups Vegetable Stock
  (see page 12) or ready-made stock
½ teaspoon sugar
salt and freshly ground black pepper
snipped chives or torn basil leaves,
  to serve

1 Heat the reserved oil in a saucepan over medium heat. Add the shallot and fry, stirring occasionally, 2 minutes. Stir in the garlic and fry 1 to 3 minutes until the shallot is softened but not colored. Stir in the tomatoes and peppers. Add the stock and sugar and season with salt and pepper. Cover and bring to a boil.

2 Lower the heat and simmer 20 minutes. Blend until smooth, then, working in batches, strain the soup into a large bowl and work it through the strainer, rubbing back and forth with a spoon and scraping the bottom of the strainer. Return the soup to the pan and adjust the salt and pepper, if necessary. Serve sprinkled with chives. You can also serve this soup chilled, adding a little extra stock to thin it and seasoning again with salt and pepper after chilling, if necessary.

049 Summer Tomato Soup with Noodles

PREPARATION TIME 15 minutes, plus making the stock and flavored oil
COOKING TIME 1½ hours

2 tablespoons butter
½ tablespoon olive or hemp oil
1 celery rib, finely chopped
1 onion, finely chopped
4 large garlic cloves, finely chopped
4¼ cups chopped juicy tomatoes
3¼ cups Vegetable Stock
  (see page 12) or ready-made stock
¼ teaspoon dried chili flakes,
  or to taste

¼ teaspoon dried oregano
3 ounces angel hair pasta
  or spaghetti, broken into
  bite-size pieces
salt and freshly ground black pepper
1 recipe quantity Crushed Basil Oil
  (see page 15), to serve
freshly grated Parmesan
  or pecorino cheese, to serve

1 Melt the butter with the oil in a saucepan over medium heat. Add the celery and onion and fry, stirring occasionally, 2 minutes. Stir in the garlic and fry 1 to 3 minutes until the onion is softened but not colored. Add the tomatoes and stir 2 minutes, then stir in the stock, chili flakes, and oregano and season with salt and pepper. Cover and bring to a boil, then reduce the heat to very low (use a heat diffuser if you have one) and simmer 1 hour.

2 Strain the soup into a large bowl and work it through the strainer to remove the tomato seeds and skins, rubbing back and forth with a spoon and scraping the bottom of the strainer. Return the soup to the pan, cover, and bring to a boil. Add the pasta and boil, uncovered, 6 to 10 minutes, or according to the package directions, until al dente. Adjust the salt and pepper, if necessary, then serve drizzled with basil oil and with Parmesan cheese on the side.

050 Edamame & Mushroom Soup

PREPARATION TIME 15 minutes, plus making the dashi, and 30 minutes soaking
the mushrooms   COOKING TIME 30 minutes

5 dried shiitake mushrooms
¾ cup frozen shelled
  edamame beans
3½ ounces enoki mushrooms,
  ends trimmed
2½ cups Vegetarian Dashi (see page
  12) or instant vegetarian dashi

soy sauce, to taste
5 ounces firm tofu, drained and diced
salt
shiso or cilantro leaves, to serve
yuzu powder or grated lemon
  or tangerine zest, to serve

1   Put the shiitake mushrooms and 3½ cups boiling water in a heatproof bowl and let
    soak 30 minutes, or until tender.
2   Meanwhile, bring a saucepan of salted water to a boil. Add the edamame and boil
    5 minutes, or until tender. Drain and immediately rinse under cold running water.
    Drain again and set aside.
3   Strain the mushrooms through a cheesecloth-lined strainer, or use a coffee filter.
    Put 2½ cups of the soaking liquid in a saucepan, add the dashi, and bring to a boil,
    covered, over high heat. Meanwhile, squeeze the shiitake mushrooms dry, cut off
    the stems, and slice the caps. Add the shiitake mushrooms and edamame to the
    dashi mixture, lower the heat and simmer, covered, 5 minutes, then season
    with soy sauce.
4   Divide the tofu into bowls. Divide the edamame and mushrooms into the bowls
    and ladle the soup over them. Serve sprinkled with shiso and yuzu.

051 Hot Tomato & Yogurt Soup

PREPARATION TIME 15 minutes, plus making the stock and preparing the tomatoes
COOKING TIME 20 minutes

¼ cup chickpea flour
½ teaspoon cayenne pepper,
  or to taste
½ teaspoon salt, plus extra to season
2 cups plain yogurt
5 large tomatoes, grated (see page 9)
2 tablespoons ghee or sunflower oil

2 garlic cloves, crushed
4 cups Vegetable Stock
  (see page 12), ready-made stock
  or water, plus extra as needed
freshly ground black pepper
Spiced Seeds (see page 15), to serve
chopped cilantro leaves, to serve

1   Mix the chickpea flour, cayenne pepper, and salt together in a large bowl and make
    a well in the middle. Add the yogurt, whisking to prevent lumps from forming, then
    stir in the tomatoes and set aside.
2   Melt the ghee in a saucepan over medium heat. Add the garlic and stir 30 seconds,
    or until very lightly colored. Watch closely so it does not burn. Remove the pan
    from the heat and slowly stir in the yogurt mixture, then stir in the stock.
3   Return the pan to the heat and bring to a boil, whisking continuously. Reduce the
    heat to very low (use a heat diffuser if you have one) and simmer 6 to 8 minutes,
    whisking occasionally, until the soup thickens and the raw flavor of the flour
    is cooked out. If it thickens too much, stir in a little extra stock or water. Season
    with pepper and adjust the salt, if necessary. Serve sprinkled with seeds and
    cilantro leaves.

052 Mushroom Miso Soup

PREPARATION TIME 10 minutes, plus making the dashi   COOKING TIME 15 minutes

1 recipe quantity Vegetarian Dashi
(see page 12) or 5 cups prepared
instant vegetarian dashi
¼ cup dark miso paste
5 shiitake mushroom caps, sliced

5 ounces shimeji or enoki
mushrooms, ends trimmed
2 scallions, finely chopped
5 ounces tofu, drained and diced
1 cilantro leaf for each bowl,
to serve

1   Put the dashi in a saucepan, cover, and bring to a boil, then lower the heat
and leave to simmer. Put the miso paste in a heatproof bowl and slowly stir
in 1 to 2 ladlefuls of the dashi to make a thin paste, then stir this mixture into the
dashi. Do not boil. Add the mushrooms and scallions and simmer 1 to 2 minutes
until the mushrooms are tender.
2   Divide the tofu into bowls. Divide the mushrooms and scallions into the bowls,
then ladle the soup over them. Top each bowl with 1 cilantro leaf and serve.

053 Wakame Miso Soup

PREPARATION TIME 5 minutes, plus making the dashi   COOKING TIME 15 minutes

1 recipe quantity Vegetarian Dashi
(see page 12) or 5 cups prepared
instant vegetarian dashi
¼ cup light miso paste
1 handful of bean sprouts, rinsed

2 tablespoons dried wakame flakes
5 ounces tofu, drained and diced
2 scallions, very finely chopped,
to serve

1   Put the dashi in a saucepan, cover, and bring to a boil, then reduce the heat
to low and leave to simmer. Put the miso paste in an heatproof bowl and stir in
1 to 2 ladlefuls of the hot dashi to blend. Stir this mixture into the dashi and add
the bean sprouts. Do not boil. Stir in the wakame, which will immediately soften.
2   Divide the tofu into bowls, then add the bean sprouts. Ladle the soup into the
bowls and serve sprinkled with scallions.

054 Hot & Sour Vegetable Soup with Tofu

PREPARATION TIME 10 minutes, plus at least 30 minutes soaking the mushrooms
and making the stock   COOKING TIME 15 minutes

2 handfuls of bean sprouts
8 dried Chinese mushrooms
5 cups Vegetable Stock (see page 12)
or ready-made stock
3 tablespoons Chinese rice vinegar
1 tablespoon light soy sauce
1 cup drained and very thinly sliced
canned bamboo shoots
4 baby corn cobs, halved lengthwise
2 large garlic cloves, finely chopped

4 snow peas, very thinly
sliced lengthwise
1 to 2 bird's-eye chilies, seeded
(optional) and sliced, to taste
1 carrot, peeled and grated
lengthwise
2 tablespoons arrowroot
9 ounces firm tofu, drained and diced
shiso or cilantro leaves, to serve

1   Put the bean sprouts in a bowl, cover with cold water, and set aside. Put the
mushrooms in a heatproof bowl, cover with boiling water, and let soak 30 minutes,
or until tender. Drain, rinse under cold water, and squeeze dry. Trim the bottom
off the stems, if necessary, slice the caps and stems and set aside.
2   Put the stock, vinegar, and soy sauce in a saucepan. Cover and bring to a boil,
then lower the heat to medium and add the bamboo shoots, corn cobs, garlic,
snow peas, chilies, carrot, and mushrooms. Cover and boil 2 minutes.
3   Put the arrowroot and 3 tablespoons cold water in a small heatproof bowl and mix
until smooth, then stir in a ladleful of the hot stock. Stir this mixture into the soup
and simmer 2 to 3 minutes until it is slightly thicker. Drain the bean sprouts, then
add them and the tofu to the pan. Warm through, then serve sprinkled with
shiso leaves.

055 Cream of Mushroom Soup

PREPARATION TIME 15 minutes, plus 30 minutes soaking the mushrooms and making the stock   COOKING TIME 25 minutes

1 ounce dried porcini mushrooms
2 tablespoons butter
1 tablespoon olive or hemp oil
1 shallot, finely chopped
7 cups trimmed and sliced cremini
    and/or portobello mushrooms
2 tablespoons all-purpose
    or wholewheat flour

6 cups Vegetable Stock (see page 12)
    or ready-made stock
1 teaspoon dried thyme
1 cup heavy cream
1 tablespoon Marsala wine,
    or to taste
salt and freshly ground black pepper
chopped parsley leaves, to serve

1   Put the porcini mushrooms and 1 cup boiling water in a heatproof bowl and leave
    to soak for 30 minutes, or until tender. Strain through a cheesecloth-lined strainer
    and set the liquid aside. Squeeze the mushrooms, then trim the stems,
    if necessary, and thinly slice the caps and stems, then set aside.
2   Melt the butter with the oil in a saucepan over medium heat. Add the shallot and
    fry, stirring occasionally, 2 minutes. Add all the mushrooms, season with salt,
    and cook, stirring occasionally, 4 to 5 minutes until the mushrooms soften and
    give off their liquid. Sprinkle in the flour and stir 2 minutes.
3   Remove the pan from the heat and slowly add the stock, stirring continuously
    to prevent lumps from forming. Return the pan to the heat, add the thyme, and
    season with pepper. Cover and bring to a boil, then boil, uncovered, 5 minutes,
    or until the liquid is reduced by about half. Stir in the cream, wine, and 1 cup of the
    reserved soaking liquid and return to a boil, stirring. Adjust the salt and pepper,
    if necessary, and serve sprinkled with parsley.

056 Tuscan "Cooked Water" Soup

PREPARATION TIME 15 minutes, plus preparing the tomatoes
COOKING TIME 50 minutes

3 tablespoons fruity extra-virgin olive
    oil, plus extra to serve
2 celery ribs, finely chopped
1 carrot, peeled and diced
1 large red onion, diced
1 red bell pepper, seeded and diced
3 large plum tomatoes, peeled
    (see page 9), seeded, and diced

1 Parmesan, pecorino, or Gruyère
    cheese rind, about 3 x 2 inches
    (see page 9; optional)
1 large egg for each bowl
1 slice of day-old ciabatta bread
    for each bowl
2 or 3 large garlic cloves, halved
freshly grated pecorino cheese,
    to serve

1   Heat the oil in a saucepan over medium heat. Add the celery, carrot, onion, and bell
    pepper and fry, stirring, 3 to 5 minutes until the onion is softened but not colored.
    Add the tomatoes, cheese rind, if using, and 5½ cups water. Season with salt and
    pepper. Cover and bring to a boil, then lower the heat and simmer 30 minutes.
2   Heat the broiler on high. Uncover the pan and lower the heat so the soup just
    simmers. Remove the cheese rind from the soup; depending on how much it has
    dissolved, you can either discard it or finely chop and set it aside.
3   Break the eggs, one by one, into a cup and then gently lower them into the
    simmering soup. Use a large metal spoon to spoon some of the liquid over each
    egg and poach 3 minutes for soft-set yolks and up to 5 minutes for firmer yolks.
    Adjust the salt and pepper, if necessary.
4   Meanwhile, toast the bread under the broiler 1 to 2 minutes on each side until crisp
    and golden brown. Rub one side of each slice with half a garlic clove, pressing
    down firmly, then set aside and keep warm while the eggs poach.
5   Divide the toast into bowls and drizzle generously with olive oil. Transfer 1 egg
    to each bowl and sprinkle with cheese and chopped rind, if using. Ladle the soup
    into the bowls and serve with extra oil for adding at the table.

057 Mixed Mushroom Broth

PREPARATION TIME 15 minutes, plus 30 minutes soaking the mushrooms and making the stock   COOKING TIME 20 minutes

½ ounce dried porcini mushrooms
3 tablespoons olive or hemp oil
1 large leek, halved lengthwise, thinly sliced, and rinsed
2 large garlic cloves, finely chopped
7 cups coarsely chopped mixed mushrooms

5½ cups Vegetable Stock (see page 12) or ready-made stock
2-inch piece of rosemary sprig
2 tablespoons sweet sherry
salt and freshly ground black pepper

1   Put the porcini mushrooms and 1 cup boiling water in a heatproof bowl and leave to soak 30 minutes, or until tender. Strain through a cheesecloth-lined strainer, and reserve the liquid. Squeeze the mushrooms, trim the stems, if necessary, and thinly slice the caps and stems, then set aside.

2   Heat the oil in a saucepan over medium heat. Add the leek and garlic and fry, stirring occasionally, 2 minutes. Add the mushrooms, season with salt and cook 5 to 8 minutes, stirring, until the mushrooms give off their liquid. Stir in the stock, rosemary, porcini mushrooms, and reserved liquid and season with salt and pepper.

3   Cover and bring to a boil, then lower the heat and simmer 8 to 10 minutes until the mushrooms are tender. Discard the rosemary sprig and stir in the sherry. Adjust the salt and pepper, if necessary, then serve.

058 Shiitake & Chinese Cabbage Soup

PREPARATION TIME 10 minutes, plus making the stock   COOKING TIME 45 minutes

5½ cups Vegetable Stock (see page 12) or ready-made stock
1-inch piece of gingerroot, peeled and smashed in one piece

½-inch piece of galangal, peeled and smashed in one piece
1 ounce dried shiitake mushrooms
light soy sauce, to taste
4½ cups shredded Chinese cabbage

1   Put the stock, ginger, and galangal in a saucepan. Cover and bring to a boil, then lower the heat and simmer 30 minutes. Meanwhile, put the shiitake mushrooms and 1 cup boiling water in a heatproof bowl and let soak 30 minutes, or until tender. Strain through a cheesecloth-lined strainer, and set the liquid aside. Squeeze the mushrooms dry, cut off the stems and slice the caps.

2   Stir the reserved liquid into the stock and season with soy sauce. Add the mushrooms and cabbage and simmer 5 to 8 minutes until the mushrooms are tender, then discard the ginger and galangal and serve.

059 Mushroom & Coconut Soup

PREPARATION TIME 15 minutes, plus making the stock and chilies
COOKING TIME 20 minutes

1 small handful of bean sprouts
3¼ cups coconut milk
2¼ cups Vegetable Stock (see page 12) or ready-made stock
½ lemongrass stem, crushed
2 tablespoons lime juice, or to taste
5 kaffir lime leaves

6 cups trimmed and sliced cremini mushrooms
2¼ cups trimmed and sliced oyster mushrooms
salt and freshly ground black pepper
Chilies in Vinegar (see page 15), to serve

1   Put the bean sprouts in a bowl, cover with cold water, and set aside.

2   Put the coconut milk, stock, lemongrass, lime juice, and lime leaves in a saucepan. Season with salt and pepper, cover, and bring to a boil. Add all the mushrooms, lower the heat and simmer, covered, 6 to 8 minutes until the mushrooms are tender. Discard the lime leaves and lemongrass.

3   Drain the bean sprouts and add them to the soup. Adjust the salt and pepper, if necessary, and add extra lime juice to taste. Serve with the chilies on the side.

060 Arame & Tofu Soup

PREPARATION TIME 25 minutes, plus making the dashi and seeds
COOKING TIME 15 minutes

¾ ounce dried arame
4½ cups Vegetarian Dashi
   (see page 12) or prepared instant
   vegetarian dashi
2 radishes, very thinly sliced
   or coarsely grated
1 carrot, peeled and coarsely grated
1 red chili, seeded and thinly chopped

1 zucchini, coarsely grated
1 tablespoon light soy sauce
1 tablespoon rice wine
14 ounces fried tofu, cut into
   ½-inch cubes
toasted sesame seeds (see page 9),
   to serve

1   Put the arame in a large bowl, cover with cold water, and let soak 15 minutes,
    or until doubled in volume, then drain.
2   Put the dashi in a saucepan over high heat, cover, and bring to a boil. Add the
    arame and boil, covered, 3 to 5 minutes until tender. Add the radishes, carrot,
    and zucchini and boil, uncovered, 30 seconds to 1½ minutes until the vegetables
    are tender. Stir in the soy sauce and rice wine. Divide the tofu into bowls and ladle
    the arame and soup over it. Serve sprinkled with sesame seeds.

061 Welsh Leek & Parsley Soup with Rarebit "Soldiers"

PREPARATION TIME 20 minutes, plus making the stock   COOKING TIME 25 minutes

1 tablespoon butter
1 tablespoon sunflower oil
1 leek, sliced and rinsed
1 large garlic clove, chopped
3¼ cups Vegetable Stock
   (see page 12) or ready-made stock
2½ cups peeled and chopped
   russet potatoes
1⅓ cups whole milk
5 ounces curly parsley, leaves and
   stems chopped, with 2 tablespoons
   leaves reserved to serve
salt and ground white pepper

RAREBIT SOLDIERS
3 slices of white
   or wholewheat bread
1½ cups grated sharp cheddar
   cheese or crumbled
   Caerphilly cheese
1½ teaspoons powdered mustard
1 tablespoon brown ale, hard cider,
   or dry white wine
vegetarian Worcestershire sauce,
   to taste

1   Heat the broiler on high and line a cookie sheet with foil. Melt the butter with the oil in a saucepan over medium heat. Add the leek and fry, stirring, 2 minutes. Stir in the garlic and fry 1 to 3 minutes until the leek is softened but not colored. Add the stock and potatoes and season well with salt. Cover and bring to a boil, then lower the heat and simmer 10 to 12 minutes until the potatoes are very tender.

2   Meanwhile, to make the "soldiers," toast the bread on one side under the broiler 1 to 2 minutes until golden brown. Put the bread on the cookie sheet, toasted-side down, and set aside. Put the cheese, powdered mustard, and ale in a small saucepan over medium heat and beat until the cheese melts and a thick paste forms. Spread the paste over the bread and splash with a few drops of Worcestershire sauce. Broil 2 minutes, or until the cheese mixture bubbles. Cut the crusts off the toast, then cut each slice into 4 fingers. Set aside and keep warm.

3   Add the milk to the soup and return to just below the boil. As it starts to bubble, stir in the parsley, then immediately turn off the heat. Let the soup stand, uncovered, about 30 seconds to soften the parsley, then blend the soup until smooth. Adjust the salt and white pepper, if necessary, and serve sprinkled with parsley and with the "soldiers" on the side. If you reheat the soup, do not boil it.

062 Forager's Nettle & Wild Garlic Soup

PREPARATION TIME 25 minutes, plus making the stock   COOKING TIME 35 minutes

9 ounces young stinging nettle tops
   (use only the top 2 to 2½ inches)
2 tablespoons butter
1 tablespoon olive or hemp oil
1 large onion
1 teaspoon sugar
5 stems of wild garlic, chopped,
   with the flowery tops reserved,
   if available, to serve

1 russet potato, peeled and chopped
5½ cups Vegetable Stock
   (see page 12) or ready-made stock
salt and freshly ground black pepper
wild garlic flowers or snipped chives,
   to serve (optional)
sour cream, to serve (optional)

1   Wearing rubber gloves, remove the nettle leaves from the stems. Tie the stems together with kitchen string and lightly crush, then set aside. Wash the leaves well in several changes of cold water, then transfer to a colander and set aside to drain.

2   Melt the butter with the oil in a saucepan over medium heat. Add the onion and sugar and fry, stirring, 10 to 12 minutes until the onions are starting to caramelize. Stir in the wild garlic and potatoes and fry 2 minutes. Add the stock and nettle leaves and stems and season with salt and pepper.

3   Cover and bring to a boil, then lower the heat and simmer, uncovered, 12 to 15 minutes until the potato is tender. Remove the nettle stems, then blend the soup until smooth, stopping to unclog the blender blades if necessary. Adjust the salt and pepper, if necessary, and serve sprinkled with wild garlic flowers and with sour cream on the side for adding at the table, if you like.

063 Rich Orange-Scented Chestnut Soup

PREPARATION TIME 25 minutes, plus making the stock   COOKING TIME 55 minutes

2 sweet cooking apples,
  peeled and chopped
1 tablespoon lemon juice
2 tablespoons sunflower, olive,
  or hemp oil
1 cup peeled and chopped
  celery root
1 onion, chopped
1 leek, chopped and rinsed
1 bay leaf

1 thyme sprig
a pinch of freshly grated nutmeg
9 ounces canned or vacuum-packed
  chestnuts, drained and chopped
4½ cups Vegetable Stock
  (see page 12) or ready-made stock
2 tablespoons orange juice
¼ cup heavy cream
salt and freshly ground black pepper
grated zest of 2 oranges, to serve

1 Put the apples in a bowl, add the lemon juice, and toss together, then set aside.
2 Heat the oil in a large saucepan over medium heat. Add the celery root, onion, leek,
   bay leaf, thyme, and nutmeg and season with salt and pepper. Cook, covered,
   8 to 10 minutes, stirring. Stir in the apples, chestnuts, stock, and orange juice.
3 Cover and bring to a boil, then lower the heat and simmer 30 to 35 minutes until
   the chestnuts are tender enough to be mashed against the side of the pan. Discard
   the bay leaf and thyme. Blend the soup until smooth, then stir in the cream and
   adjust the salt and pepper, if necessary. Serve sprinkled with orange zest.

064 Creamy Peanut & Chili Soup

PREPARATION TIME 10 minutes, plus making the stock   COOKING TIME 35 minutes

2 tablespoons sunflower oil
1 celery rib, thinly sliced
1 small onion, very finely chopped
1½ tablespoons all-purpose flour
3¼ cups Vegetable Stock
  (see page 12) or ready-made stock

a pinch of dried chili flakes,
  or to taste
½ cup natural smooth peanut butter
¾ cup light cream
salt and freshly ground black pepper

1 Heat the oil in a saucepan. Add the celery and onion and fry, stirring, 3 to 5 minutes
   until softened. Sprinkle in the flour and stir 2 minutes, then slowly stir in the stock
   and chili flakes and season with salt and pepper, stirring continuously.
2 Bring to a boil, then add the peanut butter and stir until it dissolves. Lower the heat
   and simmer, covered, 15 minutes. Stir in the cream and simmer 2 minutes. Do not
   boil. Adjust the salt and pepper, if necessary, and serve.

065 Plantain & Corn Soup

PREPARATION TIME 10 minutes, plus 30 minutes soaking the chili and making the stock
COOKING TIME 40 minutes

1 dried ancho chili pepper
4½ cups Vegetable Stock
  (see page 12) or ready-made stock
1 tablespoon butter
2 tablespoons sunflower oil
1 onion, chopped

1 green bell pepper, seeded
  and chopped
2 large garlic cloves, crushed
2 green plantains, coarsely grated
2½ cups frozen corn kernels
salt and freshly ground black pepper

1 Put the ancho chili in a heatproof bowl, cover with hot water, and let soak
   30 minutes, then drain and finely chop. Pound the chili to form a paste, adding
   a little of the stock, if necessary, then set aside.
2 Melt the butter with the oil in a saucepan over medium heat. Add the onion
   and pepper and fry, stirring, 2 minutes. Add the garlic and chili paste and fry
   1 to 3 minutes until the onion is softened. Add the plantain and remaining stock
   and season with salt and pepper. Cover and bring to a boil, then lower the heat and
   simmer, covered, 15 minutes, stirring occasionally. Stir in the corn and simmer
   10 minutes. Adjust the salt and pepper, if necessary, and serve.

066 Okra & Corn Soup

PREPARATION TIME 15 minutes, plus 30 minutes soaking the okra, making the stock and chili bon-bon, and preparing the tomatoes   **COOKING TIME** 30 minutes

1 cup sliced okra
1 tablespoon white wine vinegar
½ teaspoon salt, plus extra to season
1 tablespoon sunflower oil
1 onion, finely chopped
2 garlic cloves, chopped
5½ cups Vegetable Stock
   (see page 12) or ready-made stock
a pinch of dried chili flakes (optional)

4 large tomatoes, peeled
   (see page 9), seeded, and chopped
2⅔ cups frozen corn kernels
1 tablespoon tomato paste
2 tablespoons chopped
   curly parsley leaves
freshly ground black pepper
Chili Bon-Bon (see page 15)
   or hot pepper sauce, to serve

1   Put the okra, vinegar, and salt in a large bowl. Cover with water and let soak for
    30 minutes, then drain, rinse, drain again, and set aside. This helps to reduce the
    okra's sliminess while it cooks.
2   Heat the oil in a saucepan over medium heat. Add the onion and fry, stirring
    occasionally, 2 minutes. Add the garlic and okra and fry, stirring continuously,
    3 to 6 minutes until the onion is softened and light golden brown. Add the stock
    and chili flakes, if using, and season with salt and pepper. Cover and bring to a boil,
    then lower the heat and simmer 5 minutes.
3   Stir in the tomatoes, corn, and tomato paste and simmer 5 to 10 minutes until
    the okra is tender. Stir in the parsley and adjust the salt and pepper, if necessary.
    Serve with chili bon-bon for adding at the table.

067 Cream of Corn Soup

PREPARATION TIME 10 minutes, plus making the stock   **COOKING TIME** 35 minutes

3½ cups Vegetable Stock
(see page 12) or
ready-made stock
freshly cut kernels from 2 corn cobs,
about 2 cups, with the cobs
reserved and cut in half
2 tablespoons butter
3 tablespoons all-purpose flour

2 cups whole milk
1 roasted red pepper in olive oil,
drained and finely chopped
2 scallions, very thinly sliced
cayenne pepper (optional)
salt and freshly ground black pepper
chopped parsley leaves, to serve

1   Put the stock and corn cobs in a large saucepan and season with salt. Cover
and bring to a boil, then lower the heat and simmer at least 10 minutes.
2   Meanwhile, melt the butter in a large saucepan over medium heat. Sprinkle in
the flour and stir 2 minutes, then remove the pan from the heat and slowly stir
in the milk, stirring continuously to prevent lumps from forming.
3   Remove the corn cobs from the stock and discard. Slowly stir 2½ cups of the
stock into the white sauce and simmer 5 minutes, stirring occasionally, until
the soup is thick and smooth.
4   Stir in the corn kernels and simmer 5 minutes. Add the bell pepper and scallions
and season with cayenne pepper, if using. Season with salt and pepper, but
remember the stock was salted. Simmer 3 to 5 minutes until the corn and pepper
are tender. Serve sprinkled with parsley.

068 Onion & Mustard Soup

PREPARATION TIME 15 minutes, plus making the stock and crisps
COOKING TIME 35 minutes

3 tablespoons butter
½ tablespoon sunflower oil
3¼ cups finely chopped onions
1 leek, white part only, thinly sliced
and rinsed
⅓ fennel bulb, chopped
4½ cups Vegetable Stock
(see page 12) or ready-made stock
1 tablespoon whole grain mustard

salt and freshly ground black pepper
alfalfa sprouts, to serve
snipped chives, to serve

PARMESAN CRISPS
¾ cup finely grated fresh
Parmesan cheese
1 teaspoon all-purpose
or wholewheat flour

1   Melt the butter with the oil in a saucepan over medium heat. Add the onions, leek,
and fennel and fry, stirring occasionally, 3 to 5 minutes until the vegetables are
softened but not colored. Stir in the stock and season with salt and pepper. Cover
and bring to a boil, then lower the heat and simmer 25 to 30 minutes until the
vegetables are very tender.
2   Meanwhile, make the Parmesan crisps. Heat the oven to 375°F and line a cookie
sheet with parchment paper. Mix the cheese and flour together in a bowl, then
divide the mixture into 12 equal portions and space them out on the cookie sheet.
Bake 10 to 15 minutes until they spread and become golden brown. Use a metal
spatula to transfer the crisps to a wire rack and let cool completely.
3   Blend the soup until smooth. Working in batches, strain the soup through a fine
strainer back into the pan, rubbing back and forth with a spoon and scraping the
bottom of the strainer. Stir in the mustard and reheat. Adjust the salt and pepper,
if necessary, then serve sprinkled with alfalfa sprouts and chives and with the
cheese crisps on the side.

069 Curried Parsnip Soup

PREPARATION TIME 15 minutes, plus making the stock   COOKING TIME 30 minutes

2 tablespoons sunflower oil
1 large onion, chopped
2 garlic cloves, chopped
1 tablespoon Madras
    or other curry paste
½ teaspoon turmeric
2 cups peeled and chopped parsnips
1 large sweet cooking apple, peeled,
    cored, and chopped

2½ cups Vegetable Stock
    (see page 12) or ready-made stock
2½ cups whole milk
salt and freshly ground black pepper
plain yogurt, to serve
shredded cilantro leaves, to serve

1 Heat the oil in a saucepan over medium heat. Add the onion and fry, stirring,
   2 minutes. Add the garlic and fry 1 to 3 minutes until the onion is softened but not
   colored. Stir in the curry paste and turmeric and fry, stirring, 30 seconds. Watch
   closely so the spices do not burn. Stir in the parsnips and apple, then add the stock
   and season with salt and pepper. Cover and bring to a boil.
2 Lower the heat and simmer 12 to 15 minutes until the parsnips are tender. Stir
   in the milk and simmer 5 minutes longer. Do not boil. Blend the soup until smooth.
   Adjust the salt and pepper, if necessary, and serve topped with a swirl of yogurt
   and sprinkled with cilantro. If you reheat the soup, do not boil it.

070 Parsnip & Orange Soup

PREPARATION TIME 20 minutes, plus making the stock   COOKING TIME 35 minutes

2 tablespoons butter
1 tablespoon sunflower oil
1 large onion, chopped
1 large garlic clove, chopped
2 tablespoons all-purpose
    or wholewheat flour
4 cups Vegetable Stock (see page 12)
    or ready-made stock

2½ cups peeled and chopped parsnip
1 russet potato, peeled and chopped
½ cup orange juice
salt and freshly ground black pepper
grated zest of 2 oranges, to serve
black sesame seeds, to serve

1 Melt the butter with the oil in a saucepan over medium heat. Add the onion and fry,
   stirring occasionally, 2 minutes. Stir in the garlic and fry 1 to 3 minutes until the
   onion is softened but not colored. Sprinkle in the flour and cook, stirring, 2 minutes,
   then slowly pour in the stock, stirring continuously to prevent lumps from forming.
   Add the parsnips and potatoes and season with salt and pepper.
2 Cover and bring to a boil, then lower the heat and simmer 15 to 20 minutes until
   the parsnips are very tender. Stir in the orange juice, then blend the soup until
   smooth. Adjust the salt and pepper, if necessary, and serve sprinkled with the
   orange zest and sesame seeds.

071 Red-Hot Red Pepper Soup

PREPARATION TIME 15 minutes, plus making the stock   COOKING TIME 30 minutes

2 tablespoons butter
2 tablespoons olive or hemp oil
1 shallot, chopped
5 roasted red bell peppers in
    olive oil, drained and chopped
1 russet potato, peeled and chopped

1 red chili, sliced
5½ cups Vegetable Stock
    (see page 12) or ready-made stock
salt and freshly ground black pepper
hot pepper sauce, to serve

1 Melt the butter with the oil in a saucepan over medium heat. Add the shallot and
   fry, stirring, for 3 to 5 minutes until softened. Stir in the bell peppers, potato, and
   chili and fry, stirring, 5 minutes. Add the stock and season with salt and pepper.
2 Cover and bring to a boil, then lower the heat and simmer 10 minutes until the
   potato is very tender. Blend the soup until smooth and reheat. Adjust the salt
   and pepper, if necessary. Serve with hot pepper sauce for adding at the table.

072 Rich Pepper & Orange Soup

PREPARATION TIME 15 minutes   **COOKING TIME** 25 minutes

3 tablespoons olive or hemp oil
8 large red bell peppers, or a mix
   of red, orange, and yellow bell
   peppers, seeded and sliced
4 to 6 tablespoons lemon juice
finely grated zest of 2 large oranges

1¼ cups blood or regular
   orange juice
salt and freshly ground black pepper
thinly sliced mint leaves, to serve
hot pepper sauce, to serve (optional)

1   Heat the oil in a saucepan over medium heat. Add the bell peppers, 2 tablespoons
    of the lemon juice, and half the orange zest and season with salt and pepper. Cook,
    covered, 20 to 25 minutes, stirring frequently, until the peppers are very tender.
    Watch closely so they do not burn.
2   Remove the pan from the heat and stir in the orange juice and 2 tablespoons of the
    remaining lemon juice. Blend until smooth, then strain the soup into a large bowl
    and work it through the strainer, rubbing back and forth with a spoon and scraping
    the bottom of the strainer. Gradually stir in enough of the remaining lemon juice
    to sharpen the flavor, if necessary, tasting as you go. Adjust the salt and pepper,
    if necessary, then serve sprinkled with the orange zest and mint and with hot
    pepper sauce, if you like. You can also serve this soup chilled, adding a little extra
    stock to thin it and seasoning again with salt and pepper after chilling, if necessary.

073 Watercress Soup

PREPARATION TIME 15 minutes, plus making the stock   **COOKING TIME** 30 minutes

2 tablespoons butter
1 tablespoon sunflower oil
1 shallot, finely chopped
1 large russet potato, peeled
   and diced
5½ cups Vegetable Stock
   (see page 12) or ready-made stock

14 ounces watercress, trimmed
   and chopped
¼ cup crème fraîche or sour cream
¼ cup whole milk
freshly grated nutmeg, to taste
salt and freshly ground black pepper

1   Melt the butter with the oil in a saucepan over medium heat. Add the shallot and
    fry, stirring, 3 to 5 minutes until softened but not colored. Stir in the potato, then
    add the stock and season with salt and pepper. Cover and bring to a boil. Lower
    the heat and simmer 10 to 12 minutes until the potato is very tender. Uncover,
    add the watercress, and simmer 1 minute, then blend the soup until smooth.
2   Bring to just below the boil and stir in the crème fraîche and milk. Add the nutmeg
    and adjust the salt and pepper, if necessary, and serve. You can also serve this
    soup chilled, adding a little extra stock to thin it and seasoning again with salt and
    pepper after chilling, if necessary.

074 Spinach & Buttermilk Soup

PREPARATION TIME 10 minutes, plus making the stock   **COOKING TIME** 25 minutes

3½ cups Vegetable Stock
   (see page 12) or ready-made stock
1 pound spinach, any thick stems
   removed and leaves chopped
½ to 1 tablespoon lemon juice

1¼ cups buttermilk, plus extra
   to serve
freshly grated nutmeg, to taste
salt and freshly ground black pepper

1   Put the stock and spinach in a saucepan, add ½ tablespoon of the lemon juice
    and season with salt and pepper. Cover and bring to a boil, then lower the heat
    and simmer 10 to 12 minutes until tender.
2   Blend the soup until smooth, then strain into a bowl and work it through the
    strainer, rubbing back and forth with a spoon and scraping the bottom of the
    strainer. Return the soup to the pan, stir in the buttermilk, and season with nutmeg.
    Reheat, but do not boil it. Adjust the salt and pepper, if necessary, then add extra
    lemon juice or nutmeg, if you like. Serve with a little extra buttermilk swirled in.

075 Curried Spinach & Coconut Soup

PREPARATION TIME 15 minutes, plus making the stock   COOKING TIME 25 minutes

1 tablespoon butter
1½ tablespoons sunflower
   or peanut oil
1 leek, thinly sliced and rinsed
2 garlic cloves, finely chopped
1-inch piece of gingerroot, peeled
   and grated
1 tablespoon korma or other
   curry powder
1 teaspoon ground coriander

1 teaspoon cumin seeds,
   lightly crushed
7 ounces spinach, any thick stems
   removed and leaves chopped
3¼ cups Vegetable Stock
   (see page 12) or ready-made stock
1¾ cup coconut milk
¼ cup silken tofu
lime juice, to taste
sesame seeds, to serve

1   Melt the butter with the oil in a saucepan over medium heat. Add the leek and fry,
    stirring occasionally, 2 minutes. Stir in the garlic and ginger and fry 1 to 3 minutes
    until the leek is softened but not colored. Stir in the curry powder, coriander,
    and cumin seeds and stir 30 seconds, or until aromatic. Watch closely so the spices
    do not burn. Add the spinach and stir 3 to 5 minutes until it wilts.
2   Stir in the stock, coconut milk, and tofu. Cover and bring to just below the boil.
    Lower the heat and simmer 5 minutes, then blend until smooth. Season with
    lime juice and serve sprinkled with sesame seeds.

076 Spinach & Mung Bean Soup

PREPARATION TIME 10 minutes, plus making the stock   COOKING TIME 25 minutes

4½ cups Vegetable Stock
   (see page 12) or ready-made stock
1 cup peeled and coarsely
   grated turnip
1 tablespoon dried mint leaves
½ teaspoon ground fenugreek

a pinch of turmeric
14 ounces baby spinach leaves,
   chopped
1 cup canned mung beans,
   drained and rinsed
salt and freshly ground black pepper

1   Put the stock, turnips, mint, fenugreek, and turmeric in a saucepan. Stir in the
    spinach and season with salt and pepper. Cover and bring to a boil, then reduce
    the heat to low. Simmer 10 to 12 minutes until the vegetables are very tender.
2   Blend the soup, then stir in the mung beans and simmer 4 to 5 minutes to warm
    through. Adjust the salt and pepper, if necessary, and serve.

077 Zucchini & Arugula Soup with Croutes

PREPARATION TIME 15 minutes, plus making the stock, berry and seed mix, and croutes
COOKING TIME 20 minutes

2 tablespoons butter
1 tablespoon olive or hemp oil
2 onions, finely chopped
2 large garlic cloves, crushed
2 large zucchini, sliced
1 cup chopped arugula leaves
6 cups Vegetable Stock (see page 12)
   or ready-made stock

2 to 3 tablespoons lemon juice
salt and freshly ground black pepper
Goji Berry & Seed Mix (see page 15),
   to serve
1 recipe quantity Goat Cheese
   Croutes (see page 14), to serve

1   Melt the butter with the oil in a saucepan over medium heat. Add the onion and fry,
    stirring, 2 minutes. Add the garlic and fry 1 to 3 minutes until the onion is softened
    but not colored. Add the zucchini and fry, stirring, 2 to 3 minutes until the skins turn
    bright green. Stir in the arugula and stock, then cover and bring to a boil.
2   Lower the heat and simmer, covered, 2 to 3 minutes until the zucchini are tender.
    Stir in the lemon juice to taste and season with salt and pepper. Blend the soup
    until smooth, then serve sprinkled with the berry and seed mix and with the
    croutes on the side.

078 Spring Sorrel & Spinach Soup with Egg Butterballs

PREPARATION TIME 25 minutes, plus making the stock and cooking the eggs
COOKING TIME 40 minutes

2 tablespoons butter
1 tablespoon olive or hemp oil
1 large onion, chopped
4 large garlic cloves, chopped
1½ cups young sorrel leaves,
   stems crushed
2 handfuls of baby spinach leaves
5½ cups Vegetable Stock
   (see page 12) or ready-made stock
2 tablespoons chopped parsley leaves
salt and freshly ground black pepper

EGG BUTTERBALLS
7 tablespoons butter, at room
   temperature
2 extra-large hard-boiled egg yolks,
   chopped
a pinch of turmeric
a pinch of cayenne pepper (optional)

1   Melt the butter with the oil in a saucepan over medium heat. Add the onion and
    garlic, reduce the heat to low, and cook, covered, 10 to 12 minutes until very tender
    and just starting to turn golden. Add the sorrel and spinach and stir 3 to 5 minutes
    until they wilt. Add the stock and parsley and season with salt and pepper.
2   Bring to a boil, partially covered. Lower the heat and simmer, partially covered,
    10 to 15 minutes until the leaves are very tender.
3   Meanwhile, make the butterballs. Put the butter, egg yolks, turmeric, and cayenne
    pepper, if using, in a bowl and beat together. Season with salt and pepper, then
    divide the mixture into 12 equal portions and roll into balls. (The butterballs can
    be made up to 1 day in advance and chilled until required.)
4   Blend the soup until smooth, then work it through a strainer into a bowl,
    rubbing back and forth with a spoon and scraping the bottom of the strainer.
    Return the soup to the pan, adjust the salt and pepper, if necessary,
    and reheat. Add the butterballs and serve.

079   Butternut Squash & Chestnut Soup

PREPARATION TIME 15 minutes, plus making the stock   COOKING TIME 40 minutes

1 tablespoon olive or hemp oil
1 red onion, chopped
2 large garlic cloves, finely chopped
4¼ cups peeled, seeded, and
   chopped butternut squash
4½ cups Vegetable Stock
   (see page 12) or ready-make stock

1 bay leaf
1 cup canned chestnut puree
salt and freshly ground black pepper
Greek-style yogurt, to serve
flaxseed, lightly crushed, to serve
chopped parsley leaves, to serve

1   Heat the oil in a saucepan over medium heat. Add the onion and fry, stirring
    occasionally, 2 minutes. Add the garlic and fry 1 to 3 minutes until the onion
    is softened but not colored, then stir in the squash. Add the stock and bay leaf
    and season with salt and pepper. Cover and bring to a boil, then lower the heat
    and simmer 20 to 25 minutes until the squash is very tender.
2   Strain the stock and discard the bay leaf. Return the squash and onion to the
    pan and stir in the chestnut puree. Gradually stir in the stock until you have the
    preferred consistency. Reheat and adjust the salt and pepper, if necessary.
    Serve topped with yogurt and sprinkled with flaxseed and parsley.

080   Thai-Style Pumpkin Soup

PREPARATION TIME 25 minutes, plus making the stock   COOKING TIME 45 minutes

2 pounds pumpkin, cut into wedges
   and seeded
3 tablespoons olive or hemp oil
2 shallots, chopped
2 garlic cloves, chopped
2 tablespoons grated gingerroot
2¼ cups Vegetable Stock
   (see page 12) or ready-made stock

1 bird's-eye chili, seeded (optional)
   and chopped
1 lemongrass stalk, finely chopped,
   with outer layer removed
2¼ cups coconut milk
salt and freshly ground black pepper
chopped cilantro leaves, to serve
chopped roasted peanuts, to serve
lime wedges, to serve

1   Heat the oven to 425°F. Put the pumpkin in a baking tray, drizzle with 1 tablespoon
    of the oil, and season with salt. Toss well to coat and roast 40 to 50 minutes,
    stirring once or twice, until the pumpkin is tender. Remove from the oven and set
    aside until cool enough to handle.
2   Meanwhile, heat the remaining oil in a saucepan over medium heat. Stir in the
    shallots and fry, stirring occasionally, 2 minutes. Add the garlic and ginger and fry
    1 to 3 minutes until the shallots are softened but not colored. Add the stock, chili,
    and lemongrass and season with salt and pepper. Cover and bring to a boil, then
    lower the heat and simmer 15 minutes.
3   Scrape the pumpkin flesh from the skin and add it to the soup, then blend until
    smooth. Stir in the coconut milk, reheat, and adjust the salt and pepper, if
    necessary. Serve sprinkled with cilantro and peanuts and with lemon wedges
    for squeezing over at the table.

081   Breakfast Tea Soup

PREPARATION TIME 10 minutes, plus making the tea   COOKING TIME 2 minutes

3¼ cups whole milk
4 to 6 slices of white bread,
   buttered and crusts cut off
4 to 6 tablespoons sugar, or to taste

ground clove, to taste
cinnamon, to taste
2 cups freshly brewed tea

1   Heat the milk to just below the boil. Meanwhile, divide the bread into four
    bowls and sprinkle each portion with 1 tablespoon of the sugar and a little
    ground clove and cinnamon. Pour the tea over the bread.
2   Add the milk, stir well, and serve, sprinkling with extra sugar, if you like.

Roasted Squash & Tomato Soup

PREPARATION TIME 20 minutes, plus making the stock   **COOKING TIME** 25 minutes

3 large tomatoes, halved
1 butternut squash, about 1¼ pounds
6 large whole garlic cloves, peeled
1 red onion, quartered
½-inch piece of gingerroot, peeled
   and thinly sliced
2½ tablespoons olive or hemp oil,
   plus extra for frying the seeds

½ teaspoon ground coriander
½ teaspoon ground cumin
½ teaspoon hot paprika, or to taste
3¼ cups Vegetable Stock
   (see page 12) or ready-made stock
salt and freshly ground black pepper
chopped parsley leaves, to serve

1   Heat the oven to 425°F. Put the tomatoes, cut-sides down, in a baking tray. Cut the
squash in half, scoop out the seeds and set them aside. Coarsely chop the squash
into 2-inch pieces—there's no need to peel it—and add it to the baking tray, along
with the garlic, onion, and ginger. Add the oil, coriander, cumin, and paprika and
season with salt and pepper. Toss well to coat, then roast 20 minutes, stirring once
or twice, until the squash and onion are tender and the tomato skins have burst.

2   Meanwhile, put several layers of paper towel on a plate and set aside. Rinse the
squash seeds well and use your fingers to remove the fibers, then pat dry with
paper towels. Heat a thin layer of the oil in a skillet over high heat. Add the seeds
and stir 30 seconds to 1 minute until they start to pop and turn golden brown.
Watch closely so they do not burn. Immediately turn them out of the pan onto
the plate and set aside.

3   Transfer the vegetables from the baking tray to a large heatproof bowl or blender
and add half the stock. Blend until smooth. Working in batches, strain the soup
into a saucepan and work it through the strainer, rubbing back and forth with
a spoon and scraping the bottom of the strainer. Stir in enough of the remaining
stock to achieve the preferred consistency and reheat. (Any leftover stock can
be used in other recipes or frozen for up to 6 months.) Adjust the salt and pepper,
if necessary, then serve, sprinkled with the seeds and parsley.

083 Spiced Pumpkin & Apple Soup

PREPARATION TIME 15 minutes, plus making the stock and toasting the almonds
COOKING TIME 30 minutes

1 tablespoon butter
1 tablespoon olive or hemp oil
1 small onion, finely chopped
2 garlic cloves, very finely chopped
½ tablespoon peeled and chopped
   gingerroot
½ teaspoon cinnamon
cayenne pepper, to taste
5½ cups Vegetable Stock
   (see page 12) or ready-made stock

1 can (15-oz.) pumpkin puree
1 apple, such as Granny Smith,
   peeled, cored, and chopped
½ teaspoon dried thyme leaves
1 bay leaf
¼ cup dry sherry
¼ cup Greek-style yogurt
salt and freshly ground black pepper
toasted slivered almonds
   (see page 9), to serve

1 Heat the butter and oil in a saucepan over medium heat. Add the onion and fry, stirring, 2 minutes. Add the garlic and ginger and fry 1 to 3 minutes until the onion is softened but not colored. Add the cinnamon and cayenne pepper and stir 30 seconds, or until aromatic. Watch closely so the spices do not burn. Stir in the stock, pumpkin puree, apple, thyme, and bay leaf and season with salt and pepper. Cover and bring to a boil, then lower the heat and simmer 15 minutes.

2 Discard the bay leaf. Blend the soup until smooth. Stir in the sherry and yogurt and reheat but do not boil. Adjust the salt and pepper, if necessary, then serve sprinkled with almonds.

084 Swiss Chard & Garlic Broth

PREPARATION TIME 15 minutes, plus making the stock   COOKING TIME 35 minutes

6½ cups Vegetable Stock
   (see page 12) or ready-made stock
1 large garlic bulb, separated into
   cloves, peeled, and lightly crushed
1 onion, unpeeled and cut in half
1 russet potato, peeled and chopped
1 bay leaf

a large pinch of saffron threads
a pinch of dried chili flakes
½ teaspoon salt, plus extra to season
1 pound Swiss chard leaves,
   thick stems removed and
   leaves thinly sliced
freshly ground black pepper

1 Put the stock, garlic, onion, potato, bay leaf, saffron, chili flakes, and salt in a large saucepan over high heat. Cover and bring to a boil, then lower the heat and simmer, partially covered, 20 minutes to reduce slightly. Strain the stock into a bowl. Discard the onion and bay leaf, then press down on the garlic and potato to extract as much flavor and texture as possible.

2 Return 5½ cups of the stock to the pan and bring to a boil. Add the Swiss chard, lower the heat, and simmer 3 to 5 minutes until it wilts. Adjust the salt and pepper, if necessary, and serve.

085 Yogurt & Cilantro Soup

PREPARATION TIME 15 minutes, plus making the stock   COOKING TIME 45 minutes

4¼ cups Vegetable Stock
   (see page 12) or ready-made stock
3 large garlic cloves, chopped
1 large onion, chopped
1 large handful of cilantro, leaves
   chopped and stems separated

1 teaspoon coriander seeds,
   lightly crushed
finely grated zest of 2 limes
2 to 4 tablespoons lime juice
1¾ cups Greek yogurt, whisked
salt and freshly ground black pepper

1 Put the stock, garlic, onion, cilantro stems, coriander seeds, and lime zest in a saucepan. Season with salt and pepper, cover and bring to a boil, then lower the heat and simmer 35 minutes. Strain the stock, then return it to the pan.

2 Whisk the yogurt in a bowl with a ladleful of the hot stock, then stir it into the soup and heat. Do not boil. Stir in the leaves and lime juice to taste, adjust the salt and pepper, if necessary, then serve.

086 Amish Potato Soup with Rivvels

PREPARATION TIME 15 minutes **COOKING TIME** 25 minutes

2 cups peeled and diced
   red potatoes
1 celery rib, finely chopped
1 onion, finely chopped
2¼ cups whole milk
1 tablespoon butter
salt and freshly ground black pepper
chopped parsley leaves, to serve

RIVVELS
½ cup all-purpose flour,
   plus extra as needed
¼ teaspoon salt
1 egg, beaten

1 Put the potatoes, celery, onion, and 3 cups water in a saucepan and season
lightly with salt. Cover and bring to a boil, then lower the heat and simmer
10 to 15 minutes until the potatoes are tender.

2 Meanwhile, to make the rivvels, put the flour and salt in a bowl and make a well
in the middle. Add the egg and beat it into the flour until the mixture begins to flake
like pastry. Add extra flour, 1 tablespoon at a time, if necessary, until the mixture
flakes. Press the mixture between your thumb and fingers to make flakes slightly
less than ½ inch in size. Put the flakes in a strainer and gently shake to get rid
of any excess flour.

3 When the potatoes are tender, stir in the milk and butter and bring to just below
the boil. Drop the rivvels into the pan and cook 3 minutes, until the soup thickens
and the rivvels form dumpling-like lumps. Season with salt and pepper and serve
sprinkled with parsley.

087 Rosemary-Scented Pea & Lentil Soup

PREPARATION TIME 10 minutes, plus making the stock **COOKING TIME** 1 hour

1 tablespoon olive or hemp oil
1 shallot, chopped
seeds from 1 green cardamom pod
6 cups Vegetable Stock (see page 12)
   or ready-made stock
½ cup dried green lentils, rinsed

2 tablespoons chopped
   rosemary leaves
⅔ cup frozen peas
salt and freshly ground black pepper
Greek yogurt, to serve

1 Heat the oil in a saucepan over medium heat. Add the shallot and fry 3 to 5 minutes
until softened. Add the cardamom seeds and stir 30 seconds, or until aromatic.
Watch closely so they do not burn. Add the stock, lentils, and rosemary and season
with salt and pepper. Cover and bring to a boil, then lower the heat and simmer
30 to 40 minutes until the lentils are tender.

2 Add the peas and simmer, uncovered, 3 to 5 minutes until tender, then blend
until smooth. Adjust the salt and pepper, if necessary, and serve with yogurt.

088 Corn & Bean Broth

PREPARATION TIME 5 minutes, plus making the stock **COOKING TIME** 35 minutes

6½ cups Vegetable Stock
   (see page 12) or ready-made stock
4 garlic cloves, chopped
2 leeks, trimmed, chopped,
   and rinsed
1 bay leaf

1 can (15-oz.) navy or red kidney
   beans, drained and rinsed
1 cup frozen corn kernels
salt and freshly ground black pepper
snipped chives, to serve
chopped parsley leaves, to serve

1 Put the stock, garlic, leeks, and bay leaf in a saucepan over high heat and season
with salt and pepper. Cover and bring to a boil, then lower the heat and simmer,
partially covered, 20 minutes to reduce slightly and flavor the stock.

2 Strain the stock into a bowl. Return 5½ cups of the stock to the pan and
bring to a boil. Add the beans and corn kernels, lower the heat, and simmer
5 to 8 minutes until the corn is tender. Adjust the salt and pepper, if necessary,
then serve sprinkled with chives and parsley.

CHAPTER 2

MEAT SOUPS

It's easy to think of meat soups as substantial winter meals,

but light, spiced soups imbued with traditional flavorings

from Southeast Asia give this chapter a year-round appeal.

The recipes here include quick-cooking Asian soups, such

as Thai-inspired Beef & Coconut Soup with Pea Eggplants and

Bangkok Pork & Shrimp Soup, as well as slow-simmered,

more filling soups such as Hearty Beef & Stout Soup and

Cardamom-Scented Lamb Soup with Couscous. Substantial

soups like these will not only warm and satisfy you on cold

days but fill your kitchen with inviting aromas as well. And, like

most stews and casseroles, slow-cooked meat soups benefit

from being made a day in advance and reheated, making them

an ideal choice when friends are coming around for a meal.

Rich meat soups can be surprisingly economical, too.

Portuguese Caldo Verde, German Liver Dumpling Soup, and

Oxtail Soup with Barley make filling soups that won't cost a lot.

If the choices here leave you craving more, see the Big Bowl

Soups chapter for more meaty inspiration.

HAM & CHEESE BELGIAN ENDIVE SOUP (SEE PAGE 80)

089 Curried Beef & Potato Soup

PREPARATION TIME 20 minutes, plus making the stock   COOKING TIME 40 minutes

3 garlic cloves, finely chopped
½-inch piece of gingerroot, peeled
  and very finely chopped
2 tablespoons peanut oil
2 onions, chopped
1 tablespoon chopped cilantro leaves
1 teaspoon turmeric

½ teaspoon cayenne pepper
14 ounces ground beef
4¼ cups Beef Stock (see page 10)
  or ready-made stock
1 can (15-oz.) crushed tomatoes
4 waxy new potatoes, diced
salt and freshly ground black pepper

1 Put the garlic and ginger in a small food processor, or use a mortar and pestle.
   Season with salt and grind together to form a paste, then set aside.
2 Heat the oil in a saucepan over medium heat. Add the onions and fry, stirring
   occasionally, 2 minutes. Stir in the garlic paste, cilantro, turmeric, and cayenne and
   fry, stirring, 1 to 3 minutes until the onions are softened. Stir in the beef and fry,
   breaking up the meat, 2 to 3 minutes until it changes color. Pour off the excess fat,
   then stir in the stock and tomatoes. Season with salt and pepper and bring to a boil.
3 Skim, then simmer, covered, 10 minutes. Stir in the potatoes and add water if the
   soup is too thick. Simmer, covered, 10 to 12 minutes until they are tender. Skim
   and adjust the salt and pepper, if necessary, then serve.

090 Quick Tex-Mex Chili Soup

PREPARATION TIME 10 minutes, plus making the stock   COOKING TIME 35 minutes

2 tablespoons garlic-flavored
  sunflower oil
1 large onion, finely chopped
7 ounces ground beef
1 can (15-oz.) canned kidney beans,
  drained and rinsed
1 can (15-oz.) crushed tomatoes

4 teaspoons chili con carne
  seasoning mix
½ teaspoon sugar
2¼ cups Beef Stock (see page 10)
salt and freshly ground black pepper
sour cream, to serve
tortilla chips, to serve

1 Heat the oil in a saucepan over medium heat. Add the onion and fry, stirring,
   3 minutes. Add the beef and fry 5 to 8 minutes, breaking up the meat, until
   it changes color. Pour off the excess fat.
2 Stir in the beans, tomatoes, chili seasoning, and sugar. Add the stock and bring
   to a boil, stirring occasionally. Skim, if necessary, then lower the heat and simmer,
   covered, 15 minutes. Season with salt and pepper, if necessary, but remember
   the chili seasoning contains both. Serve with sour cream and tortilla chips.

091 Stuffed-Pepper-in-a-Bowl Soup

PREPARATION TIME 15 minutes, plus making the stock and rice
COOKING TIME 45 minutes

1 tablespoon garlic-flavored olive oil
1 onion, finely chopped
7 ounces ground beef
2¼ cups Beef Stock (see page 10)
  1 can (15-oz.) crushed tomatoes
1½ cups tomato puree
1 red bell pepper, seeded
  and chopped

2 tablespoons light brown sugar
1½ teaspoons dried thyme leaves
a pinch of ground allspice
a pinch of chili flakes, or to taste
salt and freshly ground black pepper
½ cup cooked rice
2 tablespoons chopped
  parsley leaves

1 Heat the oil in a saucepan over medium heat. Add the onion and fry, stirring,
   3 minutes. Stir in the beef and fry, breaking up the meat, 5 to 8 minutes until it is
   brown. Pour off the excess fat, then stir in the stock, tomatoes, tomato puree, bell
   peppers, sugar, thyme, allspice and chili flakes and season with salt and pepper.
2 Bring to a boil, then simmer 25 minutes. Skim and stir in the rice. Heat through,
   adjust the salt and pepper, if necessary, and serve sprinkled with parsley.

092   Red Wine Soup

PREPARATION TIME 20 minutes, plus making the stock and croutes
COOKING TIME 45 minutes

1 tablespoon butter
2 tablespoons garlic-flavored olive oil
8½ cups trimmed and thinly sliced
  cremini mushrooms
1 onion, finely chopped
2 carrots, peeled and sliced
2 celery ribs, thinly sliced
3 red potatoes, peeled and diced

1 cup dry red wine
4½ cups Beef Stock (see page 10)
  or ready-made stock
1 tablespoon cornstarch
salt and freshly ground black pepper
chopped parsley leaves, to serve
1 recipe quantity Gruyère Croutes
  (see page 14), to serve

1   Melt the butter with half the oil in a saucepan over medium heat. Add the
    mushrooms, season with salt, and fry, stirring, 5 to 8 minutes until they release
    their juices. Remove them from the pan and set aside.
2   Add the remaining oil to the fat remaining in the pan. Add the onion, lower the heat,
    and cook, covered, 10 to 12 minutes until softened and just starting to color.
    Add the carrots, celery, and potatoes and stir 2 minutes. Stir in the wine, increase
    the heat to high and cook 8 minutes, or until the wine reduces to about ¼ cup.
    Add the stock and mushrooms and season with salt and pepper. Cover and bring
    to a boil, then lower the heat and simmer 5 minutes.
3   Put the cornstarch and ½ cup cold water in a heatproof bowl and mix until the
    cornstarch dissolves. Stir a ladleful of the stock into the cornstarch mixture, then
    stir this into the soup. Bring to a boil, stirring until the soup is thickened and the
    vegetables are tender. Adjust the salt and pepper, if necessary, then serve
    sprinkled with parsley and with croutes on the side.

093   Hearty Beef & Stout Soup

PREPARATION TIME 20 minutes, plus making the stock   COOKING TIME 2 hours

1 pound 5 ounces boneless beef
  chuck, in one piece
1 tablespoon all-purpose flour
3 tablespoons sunflower oil
2 carrots, peeled and sliced
1 leek, halved lengthwise,
  thinly sliced, and rinsed
4 large garlic cloves, chopped
5 cups trimmed and thinly sliced
  cremini mushrooms

2¾ cups Beef Stock (see page 10)
  or ready-made stock
2½ cups stout, such as Guinness
1 bouquet garni made with 1 piece
  of celery rib, 1 bay leaf, and
  several parsley and thyme sprigs
  tied together
salt and freshly ground black pepper
chopped parsley leaves, to serve

1   Put the beef in a plastic bag, add the flour, and season with salt and pepper.
    Hold the top of the bag closed and shake well to coat the beef. Transfer the beef
    to a plate, shaking off any excess flour. Heat half the oil in a large saucepan over
    medium heat. Add the beef and fry 3 to 5 minutes until brown on both sides,
    then remove the beef from the pan and set aside.
2   Add the remaining oil to the pan and heat. Stir the carrots and leek into the
    pan, reduce the heat to very low (use a heat diffuser if you have one) and cook,
    covered, 8 to 10 minutes until the carrot is softened and just starting to color.
    Add the garlic and fry 30 seconds longer. Add the mushrooms, season with salt,
    and fry 5 to 8 minutes until the mushrooms release their juices.
3   Add the stock, scrape the bottom of the pan, using a spoon, and stir well. Return
    the beef and its juices to the pan, cover, and bring to a boil. Skim, then add the
    stout and bouquet garni. Season with salt and pepper, but remember the beef has
    already been seasoned. Lower the heat and simmer, covered, 1½ to 1¾ hours until
    the beef is very tender. Remove the beef and set aside until cool enough to handle.
    Discard the bouquet garni.
4   Cut the beef into fine shreds, return it to the soup, and warm through. Adjust the
    salt and pepper, if necessary, and serve sprinkled with parsley.

094 French Onion Soup

PREPARATION TIME 10 minutes, plus making the stock and croutes
COOKING TIME 40 minutes

2 tablespoons butter
2 tablespoons olive oil
4 large onions, thinly sliced
4 garlic cloves, crushed
1 teaspoon sugar
5½ cups Beef Stock (see page 10)
  or ready-made stock
6 tablespoons brandy

1 bouquet garni made with
  1 piece of celery rib, 1 bay leaf,
  4 parsley sprigs, and 4 thyme
  sprigs tied together
salt and freshly ground black pepper
1 Croute (see page 14) for each bowl,
  to serve
2½ cups grated Gruyère cheese,
  to serve

1   Melt the butter with the oil in a saucepan over medium heat. Add the onions and
    fry, stirring, 3 to 5 minutes until softened. Reduce the heat to very low (use a heat
    diffuser if you have one), stir in the garlic and sugar, and fry, stirring frequently,
    5 to 8 minutes longer until the onions are golden brown and caramelized. Add the
    stock, brandy, and bouquet garni and season with salt and pepper. Cover and bring
    to a boil, then lower the heat and simmer 15 minutes.
2   Meanwhile, heat the broiler on high. Arrange four to six flameproof soup bowls
    on a baking sheet and put 1 croute in each.
3   Discard the bouquet garni. Ladle the soup into the bowls and divide the cheese
    over the tops. Broil 2 to 3 minutes until the cheese has melted and is bubbling.
    Serve immediately.

095 Thai Beef & Cabbage Soup

PREPARATION TIME 20 minutes, plus making the stock, garlic, and chilies
COOKING TIME 2 hours

6 cups Beef Stock (see page 10)
    or ready-made stock
1 pound 5 ounces boneless beef
    brisket or chuck, in one piece,
    trimmed
1½-inch piece of galangal,
    peeled and sliced
½-inch piece of gingerroot,
    peeled and sliced
2 tablespoons light soy sauce,
    or to taste

1 kaffir lime leaf
1 cinnamon stick
¾ cup chopped green beans
3 celery ribs, thinly sliced
1¼ cups shredded Chinese cabbage
freshly ground black pepper
chopped cilantro leaves, to serve
Crisp-Fried Garlic (see page 15),
    to serve
Chilies in Vinegar (see page 15),
    to serve

1   Put the stock and beef in a saucepan. Season with pepper, cover, and bring
    to a boil. Skim, then add the galangal, ginger, soy sauce, lime leaf, and cinnamon
    stick. Lower the heat and simmer, covered, 1½ to 1¾ hours until the beef is tender.
    Remove the beef from the pan and set aside until cool enough to handle. Discard
    the galangal, ginger, lime leaf, and cinnamon stick.
2   Stir the beans and celery into the stock and simmer 10 minutes. Add the cabbage
    and simmer 3 to 5 minutes until the vegetables are tender. Remove any sinew
    from the beef and cut the flesh into bite-size pieces, then return it to the soup.
    Reheat, adjust the salt and pepper, if necessary, and serve sprinkled with cilantro
    and with the garlic and chilies on the side.

096 Beef Soup with Mushrooms & Peas

PREPARATION TIME 10 minutes, plus making the stock   COOKING TIME 2¼ hours

1 pound boneless beef brisket
    or chuck, in one piece, trimmed
1 tablespoon all-purpose
    or wholewheat flour
½ teaspoon hot paprika
3 tablespoons sunflower oil
1 large leek, sliced and rinsed
2 large garlic cloves, chopped
5¾ cups trimmed and thinly sliced
    cremini mushrooms

5½ cups Beef Stock (see page 10)
    or ready-made stock
1 bouquet garni made with 1 piece
    of celery rib, 1 bay leaf, and
    several parsley and thyme sprigs
    tied together
⅔ cup frozen peas
Worcestershire Sauce, to taste
salt and freshly ground black pepper
chopped parsley leaves, to serve

1   Put the beef in a plastic bag, add the flour and paprika, and season with salt and
    pepper. Hold the top of the bag closed and shake well to coat the beef. Transfer
    the beef to a plate, shaking off any excess flour. Heat 2 tablespoons of the oil
    in a saucepan over medium heat. Add the beef and fry 3 to 5 minutes until brown
    on both sides. Remove it from the pan and set aside.
2   Add the remaining oil to the fat remaining in the pan and heat over medium heat.
    Add the leek and fry, stirring occasionally, 2 minutes. Add the garlic and fry
    1 to 3 minutes until the leek is softened but not colored. Add the mushrooms,
    season with salt and fry 5 to 8 minutes until the mushrooms give off their juices.
    Add the stock and use a spoon to scrape the bottom of the pan.
3   Return the beef to the pan with any accumulated juices and season with salt and
    pepper—but remember that the mushrooms and beef have already been salted.
    Cover and bring to a boil. Skim, then add the bouquet garni. Lower the heat and
    simmer, covered, 1½ to 1¾ hours until the beef is tender. Remove the beef and
    set aside until cool enough to handle. Discard the bouquet garni.
4   Add the peas to the soup, bring to a boil, and boil 3 to 5 minutes until tender.
    Remove any sinew from the beef and cut the flesh into fine shreds, then return
    it to the soup and warm through. Add the Worcestershire sauce and adjust the
    salt and pepper, if necessary. Serve sprinkled with parsley.

097 Beef & Celery Root Soup

PREPARATION TIME 20 minutes, plus making the stock   COOKING TIME 2 hours

1½ tablespoons olive or hemp oil
1 small leek, sliced in half
   lengthwise, thinly sliced,
   and rinsed
1½ cups thinly sliced fennel
2 large garlic cloves, chopped
1 pound 5 ounces boneless beef
   chuck, in one piece, trimmed

3¼ cups Beef Stock (see page 10)
   or ready-made stock
1 can (15-oz.) crushed tomatoes
2 thyme sprigs
1⅓ cups peeled celery root cut into
   bite-size pieces
salt and freshly ground black pepper
chopped parsley leaves, to serve

1   Heat the oil in a saucepan over medium heat. Add the leek and fennel and fry,
    stirring occasionally, 2 minutes. Stir in the garlic and fry 1 to 3 minutes until the leek
    is softened but not colored. Add the beef, stock, tomatoes, and thyme and season
    with salt and pepper. Cover and bring to a boil. Skim, then lower the heat and
    simmer, covered, 1¼ hours, stirring occasionally.

2   Add the celery root and simmer 15 to 30 minutes until the beef and celery root are
    tender. Remove the beef and set aside until cool enough to handle. Discard the
    thyme sprigs. Remove any sinew from the beef and cut the flesh into bite-size
    pieces, then return it to the soup. Adjust the salt and pepper, if necessary,
    and serve sprinkled with parsley.

098 Beef & Bulgur Wheat Soup

PREPARATION TIME 10 minutes, plus making the stock and chili bon-bon
COOKING TIME 2¼ hours

1½ tablespoons olive or hemp oil
2 onions, chopped
2 large garlic cloves
1 pound 5 ounces boneless beef
   chuck, in one piece, trimmed
5½ cups Beef Stock (see page 10)
   or ready-made stock
1 can (15-oz.) crushed tomatoes
1 cinnamon stick
2 tablespoons tomato paste

a pinch of sugar
several cilantro sprigs, tied together
   with the stems crushed, plus extra
   chopped leaves to serve
1 carrot, peeled and sliced
2 tablespoons bulgur wheat
salt and freshly ground black pepper
Greek yogurt, to serve (optional)
Chili Bon-Bon (see page 15) or hot
   pepper sauce, to serve (optional)

1   Heat the oil in a saucepan over medium-high heat. Add the onions and fry, stirring,
    7 minutes. Add the garlic and fry 1 to 3 minutes until the onions start to color.
    Add the beef and stock, then cover and bring to a boil. Skim the suface. Add the
    tomatoes, cinnamon stick, tomato paste, sugar, and cilantro and season with salt
    and pepper. Lower the heat and simmer, covered, 1½ hours.

2   Stir in the carrot and bulgur wheat and simmer, covered, 20 to 25 minutes until
    the bulgur and beef are both tender. Remove the beef from the pan and set aside
    until cool enough to handle. Discard the cilantro sprigs and cinnamon stick.

3   Remove any sinew from the beef and cut the meat into bite-size pieces, then
    return it to the soup. Reheat and adjust the salt and pepper, if necessary. Serve
    topped with yogurt and cilantro leaves and with chili bon-bon on the side for
    adding at the table, if using.

099 Beef Consommé with Porcini Mushrooms

PREPARATION TIME 15 minutes, plus making the consommé and 30 minutes soaking the mushrooms   COOKING TIME 5 minutes

1 ounce dried porcini mushrooms
5½ cups Beef Consommé
  (see page 13)

1 tablespoon dry sherry (optional)
salt (optional)
chopped parsley leaves, to serve

1   Put the mushrooms in a heatproof bowl, cover with boiling water, and let soak 30 minutes, or until tender. Strain through a cheesecloth-lined strainer. (The soaking liquid can be used in another recipe or frozen until required.) Squeeze the mushrooms, trim the bottoms of the stems, if necessary, then thinly slice the caps and stems and divide them into serving bowls.

2   Put the consommé in a saucepan over high heat and heat to just below the boil. Stir in the sherry, if using, and season with salt, if required. Ladle the consommé over the mushrooms, sprinkle with parsley, and serve immediately.

100 Chinese Beef & Greens Soup

PREPARATION TIME 15 minutes, plus making the stock   COOKING TIME 25 minutes

5½ cups Beef Stock (see page 10)
  or ready-made stock
2 large garlic cloves, cut in half
1 handful of watercress, leaves and
  stems separated
½-inch piece of gingerroot, sliced
1 thin slice of galangal, peeled

½ tablespoon light soy sauce,
  or to taste
2 or 3 bok choy, halved or quartered
14 ounces sirloin steak, thinly sliced
  across the grain
freshly ground black pepper
toasted sesame oil, to serve

1   Put the stock, garlic, watercress stems, ginger, galangal, and soy sauce in a saucepan. Cover, bring to a boil, and boil 10 minutes. Strain, then return the stock to the pan. Bring to a slow boil, add the bok choy, and boil 3 to 5 minutes until tender. Stir in the steak.

2   Lower the heat and simmer 30 seconds, or until cooked to your liking. Stir in the watercress leaves and season with pepper. Add extra soy sauce, if necessary, then serve sprinkled with sesame oil.

101 Beef & Coconut Soup with Pea Eggplants

PREPARATION TIME 15 minutes, plus making the stock   COOKING TIME 20 minutes

1 small handful of bean sprouts
2 tablespoons sunflower oil
1 red onion, chopped
2 red bell peppers, seeded and halved
1 tablespoon red curry paste
12 ounces sirloin or topside steak,
  thinly sliced across the grain
½ cup pea eggplants

1 cup coconut milk
2 kaffir lime leaves
½ teaspoon salt
lime juice, to taste (optional)
palm sugar or light brown sugar,
  to taste (optional)
cilantro leaves, to serve
lime wedges, to serve

1   Put the bean sprouts in a bowl, cover with cold water, and set aside. Put 4½ cups water in a measuring jug and set aside.

2   Heat the oil in a large wok with a lid or a saucepan over high heat. Add the onion, bell peppers, and curry paste, lower the heat to medium, and stir-fry 2 minutes. Very slowly add 1 cup of the water and stir until the fat forms bubbles on the surface. Add the beef and pea eggplants and stir-fry 2 minutes, stirring in a little more of the water if the curry paste looks like it will burn. Slowly stir in the coconut milk, lime leaves, salt, and the remaining water and bring to a boil. Lower the heat and simmer, covered, 5 to 7 minutes until the beef, peppers, and pea eggplants are tender.

3   Drain the bean sprouts, add them to the soup, and cook 30 seconds to warm through. Stir in the lime juice and palm sugar, if using. Serve immediately, sprinkled with cilantro and with lime wedges for squeezing over.

102 Mrs. Schultz's Beef & Vegetable Soup

PREPARATION TIME 15 minutes, plus making the stock   COOKING TIME 2 hours

2 tablespoons garlic-flavored
  sunflower oil, plus extra as needed
1 pound stewing steak, cut into
  bite-size pieces and patted dry
1 onion, finely chopped
¼ teaspoon paprika
½ cup dry red wine
3¼ cups Beef Stock (see page 10)
  or ready-made stock

1 can (15-oz.) crushed tomatoes
2 bay leaves
1 carrot, peeled, halved lengthwise,
  and thickly sliced
1 russet potato, peeled and diced
½ celery rib, finely chopped
salt and freshly ground black pepper
chopped parsley leaves, to serve

1   Heat 1½ tablespoons of the oil in a saucepan over medium-high heat. Working
    in batches, if necessary, to avoid overcrowding the pan, fry the beef 2 to 3 minutes
    until brown on all sides, then transfer to a plate and set aside. Add more oil
    between batches, if necessary.

2   Add the remaining oil to the pan and heat. Add the onion and fry, stirring
    occasionally, 3 to 5 minutes until softened but not colored. Return the beef and
    any accumulated juices to the pan, and add the paprika. Stir in the wine and cook
    5 to 6 minutes until it almost evaporates.

3   Add the stock, then cover and bring to a boil. Skim the surface, then add the
    tomatoes and bay leaves and season with salt and pepper. Cover and return
    to a boil, then reduce the heat to very low (use a heat diffuser if you have one)
    and simmer 1 hour.

4   Stir in the carrot, potato, and celery and simmer, covered, 30 to 45 minutes until
    the beef and vegetables are tender. Discard the bay leaves, then adjust the salt
    and pepper, if necessary. Serve immediately, sprinkled with parsley.

103 Beef & Wild Rice Soup

PREPARATION TIME 10 minutes, plus making the stock   COOKING TIME 2 hours

1½ tablespoons olive oil
1 red onion, finely chopped
2 large garlic cloves, finely chopped
5½ cups Beef Stock (see page 10)
  or ready-made stock
1 pound 5 ounces beef brisket
  or chuck, in one piece, trimmed

1 bay leaf
½ cup wild rice
1 roasted red pepper in olive oil,
  drained and diced
1½ teaspoons Worcestershire sauce
salt and freshly ground black pepper
chopped parsley leaves, to serve

1   Heat the oil in a saucepan over medium heat. Add the onion and fry, stirring
    occasionally, 2 minutes. Stir in the garlic and fry 1 to 3 minutes until the onion
    is softened but not colored. Add the stock and beef and season with salt and
    pepper. Cover and bring to a boil. Skim the surface, then add the bay leaf.
    Lower the heat and simmer, covered, 1 hour.
2   Stir in the wild rice and simmer, covered, 35 to 40 minutes longer until the beef
    is tender and the wild rice grains are fluffy. Remove the beef and set aside until
    it is cool enough to handle.
3   Remove the sinew and cut the beef into bite-size pieces. Return it to the soup.
    Stir in the roasted pepper and Worcestershire sauce and heat through. Discard the
    bay leaf and adjust the salt and pepper, if necessary. Serve sprinkled with parsley.

104 Osso Buco Soup with Gremolata

PREPARATION TIME 15 minutes, plus making the stock and gremolata
COOKING TIME 2 hours

2 to 3 tablespoons olive oil,
  plus extra as needed
1 pound 5 ounces bone-in osso buco
  or veal shin, about 3 thick pieces
2 shallots, finely chopped
1 carrot, peeled and diced
1 celery rib, thinly chopped
4 large garlic cloves,
  very finely chopped
6 cups Beef Stock (see page 10)
  or ready-made stock

½ cup dry vermouth
2¼ cups tomato puree
1 bay leaf
1 tablespoon tomato paste
½ teaspoon sugar
a pinch of saffron threads
salt and freshly ground black pepper
1 recipe quantity Gremolata
  (see page 198), to serve

1   Heat 2 tablespoons of the oil in a saucepan over medium heat. Working in batches,
    if necessary, to avoid overcrowding the pan, fry the osso buco 2 to 3 minutes,
    turning occasionally, until brown on all sides. Remove from the pan and set aside.
    Add more oil between batches, if necessary.
2   Add the shallots, carrot, and celery and fry, stirring occasionally, 2 minutes.
    Add the garlic and fry 1 to 3 minutes until the onion is softened but not colored.
    Return the meat and any accumulated juices to the pan, then add the stock and
    vermouth and season with salt and pepper. Cover and bring to a boil.
3   Skim the surface, then add the tomato puree, bay leaf, tomato paste, sugar,
    and saffron and season again with salt and pepper. Reduce the heat to very low
    (use a heat diffuser if you have one) and simmer, covered, 1½ to 1¾ hours until
    the meat is tender. Remove the meat from the soup and set aside until cool
    enough to handle.
4   Remove the meat from the bones and finely shred it, then return it to the soup.
    Use a small spoon or knife to push the marrow out of the middle of the bones and
    stir it into the soup, if you like. Adjust the salt and pepper, if necessary, then skim
    the surface again, if necessary. Serve sprinkled with the gremolata.

105 Welsh Mountain Lamb & Leek Soup

PREPARATION TIME 20 minutes, plus making the seeds   COOKING TIME 1¾ hours

1 pound 5 ounces boneless shoulder
  of lamb, in one piece, trimmed
4 large garlic cloves, crushed
3 carrots, 2 coarsely chopped
  and 1 sliced
3 celery ribs
3 large leeks, 2 thickly sliced and
  1 thinly sliced, all rinsed and
  kept separate

1 bouquet garni made with 2 bay
  leaves and several parsley and
  rosemary sprigs tied together
2 cups peeled and chopped
  russet potatoes
salt and freshly ground black pepper
Spiced Seeds (see page 15), to serve

1   Put the lamb and 5½ cups water in a saucepan. Cover and bring to a boil. Skim
    the surface, then add the garlic, chopped carrots, celery, thickly sliced leeks,
    and bouquet garni. Season with salt and pepper, then lower the heat and simmer,
    covered, 1 hour.

2   Strain the stock and discard the vegetables and bouquet garni. Return the lamb
    and stock to the pan, then skim the fat from the surface. Add the sliced carrots,
    thinly sliced leeks, and potatoes. Cover and bring to a boil, then lower the heat and
    simmer 30 to 45 minutes until the meat is meltingly tender and the potatoes are
    falling apart. Skim again, if necessary, then remove the lamb and set aside until
    cool enough to handle.

3   Cut the lamb into bite-size pieces, return it to the soup, and reheat. Adjust the
    salt and pepper, if necessary, and serve sprinkled with the seeds.

106 Lamb Vindaloo Soup

PREPARATION TIME 25 minutes, plus at least 1 hour marinating and making the stock
COOKING TIME 2¼ hours

1 pound 5 ounces boneless leg
    or shoulder of lamb or mutton,
    trimmed and cut into large chunks
    with any bones reserved
2 tablespoons peanut
    or sunflower oil
2 onions, sliced
4 green cardamom pods, crushed
3 cloves
2 cinnamon sticks
1 teaspoon cumin seeds
5½ cups Vegetable Stock
    (see page 12) or ready-made stock
2 bay leaves

1 dried red chili, seeded (optional)
    and sliced
2 potatoes, chopped
salt and freshly ground black pepper
chopped cilantro leaves, to serve

VINDALOO MARINADE
5 tablespoons distilled white vinegar
1 tablespoon tomato paste
2 onions, grated
1-inch piece of gingerroot,
    peeled and chopped
1 large garlic clove, finely chopped
½ teaspoon turmeric

1   Mix all the ingredients for the marinade together in a large nonreactive bowl.
    Add the lamb and use your hands to rub in the marinade, then cover and chill
    at least 1 hour to marinate.
2   When ready to cook, heat the oil in a large saucepan over medium heat. Add the
    onions and fry, stirring, 10 to 12 minutes until golden brown. Add the cardamom
    pods, cloves, cinnamon sticks, and cumin seeds and stir 30 seconds, or until
    aromatic. Watch closely so the spices do not burn.
3   Stir in the lamb, marinade, and any reserved bones. Add the stock and season
    with salt and pepper. Cover and bring to a boil. Skim the surface, then add the bay
    leaves and chili. Reduce the heat to very low (use a heat diffuser if you have one)
    and simmer, covered, 1½ to 1¾ hours until the meat is very tender.
4   Remove the meat and bones and set the meat aside until cool enough to handle.
    Discard the bones. Add the potatoes to the soup and simmer, covered,
    12 to 15 minutes until they are tender. Shred the meat into bite-size pieces and
    return it to the soup. Adjust the salt and pepper, if necessary, then serve sprinkled
    with cilantro. Remember to remind your guests about the loose spices.

107 Scotch Broth

PREPARATION TIME 15 minutes   COOKING TIME 1¾ hours

2¼ pounds neck of lamb on the
    bone, trimmed and chopped
    into big pieces (ask the butcher
    to do this)
1 bouquet garni made with 1 piece
    of celery rib, 1 bay leaf, and
    several parsley and thyme sprigs
    tied together

¼ cup pearl barley
2 leeks, thinly sliced and rinsed
1 carrot, peeled and diced
1 onion, finely chopped
1 turnip, peeled and diced
2 tablespoons chopped
    parsley leaves
salt and freshly ground black pepper

1   Put the lamb and 7 cups water in a saucepan. Cover and slowly bring to just below
    the boil. Skim the surface, then add the bouquet garni. Lower the heat and simmer,
    covered, 1 hour.
2   Stir in the barley, leeks, carrot, onion, and turnip and return to just below the boil.
    Lower the heat and simmer, covered, 30 to 40 minutes until the meat and barley
    are tender. Remove the meat from the soup and set aside until cool enough
    to handle. Discard the bouquet garni.
3   Pull the meat away from the bones, cut it into small pieces, and return it to the
    soup. Reheat, if necessary, then stir in the parsley. Season with salt and pepper
    and serve.

108 Spiced Lamb & Chickpea Soup

PREPARATION TIME 15 minutes, plus soaking the chickpeas overnight and making the stock and shallots   COOKING TIME 2 hours

½ cup dried chickpeas
3¾ cups Beef Stock (see page 10)
  or ready-made stock
1 pound 5 ounces boneless shoulder
  of lamb, in one piece, trimmed
2 large garlic cloves, chopped
1 bay leaf
1 large onion, chopped
2 tablespoons lemon juice
1 tablespoon tomato paste

1 teaspoon turmeric
1½ teaspoons cinnamon
a small pinch of ground cloves
a pinch of dried chili flakes,
  or to taste
salt and freshly ground black pepper
chopped cilantro leaves, to serve
Crisp-Fried Shallots (see page 15),
  to serve
hot pepper sauce, to serve (optional)

1   Put the chickpeas in a large bowl, cover with water, and let soak overnight, then drain.
2   Put the stock, lamb, and chickpeas in another saucepan. Cover and bring to a boil. Skim the surface, then add the garlic, bay leaf, onion, lemon juice, tomato paste, turmeric, cinnamon, cloves, and chili flakes. Season with salt and pepper, then reduce the heat to very low (use a heat diffuser if you have one) and simmer, covered, 1½ hours, or until the lamb and chickpeas are tender. Skim the excess fat off the surface, then remove the lamb and set aside until cool enough to handle. Discard the bouquet garni.
3   Chop the lamb into small pieces and return it to the soup. Adjust the salt and pepper, if necessary, and serve sprinkled with the cilantro and shallots and with hot pepper sauce, if you like, for adding at the table.

109 Winter Lamb & Onion Soup

PREPARATION TIME 10 minutes, plus making the stock   COOKING TIME 55 minutes

3 tablespoons olive or hemp oil
14 ounces boneless lamb neck
  tenderloin, membrane removed
  and meat patted dry
4 large onions, thinly sliced
1 teaspoon dried mint leaves
½ teaspoon ground cumin
½ teaspoon fenugreek seeds,
  lightly crushed
½ teaspoon turmeric

2 tablespoons all-purpose
  or wholewheat flour
4½ cups Chicken Stock (see page 11)
  or ready-made stock
1 cinnamon stick, broken in half
2 tablespoons lemon juice
1 teaspoon sugar
salt and freshly ground black pepper
1 small handful of cilantro leaves,
  to serve

1   Heat 2 tablespoons of the oil in a saucepan over medium heat. Add the lamb and fry, turning often, 4 minutes, or until brown all over. Remove from the pan and set aside.
2   Add the remaining oil to the pan and heat. Add the onions and season with salt and pepper. Reduce the heat to low and cook, covered, 10 to 12 minutes, stirring occasionally, until very soft and just starting to color. Add the mint, cumin, fenugreek seeds, and turmeric and stir 30 seconds. Sprinkle in the flour and cook, stirring, 2 minutes longer. Remove the pan from the heat and slowly pour in the stock, stirring continuously, then add the cinnamon stick.
3   Bring to a boil, then reduce the heat to very low and simmer, partially covered, 15 minutes. Meanwhile, cut the lamb across the grain into very thin slices, then cut any large slices in half.
4   Add the lamb to the soup and simmer 10 minutes longer, or until the lamb is cooked to your liking. Discard the cinnamon stick and stir in the lemon juice and sugar. Adjust the salt and pepper, if necessary, then serve sprinkled with cilantro.

110 Lamb Meatball & Kale Soup

PREPARATION TIME 30 minutes, plus making the stock
COOKING TIME 35 minutes

¼ cup dried breadcrumbs
2 tablespoons milk
14 ounces ground lamb
3 scallions, very finely chopped
¼ cup very finely chopped flat-leaf
   parsley leaves, plus extra to serve
1 tablespoon finely chopped
   mint leaves
a pinch of cayenne pepper

4 garlic cloves, finely chopped
1 egg, beaten
2 tablespoons olive or hemp oil,
   plus extra for frying the meatballs
2 large shallots
5½ cups Vegetable Stock
   (see page 12) or ready-made stock
1½ cups chopped kale leaves
salt and freshly ground black pepper

1 Put the breadcrumbs in a large bowl, sprinkle with the milk, and let soak at least 10 minutes. Add the lamb, scallions, parsley, mint, cayenne pepper, and half the garlic and season with salt and pepper. Wet your hands and mix together. Work the egg, little by little, into the mixture. Divide the mixture into 6 equal portions, then divide each one into 6 smaller portions to make a total of 36. Roll into meatballs and set aside. (At this point the meatballs can be chilled up to 1 day.)

2 To fry the meatballs, heat a large skillet over high heat. When a splash of water "dances" on the surface, add a thin layer of oil, and lower the heat to medium-low. Working in batches, if necessary, to avoid overcrowding the pan, fry the meatballs 5 to 8 minutes, turning gently, until golden brown. Drain on paper towels and set aside until required.

3 Heat the oil in a saucepan over medium heat. Add the shallots and fry, stirring occasionally, 2 minutes. Add the remaining garlic and fry 1 to 3 minutes until the shallots are softened but not colored. Add the stock, cover, and bring to a boil. Add the kale, lower the heat, and simmer, uncovered, 5 minutes. Add the meatballs and season with salt and pepper, then simmer 5 minutes to warm them through and until the kale is tender. Adjust the salt and pepper, if necessary. Divide the meatballs and kale into bowls, ladle the soup over them, and serve immediately, sprinkled with parsley.

111 Spring Lamb Soup

PREPARATION TIME 15 minutes, plus making the stock   COOKING TIME 1¾ hours

2 tablespoons olive or hemp oil
1 leek, sliced and rinsed
2 garlic cloves, sliced
1½ pounds lamb shoulder chops,
   trimmed
5½ cups Vegetable Stock
   (see page 12) or ready-made stock
1 can (15-oz.) crushed tomatoes
2 tablespoons lemon juice
1 teaspoon ground fenugreek

½ teaspoon ground coriander
2 rosemary sprigs
1 bay leaf
1 tablespoon tomato paste
½ teaspoon light brown sugar
1 turnip, peeled and chopped
2 tablespoons capers in brine,
   drained and rinsed
¼ cup chopped parsley leaves
salt and freshly ground black pepper

1 Heat the oil in a saucepan over medium heat. Add the leek and garlic, cover, and reduce the heat to low. Cook 10 to 12 minutes, stirring occasionally, until softened but not colored. Stir in the lamb and stock and season with salt and pepper, then cover and bring to a boil. Skim the surface, then add the tomatoes, lemon juice, fenugreek, coriander, rosemary, bay leaf, tomato paste, and sugar. Season with salt and pepper, lower the heat, and simmer, covered, 1 hour.

2 Stir in the turnip, capers, and half the parsley and continue simmering, covered, 20 to 25 minutes until the lamb and turnip are tender. Remove the lamb, bones, and rosemary. Discard the bones and rosemary and set the lamb aside until cool enough handle.

3 Cut the lamb into bite-size pieces, return it to the soup, and warm through. Adjust the salt and pepper, if necessary, and serve sprinkled with the remaining parsley.

112 Curried Lamb & Squash Soup

PREPARATION TIME 25 minutes, plus making the stock   COOKING TIME 2¼ hours

2 to 3 tablespoons olive or hemp oil
1 pound 5 ounces boneless lamb
　shoulder, in one piece, trimmed
1 large onion, chopped
1 teaspoon curry powder
1 teaspoon ground coriander
1 teaspoon ground cumin
2 fresh curry leaves or 1 dried
6 cups Vegetable Stock (see page 12)
　or ready-made stock
2 bay leaves
1 tablespoon lemon juice

1 bird's-eye chili, seeded (optional)
　and finely chopped
finely grated zest of 2 tangerines
　or 1 orange
1½ cups peeled, seeded, and diced
　butternut squash
2 large garlic cloves, chopped
2 waxy new potatoes, peeled
　and diced
1 carrot, peeled and diced
1 handful of baby spinach leaves
salt and freshly ground black pepper

1　Heat 2 tablespoons of the oil in a saucepan over medium heat. Add the lamb and
　fry 2 to 3 minutes until brown on both sides. Remove the lamb from the pan
　and set aside.
2　Add the remaining oil, if necessary, and heat. Add the onion and fry, stirring
　occasionally, 8 to 10 minutes until golden brown. Add the curry powder, coriander,
　cumin, and curry leaves and stir 30 seconds, or until aromatic. Watch closely so the
　spices and curry leaves do not burn. Return the lamb with any accumulated juices
　to the pan. Add the stock and season with salt and pepper, then cover and bring
　to a boil. Skim, then stir in the bay leaves, lemon juice, chili, and zest. Cover, reduce
　the heat to very low (use a heat diffuser if you have one), and simmer 1½ hours.
3　Stir in the squash, garlic, potatoes, and carrot and simmer 25 to 30 minutes until
　the lamb is very tender. Add the spinach for the last 2 to 3 minutes and simmer
　until it wilts. Discard the bay and curry leaves. Adjust the salt and pepper,
　if necessary, then serve.

113 Cardamom-Scented Lamb Soup with Couscous

PREPARATION TIME 20 minutes, plus making the stock   COOKING TIME 2¼ hours

1½ tablespoons olive or hemp oil
1 cup quartered and sliced fennel
2 garlic cloves, crushed
½-inch piece of gingerroot,
　peeled and grated
2 green chilies, seeded and chopped
4½ cups Vegetable Stock
　(see page 12) or ready-made stock
1 pound 5 ounces boneless lamb
　shoulder, in one piece, trimmed

2 bay leaves
1 carrot, peeled and sliced
seeds from 8 green cardamom pods,
　wrapped in a piece of cheesecloth
¼ teaspoon turmeric
¾ cup couscous
salt and freshly ground black pepper
chopped cilantro leaves, to serve

1　Heat the oil in a saucepan over medium heat. Add the fennel and fry, stirring
　occasionally, 8 to 10 minutes until light golden brown. Add the garlic, ginger,
　and chilies and stir 30 seconds longer, or until aromatic. Watch closely so they
　do not burn.
2　Add the stock and lamb, season with salt and pepper, cover, and bring to a boil.
　Skim the surface, then stir in the bay leaves, carrot, cardamom seeds, and turmeric.
　Lower the heat and simmer, covered, 1½ to 1¾ hours until the lamb is very tender.
　Remove the lamb from the soup and set aside until cool enough to handle.
3　Stir the couscous into the soup, cover, and return the soup to a boil. Lower the
　heat and simmer 10 minutes, or until the couscous is tender.
4　Remove and discard any lamb skin, shred the meat into bite-size pieces, and return
　it to the soup. Discard the seed bundle and bay leaves and adjust the salt and
　pepper, if necessary. Serve sprinkled with cilantro.

114 Roast Lamb & Bean Soup

PREPARATION TIME 15 minutes, plus making the stock and cooking the lamb
COOKING TIME 40 minutes

1 tablespoon olive or hemp oil
1 red onion, finely chopped
3 garlic cloves, finely chopped
1 teaspoon ground coriander
½ teaspoon ground cumin
½ teaspoon turmeric
4½ cups Beef Stock (see page 10)
   or ready-made stock
1 can (15-oz.) crushed tomatoes
1 tablespoon tomato paste
½ tablespoon dried mint or dill

1 teaspoon harissa, or to taste
½ teaspoon sugar
1 lamb bone, all fat removed
   (optional)
2½ cups shredded boneless, skinless
   cooked lamb, with all fat removed
1 can (15-oz.) navy or cannellini
   beans or chickpeas, drained
   and rinsed
salt and freshly ground black pepper
chopped cilantro leaves, to serve

1   Heat the oil in a saucepan over medium heat. Add the onion and fry, stirring occasionally, 2 minutes. Add the garlic and fry 1 to 3 minutes until the onion is softened but not colored. Add the coriander, cumin, and turmeric and stir 30 seconds, or until aromatic. Watch closely so the spices do not burn.

2   Add the stock, tomatoes, tomato paste, mint, harissa, sugar, and lamb bone, if using. Season with salt and pepper, cover and bring to a boil over high heat. Lower the heat and simmer 20 minutes, stirring once or twice to break up the tomatoes. Add the lamb and beans and simmer 5 minutes to heat through. Discard the lamb bone, if used, then adjust the salt and pepper, if necessary, and add more harissa, if you like. Serve sprinkled with cilantro leaves.

115 Pork, Mushroom & Tofu Soup

PREPARATION TIME 25 minutes, plus 30 minutes soaking the mushrooms and making the stock **COOKING TIME** 45 minutes

2 dried shiitake mushrooms
1 ounce dried cloud ear mushrooms
6 cups Chicken Stock (see page 11)
  or ready-made stock
2-inch piece of gingerroot,
  peeled and sliced
3 tablespoons light soy sauce
2 tablespoons rice vinegar
1 carrot, peeled and cut into
  matchsticks

4 Chinese cabbage leaves, shredded
⅓ cup pickled preserved bamboo
  shoots, drained and chopped
2½ tablespoons cornstarch
14 ounces pork tenderloin, trimmed,
  cut into 2-inch matchstick pieces
1½ cups drained and finely chopped
  firm tofu
½ cup frozen peas
chopped cilantro leaves, to serve

1   Put the shiitake and cloud ear mushrooms in separate heatproof bowls, cover each with ⅔ cup warm water and let soak at least 30 minutes, or until tender. Meanwhile, put the stock, ginger, soy sauce, and vinegar in a saucepan, cover, and bring to a boil. Lower the heat and simmer 15 minutes. Strain the stock into a clean pan, discarding the ginger, and set aside.

2   Strain the shiitake mushrooms through a cheesecloth-lined strainer into a clean bowl and reserve the soaking liquid. Squeeze the mushrooms, cut off and discard the stems and slice the caps, then set aside. Drain the cloud ear mushrooms, discarding the soaking liquid, then trim the stems, if necessary, and slice thinly.

3   Put 4½ cups of the stock and ½ cup of the shiitake soaking liquid in the pan. Add the mushrooms, carrot, cabbage, and bamboo shoots. Put the cornstarch in a heatproof bowl, add a ladleful of the stock, and stir until a thin, smooth paste forms. Stir this mixture into the stock and bring to a boil, stirring, then lower the heat and simmer 5 minutes, or just until slightly thicker. Reduce the heat to low and add the pork, tofu, and peas, stirring gently so you don't break up the tofu. Simmer 3 to 5 minutes until the pork is cooked through and the peas are tender. Serve sprinkled with cilantro.

116 Pork, Mushroom & Snow Pea Soup

PREPARATION TIME 20 minutes, plus making the stock **COOKING TIME** 25 minutes

1 tablespoon peanut or sunflower oil
5 shiitake mushroom caps, sliced
1 large garlic clove, chopped
½-inch piece of gingerroot,
  peeled and grated
5½ cups Chicken Stock (see page 11)
14 ounces pork tenderloin, trimmed,
  cut in half lengthwise, and
  thinly sliced
1 tablespoon rice wine vinegar
2 teaspoons light soy sauce,
  or to taste

1 tablespoon arrowroot
⅓ cup snow peas
2 scallions, sliced on the diagonal
1 roasted red pepper in olive oil,
  drained and thinly sliced
Chinese five-spice powder, to taste
salt
chopped Chinese chives
  or snipped chives, to serve

1   Heat the oil in a saucepan over medium heat. Add the mushrooms, season with salt, and fry, stirring, 5 to 8 minutes until they are softened and give off their juices. Add the garlic and ginger and stir 30 seconds, or until aromatic. Watch closely so they do not burn.

2   Add the stock, pork, vinegar, and soy sauce and bring to just below the boil. Skim, if necessary, then lower the heat and simmer 2 minutes. Put the arrowroot and 3 tablespoons cold water in a small bowl and mix until smooth, then set aside.

3   Add the snow peas, scallions, pepper, and arrowroot mixture to the saucepan and simmer 2 to 3 minutes until the pork is cooked through, the vegetables are tender but still with bite, and the soup is slightly thickened. Season with five-spice powder and salt or extra soy sauce to taste. Serve sprinkled with chives.

117 Bangkok Pork & Shrimp Soup

PREPARATION TIME 20 minutes, plus making the stock   COOKING TIME 25 minutes

2 tablespoons sunflower oil
2 large garlic cloves,
   finely chopped
2 teaspoons ground coriander
14 ounces boneless pork, such
   as shoulder chops, cut into
   very fine matchstick pieces
4½ cups Chicken Stock (see page 11)
   or ready-made stock
5 shiitake mushroom caps,
   thinly sliced
4 cilantro roots, crushed

1 lemongrass stem, cut into thirds,
   with outer leaves removed
1 tablespoon soy sauce, or to taste
1½ teaspoons fish sauce, or to taste
1 bird's-eye chili, seeded (optional)
   and sliced
9 ounces large shrimp, shelled,
   deveined, and cut into thirds
4 scallions, thinly sliced
salt and freshly ground black pepper
cilantro leaves, to serve

1   Heat the oil in a large saucepan over medium heat. Add the garlic and coriander and
    fry, stirring, 1 to 2 minutes until the garlic is softened but not colored. Add the pork
    and stir-fry 2 minutes longer, then add the stock. Cover and bring to a boil, then
    skim the surface. Add the mushrooms, cilantro roots, lemongrass, soy sauce,
    fish sauce, and chili and season with salt and pepper. Lower the heat and simmer
    5 minutes.
2   Stir in the shrimp and scallions. Season again with pepper and simmer
    2 to 3 minutes until the shrimp and pork are cooked through. Discard the cilantro
    roots and lemongrass. Adjust the salt and pepper, adding extra soy sauce and
    fish sauce, if necessary. Serve sprinkled with cilantro.

118 Thai Meatball & Coconut Soup

PREPARATION TIME 25 minutes, plus making the stock, chilies, and garlic
COOKING TIME 20 minutes

14 ounces ground pork
2 cilantro sprigs, leaves and stems
   very finely chopped, plus an extra
   handful of leaves, chopped
1-inch piece of gingerroot, peeled
   and very finely chopped
1½ tablespoons cornstarch
1 tablespoon sesame oil
1 tablespoon light soy sauce
4 cups Vegetable Stock (see page 12)
   or ready-made stock

1¾ cups coconut milk
1½ tablespoons fish sauce,
   or to taste
salt and freshly ground black pepper
finely grated zest of 1 lime, to serve
Crisp-Fried Garlic (see page 15),
   to serve
Chilies in Vinegar (see page 15),
   to serve

1   Put the pork, finely chopped cilantro, ginger, cornstarch, sesame oil, and soy sauce
    in a large bowl and season with salt and pepper. Use your hands to mix together
    and divide the mixture into 6 equal portions, then divide each one into 6 smaller
    portions to make a total of 36. Roll into meatballs and set aside.
2   Put the stock in a saucepan, cover, and bring to a boil, then lower the heat so the
    liquid boils only very lightly. Working in batches, if necessary, to avoid overcrowding
    the pan, add the meatballs and cook, uncovered, 3 to 5 minutes until they pop
    to the surface and are cooked though if you cut one open. Remove the cooked
    meatballs from the pan and set them aside.
3   Put the coconut milk and fish sauce in another saucepan and bring to just below
    the boil. Season with salt and pepper, add the meatballs and slowly stir in enough
    of the meatball cooking liquid to achieve the preferred consistency. Stir in the
    chopped cilantro leaves, adjust the salt and pepper, if necessary, and add more fish
    sauce, if you like. Divide the meatballs and soup into bowls and sprinkle with the
    lime zest. Serve with the garlic and chilies on the side for adding at the table.

119 Ham & Pepper Soup

PREPARATION TIME 20 minutes, plus at least 2 hours soaking and making the stock
COOKING TIME 1½ hours

1 smoked ham hock, about 3 pounds
2 carrots, coarsely chopped
3 celery ribs, coarsely chopped
2 onions, 1 quartered and 1 diced
4 bay leaves
1 tablespoon black peppercorns,
   crushed
½ teaspoon coriander seeds, crushed
½ teaspoon salt, plus extra to season

2 tablespoons olive or hemp oil
3 red bell peppers, seeded and
   chopped
1 can (15-oz.) crushed tomatoes
1 tablespoon tomato paste
½ teaspoon light brown sugar
2½ cups Vegetable Stock
   (see page 12) or ready-made stock
freshly ground black pepper

1 Put the ham hock in a large bowl, cover with water, and let soak at least 2 hours, then drain. Change the water at least twice during soaking.
2 Put the hock in a large saucepan, cover with water, and bring to a boil. Skim, then add the carrots, celery, quartered onion, bay leaves, peppercorns, coriander seeds, and salt. Reduce the heat to very low (use a heat diffuser if you have one) and simmer, covered, 1¼ to 1½ hours until the meat is tender.
3 About 20 minutes before the end of the simmering time, heat the oil in another saucepan over medium heat. Add the bell peppers and diced onion and fry, stirring occasionally, 8 to 10 minutes until the onion has softened and turns a light golden brown. Stir in the tomatoes, tomato paste, brown sugar, and 2½ cups of the simmering cooking liquid. Cover and bring to a boil, then lower the heat and simmer 10 minutes. Blend the soup until smooth. Strain the mixture into a bowl, rubbing back and forth with a spoon and scraping the bottom of the strainer. Return the puree to the pan, stir in the vegetable stock, and reheat. If it is too thick, add a ladleful of the simmering cooking liquid.
4 Remove the ham hock from the pan and set aside until cool enough to handle. Strain the cooking liquid into a bowl and discard the flavorings. (The leftover cooking liquid can be cooled and refrigerated for up to 3 days or frozen for use in other recipes; the bone can be used in Split Pea & Ham Soup (see page 159).)
5 Cut the ham into bite-size pieces, add it to the soup, and heat through. Season with pepper and adjust the salt, if necessary, but remember that the cooking liquid was very salty. Serve.

120 Bacon & Corn Chowder

PREPARATION TIME 15 minutes   COOKING TIME 35 minutes

5 slices of bacon
1 tablespoon sunflower oil
1 celery rib, finely chopped
1 onion, finely chopped
1 green bell pepper,
   seeded and diced
3 tablespoons all-purpose flour
3½ cups whole milk

1 bay leaf
1 russet potato, peeled and diced
1 teaspoon dried thyme leaves
freshly grated nutmeg, to taste
2⅔ cups frozen corn kernels
salt and freshly ground black pepper
snipped chives, to serve

1 Put the bacon slices in a saucepan and fry over high heat, turning, 5 to 7 minutes until they brown and give off their fat. Remove the bacon from the pan and drain on paper towels, then cut into small pieces and set aside.
2 Add the oil to the fat remaining in the pan and lower the heat to medium. Add the celery, onion, and bell pepper and fry, stirring occasionally, 3 to 5 minutes until the onion is softened. Sprinkle in the flour and cook, stirring, 2 minutes. Remove the pan from the heat and slowly add the milk, stirring continuously to prevent lumps from forming.
3 Return the pan to the heat, add the bay leaf, potato, and thyme and season with nutmeg and salt and pepper. Bring to just below the boil, stirring occasionally, then lower the heat and simmer, covered, 12 minutes, stirring occasionally. Add the bacon and corn and simmer 3 to 5 minutes until both are tender. Adjust the nutmeg and salt and pepper, if necessary, then serve sprinkled with chives.

121 Portuguese Caldo Verde

PREPARATION TIME 10 minutes   **COOKING TIME** 30 minutes

3⅓ cups peeled and chopped
   russet potatoes
2 large garlic cloves, chopped
3½ cups shredded curly kale
   or savoy cabbage leaves, rinsed
1 teaspoon dried dill or thyme leaves

4 ounces chorizo, casing removed
   and meat thinly sliced
salt and freshly ground black pepper
crusty country-style bread, to serve
fruity extra-virgin olive oil, to serve

1   Put the potatoes, garlic, and 5½ cups water in a saucepan and season with salt
and pepper. Cover and bring to a boil. Lower the heat and simmer, covered,
10 to 15 minutes until the potatoes are very tender.

2   Use a potato masher or large metal spoon to coarsely mash the potatoes into
the water. Add the kale and dill and simmer, uncovered, 5 to 10 minutes until the
kale wilts. Stir in the chorizo and warm though, then adjust the salt and pepper,
if necessary. Serve with bread and olive oil for adding at the table.

122 Chorizo & Chestnut Soup

PREPARATION TIME 20 minutes, plus making the stock   COOKING TIME 40 minutes

4 ounces chorizo, casing removed
  and chopped
½ tablespoons olive or hemp oil
  (optional)
2 carrots, peeled and sliced
1 celery rib, chopped
1 onion, finely chopped
1 teaspoon ground cumin

½ teaspoon ground coriander
a pinch of chili flakes, or to taste
5½ cups Vegetable Stock
  (see page 12) or ready-made stock
1½ cups drained and chopped
  canned chestnuts
salt and freshly ground black pepper
chopped parsley leaves, to serve

1 Fry the chorizo in a saucepan over high heat, stirring, 3 to 5 minutes until slightly
   crisp. Remove it from the pan and set aside. Reduce the heat to low and add the oil
   to the pan, if necessary. Stir in the carrots, celery, and onion and cook, covered,
   10 to 12 minutes, stirring occasionally, until the vegetables are beginning to soften
   but not color. Add the cumin, coriander, and chili flakes and stir 30 seconds, or until
   aromatic. Watch closely so the spices do not burn.

2 Add the stock and chestnuts and season with salt and pepper. Cover and bring
   to a boil. Skim, then lower the heat and simmer, covered, 10 to 15 minutes until
   the vegetables and chestnuts are very tender. Blend until smooth, then adjust the
   salt and pepper, if necessary. Serve sprinkled with the parsley and fried chorizo.

123 Pea Green Soup with Ham & Blue Cheese

PREPARATION TIME 10 minutes, plus making the stock and flavored oil
COOKING TIME 20 minutes

4 cups Vegetable Stock
  (see page 12) or ready-made stock
3 cups frozen peas
2 to 3 ounces blue cheese, such
  as Roquefort or Stilton, crumbled

¾ cup diced cooked ham
salt and freshly ground black pepper
1 recipe quantity Crushed Basil
  or Mint Oil (see page 15), to serve

1 Put the stock in a saucepan. Cover and bring to a boil, then stir in the peas. Lower
   the heat and simmer, uncovered, 5 to 8 minutes until the peas are tender, then
   remove about one-third of the peas and set aside.

2 Blend the soup to the preferred consistency. Strain the soup for an even smoother
   texture, if you like. Return the soup to the pan. Return the reserved peas to the
   soup and add the cheese and ham. Reheat, stirring until the cheese melts into
   the soup. Season with salt and pepper, if necessary, but remember the cheese
   and ham are salty. Drizzle with the oil and serve.

124 Ham & Cheese Belgian Endive Soup

PREPARATION TIME 15 minutes, plus making the stock   COOKING TIME 30 minutes

2 tablespoons butter
1 tablespoon olive oil
leaves from 4 heads of Belgian
  endive, coarsely chopped
1 russet potato, peeled and diced
2½ cups Vegetable Stock
  (see page 12) or ready-made stock

1 Parmesan cheese rind, about
  3 x 2 inches (see page 9; optional)
5 tablespoons heavy cream
salt and ground white pepper
1½ ounces thinly sliced prosciutto,
  to serve
grated Gruyère cheese, to serve

1 Melt the butter with the oil in a saucepan over medium heat. Add the endive and
   potato and fry, stirring, 3 to 5 minutes until the endive wilts but does not brown.
   Add the stock, 2½ cups water, and the cheese rind, if using.

2 Cover and bring to a boil, then lower the heat and simmer 10 to 12 minutes until
   the potato is very tender. Discard the rind, then add the cream and blend the soup
   until smooth. Season with salt and white pepper, and serve sprinkled with
   prosciutto and grated cheese.

125 Smoked Ham & Celery Chowder

PREPARATION TIME 20 minutes, plus making the stock **COOKING TIME** 35 minutes

1 tablespoon butter
1½ tablespoons sunflower oil
3 cups diced lean smoked ham
2 celery ribs, finely chopped,
    with the leaves reserved to serve
1 leek, halved lengthwise, thinly
    sliced, and rinsed
1 large russet potato,
    peeled and diced
2 tablespoons all-purpose
    or wholewheat flour

2¼ cups Chicken Stock (see page 11)
    or ready-made stock
3 cups milk
2 tablespoons chopped
    parsley leaves
1 bay leaf
finely grated zest of 1 lemon
¼ cup sour cream
celery salt
freshly ground black pepper
celery seeds, to serve

1   Melt the butter with 1 tablespoon of the oil in a saucepan over medium heat.
    Add the ham and fry, stirring, 2 to 3 minutes until just starting to crisp on the
    edges. Remove it from the pan and set aside.
2   Add the remaining oil to the pan. Add the celery and leek and fry, stirring
    occasionally, 3 to 5 minutes until the leek is softened but not colored. Stir in the
    potato and return the ham to the pan, then sprinkle in the flour and stir 2 minutes.
    Slowly add half the stock, scraping the bottom of the pan and stirring continuously
    to prevent lumps from forming.
3   Stir in the remaining stock, cover, and bring to a boil, then skim. Lower the heat
    to low and stir in the milk, parsley, bay leaf, and lemon zest. Simmer, covered,
    15 to 18 minutes until the potato is starting to fall apart. Do not let the soup boil.
    Meanwhile, finely shred the reserved celery leaves.
4   Discard the bay leaf, stir in the sour cream, and warm through. Season with celery
    salt and pepper, but remember the ham is salty. Serve sprinkled with celery leaves
    and seeds.

126 Smoked Sausage & Red Cabbage Soup

PREPARATION TIME 20 minutes, plus making the stock **COOKING TIME** 35 minutes

1½ tablespoons olive or hemp oil
1 onion, finely chopped
1 large garlic clove, finely chopped
7 ounces smoked sausage, casing
    removed and sliced
1 russet potato, peeled and chopped
4½ cups Vegetable Stock
    (see page 12) or ready-made stock

1½ cups shredded red cabbage
1 sweet cooking apple, peeled, cored,
    and chopped
lemon juice, to taste (optional)
salt and freshly ground black pepper
paprika, to serve
chopped parsley leaves, to serve

1   Heat the oil in a saucepan over medium heat. Add the onion and fry, stirring
    occasionally, 2 minutes. Add the garlic and fry 1 to 3 minutes until the onion
    is softened but not colored. Stir in the sausage and potato, then add the stock and
    season with salt and pepper.
2   Cover and bring to a boil, then lower the heat and simmer 12 to 15 minutes,
    stirring occasionally, until the potato is falling apart. Stir in the cabbage and apple
    and simmer 5 to 10 minutes longer until the cabbage is tender and the apple
    is dissolving. Stir well and adjust the salt and pepper, adding lemon juice,
    if necessary. Serve immediately, sprinkled with paprika and parsley.

127 Sausage, Fennel & Bean Soup

PREPARATION TIME 15 minutes, plus overnight soaking and cooking the beans (optional) and making the stock   COOKING TIME 30 minutes

1 cup dried navy beans or 1 can (15-oz.) navy beans, drained
1½ tablespoons garlic-flavored oil
14 ounces spicy Italian sausages, casings removed
1 celery rib, finely chopped
1 bulb fennel, thinly sliced

5½ cups Beef Stock (see page 10) or ready-made stock
2 carrots, peeled and diced
2 bay leaves
salt and freshly ground black pepper
chopped parsley leaves, to serve

1   If using dried beans, put them in a bowl, cover with water, and let soak overnight, then drain. Transfer to a saucepan, add 6½ cups water, cover, and bring to a boil. Lower the heat and simmer, covered, 50 minutes to 1 hour until tender, then drain and set aside.

2   Heat the oil in a saucepan over medium heat. Add the sausage meat and fry 2 to 3 minutes, breaking up the meat, until brown all over. Remove the meat from the pan and set aside to drain on paper towels. Spoon off all but 1 tablespoon of the oil remaining in the pan. Add the celery and fennel and fry, stirring occasionally, 8 to 10 minutes until light golden brown. Add the stock, carrots, and bay leaves and season with salt and pepper.

3   Cover and bring to a boil. Skim, if necessary, then lower the heat and simmer 5 minutes. Return the sausage meat to the pan, add the beans, and simmer 2 to 3 minutes to warm through. Discard the bay leaves and skim again. Adjust the salt and pepper, if necessary, then serve sprinkled with parsley.

128 Venison & Chestnut Soup

PREPARATION TIME 25 minutes, plus at least 4 hours marinating and making the stock
COOKING TIME 1¾ hours

1 pound 5 ounces boneless venison shoulder, trimmed and cut into large chunks
1 cup full-flavored dry red wine, such as Burgundy
1 shallot, sliced
1 teaspoon juniper berries, crushed
4 large garlic cloves, chopped
1 tablespoon olive oil
1 carrot, peeled and diced
1 celery rib, chopped
½ leek, sliced and rinsed

6 cups Beef Stock (see page 10) or ready-made stock
1 bouquet garni made with 1 piece of celery rib, 1 bay leaf, several parsley sprigs, and 2 sage sprigs tied together
½ to 1 tablespoon red currant jelly (optional)
6 peeled canned or vacuum-packed chestnuts, drained and chopped
salt and freshly ground black pepper
chopped parsley leaves, to serve

1   Mix the venison, wine, shallot, juniper berries, and half the garlic together in a nonreactive bowl. Cover and chill at least 4 hours or up to 24.

2   Remove the venison from the marinade and set aside. Strain the marinade into a clean bowl and reserve.

3   Heat the oil in a saucepan over medium heat. Add the carrot, celery, and leek and fry, stirring occasionally, 2 minutes. Add the remaining garlic and fry 1 to 3 minutes until the leek is softened. Add the reserved marinade and cook 8 minutes, or until almost evaporated. Add the stock and venison and season with salt and pepper.

4   Cover and bring to a boil, then skim and add the bouquet garni. Lower the heat to very low (use a heat diffuser if you have one) and simmer, covered, 1¼ to 1½ hours until the meat is very tender. Remove the venison from the soup and set aside. Discard the bouquet garni.

5   Stir in ½ tablespoon of the jelly, if using, then blend the soup until smooth. Return the venison to the pan, add the chestnuts and warm through. Adjust the salt and pepper, if necessary, and add more jelly, if you like. Serve sprinkled with parsley.

129 Haggis Soup

PREPARATION TIME 20 minutes, plus making the stock   **COOKING TIME** 35 minutes

1 tablespoon olive or hemp oil
2 slices of bacon, chopped
1 onion, chopped
2 large garlic cloves, finely chopped
9 ounces haggis, casing removed
4 cups Beef Stock (see page 10)
   or ready-made stock

1½ cups peeled and diced rutabaga
1 bay leaf
1 carrot, peeled and diced
1 turnip, peeled and diced
salt and freshly ground black pepper
chopped parsley leaves, to serve

1   Heat the oil in a saucepan over medium heat. Add the bacon and fry, stirring occasionally, 5 to 8 minutes until it is cooked and gives off its fat. Remove the bacon from the pan and set aside to drain on paper towels.
2   Add the onion to the fat remaining in the pan and fry, stirring, 2 minutes. Add the garlic and fry 1 to 3 minutes until the onion is softened but not colored. Crumble in the haggis and stir well.
3   Add the stock and season with salt and pepper. Cover and bring to a boil. Skim, then add the rutabaga, bay leaf, carrot, and turnip. Lower the heat and simmer, covered, 10 to 15 minutes until the vegetables are tender. Meanwhile, finely chop the bacon.
4   Discard the bay leaf and adjust the salt and pepper, if necessary. Serve sprinkled with the bacon and parsley.

130 German Liver Dumpling Soup

PREPARATION TIME 25 minutes, plus 30 minutes chilling and making the stock
COOKING TIME 25 minutes

5½ cups Beef Stock (see page 10),
   Beef Consommé (see page 13),
   or ready-made stock
1¼ cups frozen peas
salt and freshly ground black pepper
chopped parsley leaves,
   to serve

LIVER DUMPLINGS
1 tablespoon sunflower oil
1 large onion, grated

9 ounces day-old bread, grated,
   or 2½ cups dried breadcrumbs
6 tablespoons milk
5 ounces calf liver,
   membrane removed
1 egg beaten with 1 extra yolk
1 tablespoon dried
   marjoram leaves
1 tablespoon chopped parsley leaves
1 teaspoon sweet or whole
   grain mustard

1   To make the dumplings, heat the oil in a saucepan over medium heat. Add the onion and fry, stirring occasionally, 8 to 10 minutes until golden brown. Transfer to a plate and set aside to cool. Meanwhile, put the bread and milk in a small bowl and let soak 10 minutes. Finely chop the calf liver in a blender or food processor and set aside. Put the bread with any leftover milk, onion, liver, and eggs in a bowl and mix together. Add the marjoram, parsley, and mustard and season with salt and pepper. (Fry a small amount in a skillet to test for seasoning, if you like.) Using a wet spoon, divide the mixture into 12 or 24 equal portions, then use wet hands to roll each portion into a ball. Cover and refrigerate at least 30 minutes.
2   Put the stock in a saucepan and season with salt and pepper. Cover and bring to a boil. Add the dumplings, then lower the heat and simmer, covered, 3 minutes. Add the peas and increase the heat to a slow boil. Boil 3 to 5 minutes until the dumplings are cooked through and the peas are tender. Adjust the salt and pepper, if necessary, then serve sprinkled with parsley.

131 Game & Barley Broth

PREPARATION TIME 20 minutes, plus making the stock and cooking the pheasant
COOKING TIME 1½ hours

3½ ounces chopped bacon
1½ tablespoons olive or hemp oil
1 carrot, chopped
1 celery rib, chopped
1 leek, white part only,
   sliced and rinsed
1 onion, sliced
½ cup dry red wine
6½ cups Game Stock (see page 11)
   or ready-made stock

1 can (15-oz.) crushed tomatoes
1 tablespoon tomato paste
1 bay leaf
a pinch of sugar
¼ cup pearl barley
2½ cups finely shredded boneless,
   skinless cooked pheasant and/or
   partridge meat
salt and freshly ground black pepper
snipped chives, to serve

1   Put the bacon in a saucepan and fry over medium heat 3 to 5 minutes, stirring,
    until it begins to crisp and the fat runs. Remove it from the pan and set aside.
2   Add the oil to the fat remaining in the pan and heat over medium heat. Add the
    carrot, celery, leek, and onion and fry, stirring occasionally, 3 to 5 minutes until
    the leek and vegetables are softened but not colored. Stir in the wine and cook
    5 to 8 minutes until it almost evaporates. Add the stock, tomatoes, tomato paste,
    bay leaf, and sugar and season with salt and pepper. Cover and bring to a boil,
    then lower the heat and simmer 20 minutes.
3   Strain the stock, pressing down on the vegetables to extract as much flavor
    as possible, then return it to the pan. Add the barley, cover and return to a boil.
    Lower the heat and simmer 30 to 40 minutes until tender.
4   Add the pheasant to the soup and simmer 2 to 3 minutes to heat through. Adjust
    the salt and pepper, if necessary, then serve sprinkled with the bacon and chives.

132 Roast Pheasant & Lentil Soup

PREPARATION TIME 20 minutes, plus cooking the pheasant and making the shallots
COOKING TIME 50 minutes

1⅓ cups dried Puy or other green
   lentils, rinsed
2 large garlic cloves, chopped
1 leek, chopped and rinsed
1 red onion, chopped
1 teaspoon juniper berries and
   1 bay leaf tied together in a
   piece of cheesecloth

2½ cups finely shredded boneless,
   skinless cooked pheasant
any leftover pheasant gravy
   (optional)
¼ cup crème fraîche or sour cream
salt and freshly ground black pepper
Crisp-Fried Shallots (see page 15),
   to serve
chopped parsley leaves, to serve

1   Put the lentils, garlic, leek, onion, spice bundle, and 7½ cups water in a saucepan
    over high heat. Cover and bring to a boil. Skim, then lower the heat and simmer
    30 to 40 minutes until the lentils are very soft. Drain, reserving the cooking liquid
    and discarding the spice bundle.
2   Put a small amount of the cooking liquid in a small saucepan over medium heat.
    Add the pheasant and simmer to warm through.
3   Meanwhile, blend the lentils with 2¼ cups of the cooking liquid until smooth, then
    season with salt and pepper. Work the soup through a strainer into a bowl, rubbing
    back and forth with a spoon and scraping the bottom of the strainer.
4   Return the soup to the pan and slowly stir in the gravy, if using, and enough of the
    remaining cooking liquid to achieve the preferred consistency. (Any leftover cooking
    liquid can be used in other recipes or frozen for up to six months.) Stir in the crème
    fraîche, then adjust the salt and pepper, if necessary. Use a slotted spoon
    to transfer the pheasant to the soup. Serve sprinkled with the shallots and parsley.

133 Oxtail Soup with Barley

PREPARATION TIME 20 minutes, plus overnight chilling (optional) **COOKING TIME** 4 hours

2 tablespoons butter

2 tablespoons sunflower or olive oil, plus extra as needed

2¼ tablespoons oxtail, cut into large pieces (ask the butcher to do this)

3 celery ribs, chopped, with the leaves reserved

2 carrots, peeled and chopped

2 onions, chopped

4 garlic cloves, finely chopped

1 bouquet garni made with the reserved celery leaves, 1 bay leaf, and several parsley and thyme sprigs tied together

⅓ cup pearl barley

Worcestershire sauce, to taste

¼ cup finely chopped parsley leaves

salt and freshly ground black pepper

1 This soup is best made a day before serving, so it can be chilled overnight and the excess fat easily removed. Melt the butter with the oil in a large saucepan over medium heat. Working in batches, fry the oxtail 2 to 3 minutes until brown on both sides, then transfer it to a plate. Add extra oil to the pan between batches, as necessary.

2 Pour off all but 1½ tablespoons of the fat from the pan. Add the celery, carrots, and onions and fry, stirring, 2 minutes. Add the garlic and fry 1 to 3 minutes until the onions are softened. Return the oxtail and any accumulated juices to the pan, add 2½ quarts water and season with salt and pepper. Cover and bring to a boil, then skim and add the bouquet garni. Reduce the heat to low and simmer, covered, 2½ to 3 hours until the meat is falling off the bones. Remove the meat and bones from the pan and set aside until cool enough to handle.

3 Strain the soup into a clean pan, discarding the vegetables, then skim the surface. Alternatively, leave the soup to cool completely, then cover and chill overnight for easier removal of the fat. (If you are chilling the soup overnight, spoon a little of the soup over the meat, cover with plastic wrap, and chill until required.)

4 Add the barley, cover, and bring to a boil. Reduce the heat to low and simmer 30 to 40 minutes until tender.

5 Meanwhile, remove any skin and all the gristle from the meat and discard, along with the bones. Shred the meat. Return the meat to the pan and reheat. Stir in the Worcestershire sauce and parsley. Adjust the salt and pepper, if necessary, and serve.

CHAPTER 3

POULTRY SOUPS

The delicate flavors of chicken and turkey give cooks an almost blank canvas for creating delicious soups bursting with myriad flavors. Thai Red Curry Chicken Soup and African-Style Chicken & Vegetable Soup, for example, have big, bold tastes, while Chicken Soup with Matzo Balls and Scottish Cock-a-Leekie are more subtle and comforting. The recipe for Chinese Egg-Drop Soup lets you recreate a restaurant favorite at home, and for anyone watching their weight, Mexican Poultry & Avocado Broth offers the exciting flavors of the country's cuisine without the traditional calories.

Chicken Noodle Soup is a universal cure-all for everything from the common cold to general malaise, and here there's also a Goji Berry & Garlic Flu Buster, made with rich chicken stock, which combines the restorative qualities of chicken soup with the health benefits of two superfoods.

Soups aren't just for everyday eating, though. Jerusalem Artichoke Soup with Duck Confit, for example, is simple but impressive for dinner parties, too.

CHICKEN NOODLE SOUP (SEE PAGE 88)

134 Chicken Noodle Soup

PREPARATION TIME 15 minutes, plus making the stock and cooking the chicken
COOKING TIME 35 minutes

5½ cups Rich Chicken Stock
  (see page 10)
1 pound 2 ounces skinless chicken
  drumsticks and/or thighs,
  or 3 cups chicken from making the
  stock, cut into bite-size pieces
2 carrots, peeled and sliced

2 celery ribs, sliced
1 leek, thinly sliced and rinsed
8 ounces thin egg noodles
¼ cup finely chopped
  parsley leaves
salt and freshly ground black pepper

1 If using raw chicken, put the stock in a saucepan, add the raw chicken and season
  with salt and pepper. Cover and bring to just below the boil. Skim, then lower the
  heat and simmer, covered, 10 to 15 minutes for thighs and 15 to 20 minutes for
  drumsticks until the chicken is cooked through and the juices run clear when you
  cut a piece. Remove the chicken from the stock and set aside until cool enough
  to handle. Meanwhile, bring a separate large pan of salted water to a boil.

2 Add the carrots, celery, and leek to the stock and return to a boil. Lower the heat
  and simmer 10 to 12 minutes until tender.

3 Meanwhile, add the noodles to the boiling water and cook 10 minutes, or according
  to the package directions, until tender. Drain, rinse under cold running water,
  and set aside.

4 Cut the chicken meat from the bones and into bite-size pieces. Add the freshly
  cooked or leftover chicken to the soup, stir in the noodles, and simmer gently
  to reheat. Adjust the salt and pepper, if necessary, stir in the parsley and serve.

135 Mexican Chicken Noodle Soup

PREPARATION TIME 35 minutes, plus making the stock and cooking the chicken
COOKING TIME 25 minutes

1 dried chipotle chili pepper
2 tablespoons garlic-flavored olive oil
1 red onion, finely chopped
1 red bell pepper, seeded and diced
4 ounces very thin egg noodles,
  such as vermicelli, broken into
  bite-size pieces
1 teaspoon ground cumin
1 teaspoon dried thyme leaves

5½ cups Chicken Stock (see page 11)
  or ready-made stock
1 cup tomato puree
a pinch of light brown sugar
3 cups boneless, skinless
  cooked chicken
salt and freshly ground black pepper
chopped cilantro leaves, to serve
hot pepper sauce, to serve
tortilla chips, to serve (optional)

1 Put the chipotle pepper in a bowl, cover with warm water, and let soak 20 minutes,
  or until tender, then drain, seed, and chop.

2 Heat half the oil in a saucepan. Add the onion and bell pepper and fry, stirring
  occasionally, 3 to 5 minutes until the onion is softened but not colored. Add the
  remaining oil to the pan and heat. Add the noodles and fry 2 to 3 minutes until
  they just start to brown. Add the chipotle, cumin, and thyme and stir 30 seconds,
  or until aromatic. Watch closely so the noodles do not overbrown and the spices
  do not burn.

3 Stir in the stock, tomato puree, and sugar and season with salt and pepper. Cover
  and bring to a boil, then boil, uncovered, 3 to 5 minutes until the noodles and red
  pepper are tender. Stir in the chicken and warm through, and adjust the salt and
  pepper, if necessary. Serve sprinkled with cilantro and with hot pepper sauce and
  tortilla chips, if you like, on the side. If reheating this soup, add a little extra stock,
  if necessary, to thin it.

136 Chicken Soup with Matzo Balls

PREPARATION TIME 25 minutes, plus 2 hours chilling and making the stock
COOKING TIME 1 ¼ hour

5½ cups Rich Chicken Stock
   (see page 10)
1 large carrot, peeled and sliced
1 leek, halved lengthwise, sliced,
   and rinsed
1½ cups shredded savoy cabbage
salt and freshly ground black pepper
chopped parsley leaves, to serve

MATZO BALLS
2 extra-large eggs
2 tablespoons butter, soft
1 cup very finely ground
   blanched almonds
1 cup medium matzo meal
4 to 5 tablespoons Rich Chicken
   Stock (see page 10)
   or ready-made stock
olive oil, if required (optional)

1   To make the matzo balls, put the eggs in a large bowl and beat with an electric mixer or a wooden spoon 2 to 3 minutes until very pale and they hold a "ribbon" on the surface when the beaters are lifted. Beat in the butter, almonds, and matzo meal and season with salt and pepper. Gradually add the stock until the mixture is thick and sticky. Cover with plastic wrap and chill 2 hours.

2   Bring a large saucepan of water to a boil. Using a wet spoon, divide the matzo mixture into 24 equal portions. Use wet hands to roll each portion into a ball. Drop the balls into the water and, just before the water returns to a boil, reduce the heat to low. Simmer 45 minutes, or until the matzo balls are cooked through when you cut one open. Gently drain and set aside. If making in advance, rub the balls lightly with oil to prevent them from sticking together.

3   Put the stock in a saucepan. Cover and bring to just below the boil. Add the carrot and leek and season with salt and pepper. Simmer, covered, 10 minutes, then stir in the matzo balls and cabbage and simmer 5 minutes, or until the carrots are very tender. Adjust the salt and pepper, if necessary, and serve sprinkled with parsley.

137 Chicken, Fennel & Saffron Soup

PREPARATION TIME 10 minutes, plus making the stock   COOKING TIME 30 minutes

1 tablespoon olive or hemp oil
2 cups quartered and thinly sliced
   fennel, with the fronds reserved
   to serve
2 large garlic cloves, finely chopped
1 teaspoon fennel seeds
5½ cups Chicken Stock (see page 11)
   or ready-made stock

1 pound 2 ounces skinless
   chicken thighs
1 bay leaf
a large pinch of saffron threads
salt and freshly ground black pepper

1   Heat the oil in a saucepan over medium heat. Add the fennel and fry, stirring occasionally, 2 minutes. Add the garlic and fry 1 to 3 minutes until the fennel is softened but not colored. Add the fennel seeds and stir 30 seconds. Watch closely so they do not burn.

2   Add the stock and chicken. Cover and bring to a boil. Skim, then add the bay leaf and saffron and season with salt and pepper. Lower the heat and simmer, covered, 10 to 15 minutes until the chicken is cooked through and the juices run clear when you cut a piece. Remove the chicken from the soup and set aside until cool enough to handle.

3   Cut the chicken into bite-size pieces, return it to the soup, and reheat. Discard the bay leaf and adjust the salt and pepper, if necessary. Serve sprinkled with the fennel fronds.

138 Scottish Cock-a-Leekie

PREPARATION TIME 10 minutes, plus making the stock   **COOKING TIME** 40 minutes

2 leeks
2 tablespoons butter
6 cups Chicken Stock (see page 11)
   or ready-made stock
1 pound 2 ounces skinless
   chicken thighs

1 bouquet garni made with 1 bay
   leaf, several parsley sprigs,
   and 1 thyme sprig tied together
6 prunes, pitted and halved
chopped parsley leaves, to serve

1   To prepare the leeks, trim them and separate the white and green parts. Slice the
    white parts thickly, then rinse and set aside. Quarter the green parts lengthwise
    and finely shred, then rinse and set aside.

2   Melt the butter in a saucepan over medium heat. Add the white part of the leeks
    and fry, stirring occasionally, 5 to 8 minutes until just starting to turn golden.
    Add the stock and chicken, cover, and bring to just below the boil. Skim, then add
    the bouquet garni and reduce the heat to low. Simmer, covered, 10 to 15 minutes
    until the chicken is cooked through and the juices run clear when you cut a piece.
    Remove the chicken from the soup and set aside until cool enough to handle.

3   Add the prunes and green parts of the leeks to the soup and simmer, uncovered,
    5 to 10 minutes until the prunes are tender. Discard the bouquet garni.

4   Cut the chicken from the bones into bite-size pieces, return it to the soup, and
    reheat. Adjust the salt and pepper, if necessary, then serve sprinkled with parsley.

139 Malay-Style Chicken Soup

PREPARATION TIME 25 minutes, plus making the stock   COOKING TIME 45 minutes

6 cups Chicken Stock (see page 11)
  or ready-made stock
½-inch piece of galangal,
  peeled and sliced
½-inch piece of gingerroot,
  peeled and sliced
2 garlic cloves, crushed
2 shallots, sliced
1 bird's-eye chili, seeded (optional)
  and sliced
1 lemongrass stem, coarsely
  chopped, with outer leaves
  removed

1 russet potato, peeled and chopped
1 pound 2 ounces skinless
  chicken thighs
1 cup peeled, seeded,
  and diced pumpkin
¾ cup chopped green beans
1 cup coconut milk
2 tablespoons lime juice, or to taste
1 tablespoon fish sauce, or to taste
salt and freshly ground black pepper
chopped cilantro leaves, to serve
finely shredded scallions, to serve

1   Put the stock, galangal, ginger, garlic, shallots, chili, lemongrass, and potato
    in a saucepan. Cover and bring to a boil, skimming as necessary. Boil, partially
    covered, 15 minutes, or until the potato is very tender. Strain into a large bowl,
    pressing down on the potato to push as much as possible through the strainer,
    then return the stock to the pan. Discard the flavorings.
2   Add the chicken, pumpkin, and green beans and season with pepper. Cover and
    bring to a boil. Lower the heat and simmer 10 to 15 minutes until the chicken
    is cooked through and the juices run clear when you cut a piece. Remove the
    chicken from the soup and set aside until cool enough to handle.
3   Cut the chicken from the bones and slice, then return it to the soup. Add the
    coconut milk, lime juice and fish sauce, and simmer over low heat, stirring,
    2 to 3 minutes. Adjust the salt and pepper and add more lime juice or fish sauce,
    if necessary. Serve sprinkled with cilantro and scallions.

140 Japanese-Style Curried Chicken Soup

PREPARATION TIME 25 minutes, plus making the stock and toasting the seeds
COOKING TIME 35 minutes

1 tart apple, peeled, cored,
  and chopped
1 tablespoon lemon juice
2 garlic cloves, chopped
1-inch piece of gingerroot,
  peeled and chopped
½ can (15-oz.) mango in light syrup,
  drained
1 onion, chopped
½ tablespoon Worcestershire Sauce,
  or to taste
2 tablespoons butter

2 tablespoons all-purpose flour
2 teaspoons curry powder
4½ cups Rich Chicken Stock
  (see page 10) or ready-made stock
1 pound 2 ounces skinless
  chicken thighs
1 carrot, peeled, halved lengthwise,
  and thinly sliced
salt and freshly ground black pepper
black sesame seeds, to serve
toasted white sesame seeds
  (see page 9), to serve

1   Toss the apple and lemon juice together in a deep bowl or blender, then add the
    garlic, ginger, mango, onion, and Worcestershire sauce. Blend until the mixture
    forms a paste but is not completely pureed, then set aside.
2   Melt the butter in a saucepan over medium heat. Stir in the apple paste, then
    sprinkle in the flour and curry powder and stir 2 minutes. Slowly add the stock,
    stirring continuously to prevent lumps from forming. Add the chicken and season
    with pepper. Cover and bring to a boil, then skim and lower the heat. Simmer,
    covered, 10 to 15 minutes until the chicken is cooked through and the juices run
    clear when you cut a piece. Remove the chicken from the soup and set aside
    until cool enough to handle.
3   Add the carrot to the soup, increase the heat to medium, and simmer 10 to 12
    minutes until it is tender. Meanwhile, cut the chicken from the bones into thin
    pieces, return it to the pan, and warm through. Adjust the salt and pepper and add
    more Worcestershire Sauce, if necessary, then serve sprinkled with sesame seeds.

141 Provençal-Style Chicken Soup

PREPARATION TIME 15 minutes, plus making the stock and croutes
COOKING TIME 25 minutes

1 tablespoon extra-virgin olive oil,
   plus extra to serve
1 red onion, finely chopped
4 garlic cloves, very finely chopped
3 cups tomato puree
2 cups Chicken Stock (see page 11)
   or ready-made stock
1 pound 2 ounces skinless
   chicken thighs

1 zucchini, halved lengthwise
   and sliced
1 bouquet garni made with 1 piece
   of celery rib, 1 bay leaf, several
   parsley and thyme sprigs,
   and 1 rosemary sprig tied together
salt and freshly ground black pepper
chopped parsley leaves, to serve
1 recipe quantity Goat Cheese
   Croutes (see page 14), to serve

1 Heat the oil in a saucepan over medium heat. Add the onion and fry 2 minutes.
   Add the garlic and fry 1 to 3 minutes until the onion is softened but not colored.
   Add the tomato puree, stock, and chicken. Cover and bring to a boil, then skim.
2 Add the zucchini and bouquet garni and season with salt and pepper. Lower the
   heat and simmer, covered, 10 to 15 minutes until the chicken is cooked through
   and the juices run clear when you cut a piece. Remove the chicken from the
   soup and set aside until cool enough to handle, then discard the bouquet garni.
3 Cut the chicken from the bones into bite-size pieces, return it to the soup,
   and reheat. Adjust the salt and pepper, if necessary, then serve drizzled with oil,
   sprinkled with parsley, and with croutes on the side.

142 Curried Chicken & Tomato Soup

PREPARATION TIME 10 minutes, plus making the stock and seeds and preparing
the tomatoes   COOKING TIME 35 minutes

2½ cups Chicken Stock (see page 11)
   or ready-made stock
1¾ cups coconut milk
2 lemongrass stems,
   cut into 3 pieces, with
   outer leaves removed
1-inch piece of gingerroot, peeled
   and smashed in one piece
1 tablespoon Madras curry paste

1 pound 2 ounces skinless
   chicken thighs
2 large tomatoes, peeled
   (see page 9), seeded, and chopped
salt and freshly ground black pepper
Spiced Seeds (see page 15), to serve
chopped cilantro leaves, to serve
mini poppadoms, warm, to serve

1 Put the stock, coconut milk, lemongrass, ginger, and curry paste in a saucepan
   over high heat. Stir until the paste dissolves, then season with salt and pepper.
   Cover and bring to a boil, then lower the heat and simmer 10 minutes. Add the
   chicken, cover, and return to a boil.
2 Skim, then lower the heat and simmer, covered, 10 minutes. Stir in the tomatoes
   and simmer, covered, 3 to 5 minutes longer until the chicken is cooked through
   and the juices run clear when you cut a piece. Remove the chicken and set aside
   until cool enough to handle. Discard the lemongrass and ginger.
3 Cut the chicken from the bones into bite-size pieces, return it to the soup,
   and reheat, if necessary. Adjust the salt and pepper, if necessary, then serve
   sprinkled with seeds and cilantro and with poppadoms on the side.

143 Mexican-Style Chicken Soup

PREPARATION TIME 15 minutes, plus making the stock   COOKING TIME 35 minutes

1½ tablespoons sunflower oil
1 large onion, chopped
2 red or green bell peppers,
   seeded and diced
2 garlic cloves, chopped
1 teaspoon ancho chili powder,
   or to taste
3½ cups Chicken Stock (see page 11)
   or ready-made stock

14 ounces boneless, skinless
   chicken breast halves
2⅔ cups frozen corn kernels
½ can (15-oz.) kidney beans,
   drained and rinsed
salt and freshly ground black pepper
chopped cilantro leaves, to serve
lime wedges, to serve
tortilla chips, to serve (optional)

1   Heat the oil in a large saucepan over medium heat. Add the onion and bell
    peppers and fry, stirring occasionally, 2 minutes. Stir in the garlic and fry
    1 to 3 minutes until the onion is softened but not colored. Add the chili powder
    and stir 30 seconds, or until aromatic. Watch closely so it does not burn.
2   Add the stock and chicken and season with salt and pepper, then cover
    and bring to a boil. Skim, then lower the heat, and simmer, covered,
    12 to 15 minutes until the chicken is cooked through and the juices run clear when
    you cut a piece. Remove the chicken from the soup and set aside until cool enough
    to handle.
3   Add the corn to the soup and boil 3 to 5 minutes until tender. Thinly slice the
    chicken breasts, return them to the soup, add the kidney beans, and reheat until
    both are warm. Adjust the salt and pepper, if necessary, then serve sprinkled
    with cilantro and with lime wedges for squeezing over and tortilla chips on the
    side, if you like.

144 Chicken & Chickpea Soup

PREPARATION TIME 10 minutes, plus overnight soaking and cooking the chickpeas
(optional), making the stock, and toasting the seeds   COOKING TIME 35 minutes

1 cup dried chickpeas or 1 can
   (15-oz.) chickpeas, drained
   and rinsed
1 tablespoon garlic-flavored olive oil
1 leek, sliced and rinsed
1½ teaspoons ground cumin
a pinch of chili flakes, or to taste
a pinch of turmeric
6 cups Chicken Stock (see page 11)
   or ready-made stock

1 pound 2 ounces skinless
   chicken thighs
1 handful of baby spinach leaves
salt and freshly ground black pepper
toasted sesame seeds (see page 9),
   to serve
chopped cilantro leaves, to serve

1   If using dried chickpeas, put them in a bowl, cover with water and let soak
    overnight, then drain. Transfer to a saucepan and add 6½ cups water. Cover and
    bring to a boil, then lower the heat and simmer, covered, 50 minutes to 1 hour,
    then drain.
2   Heat the oil in a saucepan over medium heat. Add the leek and fry, stirring
    occasionally, 3 to 5 minutes until softened but not colored. Stir in the cumin, chili
    flakes, and turmeric and fry 30 seconds. Watch closely so the spices do not burn.
    Add the stock and chicken and season with salt and pepper. Cover and bring
    to a boil, then skim.
3   Lower the heat and simmer, covered, 10 to 15 minutes until the chicken is cooked
    through and the juices run clear when you cut a piece. Remove the chicken from
    the stock and set aside until cool enough to handle.
4   Add the spinach and half the chickpeas to the pan and simmer 3 to 5 minutes until
    the spinach wilts. Blend the soup until smooth, then add the remaining chickpeas
    and return to a simmer.
5   Cut the chicken from the bones into bite-size pieces, return it to the soup,
    and warm through. Adjust the salt and pepper, if necessary, then serve sprinkled
    with sesame seeds and cilantro.

145 Chicken, Pepper & Rice Soup

PREPARATION TIME 15 minutes, plus making the stock and rice
COOKING TIME 30 minutes

1 tablespoon garlic-flavored olive oil
1 onion, finely chopped
5½ cups Chicken Stock (see page 11)
  or ready-made stock
1 pound 2 ounces skinless
  chicken thighs
1 green bell pepper, seeded
  and diced

1 red bell pepper,
  seeded and diced
a pinch of chili flakes, or to taste
  (optional)
½ cup frozen corn kernels
1 cup long-grain rice, cooked
salt and freshly ground black pepper
chopped cilantro or parsley leaves,
  to serve

1   Heat the oil in a saucepan over medium heat. Add the onion and fry, stirring
    occasionally, 3 to 5 minutes until softened but not colored. Add the stock and
    chicken and season with salt and pepper. Cover and bring to a boil. Skim, then
    lower the heat and simmer, covered, 5 minutes.
2   Add the peppers and chili flakes, if using, and simmer, covered, 5 to 10 minutes
    longer until the peppers are tender and the chicken is cooked through and
    the juices run clear when you cut a piece. Remove the chicken from the soup
    and set aside until it is cool enough to handle.
3   Add the corn kernels to the pan, bring to a slow boil, and boil 3 to 5 minutes
    until tender. Cut the chicken from the bones into bite-size pieces, return it to the
    soup with the rice, and heat through. Adjust the salt and pepper, if necessary,
    then serve sprinkled with cilantro.

146 African-Style Chicken & Vegetable Soup

PREPARATION TIME 20 minutes, plus making the stock   COOKING TIME 40 minutes

1½ tablespoons peanut
  or sunflower oil
1 large onion, chopped
4½ cups Chicken Stock (see page 11)
  or ready-made stock
1 pound 2 ounces skinless
  chicken thighs
½ cup natural chunky peanut butter
1 can (15-oz.) crushed tomatoes

a pinch of chili flakes, or to taste
1 cup peeled and seeded pumpkin
  cut into bite-size pieces
¾ cup cored and shredded
  white cabbage
½ cup chopped green beans
1 carrot, peeled and sliced
salt and freshly ground black pepper
chopped cilantro leaves, to serve

1   Heat the oil in a saucepan over medium heat. Add the onion and fry, stirring
    occasionally, 3 to 5 minutes until softened but not colored. Add the stock and
    chicken and season with salt and pepper. Cover and bring to a boil, then skim the
    surface. Add the peanut butter, stirring until it dissolves, then add the tomatoes
    and chili flakes, if using. Lower the heat and simmer, covered, 10 to 15 minutes
    until the chicken is cooked through and the juices run clear when you cut a piece.
    Remove the chicken from the soup and set aside until cool enough to handle.
2   Add the pumpkin, cabbage, green beans, and carrot to the pan and return the
    soup to a boil. Lower the heat and simmer, uncovered, 10 to 12 minutes until
    the vegetables are tender.
3   Cut the chicken from the bones into bite-size pieces, return it to the soup,
    and heat through. Adjust the salt and pepper, if necessary, then serve sprinkled
    with cilantro.

147 Thai Red Curry Chicken Soup

PREPARATION TIME 15 minutes, plus making the chilies   **COOKING TIME** 30 minutes

2 tablespoons sunflower oil
2 large shallots, sliced
1 tablespoon red curry paste
1 pound 2 ounces skinless
   chicken thighs
1¾ cups coconut milk
1-inch piece of gingerroot,
   peeled and sliced

4 kaffir lime leaves, torn
lime juice, to taste (optional)
palm sugar or light brown sugar,
   to taste (optional)
chopped cilantro leaves, to serve
Chilies in Vinegar (see page 15),
   to serve
lime wedges, to serve (optional)

1 Measure 4½ cups water into a large measuring jug and set aside.
2 Heat the oil in a large wok with a lid or a saucepan over high heat. Add the
   shallots and curry paste, lower the heat to medium, and stir-fry 2 minutes. Very
   slowly stir in 1 cup of the water and stir 1 to 2 minutes until the fat forms bubbles
   on the surface. Add the chicken and fry, turning occasionally, 5 minutes, gradually
   stirring in a little more of the measured water if the curry paste looks like it will
   burn. Add the coconut milk, ginger, lime leaves, and remaining water, then cover
   and bring to a boil.
3 Lower the heat and simmer 10 to 15 minutes until the chicken is cooked through
   and the juices run clear when you cut a piece. Remove the chicken from the soup
   and set aside until cool enough to handle.
4 Cut the chicken from the bones into bite-size pieces and return it to the soup.
   Stir in the lime juice and palm sugar to temper the heat of the curry paste,
   if you like, and reheat the soup. Serve sprinkled with cilantro, topped with chilies,
   and with lime wedges for squeezing over, if you like.

148 Middle Eastern-Spiced Chicken & Rice Soup

PREPARATION TIME 15 minutes, plus making the stock   **COOKING TIME** 50 minutes

6 cups Chicken Stock (see page 11)
 or ready-made stock
1 pound 2 ounces skinless
 chicken thighs
1 large carrot, cut in several pieces
1 onion, unpeeled and halved
1 teaspoon ground coriander

1 teaspoon ground cumin
several mint sprigs, tied together
½ cup long-grain rice
salt and freshly ground black pepper
1 teaspoon finely chopped mint
 leaves for each bowl, to serve
lemon wedges, to serve

1   Put the stock in a saucepan over medium heat. Add the chicken, carrot, onion, coriander, cumin, and mint sprigs and season with salt and pepper. Cover and bring to a boil, then skim. Lower the heat and simmer, covered, 15 to 20 minutes until the chicken is cooked through and the juices run clear when you cut a piece. Remove the chicken, carrot, onion, and mint sprigs from the stock. Set the chicken aside until cool enough to handle and discard the vegetables.

2   Cover and return to a boil. Stir in the rice, lower the heat, and simmer, covered, 15 to 20 minutes until the rice is tender. Skim as necessary. Meanwhile, cut the chicken from the bones into bite-size pieces, return it to the soup and reheat. Adjust the salt and pepper, if necessary.

3   Put a teaspoon of chopped mint in each bowl, ladle the soup over it, and serve with lemon wedges for squeezing over. If reheating this soup, add a little extra stock to thin it.

149 Creamy Chicken & Mushroom Soup

PREPARATION TIME 15 minutes, plus making the stock   **COOKING TIME** 40 minutes

4½ cups Chicken Stock (see page 11)
 or ready-made stock
1 pound 2 ounces skinless
 chicken thighs
1 bouquet garni made with 1 bay
 leaf, several parsley sprigs, and
 1 thyme sprig tied together
2 tablespoons butter
1 tablespoon olive or hemp oil

1 leek, halved lengthwise,
 thinly sliced, and rinsed
4 large portobello mushrooms,
 trimmed and sliced
¼ cup all-purpose
 or wholewheat flour
½ cup light cream
2 tablespoons sweet sherry
salt and freshly ground black pepper
chopped parsley leaves, to serve

1   Put the stock and chicken in a saucepan and season with salt and pepper. Cover and bring to just below the boil. Skim, then lower the heat, add the bouquet garni, and simmer, covered, 10 to 15 minutes until the chicken is cooked through and the juices run clear if you cut a piece. Remove the chicken from the stock and set aside until cool enough to handle. Discard the bouquet garni.

2   Cut the chicken from the bones into bite-size pieces and set aside.

3   Meanwhile, melt the butter with the oil in another saucepan over medium heat. Add the leek and fry, stirring occasionally, 3 minutes. Add the mushrooms, season with salt, and fry 5 to 8 minutes until the mushrooms are softened and give off their juices. Sprinkle in the flour and cook, stirring, 2 minutes. Slowly stir in enough of the stock to achieve the preferred consistency, stirring continuously to prevent lumps from forming.

4   Bring the soup to a boil, stirring, then reduce the heat to low and stir in the cream and sherry. Add the chicken and simmer until warmed through, then skim and adjust the salt and pepper, if necessary. Serve sprinkled with parsley. If you reheat this soup, do not boil it.

150 "Velvet" Chicken & Edamame Soup

PREPARATION TIME 25 minutes, plus making the stock   COOKING TIME 20 minutes

14 ounces boneless chicken thighs
6 cups Rich Chicken Stock
  (see page 10) or ready-made stock
1½-inch piece of gingerroot,
  peeled and grated
1 thin slice of galangal, smashed
¾ cup frozen shelled
  edamame beans

½ teaspoon salt
½ cup drained and finely chopped
  canned water chestnuts
3 scallions, thinly sliced
  on the diagonal
2 teaspoons light soy sauce,
  or to taste

1   Up to 2 hours in advance, prepare the chicken. Put the chicken, skin-side down,
    on a cutting board and use the flat side of a cleaver or large chef's knife to pound
    it several times to flatten. Next, use the flat edge along the top of the cleaver
    or knife to pound the meat until it looks like it has been ground, then use the sharp
    edge of the knife to scrape the meat away from the skin. Discard the skin. Finely
    chop the meat, occasionally adding 1 teaspoon cold water until it becomes almost
    white and fluffy. (You can add up to 3 tablespoons cold water.) Cover and chill until
    required. Alternatively, skin and very thinly slice the thighs.
2   When ready to cook, bring a small saucepan of water to a boil for the edamame.
    Put the stock in a separate saucepan, cover, and bring to just below the boil.
    Add the ginger and galangal to the stock, reduce the heat to very low, and simmer
    while you cook the edamame.
3   Add the edamame and salt to the boiling water and boil 5 minutes, or until tender.
    Drain and immediately rinse under cold running water to stop the cooking.
4   Add the chicken, edamame, water chestnuts, and scallions to the stock and
    simmer 2 to 3 minutes until the chicken is cooked through. Discard the galangal.
    Stir in the soy sauce, adding extra to taste, if you like, then serve.

151 Sweet-and-Sour Chicken Soup

PREPARATION TIME 15 minutes, plus making the stock, chilies, and garlic
COOKING TIME 50 minutes

6 cups Rich Chicken Stock
  (see page 10) or ready-made stock
½-inch piece of gingerroot,
  peeled and sliced
2 garlic cloves, halved
5 Thai basil leaves, plus extra
  to serve
1 tablespoon sunflower oil
3 shallots, finely chopped
1 pound 2 ounces skinless
  chicken thighs

1½ tablespoons fish sauce,
  or to taste
1 tablespoon lime juice, or to taste
2 teaspoons palm sugar or light
  brown sugar, or to taste
salt and freshly ground black pepper
Chilies in Vinegar (see page 15),
  to serve
Crisp-Fried Garlic (see page 15),
  to serve

1   Put the stock, ginger, garlic, and basil in a saucepan, cover, and bring to a boil.
    Lower the heat and simmer 20 minutes, then strain into a bowl and set aside.
2   Heat the oil in the rinsed-out and dried saucepan. Add the shallots and fry
    3 to 5 minutes until softened but not colored. Add the stock and chicken. Cover
    and bring to a boil, then skim the surface and stir in the fish sauce, lime juice,
    and sugar. Lower the heat and simmer, covered, 10 to 15 minutes until the chicken
    is cooked through and the juices run clear when you cut a piece. Remove the
    chicken from the soup and set aside until cool enough to handle.
3   Cut the chicken from the bones into bite-size pieces, return it to the soup, and
    warm through. Adjust the salt and pepper and add extra fish sauce, lime juice,
    or sugar, if you like. Serve with the chilies in vinegar and fried garlic on the side
    for adding at the table.

152 Cream of Chicken Soup with Tarragon & Lemon

PREPARATION TIME 15 minutes, plus making the stock   **COOKING TIME** 30 minutes

4½ cups Rich Chicken Stock
  (see page 10) or ready-made stock
1 pound 2 ounces skinless
  chicken thighs
4 tarragon sprigs, plus extra leaves,
  chopped, to serve
1 bay leaf
1 leek, chopped and rinsed

2 tablespoons butter
1 tablespoon sunflower oil
2 shallots, finely chopped
¼ cup all-purpose flour
½ cup heavy cream
finely grated zest of 1 lemon
salt and ground white pepper

1. Put the stock and chicken in a saucepan and season with salt and white pepper. Cover and bring to a boil, then skim. Add the tarragon, bay leaf, and leek, lower the heat and simmer, covered, 10 to 15 minutes until the chicken is cooked through and the juices run clear when you cut a piece. Remove the chicken from the stock and set aside until cool enough to handle. Strain the stock and set aside.

2. Melt the butter with the oil in another saucepan. Add the shallots and fry, stirring occasionally, 3 to 5 minutes until softened but not colored. Sprinkle in the flour and stir 2 minutes, then slowly add the stock, stirring continuously, to prevent lumps from forming. Leave to simmer while you prepare the chicken.

3. Cut the chicken from the bones into thin pieces and return it to the soup. Stir in the cream and lemon zest and reheat. Adjust the salt and pepper, if necessary, then serve sprinkled with tarragon.

153 Chicken & Purple Broccoli Soup

PREPARATION TIME 20 minutes, plus making the stock   COOKING TIME 40 minutes

5½ cups Chicken Stock (see page 11)
   or ready-made stock
1 large garlic clove, finely chopped
1 onion, grated
1 bouquet garni made with 1 piece
   of celery rib with its leaves,
   1 bay leaf and several parsley
   and thyme sprigs tied together
1 red bell pepper, seeded
   and chopped

2⅔ cups frozen corn kernels
14 ounces boneless, skinless chicken
   breasts, thinly sliced
2 cups purple sprouting broccoli,
   or ordinary broccoli, cut into
   bite-size pieces
2 tablespoons chopped mixed herbs,
   such as chives, dill, parsley
   and/or tarragon
salt and freshly ground black pepper

1   Put the stock, garlic, onion, and bouquet garni in a saucepan, cover, and bring
    to just below the boil. Lower the heat and simmer 10 minutes. Add the bell pepper
    and corn and simmer, covered, 3 minutes, then stir in the chicken and season with
    salt and pepper. Simmer, covered, 5 minutes, then add the broccoli and simmer,
    uncovered, 5 minutes longer. Discard the bouquet garni.
2   Stir in the herbs and simmer 3 to 5 minutes until the chicken is cooked through
    and the broccoli is tender. Adjust the salt and pepper, if necessary, and serve.

154 Chicken & Pumpkin Broth

PREPARATION TIME 15 minutes, plus making the stock   COOKING TIME 35 minutes

6 cups Chicken Stock (see page 11)
   or ready-made stock
6 garlic cloves, peeled but left whole
1 bouquet garni made with 1 piece
   of celery rib with its leaves, 1 bay
   leaf, and several parsley and
   thyme sprigs tied together

1 pound 2 ounces skinless chicken
1¾ cups peeled, seeded, and
   diced pumpkin
½ cup chopped green beans
⅓ cup frozen peas
2 tablespoons chopped
   parsley leaves
salt and freshly ground black pepper

1   Put the stock, garlic, and bouquet garni in a saucepan. Cover and bring to a boil.
    Boil 10 minutes, then lower the heat to medium, add the chicken, and season with
    salt and pepper. Cover and return to a boil, then skim. Add the pumpkin, lower the
    heat and simmer, covered, 10 minutes.
2   Add the beans and peas and simmer 5 to 8 minutes until the vegetables are tender
    and the chicken is cooked through and the juices run clear when you cut a piece.
    Remove the chicken from the soup and set aside until cool enough to handle.
    Discard the bouquet garni and garlic.
3   Cut the chicken from the bones into bite-size pieces and return it to the soup.
    Adjust the salt and pepper, if necessary, then serve.

155 Chicken, Leek & Tarragon Soup

PREPARATION TIME 10 minutes, plus making the stock   COOKING TIME 30 minutes

1½ tablespoons olive or hemp oil
2 cups leeks halved lengthwise,
   sliced, and rinsed
1¼ pounds skinless chicken thighs

5½ cups Chicken Stock (see page 11)
   or ready-made stock
1½ tablespoons torn tarragon leaves
salt and freshly ground black pepper

1   Heat the oil in a saucepan over medium heat. Stir in the leeks, lower the heat
    to low, and cook, covered, 8 to 10 minutes until tender. Add the chicken and stock
    and season with salt and pepper. Cover and bring to a boil, then skim and reduce
    the heat to low. Stir in the tarragon and simmer, covered, 12 to 15 minutes until the
    chicken is cooked through and the juices run clear when you cut a piece. Remove
    the chicken from the soup and set aside until cool enough to handle.
2   Cut the chicken from the bones into bite-size pieces, return it to the soup, and heat
    through. Adjust the salt and pepper, if necessary, then serve.

156 Chicken & Corn Soup

PREPARATION TIME 10 minutes, plus making the stock   **COOKING TIME** 25 minutes

2 tablespoons arrowroot
4½ cups Rich Chicken Stock
   (see page 10) or ready-made stock
14 ounces boneless, skinless
   chicken breasts
1 can (15-oz.) creamed corn

½ teaspoon sugar
1 egg, beaten
salt and freshly ground black pepper
2 scallions, finely chopped,
   to serve

1   Put the arrowroot and 3 tablespoons cold water in a small heatproof bowl and
    mix until smooth, then set aside.
2   Put the stock and chicken in a saucepan and season with salt and pepper. Cover
    and bring to a boil, then lower the heat and simmer 10 to 12 minutes until the
    chicken is cooked through and the juices run clear when you cut a piece.
    Remove the chicken from the stock and set aside until cool enough to handle.
3   Add the corn and sugar to the pan. Stir a ladleful of the hot stock into the
    arrowroot mixture, then stir this mixture into the pan. Return to a boil, then boil
    2 to 3 minutes until the soup thickens slightly.
4   Meanwhile, shred the chicken, return it to the soup, and reduce the heat to low.
    Slowly add the egg, stirring quickly with a fork until it sets in small pieces—
    the quicker you stir, the finer the pieces will be. Adjust the salt and pepper,
    if necessary, then serve sprinkled with the scallions. If you reheat the soup,
    do not boil it or the eggs will scramble.

157 Thai Green Curry Chicken & Bean Soup

PREPARATION TIME 15 minutes   COOKING TIME 40 minutes

2 tablespoons sunflower oil
1 tablespoon green curry paste
9 ounces skinless chicken thighs
1 tablespoon fish sauce
1½ cups chopped green beans
1 scallion, chopped

lime juice, to taste (optional)
palm sugar or light brown sugar,
   to taste
Thai basil leaves, shredded, to serve
lime wedges, to serve

1   Measure 5½ cups water and set aside. Heat the oil in a large wok with a lid over
    high heat. Add the curry paste, lower the heat, and stir 2 minutes. Slowly add
    1 cup of the water and stir until the fat forms bubbles.
2   Add the chicken and fry, turning occasionally, for 5 minutes, stirring in a little more
    of the measured water if the paste looks like it will burn. Add the remaining water
    and the fish sauce and bring to a boil, then simmer, covered, 10 minutes. Add the
    beans and scallion and simmer, uncovered, 5 to 10 minutes until the chicken
    is cooked through. Remove the chicken and set aside.
3   Cut the chicken into bite-size pieces and return it to the soup. Stir in the lime juice
    and/or palm sugar to temper the heat of the curry paste, if you like. Serve sprinkled
    with Thai basil and with lime wedges for squeezing over.

158 Chicken & Spring Vegetable Soup

PREPARATION TIME 15 minutes, plus making the stock and cooking the chicken
COOKING TIME 25 minutes

1 tablespoon butter
1 tablespoon garlic-flavored olive oil
2 celery ribs, finely chopped
1 onion, very finely chopped
4½ cups Vegetable Stock
   (see page 12) or ready-made stock
5 new potatoes, diced
2 ounces asparagus tips
⅓ cup shelled fava beans

⅓ cup frozen peas
3 cups boneless, skinless cooked
   chicken cut into bite-size pieces
1 tablespoon chopped mint leaves
1 tablespoon chopped parsley leaves
salt and freshly ground black pepper
pesto, to serve
freshly grated Parmesan cheese,
   to serve

1   Melt the butter with the oil in a saucepan over medium heat. Add the celery and
    onion and fry, stirring occasionally, 3 to 5 minutes until the onion is softened.
    Add the stock and potatoes and season with salt and pepper. Cover and bring
    to a boil, then lower the heat and simmer 10 minutes. Add the asparagus, beans,
    and peas and simmer 2 to 3 minutes until the vegetables are tender.
2   Stir in the chicken and warm though. Add the mint and parsley and adjust the salt
    and pepper, if necessary. Serve topped with pesto and Parmesan cheese.

159 Chicken & Asian Mushroom Soup

PREPARATION TIME 15 minutes, plus making the stock   COOKING TIME 45 minutes

6 cups Chicken Stock (see page 11)
   or ready-made stock
14 ounces honshimeji or shiitake
   mushrooms, stems removed and
   reserved and caps thinly sliced
¼ cup chopped gingerroot,
2 large garlic cloves, chopped

2 star anise
1 thin slice of galangal, smashed
3 cups thinly sliced boneless,
   skinless chicken
light soy sauce, to taste
2 scallions, sliced, to serve
toasted sesame oil, to serve

1   Put the stock, mushroom stems, ginger, garlic, star anise, and galangal
    in a saucepan, cover, and bring to a boil. Lower the heat and simmer 30 minutes,
    then strain the stock and return it to the pan. Return the stock to a boil.
2   Lower the heat, add the chicken and mushroom caps, and simmer 4 to 5 minutes
    until the chicken is cooked through. Season with soy sauce.
3   Serve topped with the scallions and drizzled with sesame oil.

160 Zucchini & Pea Chicken Soup

PREPARATION TIME 15 minutes, plus cooking the chicken and making the stock and shallots   **COOKING TIME** 25 minutes

1½ tablespoons olive or hemp oil
1 carrot, peeled and sliced
1 celery rib, thinly sliced
1 onion, finely chopped
2⅔ cups tomato puree
2½ cups Chicken Stock (see page 10)
  or ready-made stock
1 zucchini, sliced

1 teaspoon dried thyme leaves
½ teaspoon sugar
3 cups shredded cooked chicken
½ cup frozen peas
salt and freshly ground black pepper
Crisp-Fried Shallots (see page 15),
  to serve

1   Heat the oil in a saucepan over medium heat. Add the carrot, celery, and onion and fry, stirring, 3 to 5 minutes until the onion is softened. Add the tomato puree and stock and season with salt and pepper. Cover and bring to a boil, then stir in the zucchini, thyme, and sugar. Lower the heat and simmer, covered, 5 minutes.

2   Add the chicken and peas and simmer, uncovered, 3 to 5 minutes until the peas are tender. Adjust the salt and pepper, if necessary, and serve with the shallots.

161 Sunday Night Chicken & Ham Soup

PREPARATION TIME 15 minutes, plus making the stock and cooking the chicken
COOKING TIME 35 minutes

6 cups Chicken Stock (see page 11)
  or ready-made stock
1 bouquet garni made with 1 bay leaf
  and several parsley and thyme
  sprigs tied together
½ cup long-grain rice

4 garlic cloves, halved
4 sun-dried tomatoes in oil, chopped
1½ cups diced cooked chicken
1½ cups diced cooked ham
salt and freshly ground black pepper

1   Put the stock, bouquet garni, rice, garlic, and sun-dried tomatoes in a saucepan and season with salt and pepper. Cover and bring to a boil, then skim.

2   Reduce the heat to low. Simmer, covered, 10 to 15 minutes until the rice is tender. Add the chicken and ham and heat through. Discard the bouquet garni and garlic and adjust the salt and pepper, if necessary, and serve.

162 Colombian Chicken & Corn Soup

PREPARATION TIME 15 minutes, plus making the stock   **COOKING TIME** 40 minutes

1½ tablespoons sunflower oil
1 large onion, finely chopped
2 teaspoons dried oregano
1 pound 2 ounces skinless
  chicken thighs
6 cups Chicken Stock (see page 11)
  or ready-made stock
1 russet potato, peeled and grated
1 waxy potato, peeled and diced

3 corn cobs, husked and each cut
  into 2 or 3 pieces
salt and freshly ground black pepper
2 avocados, to serve
1 tablespoon lemon juice, to serve
chopped cilantro leaves, to serve
rinsed capers, to serve
double cream, to serve

1   Heat the oil in a saucepan over medium heat. Add the onion and fry, stirring, 3 to 5 minutes until softened. Stir in the oregano, chicken, stock, and grated potato and season with salt and pepper. Cover and bring to a boil, then lower the heat and simmer 10 to 15 minutes until the chicken is cooked through. Remove the chicken from the pan and set aside until cool enough to handle.

2   Add the diced potato and corn to the pan, cover, and return to a boil. Lower the heat and simmer 10 to 12 minutes until the vegetables are tender.

3   Meanwhile, peel, seed, and chop the avocados and toss with the lemon juice, then set aside. Cut the chicken into bite-size pieces, return it to the soup, and heat through. Adjust the salt and pepper, if necessary. Divide the corn pieces into bowls and ladle the soup over them. Serve sprinkled with cilantro and with the avocado, and capers on the side.

163 Chicken Mulligatawny Soup

PREPARATION TIME 20 minutes, plus making the stock and cooking the chicken and rice
(optional)   **COOKING TIME** 35 minutes

1 tablespoon peanut or sunflower oil
1 apple, peeled, cored, and chopped
1 carrot, peeled and chopped
1 celery rib, thinly sliced
1 onion, finely chopped
1 green or red bell pepper,
  seeded and chopped
1 tablespoon all-purpose
  or wholewheat flour
1 teaspoon curry powder

½ teaspoon powdered mustard
5½ cups Rich Chicken Stock
  (see page 10) or ready-made stock
3 cups boneless, skinless cooked
  chicken cut into bite-size pieces
salt and freshly ground black pepper
cooked white or brown basmati rice,
  hot, to serve (optional)
chopped cilantro or parsley leaves,
  to serve

1   Heat the oil in a saucepan over medium heat. Add the apple, carrot, celery, onion,
    and bell pepper and fry, stirring occasionally, 3 to 5 minutes until the vegetables
    are softened. Sprinkle in the flour, curry powder, and mustard and stir 2 minutes.
    Slowly add the stock, stirring continuously to prevent lumps from forming.

2   Season with salt and pepper, cover, and bring to a boil. Lower the heat and simmer
    20 minutes, or until the apple breaks down, the vegetables are tender, and the
    soup has thickened slightly. Add the chicken and heat through, then adjust the salt
    and pepper, if necessary.

3   Put a portion of hot rice, if using, in each bowl. Ladle the soup over it, sprinkle
    with cilantro, and serve.

164 Roast Chicken Soup

PREPARATION TIME 10 minutes, plus making the stock and roasting the chicken
COOKING TIME 30 minutes

1 tablespoon olive or hemp oil
2 carrots, peeled and diced
1 leek, halved lengthwise, thinly
   sliced, and rinsed
5½ cups Chicken Stock (see page 11)
   or ready-made stock
1 bay leaf

2 tablespoons chicken gravy
   (optional)
½ cup frozen corn kernels
3 cups boneless, skinless roast
   chicken cut into bite-size pieces
salt and freshly ground black pepper

1   Heat the oil in a saucepan over medium heat. Add the carrot and leek and fry,
    stirring occasionally, 3 to 5 minutes until the leek is softened but not colored.
    Stir in the stock, bay leaf, and gravy, if using, and season with salt and pepper,
    then cover and bring to a boil. Reduce the heat to low, add the corn and simmer,
    covered, 10 to 15 minutes until the carrots and are tender.
2   Stir in the chicken and simmer 3 to 5 minutes to warm through. Discard the bay
    leaf, adjust the salt and pepper, if necessary, and serve.

165 Chicken & Barley Soup

PREPARATION TIME 20 minutes, plus making the stock and cooking the chicken
COOKING TIME 50 minutes

1 tablespoon sunflower oil
1 celery rib, chopped
1 onion, finely chopped
2 garlic cloves, finely chopped
½ teaspoon turmeric
5½ cups Chicken Stock (see page 11)
   or ready-made stock
¼ cup pearl barley
2 bay leaves

1½ cups peeled and diced mixed root
   vegetables, such as carrot, potato,
   rutabaga, sweet potato, turnip,
   or pumpkin
3 cups diced boneless, skinless
   cooked chicken
1 zucchini, coarsely grated
salt and freshly ground black pepper
chopped parsley leaves, to serve

1   Heat the oil in a saucepan over medium heat. Add the celery and onion and fry,
    stirring occasionally, 2 minutes. Stir in the garlic and fry 1 to 3 minutes until the
    onion is softened but not colored. Stir in the turmeric, then add the stock and
    season with salt and pepper. Cover and bring to a boil. Skim the surface, then
    stir in the barley and bay leaves, cover, and return to a boil.
2   Lower the heat and simmer 20 minutes. Stir in the vegetables and simmer
    10 to 20 minutes longer until the barley is tender. Stir in the chicken and zucchini
    and warm through. Discard the bay leaves and adjust the salt and pepper,
    if necessary, then serve sprinkled with parsley.

166 Soothing Lemon Thyme & Garlic Broth

PREPARATION TIME 5 minutes, plus at least 15 minutes infusing and making the stock
COOKING TIME 15 minutes

6½ cups Rich Chicken Stock
   (see page 10), Chicken Stock
   (see page 11) or ready-made stock
8 large garlic cloves, sliced

1 bunch of lemon thyme, about
   1 ounce, tied together
salt and freshly ground black pepper
   (optional)

1   Put the stock, garlic, and lemon thyme in a saucepan, cover, and bring to a boil.
    Uncover and boil 5 minutes to reduce slightly, then turn off the heat, cover, and let
    infuse for at least 15 minutes, or up to several hours, depending on how strongly
    flavored you want the broth.
2   Strain the broth, then return it to the pan and reheat. Season with salt and pepper,
    if you like, but it should be well flavored as it is, then serve.

167 Greek Lemon & Egg Soup With Orzo

PREPARATION TIME 5 minutes, plus making the stock   COOKING TIME 25 minutes

5½ cups Chicken Stock (see page 11)
   or ready-made stock
½ teaspoon salt, plus extra to season
¾ cup orzo

2 eggs
6 tablespoons lemon juice
freshly ground black pepper
chopped parsley leaves, to serve

1 Put the stock and salt in a saucepan, cover, and bring to a boil. Stir in the orzo
and boil 15 to 17 minutes, or according to the package directions, stirring
frequently, until tender, then reduce the heat to low.

2 Beat the eggs and lemon juice in a heatproof bowl with a ladleful of the hot stock.
Remove the pan from the heat and whisk the egg mixture into the soup. Season
with salt and pepper and serve sprinkled with parsley. If you reheat the soup,
do not boil it, or the eggs will scramble.

168 Chicken Liver & Sweet Onion Soup

PREPARATION TIME 15 minutes, plus making the stock   COOKING TIME 35 minutes

1 tablespoon butter
3 tablespoons olive or hemp oil
2 large onions, finely chopped
1 teaspoon sugar
7 ounces chicken livers,
   trimmed and patted dry

1 sage sprig
5½ cups Chicken Stock (see page 11)
   or ready-made stock
½ cup small pasta shapes
2 tablespoons chopped parsley leaves
salt and freshly ground black pepper

1 Melt the butter with half the oil in a saucepan over medium heat. Add the onions
and fry, stirring, 3 to 5 minutes until softened. Reduce the heat to very low
(use a heat diffuser if you have one), stir in the sugar, and fry, stirring frequently,
10 to 15 minutes until the onions are caramelized. Remove them and set aside.

2 Heat the remaining oil with the fat remaining in the pan over medium heat.
Add the chicken livers and fry, stirring, 3 to 5 minutes until cooked through and
firm. Remove the chicken livers from the pan and chop.

3 Put the sage and stock in the rinsed-out saucepan and season with salt and pepper.
Cover and bring to a boil. Add the pasta and boil, uncovered, 4 to 6 minutes,
or according to the package directions, until al dente. Discard the sage and add
the livers, onions and parsley. Warm through, adjust the salt and pepper,
if necessary, and serve.

169 Chinese Egg-Drop Soup

PREPARATION TIME 10 minutes, plus making the stock   COOKING TIME 25 minutes

6 cups Chicken Stock (see page 11)
   or ready-made stock
2-inch piece of gingerroot, sliced
3 scallions, chopped
1 thin slice of galangal, crushed
1 tablespoon light soy sauce

2 tablespoons arrowroot
2 eggs
1½ teaspoons toasted sesame oil
salt and ground white pepper
snipped chives, to serve

1 Put the stock, ginger, scallions, and galangal in a saucepan, cover, and bring
to a boil. Boil 10 minutes to reduce slightly, then strain the stock and return
it to the pan. Add the soy sauce, cover, and return to a boil. Put the arrowroot
and 3 tablespoons cold water in a small heatproof bowl and mix until smooth.

2 Stir a ladleful of the hot stock into the arrowroot mixture. Reduce the heat to low,
then stir the arrowroot mixture into the pan and simmer for 2 to 3 minutes until
the soup thickens slightly. Season with salt and white pepper.

3 Meanwhile, beat the eggs and sesame oil together in a small bowl until blended
but not frothy. Remove the soup from the heat and pour the egg mixture
in a steady stream into the middle with one hand while beating continuously
in a circular motion with a chopstick or fork in the other hand until long, thin strands
of egg form. Serve immediately, sprinkled with chives.

170 Roasted Pepper, Garlic & Egg Soup

PREPARATION TIME 10 minutes, plus making the stock and croutes
COOKING TIME 15 minutes

6 tablespoons fruity extra-virgin olive
   oil, plus extra for drizzling
1 large garlic bulb, cloves peeled and
   smashed in one piece
6½ cups Rich Chicken Stock
   (see page 10) or ready-made stock
2 roasted peppers in olive oil,
   drained and chopped

a pinch of saffron threads
a pinch of smoked or sweet paprika
1 recipe quantity Croutes
   (see page 14)
1 egg for each bowl, at room
   temperature
salt and freshly ground black pepper
chopped parsley leaves, to serve

1 Heat the oil in a saucepan over medium heat. Add the garlic, reduce the heat
to low, and stir 30 seconds just until golden brown. Watch closely so it doesn't
burn. Immediately add the stock, cover, and bring to a boil. Skim, if necessary, then
stir in the peppers, saffron, and paprika and season with salt and pepper. Boil
5 minutes until it reduces slightly.

2 Put 1 croute in each bowl and drizzle generously with oil. Gently crack 1 egg over
each croute, taking care not to break the yolks.

3 Divide the peppers into the bowls, then ladle the boiling soup over them. At this
point you can either let the stock lightly poach the eggs or beat each egg with
a fork so it lightly scrambles. Sprinkle with parsley and serve.

171 Chicken & Parsley Dumpling Soup

PREPARATION TIME 10 minutes, plus making the stock and dumplings
COOKING TIME 45 minutes

6 cups Chicken Stock (see page 11)
   or ready-made stock
2 garlic cloves, halved
1 leek, thinly sliced and rinsed
14 ounces boneless, skinless chicken
   thighs, cut into thin strips

1 cup frozen peas
1 recipe quantity Parsley Dumplings
   (see page 13)
salt and freshly ground black pepper
chopped parsley leaves, to serve

1 Put the stock, garlic, and leek in a saucepan over high heat. Cover and bring to just
below the boil. Lower the heat and simmer 20 minutes. Strain the stock.

2 Return the stock to the pan, add the chicken and peas, and season with salt and
pepper. Return the stock to just below the boil. Skim, then lower the heat and
simmer, covered, 10 to 12 minutes until the chicken is cooked through.

3 Add the dumplings and simmer to reheat. Adjust the salt and pepper, if necessary,
then serve sprinkled with parsley.

172 Chicken & Leek Broth

PREPARATION TIME 5 minutes, plus making the stock   COOKING TIME 25 minutes

1 tablespoon garlic-flavored olive oil
2 leeks, thinly sliced and rinsed
5½ cups Rich Chicken Stock
   (see page 10) or ready-made stock

1¼ pounds skinless chicken thighs
1 large bay leaf, torn
salt and freshly ground black pepper
snipped chives, to serve

1 Heat the oil in a saucepan over medium heat. Add the leeks and fry, stirring,
2 minutes. Add the garlic and fry 1 to 3 minutes until the leeks are softened.

2 Add the stock and chicken. Cover and bring to a boil. Skim, then add the bay
leaf and season with salt and pepper. Lower the heat and simmer, covered,
10 to 15 minutes until the chicken is cooked through. Remove the chicken from the
pan and set aside until cool enough to handle. Cut the chicken from the bones into
bite-size pieces, return it to the soup, and reheat. Remove the bay leaf and adjust
the salt and pepper, if necessary. Serve sprinkled with chives.

173 Roman Egg Soup

PREPARATION TIME 5 minutes, plus making the stock   COOKING TIME 10 minutes

5½ cups Chicken Stock (see page 11)
or ready-made stock
2 eggs
1 cup freshly grated
Parmesan cheese

2 tablespoons very finely chopped
parsley leaves
2 tablespoons lemon juice
salt and freshly ground black pepper

1   Bring the stock to just below the boil in a large saucepan over high heat, then
reduce the heat to low.

2   Beat the eggs, Parmesan cheese, and parsley together in a heatproof bowl. Slowly
pour this mixture into the simmering stock, whisking continuously and quickly with
a fork until the eggs set in small pieces—the quicker you whisk the finer the pieces
will be. Stir in the lemon juice, season with salt and pepper and serve immediately.
If you reheat the soup, do not boil it or the eggs will scramble.

174 Mexican Poultry & Avocado Broth

PREPARATION TIME 20 minutes, plus making the stock and preparing the tomato
COOKING TIME 30 minutes

6 cups Chicken Stock (see page 11)
or ready-made stock
4 garlic cloves, finely chopped
2 jalapeño chilies, seeded and sliced
14 ounces boneless, skinless chicken
or turkey breasts, thinly sliced
1 large tomato, peeled (see page 9),
seeded, and diced

1 avocado
½ tablespoon lime juice, or to taste
salt and freshly ground black pepper
shredded cilantro leaves, to serve
hot pepper sauce, to serve
tortilla chips, to serve

1   Put the stock, garlic, and chilies in a saucepan, cover, and bring to a boil. Boil
10 minutes, then add the chicken and season with salt and pepper. Cover and
return to a boil. Skim, then lower the heat and simmer 10 to 12 minutes until the
chicken is cooked through and the juices run clear when you cut a piece.

2   Meanwhile, peel the avocado, discard the seed, and chop. Put the flesh in a bowl,
toss with the lime juice, and divide it into serving bowls, then set aside.

3   Stir the tomato into the soup and warm through. Taste and add a little lime juice,
if you like. Adjust the salt and pepper, if necessary, then ladle the soup over the
avocado and sprinkle with cilantro. Serve with hot pepper sauce and tortilla chips.

175 Turkey & Orzo Soup

PREPARATION TIME 15 minutes, plus making the stock and cooking the turkey
COOKING TIME 30 minutes

1½ tablespoons garlic-flavored
olive oil
1 red onion, finely chopped
1 carrot, peeled and finely chopped
5½ cups Turkey Stock (see page 11)
or ready-made stock

¾ cup orzo
4 cups shredded spinach leaves
¾ cup diced boneless, skinless
cooked turkey
salt and freshly ground black pepper
chopped parsley leaves, to serve

1   Heat the oil in a saucepan over medium heat. Add the onion and fry, stirring
occasionally, 3 to 5 minutes until softened but not colored. Stir in the carrot,
then add the stock and season with salt and pepper. Cover and bring to a boil.

2   Add the orzo and boil, uncovered, 15 to 17 minutes, or according to the package
directions, until tender. Two minutes before the end of this cooking time, stir in
the spinach and turkey and warm through. Adjust the salt and pepper, if necessary,
then serve sprinkled with parsley.

176 Goji Berry & Garlic Flu Buster

PREPARATION TIME 15 minutes, plus making the stock   **COOKING TIME** 35 minutes

6½ cups Rich Chicken Stock
   (see page 10) or Chicken Stock
   (see page 11)
1 large garlic bulb, separated
   into cloves
2 leeks, halved lengthwise, sliced,
   and rinsed
½-inch piece of gingerroot, peeled
   and grated

a pinch of chili flakes, or to taste
grated zest of 1 lemon
2 tablespoons medium rolled oats
1 tablespoon honey
2 to 4 tablespoons lemon juice
2 tablespoons dried goji berries
1 large handful of watercress leaves,
   torn
snipped chives, to serve

1   Put the stock and garlic in a saucepan, cover, and bring to a boil. Boil 15 minutes,
    or until the garlic is very tender. Use a fork to mash the garlic against the sides
    of the pan, then stir in the leeks, ginger, chili flakes, lemon zest, and oats. Lower
    the heat and simmer, covered, 8 to 10 minutes until thickened slightly and the
    oats are tender.
2   Stir in the honey and 1 tablespoon of the lemon juice, then add the remaining juice
    to taste. Stir in the goji berries and watercress and simmer, uncovered, 1 minute,
    or until the berries soften. Serve sprinkled with chives.

177 Turkey & Rice Soup

PREPARATION TIME 10 minutes, plus making the stock and cooking the turkey
COOKING TIME 35 minutes

6 cups Turkey Stock (see page 11)
  or ready-made stock
2 celery ribs, halved
a pinch of chili flakes, or to taste
⅓ cup long-grain white rice
⅔ cup frozen corn kernels
2 cups shredded savoy cabbage

1½ cups dice boneless, skinless
  cooked turkey
1 roasted red pepper in olive oil,
  drained and diced
2 tablespoons chopped
  parsley leaves
salt and freshly ground black pepper

1 Put the stock, celery, and chili flakes in a saucepan and season with salt and pepper. Cover, bring to a boil and boil 10 minutes, then discard the celery.
2 Cover and return the stock to a boil. Add the rice and boil, uncovered, 10 minutes. Stir in the corn and cabbage and continue boiling 5 minutes, or until the rice is tender.
3 Stir in the turkey, red pepper, and parsley and warm through. Adjust the salt and pepper, if necessary, and serve.

178 Turkey Meatball & Rice Soup

PREPARATION TIME 30 minutes, plus 30 minutes chilling and making the stock
COOKING TIME 50 minutes

⅓ cup basmati rice, rinsed until the
  water runs clear
14 ounces ground turkey
2 shallots, very finely chopped
2 tablespoons finely chopped
  parsley leaves
2 teaspoons dried thyme leaves
½ teaspoon ground coriander
½ teaspoon ground cumin
finely grated zest of 1 lemon
a pinch of cayenne pepper

1 tablespoon olive or hemp oil
1 onion, quartered and thinly sliced
7 cups Vegetable Stock (see page 12)
  or ready-made stock, plus extra
  as needed
1 leek, halved lengthwise, sliced,
  and rinsed
½ tablespoon dried mint leaves
¼ teaspoon turmeric
salt and freshly ground black pepper
chopped cilantro leaves, to serve

1 Put the rice in a bowl, cover with water, and let soak until required.
2 Put the turkey, shallots, parsley, thyme, coriander, cumin, lemon zest, and cayenne pepper in a bowl. Season with salt and pepper and mix well with wet hands. (Fry a small piece, then taste to test the seasoning, if you like.) Divide the mixture into 36 equal portions and roll into meatballs. Put them on a plate, cover with plastic wrap, and chill at least 30 minutes. (The meatballs can be made up to a day ahead.)
3 Heat the oil in a saucepan over medium heat. Add the onion, reduce the heat to low, and cook, covered, 8 to 10 minutes, stirring occasionally, until the onion turns golden brown. Watch closely so it does not burn. Add half the stock and bring to a slow boil. Working in batches, if necessary, gently boil the meatballs 2 minutes. Skim, then add the remaining stock.
4 Drain the rice and add it to the soup, along with the leek, mint, and turmeric. Season with salt and pepper, then cover, and bring to a boil. Uncover and boil 20 to 25 minutes until the rice is tender. If too much stock evaporates, stir in a little extra stock or water. Adjust the salt and pepper, if necessary, and serve sprinkled with cilantro leaves.

179 Onion, Tomato & Chicken Soup

PREPARATION TIME 10 minutes, plus making the stock and croutes and cooking the chicken   COOKING TIME 1¼ hours

3 tablespoons olive or hemp oil
2 ounces chopped
 unsmoked bacon
4 cups thinly sliced onions
4¼ cups Chicken Stock (see page 11)
 or ready-made stock
1 can (15-oz.) crushed tomatoes
1 red chili, seeded (optional)
 and chopped

1 cup thinly sliced boneless,
 skinless cooked chicken
salt and freshly ground black pepper
1 recipe quantity Garlic Croutes
 (see page 14), to serve
basil leaves, torn, to serve
freshly grated Parmesan cheese,
 to serve

1   Heat the oil in a saucepan over medium heat. Add the bacon and fry 3 to 5 minutes until it is beginning to crisp but not browned. Stir in the onions, reduce the heat to very low (use a heat diffuser if you have one), and cook 45 minutes, stirring occasionally, until the onions are very soft. Watch closely so they do not brown.

2   Add the stock, tomatoes, and chili and season with salt and pepper. Cover and bring to a boil, then lower the heat and simmer 20 minutes until the flavors are blended. Add the chicken and warm through. Adjust the salt and pepper, if necessary.

3   Divide the croutes into bowls and ladle the soup over them. Sprinkle with basil leaves and serve with Parmesan cheese on the side.

180 Duck in Ginger Broth

PREPARATION TIME 25 minutes   COOKING TIME 1¼ hours

3-inch piece of gingerroot, peeled
 and sliced
4 cilantro sprigs, roots and stems
 coarsely chopped, with the leaves
 reserved to serve
2 carrots, peeled and thickly sliced,
 plus an extra ½ carrot, peeled and
 cut into matchsticks
2 large garlic cloves, chopped
2 star anise
1 large onion, unpeeled and halved

1 large leek, half thickly sliced and
 rinsed, and the rest cut into
 matchsticks and rinsed
14 ounces boneless, skinless
 duck breasts
4 shiitake mushroom caps,
 thinly sliced
2 Chinese cabbage leaves, rolled and
 thinly sliced
2 scallions, sliced on the diagonal
light soy sauce, to taste

1   Put the ginger, cilantro, sliced carrots, garlic, star anise, onion, sliced leek, and 6½ cups water in a large saucepan. Cover and bring to a boil, then boil, uncovered, 10 minutes to reduce slightly.

2   Reduce the heat to low. Add the duck and slowly return the liquid to just below the boil, skimming as necessary. Just before the liquid boils, reduce the heat to very low (use a heat diffuser if you have one) and simmer, covered, 40 to 45 minutes until the duck is very tender. Remove the duck from the soup and set aside until cool enough to handle.

3   Strain the stock into a bowl and discard the flavorings. Return the stock to the washed pan, cover, and return to a boil. Thinly slice the duck and set aside.

4   Lower the heat to a simmer, then add the carrot and leek matchsticks, mushrooms, cabbage, and scallions and simmer 5 to 8 minutes until they are all tender. Return the duck to the pan and reheat. Season with soy sauce and serve sprinkled with cilantro leaves.

181 Jerusalem Artichoke Soup with Duck Confit

PREPARATION TIME 20 minutes   **COOKING TIME** 50 minutes

1¾ pounds Jerusalem artichokes,
   unpeeled but well scrubbed
3 lemon slices
2 tablespoons butter
1 large onion, finely chopped
2¼ cups whole milk

14 ounces duck confit, skin and
   bones removed and meat finely
   shredded, with a little of the
   surrounding fat reserved
⅔ cup light cream
1½ tablespoons lemon juice
salt and ground white pepper
finely shredded watercress leaves,
   to serve

1   Put the artichokes, lemon slices, and 3 cups water in a saucepan, adding extra
    water, if needed to cover the artichokes. Cover and bring to a boil, then lower the
    heat and simmer 20 to 25 minutes until the artichokes are tender but still holding
    their shape. Drain, reserving 2½ cups of the cooking liquid, then set the artichokes
    aside until cool enough to handle.
2   Use your fingers to peel the artichokes, then mash them with a fork and set aside.
3   Melt the butter in the washed and dried pan over medium heat. Add the onion and
    fry, stirring occasionally, 3 to 5 minutes until softened. Stir in the artichokes, milk,
    and reserved cooking liquid and season with salt and white pepper. Cover and bring
    to just below the boil, then lower the heat and simmer 5 minutes. Meanwhile, heat
    the duck with a little of its fat in a small skillet over medium heat.
4   Blend the soup until smooth and reheat, if necessary. Stir in the cream and
    1 tablespoon of the lemon juice, then adjust the salt and pepper and add extra lemon
    juice, if necessary. Serve sprinkled with watercress and topped with the duck confit.

CHAPTER 4

SEAFOOD SOUPS

Seafood soups can range from simple to extravagant, but they all have an essential common feature: for optimum results they must be made with the freshest, best-quality fish and shellfish.

This chapter contains recipes for many familiar fish—cod, haddock, monkfish, and salmon—but also includes soups using some of the lesser-known varieties that help promote seafood sustainability. Recipes like Hake & Mixed Herb Soup, Pollock Quenelle Soup, and Tilapia & Cilantro Soup can satisfy your palate as well as your conscience and your budget. For an even more purse-friendly treat, try Shrimp Bisque. If you plan ahead and remember to freeze the shrimp shells and heads from other recipes, this rich, sophisticated soup is almost free to make.

Here, too, you will find a selection of delicious seafood recipes from around the world, from creamy North American soup-stews, such as the ever popular New England and Manhattan clam chowders, to Irish Oyster Soup, Scandinavian Salmon & Shrimp Soup, and ultrastylish Japanese Scallop Soup.

NEW ENGLAND CLAM CHOWDER (SEE PAGE 114)

182 New England Clam Chowder

PREPARATION TIME 20 minutes   **COOKING TIME** 45 minutes

⅓ cup diced bacon
2 tablespoons butter
2 celery ribs, finely chopped
2 onions, finely chopped
1 tablespoon all-purpose flour
2½ cups whole milk
2¾ cups peeled and diced
   russet potatoes

48 live littleneck clams, rinsed and
   soaked in cold water to cover
2 teaspoons dried thyme leaves
2½ cups light cream
salt and freshly ground black pepper
cayenne pepper, to serve
oyster crackers, to serve (optional)

1 Put the bacon in a saucepan over high heat and fry, stirring, 5 to 8 minutes until it crisps and gives off its fat. Remove it from the pan and set aside.

2 Melt the butter in the fat remaining in the pan. Stir in the celery and onions, cover, reduce the heat to low, and cook 8 to 10 minutes until softened but not colored. Increase the heat to medium, sprinkle in the flour, and stir 2 minutes, then slowly add the milk, stirring continuously to prevent lumps from forming. Add the potatoes and season with salt and pepper. Cover and bring to just below the boil, then lower the heat and simmer 15 to 20 minutes until the potatoes are tender.

3 Meanwhile, discard any clams with broken shells or open ones that do not close when tapped. Shuck the clams over a bowl to catch the juices. Discard the shells and chop the clams, then stir them together with the juices, thyme and bacon into the soup.

4 Cover and simmer 1 minute. Stir in the cream and simmer 1 to 2 minutes until the clams are cooked through. Adjust the salt and pepper, if necessary, then serve sprinkled with cayenne pepper and with oyster crackers on the side, if you like.

183 Manhattan Clam Chowder

PREPARATION TIME 10 minutes   **COOKING TIME** 40 minutes

10 ounces canned or jarred clams,
   drained and juices reserved
½ cup diced bacon
1 tablespoon butter
2 onions, finely chopped
1 tablespoon all-purpose
   or wholewheat flour
2 cans (15-oz.) crushed tomatoes

2 waxy potatoes, peeled and diced
1 red bell pepper, seeded and diced
1 tablespoon tomato paste
1 teaspoon sugar
lemon juice, to taste
salt and freshly ground black pepper
chopped parsley leaves or dill,
   to serve

1 Add enough water to the reserved clam juice to make 2¼ cups liquid, if necessary, then set aside.

2 Put the bacon in a saucepan over high heat and fry, stirring, 5 to 8 minutes until it crisps and gives off its fat. Remove it from the pan and set aside. Lower the heat to medium and melt the butter with the fat remaining in the pan. Add the onions and fry, stirring occasionally, 3 to 5 minutes until softened but not colored. Sprinkle in the flour and stir 2 minutes, then slowly add the clam liquid, stirring continuously to prevent lumps from forming.

3 Add the tomatoes, potatoes, pepper, tomato paste, and sugar and season with salt and pepper. Bring to a boil, then reduce the heat to low and simmer, covered, 15 to 20 minutes until the potatoes are tender. Stir in the clams and bacon and simmer 2 minutes to warm through. Add lemon juice and adjust the salt and pepper, if necessary, then serve sprinkled with parsley.

184 Salt Cod Soup

PREPARATION TIME 20 minutes, plus 24 hours soaking   COOKING TIME 40 minutes

8 ounces salted cod
1 bay leaf
2 lemon slices
2 leeks, thinly sliced and rinsed
2 large garlic cloves, finely chopped
1 russet potato, peeled and diced

a pinch of saffron threads
1 large roasted red pepper in olive
    oil, drained and chopped
salt and freshly ground black pepper
lemon wedges, to serve
extra-virgin olive oil, to serve

1   Put the salted cod in a bowl, cover with cold water, and let soak 24 hours,
    changing the water several times, then drain.
2   Put the cod and 2½ cups water in a skillet, cover, and bring to a boil. Skim,
    then add the bay leaf and lemon slices. Reduce the heat to low and simmer,
    covered, 10 to 15 minutes until the fish flakes easily.
3   Remove the fish from the pan and set aside. Strain the liquid through
    a cheesecloth-lined strainer into a saucepan. Add the leeks, garlic, potato, saffron,
    and another 2½ cups water. Cover and return to a boil, then lower the heat and
    simmer 15 to 18 minutes until the potatoes are starting to fall apart.
4   Meanwhile, flake the cod, discarding all skin and bones. Return it to the soup,
    add the roasted pepper and heat through. Adjust the salt and pepper, if necessary,
    but remember the cod might still be very salty. Serve with lemon wedges for
    squeezing over and extra-virgin olive oil for drizzling at the table.

185 Spicy Tomato & Crab Soup

PREPARATION TIME 10 minutes, plus making the stock and flavored oil
COOKING TIME 25 minutes

4 cups tomato puree
2 cups Fish Stock (see page 11)
    or ready-made stock
1 bay leaf
1 tablespoon lemon juice
1 tablespoon tomato paste
1 teaspoon sugar
finely grated zest of ½ lemon

a pinch of chili flakes, or to taste
1 crab shell (optional)
14 ounces shelled white crabmeat,
    picked over and flaked
salt and freshly ground black pepper
1 recipe quantity Crushed Basil Oil
    (see page 15), to serve

1   Put the tomato puree, stock, bay leaf, lemon juice, tomato paste, sugar, lemon
    zest, chili flakes, and crab shell, if using, in a saucepan and season with salt and
    pepper. Cover and bring to a boil, then lower the heat and simmer 10 minutes.
    Discard the bay leaf and crab shell, if used, and blend the soup until smooth.
2   Stir the crabmeat into the soup and simmer 3 minutes, or until cooked through.
    Adjust the salt and pepper, if necessary, then serve with basil oil.

186 Smoked Eel & Kale Soup

PREPARATION TIME 15 minutes, plus making the stock   COOKING TIME 35 minutes

6 cups Fish Stock (see page 11)
    or ready-made stock
5¾ cups chopped kale leaves, rinsed
1 leek, halved lengthwise, thinly
    sliced, and rinsed
1 tablespoon chopped dill

1 long strip of lemon zest,
    all bitter white removed
a pinch of chili flakes, or to taste
1 pound smoked eel or mackerel,
    skinned, boned, and flaked
salt and freshly ground black pepper

1   Put the stock, kale, leek, dill, lemon zest, and chili flakes in a saucepan and season
    with salt and pepper. Cover and bring to a boil, then lower the heat and simmer
    25 minutes, or until the kale is very tender.
2   Add the eel and warm through. Adjust the salt and pepper, if necessary, and serve.

187 Crab & Asparagus Soup

PREPARATION TIME 10 minutes, plus making the stock   **COOKING TIME** 25 minutes

2 tablespoons arrowroot
5½ cups Chicken Stock (see page 11)
   or ready-made stock
1 tablespoon fish sauce
½ teaspoon salt, plus extra to season
2½ cups trimmed asparagus cut into
   bite-size pieces, with the tips
   reserved

1 egg
6 ounces shelled white crabmeat,
   thawed if frozen, picked over and
   flaked
ground white pepper
toasted sesame oil, to drizzle

1   Put the arrowroot and 2 tablespoons of the stock in a bowl and mix until smooth,
    then set aside. Put the remaining stock in a saucepan over medium heat and bring
    to a simmer. Pour the arrowroot mixture into the stock, whisking continuously, then
    bring to just below the boil, stirring. Stir in the fish sauce and salt, lower the heat,
    and simmer 2 to 3 minutes, stirring, until the soup thickens slightly.

2   Add the asparagus stalks and simmer 3 minutes, then add the asparagus tips and
    simmer 3 to 5 minutes longer until all the asparagus is tender but still has a little bite.
    Return the soup to a boil.

3   Meanwhile, beat the egg in a heatproof bowl, add a ladleful of the hot stock,
    and whisk together.

4   Remove the pan from the heat and pour the egg mixture in a steady stream into
    the middle of the soup with one hand while beating continuously in a circular motion
    with a chopstick or fork in the other hand until long, thin strands of egg form. Stir
    in the crab and cook over very low heat 2 to 3 minutes until the crabmeat is cooked
    through. Season with salt and white pepper and serve drizzled with sesame oil.

188 Rich Crab Soup with Dill Croutons

PREPARATION TIME 25 minutes, plus making the stock and croutons
COOKING TIME 35 minutes

6 cups Fish Stock (see page 11)
   or ready-made stock
6 tablespoons dry white wine
1 bay leaf
crab shells (ask the fish merchant
   for these)
2 tablespoons butter
½ tablespoon olive or hemp oil
1 carrot, peeled and finely diced
1 celery rib, very finely chopped
1 onion, finely chopped
1 large garlic clove, finely chopped

¼ cup all-purpose flour
2 tablespoons tomato paste
1 tablespoon chopped parsley leaves
several thyme sprigs, tied together
2 tablespoons brandy
5 ounces shelled brown crabmeat,
   thawed if frozen, and picked over
9 ounces shelled white crabmeat,
   thawed if frozen, and picked over
salt and freshly ground black pepper
1 recipe quantity Dill Croutons
   (see page 14), hot, to serve

1   Put the stock, wine, bay leaf, and crab shells in a saucepan. Cover and bring to
    a boil. Lower the heat and simmer 10 minutes, then strain, set the stock aside,
    and discard the flavorings.
2   Meanwhile, melt the butter with the oil in another saucepan. Add the carrot,
    celery, and onion and fry, stirring occasionally, 2 minutes. Add the garlic and fry
    1 to 3 minutes until the onion is softened but not colored, then sprinkle in the flour
    and stir 2 minutes. Stir in the tomato paste, parsley, and thyme and season with
    salt and pepper. Slowly add the stock, stirring continuously to prevent lumps
    from forming.
3   Add the brandy, cover, and return to a boil, then boil, uncovered, 4 to 6 minutes
    until it evaporates. Stir in the brown crabmeat and simmer 2 minutes. Discard the
    thyme sprigs. Blend the soup until smooth, then add the white crabmeat and
    simmer 2 to 3 minutes until all the crab is cooked through. Adjust the salt and
    pepper, if necessary, and serve sprinkled with croutons.

189 Shellfish Chowder with Herbs

PREPARATION TIME 30 minutes   COOKING TIME 35 minutes

24 live clams or cockles, soaked
   in cold water to cover
24 live mussels, scrubbed, with
   "beards" removed and soaked
   in cold water to cover
2 garlic cloves, coarsely chopped
1 leek, sliced and rinsed
3 carrots, peeled and finely diced

2 shallots, finely chopped
2 cups diced russet potatoes
scant 1 cup milk
1 tablespoon snipped chives
1 tablespoon chopped parsley
   leaves, plus extra to serve
½ tablespoon thyme leaves
salt and freshly ground black pepper

1   Discard any clams or mussels with broken shells or open ones that do not close
    when tapped. Put the clams, mussels, garlic, and leek in a saucepan with at least
    4½ cups water to cover over high heat. Cook, covered, 3 to 5 minutes, shaking
    the pan frequently, until all the shells open. Strain the cooking liquid through a
    cheesecloth-lined strainer into a large bowl and set aside. Discard the flavorings.
    When the clams and mussels are cool enough to handle, discard any that remain
    closed. Remove the flesh from the shells and set aside.
2   Meanwhile, put the carrots, shallots, potatoes, and 4½ cups of the reserved
    cooking liquid in the rinsed-out saucepan and season with salt and pepper. Cover
    and bring to a boil. Lower the heat and simmer 10 to 12 minutes until the
    vegetables are tender.
3   Add the milk, chives, parsley, and thyme and simmer, covered, 10 minutes, but
    do not let the liquid boil. Stir in the clams and mussels and gently reheat. Adjust
    the salt and pepper, if necessary, then serve sprinkled with parsley. If you reheat
    the soup, do not boil it.

190 Smoked Haddock & Sweet Potato Chowder

PREPARATION TIME 10 minutes, plus making the stock   COOKING TIME 35 minutes

2 slices of bacon, chopped
½ tablespoon sunflower oil
1 onion, finely chopped
2 tablespoons all-purpose flour
1¾ cups Fish Stock (see page 11)
   or ready-made stock
1 large sweet potato, peeled and
   finely diced

14 ounces undyed smoked haddock
1 cup whole milk
⅔ cup light cream
freshly grated nutmeg, to taste
cayenne pepper, to taste
salt and ground white pepper
chopped parsley leaves, to serve

1   Put the bacon in a saucepan over high heat and fry 3 minutes. Remove from the pan and set aside. Add the oil and onion to the pan and fry 3 to 5 minutes until the onion is softened. Sprinkle in the flour and stir 2 minutes, then add the stock, stirring continuously.

2   Add the sweet potatoes and season with white pepper. Cover and bring to a boil, then lower the heat and simmer 3 to 5 minutes until the potato is just soft.

3   Calculate the haddock's cooking time at 10 minutes per 1 inch of thickness. Add the fish, flesh-side down, and the milk and simmer for the calculated time, or until the flesh flakes easily. Remove the fish and set aside. Continue simmering until the potatoes are tender. Do not boil.

4   Skin and bone the fish, then flake it into the soup. Add the bacon, cream, nutmeg, and cayenne pepper, then season with salt and return to just below the boil. Adjust the pepper, if necessary, and serve sprinkled with parsley.

191 Scottish Cullen Skink

PREPARATION TIME 15 minutes   COOKING TIME 50 minutes

14 ounces cold-smoked haddock,
   traditionally finnan haddock but
   other smoked haddock is fine
1 onion, chopped
2½ cups whole milk

5 cups coarsely chopped
   russet potatoes
¼ teaspoon salt, plus extra to season
2 tablespoons butter
freshly ground black pepper

1   Calculate the fish's cooking time at 10 minutes per 1 inch of thickness. Put the haddock and at least 4 cups water in a large skillet and bring to just below the boil, skimming as necessary. Reduce the heat to low, add the onion and simmer, covered, for the calculated time, or until the fish flakes. Remove the fish and set aside. Strain the cooking liquid and reserve; discard the onion. Remove the skin and any bones from the fish, reserving the bones and discarding the skin. Flake the fish into a bowl, cover with a little of the reserved cooking liquid and set aside.

2   Return the bones and remaining cooking liquid to the pan and simmer, covered, while you cook the potatoes.

3   Meanwhile, put the potatoes and salt in a saucepan with water to cover. Cover and bring to a boil, then boil, uncovered, 15 to 20 minutes until the potatoes are tender. Drain, then return them to the pan. Add the butter and a ladleful of the simmering cooking liquid and mash until smooth. Slowly stir in enough of the cooking liquid, without any bones, to achieve the preferred consistency. Add the flaked fish to the soup and reheat, then adjust the salt and pepper, if necessary, and serve.

192 Mackerel in Chili-Lime Broth

PREPARATION TIME 10 minutes, plus making the stock   COOKING TIME 25 minutes

6 cups Fish Stock (see page 11)
  or ready-made stock
6 kaffir lime leaves, lightly crushed
1-inch piece of gingerroot, peeled
  and grated
1 red chili, seeded and sliced
2 tablespoons light soy sauce

1 tablespoon fish sauce
14 ounces mackerel fillets
finely grated zest of 1 lime
freshly ground black pepper
shiso leaves or cilantro leaves,
  to serve
lime wedges, to serve

1   Put the stock, lime leaves, ginger, chili, soy sauce, and fish sauce in a saucepan.
    Cover and bring to a boil, then lower the heat and simmer 10 minutes. Add the
    mackerel and simmer, covered, 2 to 3 minutes until the fillets flake easily. Remove
    the mackerel from the pan and remove the skin.
2   Flake the fish into the soup, add the lime zest, and season with pepper. Serve
    topped with shiso leaves and with lime wedges for squeezing over.

193 Mackerel & Fennel Soup

PREPARATION TIME 15 minutes, plus making the stock and preparing the tomatoes
COOKING TIME 30 minutes

2 tablespoons chili-flavored olive oil
2 fennel bulbs, sliced
2 large garlic cloves, finely chopped
½ teaspoon fennel seeds
6 cups Fish Stock (see page 11)
  or ready-made stock
2 bay leaves
½ tablespoon dried dill

2 large tomatoes, peeled
  (see page 9), seeded, and diced
1 tablespoon tomato paste
a pinch of sugar
14 ounces mackerel fillets, cut into
  thin strips
salt and freshly ground black pepper

1   Heat the oil in a saucepan over medium heat. Add the fennel and fry, stirring,
    2 minutes. Stir in the garlic and fry 1 to 3 minutes until the fennel is softened.
    Add the seeds and stir 30 seconds. Add the stock and bay leaves and season
    with salt and pepper.
2   Bring to a boil, then simmer 5 minutes. Stir in the dill, tomatoes, tomato paste,
    and sugar and simmer 5 minutes. Add the mackerel and simmer, uncovered,
    2 to 3 minutes until it flakes easily. Discard the bay leaves, adjust the salt and
    pepper, if necessary, and serve.

194 White Fish Soup

PREPARATION TIME 15 minutes, plus making the stock and preparing the tomatoes
COOKING TIME 40 minutes

1 tablespoon butter
1 tablespoon olive oil
1 large onion, finely chopped
2 large garlic cloves, finely chopped
4 large tomatoes, peeled
  (see page 9), seeded, and diced
1 long strip of orange zest, all bitter
  white pith removed

¼ cup dry white wine
6 cups Fish Stock (see page 11)
  or ready-made stock
14 ounces boneless, skinless cod,
  cusk, pollock, or other white fish,
  cut into large chunks
2 tablespoons shredded basil leaves
salt and freshly ground black pepper

1   Melt the butter with the oil in a saucepan over medium heat. Add the onion and fry,
    stirring, 2 minutes. Add the garlic and fry 1 to 3 minutes until the onion is softened.
    Stir in the tomatoes, orange zest, and wine and cook 2 to 4 minutes until the wine
    evaporates. Add the stock and season with salt and pepper, then cover and bring
    to a boil. Skim, then simmer, covered, 10 minutes.
2   Add the fish and simmer, covered, 4 to 7 minutes. Stir in the basil and simmer
    1 minute longer, or until the fish is cooked through and the flesh flakes easily.
    Discard the zest and adjust the salt and pepper, if necessary, then serve.

195 Aegean Red Mullet Soup

PREPARATION TIME 20 minutes, plus preparing the tomatoes
COOKING TIME 30 minutes

1½ tablespoons olive oil
3 garlic cloves, finely chopped
1 leek, halved lengthwise, sliced,
    and rinsed
1 carrot, peeled and finely chopped
1 celery rib, finely chopped
1 fennel bulb, thinly sliced
1 tablespoon aniseed-flavored spirit,
    such as Pernod
1 pound red mullet, dressed, head
    and tail removed, rinsed, and cut
    into serving pieces on the bone

2 large tomatoes, grated
    (see page 9)
1 bay leaf
2 tablespoons orange juice
1 tablespoon tomato paste
grated zest of 1 orange
a pinch of saffron threads
a small pinch of chili flakes
2 tablespoons chopped
    parsley leaves
salt and freshly ground black pepper

1   Heat the oil in a saucepan over medium heat. Stir in the garlic, leek, carrot, celery,
    and fennel, then reduce the heat to low and cook, covered, 8 to 10 minutes until
    softened but not colored. Add the aniseed spirit, increase the heat to high,
    and cook 30 seconds to 1 minute until it evaporates.

2   Add the fish and 5½ cups water and season with salt and pepper. Cover and bring
    to just below the boil, then skim. Stir in the tomatoes, bay leaf, orange juice,
    tomato paste, orange zest, saffron, and chili flakes. Lower the heat and simmer,
    covered, 8 to 10 minutes until the fish flakes easily. Stir in the parsley and adjust
    the salt and pepper, if necessary, then serve.

196 New England Seafood Chowder

PREPARATION TIME 20 minutes   COOKING TIME 40 minutes

1 pound 2 ounces mixed boneless,
  skinless fish, such as haddock,
  halibut, and scrod
2 lemon slices
1 tablespoon butter
1 tablespoon sunflower oil
1 carrot, peeled and grated
1 celery rib, finely chopped

1 onion, finely chopped
1 russet potato, peeled and
  finely chopped
2½ cups whole milk
¼ cup evaporated milk
½ tablespoon chopped dill
salt and freshly ground black pepper
sweet paprika, to serve

1   Calculate the cooking time for the fish at 10 minutes per 1 inch of thickness.
    Put the fish, lemon, and 4 cups water in a large skillet and season with salt and
    pepper. Cover and slowly bring to just below the boil. Skim, then lower the heat
    and simmer, covered, for the calculated time, or until the fish flakes easily.
    Add the fish in stages, if necessary, starting with the thickest pieces. Remove the
    fish, set aside, and cover. Strain and reserve the cooking liquid.
2   Melt the butter with the oil in a saucepan over medium heat. Add the carrot,
    celery, onion, and potato and fry, stirring occasionally, 3 to 5 minutes until the
    onion is softened but not colored. Stir in the milk, evaporated milk, and 2 cups
    of the reserved cooking liquid, then cover and bring to just below the boil. Lower
    the heat and simmer 10 to 12 minutes until the potato is tender. Meanwhile,
    remove the skin and any bones from the fish.
3   Flake the fish into the soup and heat through. Add the dill, adjust the salt and
    pepper, if necessary, and serve sprinkled with paprika.

197 Soupe de Poissons

PREPARATION TIME 30 minutes, plus making the stock, croutes, and rouille
COOKING TIME 1 hour

3 tablespoons olive oil
2 onions, sliced
4 garlic cloves, chopped
4 large tomatoes, chopped
6 tablespoons long-grain white rice
2 pounds mixed fish, such as mullet,
  haddock, and monkfish, dressed,
  heads removed, and trimmed
  but not boned
9 ounces large raw shrimp, shelled
  and deveined, with the heads and
  shells reserved
¼ cup dry white wine
5½ cups Fish Stock (see page 11)
  or ready-made stock

1 bouquet garni made with 1 piece
  of celery rib with its leaves, 1 bay
  leaf, and several parsley and
  thyme sprigs tied together
1 long strip of orange zest, all bitter
  white pith removed
a pinch of saffron threads
3 tablespoons tomato paste
salt and freshly ground black pepper
1 recipe quantity Croutes
  (see page 14), hot, to serve
½ cup grated Gruyère cheese,
  to serve
1 recipe quantity Rouille
  (see page 14), to serve

1   Heat the oil in a large saucepan over medium heat. Add the onions and fry, stirring
    occasionally, 3 to 5 minutes until softened but not colored. Add the garlic and
    tomatoes and fry 3 minutes, then add the rice, fish, and shrimp, including the heads
    and shells. Stir in the wine and cook 30 seconds to 1 minute until it evaporates.
    Add the stock and season with salt and pepper.
2   Cover and bring to a boil, then skim the surface. Stir in the bouquet garni,
    orange zest, saffron, and tomato paste. Lower the heat and simmer, covered,
    30 to 45 minutes until the fish comes off the bones and is starting to fall apart.
3   Discard the bouquet garni and blend the soup, including the bones and shrimp
    trimmings. Work the soup through a strainer into a bowl, pressing down with
    a spoon to extract as much flavor as possible. Rub back and forth with the spoon
    and scrape the bottom of the strainer. Return the soup to the rinsed-out pan and
    reheat. Adjust the salt and pepper, if necessary.
4   Divide the croutes into bowls and top with the cheese. Ladle the soup into the
    bowls and serve immediately with the rouille for stirring in at the table.

198 Shrimp Bisque

PREPARATION TIME 15 minutes, plus making the stock   COOKING TIME 50 minutes

3 tablespoons butter
1 tablespoon olive or hemp oil
2 shallots, finely chopped
1 carrot, peeled and chopped
1 celery rib, thinly sliced
heads and shells from 1 pound
    5 ounces raw shrimp, with 12 of
    the shrimp deveined and reserved
    (the remaining shrimp can be
    frozen to use in other recipes)
2 tablespoons brandy
1 can (15-oz.) crushed tomatoes

¼ cup dry vermouth
1 tablespoon tomato paste
6 cups Fish Stock (see page 11)
    or ready-made stock
6 tablespoons long-grain white rice
1 bay leaf
a pinch of chili flakes, or to taste
½ tablespoon salt
1 to 2 tablespoons lemon juice
1 tablespoon chopped dill, to serve
freshly ground black pepper
lemon wedges, to serve

1   Melt 2 tablespoons of the butter with the oil in a saucepan over medium heat.
    Add the shallots, carrot, and celery and fry, stirring occasionally, 8 to 10 minutes
    until the shallots are light golden brown. Add the shrimp shells and heads and
    pound them into the vegetables with a wooden spoon. Add the brandy and cook
    2 to 4 minutes until it evaporates. Add the tomatoes, vermouth, and tomato paste.
    Bring to a boil and boil 1 to 2 minutes, then add the stock, rice, and bay leaf. Cover
    and return to a boil. Skim, add the chili flakes, and season with salt and pepper.
    Lower the heat and simmer, covered, 15 to 18 minutes until the rice is very tender.
2   Meanwhile, bring a small saucepan of water to a boil and add the salt. Reduce the
    heat to low, add the shrimp, and simmer 2 to 3 minutes until they turn pink and
    curl. Drain, slice in half lengthwise, and set aside.
3   Blend the soup until smooth, then work it through a strainer into a bowl, rubbing
    back and forth with a spoon and scraping the bottom of the strainer. Return the
    soup to the rinsed-out pan, add the lemon juice and reheat.
4   Melt the remaining butter in the small pan. Add the shrimp and dill and toss
    together just to warm through. Do not overcook or the shrimp will toughen. Adjust
    the salt and pepper and add extra lemon juice, if necessary. Divide the shrimp into
    bowls, ladle the soup over, and serve with lemon wedges for squeezing over.

199 Haddock Chowder with Spinach

PREPARATION TIME 20 minutes   COOKING TIME 45 minutes

14 ounces haddock or cod fillet
2¼ cups whole milk
2 bay leaves
2 tablespoons butter
1 celery rib, finely chopped
1 onion, diced
1 red bell pepper, seeded and diced
½ cup diced waxy potatoes

½ cup heavy cream
½ tablespoon dried dill
freshly grated nutmeg, to taste
1 large handful of baby spinach
    leaves, rinsed
salt and freshly ground black pepper
finely grated lemon zest, to serve
chopped parsley leaves, to serve

1   Calculate the haddock's cooking time at 10 minutes per 1 inch of thickness.
    Put the haddock, milk, bay leaves, and enough water to cover the fish in a skillet
    over medium-high heat and season with salt and pepper. Cover and bring to just
    below the boil. Lower the heat and simmer for the calculated time, or until the flesh
    turns opaque and flakes easily. Remove the fish from the pan and set aside.
    Discard the bay leaves and reserve the cooking liquid.
2   Melt the butter in a saucepan over medium heat. Stir in the celery, onion, pepper,
    and potatoes and fry, stirring occasionally, 3 to 5 minutes until the vegetables are
    softened but not colored. Add 3½ cups of the reserved cooking liquid, cover, and
    bring to a boil. Lower the heat and simmer 10 to 12 minutes until the potatoes are
    tender. Stir in the cream, dill, and nutmeg and return to just below the boil. Add the
    spinach and simmer 2 to 3 minutes until it wilts. Meanwhile, remove the skin and
    any bones from the fish.
3   Flake the fish into the soup and warm through. Adjust the salt and pepper,
    if necessary, then serve sprinkled with lemon zest and parsley.

200 Brazilian Fish Soup

PREPARATION TIME 20 minutes, plus making the stock and preparing the tomatoes
COOKING TIME 35 minutes

1½ tablespoons sunflower oil
1 onion, chopped
1 green bell pepper,
   seeded and chopped
1 red bell pepper,
   seeded and chopped
2 large garlic cloves, chopped
1 thick red chili, seeded and chopped
4½ cups Fish Stock (see page 11)
   or ready-made stock

2 tomatoes, peeled (see page 9),
   seeded, and chopped
1 tablespoon tomato paste
scant 1 cup coconut milk
1 pound boneless, skinless firm fish,
   such as hake or swordfish
1 tablespoon dendê (red palm oil)
   or olive oil
salt and freshly ground black pepper
chopped cilantro leaves, to serve

1   Heat the oil in a saucepan over medium heat. Add the onion and bell peppers and
    fry, stirring, 2 minutes. Stir in the garlic and chili and fry 1 to 3 minutes until the
    onion is softened but not colored. Add the stock, tomatoes, and tomato paste and
    season with salt and pepper. Cover and bring to a boil, then reduce the heat to low,
    stir in the coconut milk, and simmer, covered, 10 minutes. Meanwhile, calculate
    the hake's cooking time at 10 minutes per 1 inch of thickness.
2   Add the hake to the soup and simmer for the calculated time, or until it is cooked
    through and flakes easily. Adjust the salt and pepper, if necessary, then stir in the
    palm oil. Serve sprinkled with cilantro.

201 Hake & Mixed Herb Soup

PREPARATION TIME 10 minutes, plus making the stock and preparing the tomatoes
COOKING TIME 35 minutes

1 tablespoon olive or hemp oil
1 large shallot, sliced
⅔ cup dry white wine
1 pound 2 ounces hake or cod steaks
4½ cups Fish Stock (see page 11)
   or ready-made stock
2 tomatoes, grated (see page 9)
1½ tablespoons tomato paste

4 scallions, thinly sliced
   on the diagonal
2 tablespoons finely chopped
   parsley leaves
1 tablespoon snipped chives
salt and freshly ground black pepper
basil leaves, torn, to serve
extra-virgin olive oil, to serve

1   Heat the oil in a saucepan over medium heat. Add the shallot and fry, stirring
    occasionally, 3 to 5 minutes until softened. Stir in the wine and cook 5 to 6 minutes
    until it almost evaporates. Meanwhile, calculate the fish's cooking time
    at 10 minutes per 1 inch of thickness.
2   Add the stock to the pan and season with salt and pepper. Cover and bring
    to a boil, then reduce the heat to low and add the hake, tomatoes, and tomato
    paste. Simmer, covered, for the calculated cooking time, or until the hake flesh
    flakes easily. Remove the hake from the soup and set aside. Add the scallions
    to the pan and simmer while you remove the hake skin and any bones. Flake the
    fish into the soup and stir in the parsley and chives. Adjust the salt and pepper,
    if necessary, and serve sprinkled with basil and drizzled with extra-virgin olive oil.

North Sea Haddock & Pea Soup

PREPARATION TIME 10 minutes, plus making the stock   **COOKING TIME** 30 minutes

3¼ cups Fish Stock (see page 11)
  or ready-made stock
1¾ cups heavy cream
2 large garlic cloves, finely chopped
1 bay leaf
finely grated zest of ½ lemon

a pinch of ground cardamom
14 ounces haddock fillet
1¼ cups frozen peas
salt and freshly ground black pepper
smoked paprika, to serve

1 Put the stock, cream, garlic, bay leaf, lemon zest, and cardamom in a saucepan
   and season with salt and pepper. Cover and bring to a boil, then lower the heat
   and simmer 10 minutes.

2 Calculate the haddock's cooking time at 10 minutes per 1 inch of thickness.
   Add the haddock and simmer, covered, for the calculated time, or until it is cooked
   through and flakes easily. Five minutes before the end of the calculated cooking
   time, add the peas and simmer, uncovered. Remove the haddock and set aside
   until cool enough to handle. Discard the bay leaf.

3 Bring the soup to a boil, and boil 1 to 2 minutes until the peas are very soft.
   Use a slotted spoon to transfer half the peas to a bowl. Blend the soup until
   smooth and rub it through a strainer for an even smoother texture, if you like.
   Return the peas to the pan. Remove the skin and any small bones from the fish and
   flake it into large pieces into the soup. Reheat and adjust the salt and pepper,
   if necessary. Serve very lightly sprinkled with paprika.

203 Mackerel & Shiitake Miso Soup

PREPARATION TIME 10 minutes, plus making the dashi   COOKING TIME 20 minutes

1 recipe quantity Dashi (see page 12)
  or 5½ cups prepared instant dashi
¼ cup dark miso paste
5 shiitake mushroom caps, sliced
3-inch piece of daikon, peeled and
  grated, or 2 radishes, grated

5 mackerel fillets, cut into bite-size
  pieces
light soy sauce, to taste
1 watercress leaf per bowl, to serve

1   Put the dashi in a saucepan, cover, and bring to a boil. As soon as it boils, lower
    the heat and simmer, uncovered.
2   Put the miso paste in an heatproof bowl and slowly stir in a ladleful or two
    of the hot dashi to form a thin paste, then stir the paste into the dashi. Do not allow
    the soup to boil from this point. Add the mushrooms and daikon and simmer
    3 minutes, then add the mackerel and soy sauce. Simmer 4 to 6 minutes until
    the fish flakes easily. Serve immediately, topped with the watercress leaves.

204 Hoki Soup with Pesto

PREPARATION TIME 10 minutes, plus making the stock   COOKING TIME 40 minutes

2 tablespoons garlic-flavored olive oil
1 fennel bulb, chopped
4 large garlic cloves
½ cup dry white wine
2½ cups Fish Stock (see page 11)
  or ready-made stock

2⅔ cups tomato puree
finely grated zest of 1 lemon
14 ounces hoki or cod fillet
lemon juice, to taste
salt and freshly ground black pepper
pesto, to serve

1   Heat the oil in a saucepan over medium heat. Add the fennel and fry, stirring
    occasionally, 3 to 5 minutes until softened but not colored. Add the garlic and fry
    1 minute. Stir in the wine and cook 5 to 6 minutes until it almost evaporates, then
    add the stock, tomato puree, and lemon zest and season with salt and pepper.
    Cover and bring to a boil. Lower the heat and simmer 10 minutes. Meanwhile,
    calculate the hoki's cooking time at 10 minutes per 1 inch of thickness.
2   Add the fish and simmer for the calculated cooking time, or until it is cooked
    through and flakes easily, then remove it from the pan. When it is cool enough
    to handle, remove the skin and any bones. Flake the fish into the soup, reheat and
    adjust the salt and pepper, if necessary, then serve topped with pesto.

205 Mediterranean Swordfish Soup

PREPARATION TIME 15 minutes, plus making the stock   COOKING TIME 40 minutes

3 tablespoons olive oil
1 celery rib, very finely chopped
1 onion, very finely chopped
2 large garlic cloves, crushed
1 can (15-oz.) crushed tomatoes
1 cup dry white wine
1 tablespoon brined capers, rinsed

5½ cups Fish Stock (see page 11)
  or ready-made stock
2 tablespoons lemon juice
1 teaspoon dried oregano leaves
1 teaspoon dried thyme leaves
1 pound 2 ounces swordfish steaks
salt and freshly ground black pepper

1   Heat the oil in a saucepan over medium heat. Add the celery and onion and fry,
    stirring occasionally, 2 minutes. Stir in the garlic and fry 1 to 3 minutes until the
    onion is softened but not colored. Add the tomatoes, wine, and capers and cook
    8 minutes, stirring to break up the tomatoes.
2   Add the stock, lemon juice, oregano, and thyme and season with salt and pepper.
    Cover and bring to a boil, then lower the heat and simmer 10 minutes.
3   Calculate the swordfish's cooking time at 10 minutes per 1 inch of thickness,
    then add it to the soup and simmer, covered, for the calculated time, or until the
    swordfish flakes easily. Adjust the salt and pepper, if necessary. Remove the fish
    from the soup and remove any skin or bones, then flake or cut into large pieces.
    Divide the swordfish into bowls, ladle the soup over it, and serve immediately.

206 Pollock Quenelle Soup

PREPARATION TIME 30 minutes, plus making the stock   COOKING TIME 30 minutes

6 cups Fish Stock (see page 11)
  or ready-made stock
1½ cups sliced fennel
4 dill sprigs, leaves finely chopped,
  stems lightly crushed and both
  kept separate
2 tablespoons tomato paste
1 tablespoon coriander seeds,
  crushed
1 long strip of lemon zest, all bitter
  white pith removed

a pinch of sugar
12 ounces pollock or pike fillets,
  skinned with small bones removed
1 large egg white, chilled
2 to 4 tablespoons heavy cream
1 teaspoon lemon juice
2 tablespoons very finely chopped
  parsley leaves, plus extra to serve
¼ cup crème fraîche or sour cream
salt and ground white pepper

1   Put the stock, fennel, half the dill leaves and all the stems, tomato paste, coriander
    seeds, lemon zest, and sugar in a skillet and season with salt and white pepper.
    Cover and bring to a boil. Lower the heat and simmer 5 minutes, then remove from
    the heat and set aside, covered.
2   To make the quenelles, blend the pollock in a blender or food processor until
    it forms a smooth, thick paste. Add the egg white and blend again until well mixed,
    then add 2 tablespoons of the cream and blend. The paste will be softer but should
    still hold its shape. Slowly beat in the remaining cream but take care that the paste
    doesn't become too thin. Add the lemon juice, season with salt and white pepper,
    and blend again, then stir in the parsley and remaining dill. Use 2 wet tablespoons
    to shape the mixture into 12 quenelles, or long, egg-shaped ovals, and set aside
    on a plate. Alternatively, roll the mixture into 12 balls with wet hands.
3   Strain the stock, then return it to the pan and bring to a simmer. Do not boil.
    Gently lower the quenelles into the stock and poach 10 minutes, rolling them
    over after 5 minutes. Stir in the crème fraîche and warm through, then adjust the
    salt and pepper, if necessary. Divide the quenelles into bowls, ladle the soup over
    them, and serve sprinkled with parsley.

207 Whiting & Anchovy Soup

PREPARATION TIME 15 minutes, plus making the stock   COOKING TIME 35 minutes

1 tablespoon butter
1 tablespoon olive or hemp oil
2 shallots, chopped
5½ cups Fish Stock (see page 11)
  or ready-made stock
2 cups peeled and diced
  russet potatoes
2 bay leaves
1 long strip of lemon zest, all bitter
  white pith removed

½ teaspoon dried thyme leaves
½ teaspoon dried marjoram leaves
14 ounces boneless, skinless whiting
  or haddock, cut into large chunks
4 anchovy fillets in oil, drained
  and chopped
2 tablespoons chopped
  parsley leaves
salt and freshly ground black pepper

1   Melt the butter with the oil in a saucepan over medium heat. Add the shallots
    and fry, stirring occasionally, 5 minutes until softened but not colored. Add the
    stock, potatoes, bay leaves, lemon zest, thyme, and marjoram, then cover and
    bring to a boil. Lower the heat and simmer 10 minutes. Meanwhile, calculate the
    whiting's cooking time at 10 minutes per 1 inch of thickness.
2   Add the whiting to the soup and simmer for the calculated time, or until it is cooked
    through and flakes easily and the potatoes are tender. Remove the whiting from
    the pan if it is cooked before the potatoes. Stir in the anchovies and parsley, then
    return the whiting to the pan, if necessary. Discard the bay leaves. Season with salt
    and pepper, but remember the anchovies are salty. Serve immediately.

208 Saffron-Scented Mussel Soup

PREPARATION TIME 30 minutes, plus making the stock   COOKING TIME 45 minutes

4½ cups Fish Stock (see page 11)
  or ready-made stock
a large pinch of saffron threads
2¾ pounds live mussels, scrubbed,
  with "beards" removed, and
  soaked in cold water to cover
3 tablespoons olive or hemp oil
2 large garlic cloves,
  finely chopped
1 carrot, peeled and diced
1 celery rib, thinly sliced

1 fennel bulb, sliced
1 leek, halved lengthwise, sliced,
  and rinsed
⅔ cup dry white wine
1 bouquet garni made with
  1 bay leaf, 1 parsley sprig,
  1 rosemary sprig, and
  1 thyme sprig tied together
lemon juice, to taste
salt and freshly ground black pepper

1 Put the stock and saffron in a saucepan, cover, and bring to a boil, then remove
  from the heat and set aside, covered, for the flavors to blend.
2 Discard any cracked mussels or open ones that do not close when tapped.
  Put the mussels and 1 cup water in another saucepan and cook, covered, over
  medium heat 5 to 8 minutes, shaking the pan frequently, until they all open. Strain
  the cooking liquid through a cheesecloth-lined strainer, then add it to the saffron-
  flavored stock. Set the mussels aside until cool enough to handle, then discard
  any that are still closed. Remove the mussels from the shells and set aside.
3 Meanwhile, heat the oil in the rinsed-out pan over medium heat. Add the garlic,
  carrot, celery, fennel, and leek and fry, stirring, 2 minutes. Reduce the heat
  to low and cook, covered, 8 to 10 minutes, stirring occasionally, until all the
  vegetables are softened but not colored. Add the stock, white wine, and bouquet
  garni and season with salt. Cover and bring to a boil, then lower the heat and
  simmer 5 minutes.
4 Discard the bouquet garni and stir the mussels into the soup to warm through—
  take care not to overcook or they will toughen. Adjust the salt and pepper and add
  lemon juice, if necessary, then serve.

209 Mussel & Basil Soup

PREPARATION TIME 25 minutes, plus making the stock   COOKING TIME 30 minutes

¼ cup garlic-flavored olive oil
3 celery ribs, thinly sliced, with the
  leaves reserved
1 large onion, finely chopped
1 green bell pepper, seeded and
  finely chopped
2½ cups Fish Stock (see page 11)
  or ready-made stock
2¼ cups dry white wine
1 can (15-oz.) crushed plum tomatoes
1 tablespoon tomato paste

1 bouquet garni made with the
  reserved celery leaves, 1 bay leaf,
  and several parsley sprigs tied
  together
½ teaspoon sugar
2¾ pounds live mussels, scrubbed,
  with "beards" removed, and
  soaked in cold water to cover
1 large handful of basil leaves, torn
salt and freshly ground black pepper

1 Heat the oil in large saucepan over high heat. Add the celery, onion, and bell pepper
  and fry, stirring, 3 to 5 minutes until softened. Add the stock, wine, tomatoes,
  tomato paste, bouquet garni, and sugar and season with salt and pepper. Cover and
  bring to a boil, then boil, partially covered, 10 minutes to reduce slightly.
2 Discard any cracked mussels or open ones that do not close when tapped. Reduce
  the heat to low, add the mussels to the pan, and simmer, covered, 5 to 8 minutes,
  shaking the pan frequently, until they all open. Strain the soup through a large
  cheesecloth-lined colander and return it to the pan. Discard any mussels that
  remain closed, then set the rest aside until cool enough to handle.
3 Reserve a few mussels in their shells for decorating the bowls. Remove the
  remaining mussels from the shells and add them to the soup. Simmer gently just
  long enough to warm the mussels through—take care not to overcook or they will
  toughen. Adjust the salt and pepper, if necessary, then sprinkle the basil into the
  soup. Serve immediately, topped with the mussels in their shells.

210 Golden Monkfish Soup

PREPARATION TIME 25 minutes, plus making the stock   COOKING TIME 45 minutes

1 tablespoon butter
1 tablespoon olive or hemp oil
1 carrot, peeled and finely diced
1 leek, sliced and rinsed
1 onion, finely diced
⅔ cup dry sherry
4½ cups Fish Stock (see page 11)
   or ready-made stock
5 tablespoons long-grain white rice
a large pinch of saffron threads

1 pound monkfish tail or other
   white fish, thin membrane
   removed, central bone cut out,
   if necessary, and flesh cut into
   bite-size chunks
finely grated zest of 1 lemon
salt and ground white pepper
1 roasted red pepper in olive oil,
   drained and very finely chopped,
   to serve
chopped dill, to serve

1   Melt the butter with the oil in a saucepan over medium heat. Stir in the carrot, leek, and onion and fry, stirring frequently, 3 to 5 minutes until the leek and onion are softened but not colored. Stir in the sherry and cook 5 to 6 minutes until it almost evaporates. Add the stock, rice, and saffron and season with salt and white pepper. Cover and bring to a boil, then lower the heat and simmer 10 to 15 minutes until the rice is tender. Meanwhile, calculate the monkfish's cooking time at 10 minutes per 1 inch of thickness.

2   Add the monkfish and lemon zest and simmer for the calculated time, or until the monkfish is cooked through and breaks into large flakes easily. Remove the fish from the pan, cover, and keep warm. Blend the soup until smooth. Rub the soup through a strainer for an even smoother texture, if you like.

3   Return the monkfish to the soup and warm through. Adjust the salt and pepper, if necessary, and serve sprinkled with the roasted pepper and dill.

211 Tuna Escabeche Soup

PREPARATION TIME 20 minutes, plus making the soup and at least 24 hours marinating
COOKING TIME 20 minutes

1 recipe quantity Slow-Cooked
   Tomato & Orange Soup
   (see page 40)
salt and freshly ground black pepper
finely chopped parsley leaves,
   to serve

TUNA ESCABECHE
1 cup olive oil
14 ounces tuna steaks, about
   ¾ inch thick

1 red onion, finely chopped
1 cup red wine vinegar
1 large bay leaf
1 large carrot,
   peeled and diced
2 large garlic cloves,
   finely chopped
a pinch of chili flakes, or to taste
1 tablespoon coriander seeds,
   lightly crushed

1   At least one day and up to five days before you plan to serve, make the tuna escabeche. Heat 2 tablespoons of the oil in a skillet over medium heat. Add the tuna and fry 2 minutes on each side, or until medium-rare. Remove the tuna from the pan and drain on paper towels, then set side.

2   Add the remaining oil to the pan and heat over medium heat. Add the onion and fry, stirring, 3 to 5 minutes until softened but not colored. Reduce the heat to very low (use a heat diffuser if you have one) and add the vinegar, bay leaf, carrot, garlic, chili flakes, and coriander seeds and season with salt and pepper. Simmer 10 minutes, watching closely so none of the ingredients brown.

3   Meanwhile, flake the tuna into a nonreactive bowl, add the oil and vegetable mixture, and very gently mix together, taking care not to break up the tuna too much. Let cool completely, then cover and chill until required.

4   When ready to serve, reheat the soup and adjust the salt and pepper, if necessary. Remove the tuna from the escabeche mixture, making sure you don't include the bay leaf or any of the coriander seeds, and divide it into bowls. Ladle the hot soup over it, sprinkle with parsley, and serve.

212 Irish Oyster Soup

PREPARATION TIME 20 minutes   COOKING TIME 30 minutes

12 live oysters
up to 5 cups whole milk
¼ cup (½ stick) butter
1 tablespoon olive or hemp oil
2 leeks, halved lengthwise, thinly
 sliced, and rinsed
1 celery rib, finely chopped

1 large garlic clove, finely chopped
2 tablespoons all-purpose flour
2 bay leaves
2 tablespoons chopped parsley
 leaves, plus extra to serve
salt and ground white pepper
smoked or sweet paprika, to serve

1   Shuck the oysters over a bowl to catch the juices, then cut each one into
    2 or 3 pieces and set aside. Strain the juices through a cheesecloth-lined strainer
    into a measuring jug. Add enough milk to make 5 cups, then set aside.
2   Melt the butter with the oil in a saucepan over medium heat. Stir in the leeks and
    celery and cook, covered, 7 minutes, stirring occasionally. Add the garlic and stir
    1 to 3 minutes until the vegetables are softened and light golden brown. Sprinkle
    in the flour and cook, stirring, 2 minutes. Slowly add in the milk mixture, stirring
    continuously to prevent lumps from forming.
3   Add the bay leaves and parsley and bring to just below the boil, then lower the
    heat and simmer, covered, 5 minutes. Add the oysters and simmer 2 to 3 minutes
    until cooked through, but take care not to overcook or they will toughen. Discard
    the bay leaves and season with salt and white pepper, then serve sprinkled with
    parsley and paprika.

213 Caribbean Callaloo

PREPARATION TIME 15 minutes, plus making the stock   COOKING TIME 40 minutes

1 tablespoon butter
2 tablespoons sunflower
 or peanut oil
1 large onion, chopped
2 garlic cloves, finely chopped
1 pound 5 ounces callaloo greens
 or spinach leaves, chopped
5½ cups Chicken Stock (see page 11)
 or ready-made stock

3½ cups coconut milk
2¾ cups peeled and chopped
 russet potatoes
12 ounces shelled white crabmeat
salt and freshly ground black pepper
hot or sweet paprika, to serve
hot pepper sauce, to serve

1   Melt the butter with the oil in a saucepan over medium heat. Add the onion and
    fry, stirring, 2 minutes. Stir in the garlic and fry 1 to 3 minutes until the onion
    is softened. Add the greens and stir 5 minutes, or until they wilt, then remove them
    from the pan and set aside. Add the stock, coconut milk, and potatoes to the pan
    and season with salt and pepper. Cover and bring to a boil, then lower the heat
    and simmer, partially covered, 10 to 12 minutes until the potatoes are tender.
2   Return the greens to the pan and simmer, uncovered, 5 to 8 minutes until they are
    tender. Stir in the crabmeat and simmer 3 minutes until cooked, then adjust the salt
    and pepper, if necessary. Serve sprinkled with paprika and with hot pepper sauce
    on the side for adding at the table.

214 Oyster & Salmon Soup

PREPARATION TIME 20 minutes, plus making the stock   COOKING TIME 35 minutes

12 live oysters
7 cups Fish Stock (see page 11)
    or ready-made stock
14 ounces skinless salmon fillet,
    any small bones removed,
    and cut into bite-size pieces
12 raw large shrimp, shelled
    and deveined
3 tablespoons butter

1 shallot, finely chopped
1 cup dry vermouth or dry
    white wine
⅔ cup heavy cream
2 tablespoons chopped mixed herbs,
    such as chervil, chives, dill,
    and parsley
lemon juice, to taste
salt and freshly ground black pepper

1   Shuck the oysters over a bowl to catch the juices, then set aside. Put the juices
    and fish stock in a saucepan and bring to a simmer over medium heat. Add the
    salmon and simmer 1 minute, then add the oysters and shrimp and simmer
    2 to 3 minutes longer until the oysters are cooked through and the shrimp turn pink
    and curl. Watch closely so the oysters and shrimp do not overcook and toughen.
    Remove the seafood from the pan, cover with a little of the cooking liquid, and set
    aside. Strain the cooking liquid through a cheesecloth-lined strainer and set aside.
2   Melt 2 tablespoons of the butter in the rinsed-out pan. Add the shallot and fry,
    stirring occasionally, 5 minutes until softened but not colored. Stir in the vermouth
    and cook 6 to 8 minutes until it almost evaporates. Add the cooking liquid and
    bring to a boil, then boil until reduced by half. Stir in the cream and boil until
    reduced by half again.
3   Reduce the heat to low and stir in the remaining butter. Return the seafood
    to the pan and simmer to warm through. Stir in the herbs, add lemon juice to taste,
    and season with salt and pepper, then serve.

215 Shrimp & Orzo Soup

PREPARATION TIME 25 minutes, plus making the stock   COOKING TIME 30 minutes

24 large raw shrimp,
    shelled and deveined,
    with heads and shells reserved
6 cups Fish Stock (see page 11)
    or ready-made stock
¼ cup dry vermouth
2 large garlic cloves, crushed
2 large tomatoes, chopped
1 bay leaf
1 celery rib, chopped

1 teaspoon marjoram leaves
    or ½ teaspoon dried marjoram
1 large handful of basil leaves,
    chopped
pared zest of 1 lemon
a pinch of chili flakes, or to taste
¼ teaspoon salt, plus extra to season
½ cup orzo
freshly ground black pepper
lemon-flavored olive oil, to serve

1   Put the shrimp heads and shells, stock, vermouth, garlic, tomatoes, bay leaf,
    celery, marjoram, half the basil, lemon zest, chili flakes, and salt in a large saucepan
    and season with pepper. Cover and bring to a boil. Lower the heat and simmer
    10 minutes, then strain, pressing down on the flavorings and rubbing back and forth
    to extract as much flavor as possible. Discard the flavorings, return the stock to the
    pan, cover, and set aside.
2   Meanwhile, bring a saucepan of salted water to a boil. Add the orzo and boil
    15 to 18 minutes, or according to the package directions, until al dente.
3   Shortly before the orzo is finished cooking, return the stock to a simmer, add the
    shrimp and cook 2 to 3 minutes until they turn pink and curl. If the orzo still isn't
    finished cooking, remove the shrimp and set aside so they do not become tough.
4   Drain the orzo, then add it to the soup with the remaining basil and the shrimp.
    Adjust the salt and pepper, if necessary, but remember the stock has already
    been salted. Serve drizzled with lemon olive oil.

216 Shrimp Ball Soup

PREPARATION TIME 30 minutes, plus making the dashi   **COOKING TIME** 25 minutes

1 recipe quantity Dashi (see page 12)
   or 5½ cups prepared instant dashi
14 ounces raw shrimp, shelled,
   deveined, and finely chopped, with
   heads and shells reserved
1 small egg, beaten

1 tablespoon cornstarch
2 teaspoons salt
1 teaspoon sesame oil
cilantro leaves or baby shiso leaves,
   to serve
julienned zest of 1 lemon, to serve

1   Put the shrimp in a bowl and use your fingers to gradually incorporate the egg
to make a sticky paste—you might not need all the egg. Sprinkle in the cornstarch,
mix again, and shape into a loose ball, which will be a moist, pastelike mixture.
"Throw" this ball against the inside of the bowl several times to soften the mixture
and help it stick together more, then cover and chill at least 15 minutes.

2   Meanwhile, put the dashi and shrimp heads and shells in a saucepan. Cover and
bring to just below the boil, then reduce the heat to very low (use a heat diffuser
if you have one) and simmer while you prepare the shrimp balls. Do not boil.

3   Divide the salt between two saucepans of water, cover, and bring to a boil. Put the
shrimp ball on a plate and sprinkle with the sesame oil, letting the excess slide onto
the plate—this helps make it easy to roll the mixture into balls without it sticking
to your fingers. Divide the mixture into 36 equal portions and roll them into balls.

4   Divide the shrimp balls between the two pans of slowly boiling water and boil
1½ to 2 minutes until they float. Remove from the water and set aside.

5   Strain the dashi into one of the rinsed-out pans and return to just below
the boil. Immediately reduce the heat to low, add the shrimp balls,
and warm through. Divide the shrimp balls into bowls, ladle the
soup over them, and serve topped with cilantro and lemon zest.

217 Thai Hot-and-Sour Soup with Shrimp

PREPARATION TIME 20 minutes   COOKING TIME 20 minutes

4 lemongrass stalks, cut into 3 pieces
  and lightly crushed, with outer
  leaves removed
4 cilantro sprigs, including roots and
  stems, cut in half, plus extra
  chopped leaves to serve
6 kaffir lime leaves, torn
12 button mushrooms, sliced

1 teaspoon salt
24 large raw shrimp, shelled
  and deveined
3 tablespoons lime juice
2 tablespoons fish sauce
1 to 2 bird's-eye chilies, seeded
  (optional) and diagonally sliced
lime wedges, to serve

1   Bring 5½ cups water to a boil in a saucepan. Add the lemongrass, cilantro, lime
    leaves, mushrooms, and salt and boil, covered, 5 minutes.
2   Reduce the heat to low, add the shrimp and simmer 2 to 3 minutes until they turn
    pink and curl. Immediately stir in the lime juice, fish sauce, and chilies. Discard the
    lemongrass, lime leaves and cilantro. Serve sprinkled with cilantro leaves and with
    lime wedges for squeezing over.

218 Scottish Poached Salmon & Cabbage Soup

PREPARATION TIME 20 minutes, plus making the stock and cooking the salmon
COOKING TIME 35 minutes

1 tablespoon butter
1 tablespoon olive or hemp oil
1 leek, halved lengthwise,
  thinly sliced, and rinsed
5½ cups Fish Stock (see page 11)
  or ready-made stock
1 carrot, peeled and diced
1 potato, peeled and diced

1 cup finely shredded
  savoy cabbage
2½ cups flaked boneless,
  skinless poached salmon
  with all fat removed
salt and freshly ground black pepper
chopped dill, to serve

1   Melt the butter with the oil in a saucepan over medium heat. Add the leek and
    fry, stirring occasionally, 3 to 5 minutes until softened but not colored. Add the
    stock, carrot, and potato and season with salt and pepper.
2   Cover and bring to a boil, then lower the heat and simmer 10 to 12 minutes
    until the potatoes are tender. Add the cabbage and simmer, uncovered,
    5 minutes. Stir in the salmon and simmer 2 to 3 minutes until it is warmed
    through and the cabbage is tender. Adjust the salt and pepper, if necessary,
    then serve sprinkled with dill.

219 Vietnamese-Style Scallop & Shrimp Soup

PREPARATION TIME 20 minutes, plus making the stock   COOKING TIME 25 minutes

1 small handful of bean sprouts
6 cups Fish Stock (see page 11)
  or ready-made stock
12 button mushrooms, trimmed
  and quartered
1 lemongrass stalk, crushed and cut
  in half, with outer leaves removed

1 tablespoon fish sauce, or to taste
1 tablespoon lime juice, or to taste
1 long red chili, seeded (optional)
  and thinly sliced
9 ounces shelled raw queen scallops
9 ounces large raw shrimp, peeled
  and deveined

1   Put the bean sprouts in a bowl, cover with cold water, and set aside. Put the stock,
    mushrooms, lemongrass, fish sauce, lime juice, and chili in a saucepan. Cover
    and bring to a boil, then boil, partially covered, 10 minutes to reduce slightly.
    Reduce the heat to low.
2   Add the scallops and shrimp and simmer 2 to 3 minutes until the shrimp turn pink
    and curl and the scallops are cooked through when you cut one open. Add more
    fish sauce and lime juice, if necessary. Drain the bean sprouts and add them
    to the soup to warm through, then serve.

220 Cream of Smoked Trout Soup

PREPARATION TIME 20 minutes, plus making the stock and toasting the seeds
COOKING TIME 30 minutes

1 cup plus 2 tablespoons whole milk
2 parsley sprigs, stalks crushed
1 bay leaf
3¾ cups Fish Stock (see page 11)
   or ready-made stock
14 ounces skinless hot-smoked
   trout fillets with all small
   bones removed

1 large onion, chopped
1 large sweet potato,
   peeled and diced
salt and freshly ground black pepper
toasted white sesame seeds
   (see page 9)
black sesame seeds, to serve
chives, to serve

1   Put the milk, parsley, and bay leaf in a small saucepan and bring to just below
    the boil. Cover and set aside to infuse.
2   Put the stock, trout, onion, and sweet potato in another saucepan and season
    with salt and pepper. Cover and bring to just below the boil, then lower the heat
    and simmer 10 to 12 minutes until the potato is tender. Remove about one-quarter
    of the trout and set aside.
3   Blend the soup until smooth. Slowly strain in enough of the infused milk to achieve
    the preferred consistency. Adjust the salt and pepper, if necessary, but remember
    the trout might be salty. Divide the soup into bowls and flake the reserved trout
    over. Serve sprinkled with sesame seeds and chives.

221 Elegant Japanese Scallop Soup

PREPARATION TIME 5 minutes, plus making the dashi   COOKING TIME 10 minutes

1 recipe quantity Dashi (see page 12)
  or 5½ cups prepared instant dashi
4 teaspoons soy sauce
2 teaspoons sake or dry sherry
½ teaspoon salt, plus extra to season

1 large shelled queen scallop for
  each bowl, coral removed and
  reserved and each scallop cut
  into 3 equal horizontal slices
shiso or cilantro leaves, to serve
grated yuzu or lemon zest, to serve

1 Put the dashi, soy sauce, sake, and salt in a saucepan. Cover and bring to just
   below the boil. Lower the heat and simmer 1 minute. Adjust the salt, if necessary.
2 Arrange the scallop slices and coral in bowls and ladle the soup over them.
   Add a shiso leaf to each, sprinkle with yuzu zest and serve.

222 Tilapia & Cilantro Soup

PREPARATION TIME 15 minutes, plus making the stock and preparing the tomato
COOKING TIME 25 minutes

2 tablespoons peanut
  or sunflower oil
1 large red onion, chopped
2 large garlic cloves, finely chopped
1 celery rib, thinly sliced
1 large tomato, peeled (see page 9),
  seeded, and chopped
14 ounces black tilapia fillets, any
  small bones removed and fish cut
  into bite-size pieces (no need
  to skin as the skin is edible)

4½ cups Fish Stock (see page 11)
  or ready-made stock
2 tablespoons fish sauce,
  or to taste
a pinch of sugar
1 handful of cilantro leaves,
  coarsely torn
freshly ground black pepper

1 Heat the oil in a saucepan over medium heat. Add the onion and cook, stirring,
   2 minutes. Add the garlic and cook, stirring, 1 to 3 minutes until the onion is
   softened but not colored. Add the celery and tomato and cook 3 to 5 minutes
   longer until the tomato is soft.
2 Add the tilapia and gently stir 1 minute, or until the flesh turns white. Add the stock,
   fish sauce, and sugar and season with pepper. Cover, bring to a boil, then lower the
   heat and simmer 3 to 5 minutes until the fish is cooked through and flakes easily.
   Stir in the cilantro, then adjust the fish sauce and pepper, if necessary, and serve.

223 Lightly Spiced Scallop & Spinach Soup

PREPARATION TIME 15 minutes, plus making the stock   COOKING TIME 15 minutes

2 teaspoons sunflower oil
2 large garlic cloves, finely chopped
1 green chili, seeded (optional)
  and finely chopped
1-inch piece of gingerroot,
  peeled and finely chopped
2 teaspoons dried curry leaves
3¼ cups coconut milk

2½ cups Fish Stock (see page 11)
  or ready-made stock
14 ounces shelled bay scallops,
  rinsed
2 large handfuls of baby
  spinach leaves
salt and freshly ground black pepper
lemon wedges, to serve

1 Heat the oil in a saucepan over medium heat. Add the garlic, chili, ginger, and curry
   leaves and stir 30 seconds, or until fragrant. Watch closely so the garlic and ginger
   do not brown. Add the coconut milk and stock and season with salt and pepper,
   then bring to a boil, uncovered.
2 Reduce the heat to low, add the scallops and spinach, and simmer 3 to 4 minutes
   until the scallops are cooked through when you cut one open. Adjust the salt and
   pepper, if necessary, and serve with lemon wedges on the side for squeezing over.

224 Scandinavian Salmon & Shrimp Soup

PREPARATION TIME 20 minutes, plus making the stock and preparing the tomato
COOKING TIME 30 minutes

1 tablespoon butter
1 tablespoon sunflower oil
½ leek, halved lengthwise, thinly
  sliced, and rinsed
1 russet potato, peeled and chopped
1 large ripe tomato, peeled
  (see page 9), seeded, and diced
14 ounces skinless salmon fillet,
  any small bones removed

4½ cups Fish Stock (see page 11)
  or ready-made stock
1 bay leaf
a pinch of cayenne pepper
a pinch of ground cardamom
9 ounces medium raw shrimp,
  shelled and deveined
3 tablespoons chopped dill
salt and freshly ground black pepper

1 Melt the butter with the oil in a saucepan over medium heat. Stir in the leek, potato, and tomato, reduce the heat to low, and cook, covered, 10 minutes, or until the vegetables are softened but not colored. Meanwhile, calculate the salmon's cooking time at 10 minutes per 1 inch of thickness.

2 Add the stock, bay leaf, cayenne pepper, and cardamom and season with salt and pepper. Cover and bring to a boil. Reduce the heat to low, add the salmon and simmer, covered, 3 minutes less than the calculated time.

3 Stir in the shrimp and simmer 2 to 3 minutes until they turn pink and curl and the salmon flakes easily. If the shrimp are cooked before the salmon, remove them from the pan and set aside. Discard the bay leaf, then stir in the dill and return the shrimp, if necessary. Adjust the salt and pepper, if necessary, and serve.

225 Spiced Halibut & Sweet Potato Soup

PREPARATION TIME 25 minutes, plus making the stock   **COOKING TIME** 35 minutes

1 tablespoon butter
1 tablespoon olive oil
1 celery rib, thinly sliced
1 leek, halved lengthwise, thinly
  sliced, and rinsed
1 onion, finely chopped
1 green bell pepper, seeded and
  finely chopped
1 sweet potato, peeled and diced
2 garlic cloves, crushed
1 teaspoon ground coriander
1 teaspoon fennel seeds

½ teaspoon ground cumin
a large pinch of saffron threads
a pinch of chili flakes, or to taste
4 cups Fish Stock (see page 11)
  or ready-made stock
¼ cup dry white wine
1 long pared strip of orange zest,
  all bitter white pith removed
14 ounces skinless halibut steaks
12 large raw shrimp, shelled
  and deveined
salt and freshly ground black pepper

1 Melt the butter with the oil in a saucepan over medium heat. Add the celery, leek, onion, green pepper, and sweet potato and fry, stirring occasionally, 2 minutes. Add the garlic, coriander, fennel seeds, cumin, saffron, and chili flakes and stir 30 seconds, or until aromatic. Watch closely so the spices do not burn.

2 Add the stock, wine, and orange zest and season with salt and pepper. Cover and bring to a boil, then lower the heat and simmer 10 minutes to blend the flavors. Meanwhile, calculate the halibut's cooking time at 10 minutes per 1 inch of thickness.

3 Add the halibut steaks to the pan and simmer, covered, 3 minutes less than the calculated time. Add the shrimp and simmer 2 to 3 minutes until the halibut is cooked through and flakes easily and the shrimp turn pink and curl. If the shrimp are cooked before the halibut, remove them from the pan and set aside. Adjust the salt and pepper, if necessary.

4 Remove the halibut from the soup. Divide the shrimp into bowls, then ladle the soup over them. Flake the halibut over each portion and serve.

CHAPTER 5

PASTA, LEGUME & GRAIN SOUPS

With a well-stocked pantry, the recipes in this chapter give you a taste of delicious, satisfying soups from around the world. A variety of pasta shapes, legumes, and grains are paired with a colorful mix of vegetables in most recipes. This is your visual clue that these soups not only taste great but are good for you, too. Many of them fit in the category of "comfort food," ideal for fighting off the chill on dreary gray days. Greeks swear by Greek Lentil & Garlic Soup with loads of garlic and onions to keep colds at bay, and Chickpea & Pasta Soup and Winter Minestrone are two more of the appetizing and hearty winter warmers you'll find in this chapter.

Rice is a popular pantry staple. You might be in the habit of only cooking long-grain rice, such as basmati, but why not try something new with Red Rice & Wild Arugula Soup or Beef & Wild Rice Soup? Or, be even more adventurous and use one of the often overlooked grains, such as spelt, quinoa, and millet—they make fantastic soups, and this chapter includes recipes for all of them.

WINTER MINESTRONE (SEE PAGE 142)

226 Chickpea & Pasta Soup

PREPARATION TIME 15 minutes, plus soaking the chickpeas overnight, making
the flavored oil (optional) and preparing the tomatoes   COOKING TIME 2¼ hours

1 cup dried chickpeas
2 large bay leaves
2 carrots, cut in half
2 celery ribs, cut in half
2 large garlic cloves, smashed
2 onions, halved
2 rosemary sprigs
½ cup tubetti or other small
   soup pasta

2 large, juicy tomatoes, grated
   (see page 9)
salt and freshly ground black pepper
1 recipe quantity Crushed Basil Oil
   (see page 15) or extra-virgin
   olive oil, to serve
freshly grated Parmesan cheese,
   to serve

1   Put the chickpeas in a bowl, cover with water, and let soak overnight, then drain.
    Transfer to a saucepan and add 7 cups water. Cover and bring to a boil. Skim,
    if necessary, then add the bay leaves, carrots, celery, garlic, onions, and rosemary.
    Lower the heat and simmer, covered, 1½ to 2 hours until the chickpeas are tender.
2   Strain the cooking liquid into a bowl. Discard the flavorings and set the chickpeas
    aside. Skim the liquid, then blend half the chickpeas and 5½ cups of the cooking
    liquid until smooth and return the mixture to the pan.
3   Add the pasta and tomatoes and season with salt and pepper. Cover and bring
    to a boil, then boil, uncovered, 10 to 12 minutes, or according to the package
    directions, until the pasta is al dente. Stir occasionally to prevent the pasta from
    sticking to the bottom of the pan.
4   Stir in the remaining chickpeas and warm through. Adjust the salt and pepper,
    if necessary, and serve drizzled with oil and with cheese.

227 Broccoli, Orecchiette & Anchovy Soup

PREPARATION TIME 15 minutes, plus making the stock and crisps
COOKING TIME 35 minutes

1 tablespoon extra-virgin olive oil,
   plus extra to serve
1 onion, finely chopped
2 large garlic cloves, chopped
2 canned anchovy fillets, drained
   and chopped
3 cups tomato puree
2½ cups Vegetable Stock
   (see page 12) or ready-made stock

2 cups small broccoli florets and
   thinly sliced stems
a pinch of chili flakes (optional)
½ cup orecchiette
salt and freshly ground black pepper
freshly grated Parmesan cheese,
   to serve
1 recipe quantity Parmesan Crisps
   (see page 51), to serve (optional)

1   Heat the oil in a saucepan over medium heat. Add the onion and fry, stirring,
    2 minutes. Add the garlic and anchovies and stir 1 to 3 minutes until the onion
    is softened and the anchovies break down. Add the tomato puree, stock, broccoli
    stems, and chili flakes, if using, and season with pepper. Cover and bring to a boil,
    then lower the heat and simmer 5 minutes.
2   Uncover and increase the heat to a slow boil. Add the broccoli florets and
    orecchiette and boil 12 to 15 minutes, or according to the package directions, until
    the pasta and the florets are tender. Adjust the pepper, if necessary, and season
    with salt, but remember the anchovies are salty so you might not need any.
    Serve with cheese, olive oil, and Parmesan crisps, if you like, on the side.

228 Thai Wonton Soup

PREPARATION TIME 25 minutes, plus making the stock   COOKING TIME 30 minutes

5½ cups Rich Chicken Stock
  (see page 10) or ready-made stock
4 leaves Chinese cabbage, rolled and
  thinly sliced
salt and freshly ground black pepper
1 scallion, finely chopped, to serve

THAI WONTONS
3 ounces finely ground pork
2 ounces small, shelled raw shrimp,
  very finely chopped

½ tablespoon finely chopped
  cilantro leaves, plus 24 small
  whole leaves
½ teaspoon sweet soy sauce
½ teaspoon cornstarch
½ teaspoon sesame oil, plus
  extra as needed
24 wonton wrappers, thawed
  if frozen
1 small egg yolk, beaten

1   To make the wontons, put the pork, shrimp, chopped cilantro, and soy sauce
    in a bowl and use your fingers to mix together. Sprinkle in the cornstarch, mix again
    and shape into a ball. Put the ball on a plate and sprinkle with the sesame oil to help
    make it easier to roll into balls. Divide and roll the mixture into 24 equal balls.
2   Bring a large saucepan of water to a boil. Meanwhile, position 1 wonton wrapper
    in a diamond shape on the countertop and put 1 cilantro leaf in the middle, then
    top with 1 ball of the filling. Fold the bottom corner of the wrapper over the filling
    to make a triangle. Seal the edges with the egg yolk, then fold both side points over
    the filling and seal. Repeat with the remaining wontons.
3   Working in batches to avoid overcrowding the pan, boil the wontons until they
    float to the surface, then cook 1 minute longer to make sure the filling is cooked
    through. Remove with a slotted spoon and set aside. If not using immediately,
    sprinkle with sesame oil to prevent them from sticking together.
4   Bring the stock to a boil. Add the cabbage and boil 1 to 2 minutes until tender.
    Reduce the heat to low, add the wontons to just warm through, then season
    with salt and pepper. Divide the wontons and cabbage into bowls, add the stock,
    and serve sprinkled with scallion.

229 Green Tea Noodle Soup

PREPARATION TIME 20 minutes, plus making the stock and toasting the seeds
COOKING TIME 35 minutes

5½ cups Rich Chicken Stock
  (see page 10)
2 large garlic cloves, finely chopped
½-inch piece of gingerroot, peeled
  and smashed in one piece
¼-inch piece of galangal, peeled and
  smashed in one piece
½ tablespoon light soy sauce,
  or to taste
½ tablespoon mirin
5 ounces green tea noodles

2 teaspoons toasted sesame oil
3 cups boneless, skinless chicken
  thighs cut into thin strips
5 shiitake mushroom caps, sliced
6 tablespoons frozen corn kernels
2 scallions, finely shredded
salt and freshly ground black pepper
finely shredded mint leaves, to serve
black sesame seeds, to serve
white sesame seeds, toasted
  (see page 9), to serve

1   Put the stock, garlic, ginger, galangal, soy sauce, and mirin in a saucepan.
    Cover and bring to a boil. Lower the heat and simmer 10 minutes.
2   Meanwhile, bring another saucepan of water to a boil. Add the noodles, return
    to a boil, and boil 6 minutes, or according to the package directions, until tender.
    Drain, rinse under cold running water, and drain again. Toss with the sesame oil
    and set aside. Remove and discard the ginger and galangal from the stock.
3   Add the chicken to the stock, cover, and bring to just below the boil. Skim, then
    add the mushrooms, lower the heat, and simmer, covered, 5 minutes. Add the corn
    and scallions and simmer 3 to 5 minutes until the chicken is cooked through and
    the juices run clear when you cut a piece. Add the noodles and warm through.
    Adjust the salt and pepper and add extra soy sauce, if necessary. Serve sprinkled
    with mint leaves and sesame seeds.

Orzo Primavera Soup

PREPARATION TIME 15 minutes, plus making the stock   **COOKING TIME** 40 minutes

6 cups Vegetable Stock (see page 12)
   or ready-made stock
1 bouquet garni made with
   1 piece of celery rib with its leaves,
   1 rosemary sprig, and several
   parsley and thyme sprigs
   tied together
1 young carrot, diced

1 young turnip, peeled and diced
½ cup orzo
¾ cup chopped green beans
½ cup frozen peas
1 teaspoon finely grated lemon zest
2 tablespoons chopped
   parsley leaves
salt and freshly ground black pepper

1   Put the stock and bouquet garni in a saucepan over high heat and season with salt and pepper. Cover and bring to a boil, then lower the heat and simmer 10 minutes.

2   Return the stock to a boil, add the carrot and turnip, and boil 2 minutes. Stir in the orzo and boil 11 minutes, then add the green beans and peas and boil 4 to 6 minutes longer until the orzo and vegetables are tender. Discard the bouquet garni. Stir in the lemon zest and adjust the salt and pepper, if necessary. Stir in the parsley and serve.

231 Buckwheat Noodle Soup with Nori

PREPARATION TIME 5 minutes   COOKING TIME 20 minutes

5 ounces buckwheat noodles
1 recipe quantity Dashi, Vegetarian
   Dashi (see page 12), or 5½ cups
   prepared instant dashi
6 tablespoons soy sauce, or to taste
2 tablespoons sugar

2 tablespoons mirin or sweet sherry
2 teaspoons salt, plus extra to season
½ sheet nori, finely shredded or torn,
   to serve
wasabi paste, to serve

1   You need a large saucepan for the noodles because they foam up during cooking.
    Fill it three-quarters of the way with water, cover, and bring to a boil. Set aside
    a bowl of cold water. Add the noodles to the boiling water and return to a boil.
    As soon as the liquid foams and rises, add a ladleful of the cold water. Return
    the water to just below the boil, then lower the heat and simmer the noodles
    2 to 5 minutes, or according to the package directions, until tender. Drain, rinse
    immediately in cold water, and set aside.
2   Meanwhile, in a separate saucepan, mix together the dashi, soy sauce, sugar,
    mirin, and salt, stirring to dissolve the sugar. Bring to just below the boil, then turn
    off the heat and keep warm if the noodles haven't finished cooking. Adjust the
    seasoning, adding extra soy sauce or salt, if necessary. Divide the noodles and
    soup into bowls, sprinkle with nori, and serve with wasabi paste.

232 Pasta & Potato Soup

PREPARATION TIME 20 minutes   COOKING TIME 45 minutes

3 tablespoons extra-virgin olive oil,
   plus extra to serve
1 carrot, peeled and diced
1 celery rib, finely chopped, with the
   leaves reserved
1 onion, diced
1 bouquet garni made with
   1 bay leaf, the celery leaves,
   and several parsley and
   thyme sprigs tied together

2 cups peeled and diced
   russet potatoes
1 Parmesan or pecorino cheese rind,
   about 2 x 3 inches, or 1 heel
   of prosciutto (see page 9)
⅔ cup dried macaroni
½ cup freshly grated
   Parmesan cheese
salt and freshly ground black pepper
chopped parsley leaves, to serve

1   Heat the oil in a saucepan over medium heat. Add the carrot, celery, and onion
    and fry, stirring occasionally, 3 to 5 minutes until softened.
2   Add the bouquet garni, potatoes, cheese rind, and 6 cups water and season with
    salt and pepper but remember the rind is salty. Cover and bring to a boil. Lower
    the heat and simmer 15 to 20 minutes until all the vegetables are very tender,
    then discard the bouquet garni and cheese rind.
3   Blend the soup until semi-smooth with small pieces of carrot and potato
    remaining. Add the pasta to the soup and return it to a boil, then boil, uncovered,
    10 to 12 minutes until just al dente. Stir frequently to prevent the pasta from
    sticking to the bottom of the pan. Stir in half the cheese and adjust the salt
    and pepper, if necessary, but remember the cheese is salty. Serve with extra
    oil and cheese.

233 Mediterranean Minestrone

PREPARATION TIME 20 minutes, plus overnight soaking and cooking the beans and preparing the tomatoes **COOKING TIME** 45 minutes

½ cup dried cannellini or navy beans
3 tablespoons fruity extra-virgin
   olive oil, plus extra to serve
1 onion, finely chopped
1 leek, thinly sliced and rinsed
1 carrot, peeled and diced
2 new potatoes, peeled and diced
4 thyme sprigs
1 piece of Parmesan cheese rind,
   about 2 x 3 inches
1 zucchini, diced

½ cup thin green beans cut into
   bite-size pieces
2 beefsteak tomatoes, peeled
   (see page 9), seeded, and chopped
1 tablespoon tomato paste
½ cup vermicelli broken into
   bite-size pieces
½ teaspoon sugar (optional)
salt and freshly ground black pepper
pesto, to serve
freshly grated Parmesan cheese,
   to serve

1 Put the beans in a bowl, cover with water, and let soak overnight, then drain. Transfer to a saucepan, add 7 cups water, cover, and bring to a boil. Lower the heat and simmer, covered, 50 minutes to 1 hour until almost tender, then drain.

2 Heat the oil in a saucepan over low heat. Stir in the onion and leek and fry, covered, 10 to 12 minutes until softened. Stir in the carrot, potatoes, thyme, and cheese rind. Season with salt and pepper, but remember the cheese rind is salty. Add 6 cups water and bring to a boil. Skim, then lower the heat and simmer, covered, 10 minutes. Discard the cheese rind.

3 Stir in the cannellini beans, zucchini, green beans, tomatoes, tomato paste, vermicelli, and sugar, if using. Return to a boil, then boil, uncovered, 10 to 15 minutes until the beans are tender and the pasta is al dente. Stir frequently to prevent the pasta from sticking to the bottom of the pan. Adjust the salt and pepper, if necessary, and serve immediately with pesto, cheese, and olive oil for adding at the table.

234 Winter Minestrone

PREPARATION TIME 20 minutes, plus overnight soaking and cooking the beans
COOKING TIME 45 minutes

½ cup dried cannellini or navy beans
5 ounces pancetta, skinned,
   if necessary, and chopped
1 large onion, finely chopped
4 large garlic cloves, chopped
1½ cups shredded white cabbage
1 carrot, peeled, halved lengthwise,
   and sliced
1 zucchini, halved lengthwise
   and sliced

1 russet potato, peeled and chopped
1 Parmesan cheese rind, about
   2 x 3 inches (see page 9)
½ cup Arborio rice
salt and freshly ground black pepper
extra-virgin olive oil, to serve
freshly grated Parmesan cheese,
   to serve

1 Put the beans in a bowl, cover with water, and let soak overnight, then drain. Transfer to a saucepan, add 7 cups water, cover, and bring to a boil. Lower the heat and simmer, covered, 50 minutes to 1 hour until almost tender, then drain.

2 Put the pancetta in a saucepan over medium-high heat and fry, stirring, until the fat runs. Add the onion and fry, stirring, 5 to 8 minutes until softened and turning golden. Add the garlic, cabbage, carrot, zucchini, and potato and stir 1 to 2 minutes. Add the cheese rind and 6 cups water.

3 Cover and bring to a boil. Season with salt and pepper but remember the rind is salty. Lower the heat and simmer, covered, 10 minutes. Stir in the cooked dried beans and rice, return the soup to a boil, uncovered, then lower the heat slightly and slowly boil 10 to 15 minutes until the beans and rice are tender. Discard the cheese rind, then adjust the salt and pepper, if necessary. Serve with oil and cheese.

235 Alphabet Soup

PREPARATION TIME 5 minutes, plus making the stock   COOKING TIME 15 minutes

3 cups Vegetable Stock (see page 12)
  or ready-made stock
3 cups tomato puree
1 cup small pasta letters or
  other small soup pasta
1 cup frozen corn kernels

salt and freshly ground black pepper
chopped parsley leaves,
  to serve
freshly grated Parmesan cheese,
  to serve

1   Put the stock and tomato puree in a saucepan. Cover and bring to a boil. Add the
    pasta and corn, and season with salt and pepper. Return to a boil, then boil,
    uncovered, 3 to 5 minutes until the pasta is al dente and the corn is tender.
2   Adjust the salt and pepper, if necessary. Serve sprinkled with parsley and cheese.

236 Very Garlicky Pasta & Cavolo Nero Soup

PREPARATION TIME 10 minutes, plus making the stock   COOKING TIME 30 minutes

1 tablespoon fruity extra-virgin olive
  oil, plus extra to serve
1 red onion, finely chopped
4 large garlic cloves, chopped
6½ cups Vegetable Stock
  (see page 12) or ready-made stock

1½ cups shredded cavolo nero
  or savoy cabbage, shredded
1 cup tubetti or other small
  soup pasta
a pinch of chili flakes, or to taste
salt and freshly ground black pepper

1   Heat the oil in a saucepan over medium heat. Add the onion and fry, stirring,
    2 minutes. Add the garlic and fry 1 to 3 minutes until the onion is softened.
    Stir in the stock, cavolo nero, and chili flakes and season with salt and pepper.
    Cover and bring to a boil. Uncover and lower the heat to a slow boil, then boil
    8 to 10 minutes until the cavolo nero is very tender.
2   Add the pasta for the final 4 to 6 minutes, or according to the pasta package
    directions, and cook until it is al dente. Adjust the salt and pepper, if necessary.
    Serve with olive oil on the side for drizzling.

237 Cuban Black Bean Soup

PREPARATION TIME 5 minutes   COOKING TIME 2½ hours

1⅔ cups dried black beans
5 ounces chopped bacon
1 long green chili, seeded (optional)
  and sliced
2 tablespoons ground cumin
1 tablespoon ground coriander
¼ cup olive or hemp oil
¼ cup white distilled vinegar
salt and freshly ground black pepper

TO SERVE
1 avocado
1 tablespoon lemon juice
shredded cilantro leaves
tortilla chips
sour cream
lime wedges

1   Put the beans in a saucepan and add enough water to cover by 3 inches.
    Cover, bring to a boil, and boil 10 minutes, then drain and set aside.
2   Meanwhile, put the bacon in another large saucepan and fry, stirring occasionally,
    2 to 4 minutes until it browns and crisps. Stir in the chili, then add the beans and
    2½ quarts water. Cover and bring to a boil, then lower the heat and simmer 1 hour.
3   Stir in the cumin, coriander, olive oil, and vinegar and simmer, covered, 45 minutes
    to 1 hour, stirring occasionally and topping up the water, if necessary, until
    the beans are tender and the soup thickens. If the soup is too thin, simmer
    15 minutes, uncovered.
4   Just before serving, peel, seed, and dice the avocado and toss it with the lemon
    juice. Season the soup with salt and pepper and serve topped with cilantro leaves
    and with the avocado, tortilla chips, sour cream, and lime wedges on the side.

238 Black-Eye Pea & Rice Soup

PREPARATION TIME 10 minutes, plus soaking the beans overnight and making the stock
COOKING TIME 55 minutes

1 cup dried black-eye peas
4½ cups Vegetable Stock
   (see page 12) or ready-made stock
2¼ cups tomato puree
2 large garlic cloves, finely chopped
1 celery rib, thinly sliced, with the
   leaves reserved and torn to serve

1 bouquet garni made with 1 bay leaf
   and several parsley and thyme
   sprigs tied together
a pinch of chili flakes, or to taste
½ cup white or brown long-grain rice
salt and freshly ground black pepper
chopped parsley leaves, to serve

1   Put the beans in a bowl, cover with water, and let soak overnight, then drain.
2   Put the beans, stock, tomato puree, garlic, celery, bouquet garni, and chili flakes, if using, in a saucepan. Cover and bring to a boil, then boil 10 minutes. Lower the heat and simmer 20 minutes.
3   Add the rice, season with salt and pepper, and increase the heat to a slow boil. Boil, uncovered, 10 to 20 minutes, depending on the type of rice, stirring often to prevent the rice from sticking to the bottom of the pan, until the beans and rice are tender.
4   Discard the bouquet garni and adjust the salt and pepper, if necessary, then serve sprinkled with the parsley and celery leaves. If reheating this soup, add a little extra stock, if necessary, to thin.

239 Borlotti Bean & Fennel Soup

PREPARATION TIME 10 minutes, plus overnight soaking and cooking the beans (optional) and making the stock   **COOKING TIME** 50 minutes

1 cup dried borlotti beans or
   1 can (15-oz.) borlotti beans,
   drained and rinsed
1½ tablespoons garlic-flavored
   olive oil
2 cups thinly sliced fennel
1 shallot, chopped
5½ cups Vegetable Stock
   (see page 12) or ready-made stock

1 can (15-oz.) crushed tomatoes
1 Parmesan or cheddar cheese rind,
   about 2 x 3 inches (see page 9)
1 tablespoon tomato paste
½ teaspoon sugar
2 handfuls of baby spinach leaves
freshly grated nutmeg, to taste
salt and freshly ground black pepper
chopped parsley leaves, to serve

1   If using dried beans, put them in a bowl, cover with water, and let soak overnight, then drain. Transfer to a saucepan, add 7 cups water, cover, and bring to a boil. Lower the heat and simmer, covered, 1 hour, then drain.
2   Heat the oil in a saucepan over medium heat. Add the fennel and shallot and fry, stirring occasionally, 5 to 8 minutes until softened and golden. Stir in the stock, tomatoes, cheese rind, tomato paste, and sugar and season with salt and pepper but remember the rind is salty. Cover and bring to a boil, then lower the heat and simmer 30 minutes.
3   Stir in the beans and simmer 3 minutes to warm through. Add the spinach and simmer 1 to 2 minutes until it wilts. Discard the cheese rind, add the nutmeg and adjust the salt and pepper, if necessary. Serve sprinkled with parsley.

Halloween Bean Soup

PREPARATION TIME 15 minutes, plus overnight soaking and cooking the beans
(optional), making the stock, and toasting the seeds   **COOKING TIME** 1 ½ hours

½ cup dried black beans or 1 cup
   canned black beans, drained
   and rinsed
1 tablespoon hemp or olive oil
1 large red onion, quartered and
   thinly sliced
2 large garlic cloves, chopped
5½ cups Vegetable Stock
   (see page 12) or ready-made stock
2 bay leaves
a pinch of chili flakes, or to taste

1 Parmesan or Cheddar cheese rind,
   about 2 x 3 inches (see page 9;
   optional)
2 cups peeled, seeded, and
   chopped pumpkin
2 handfuls of baby spinach leaves
salt and freshly ground black pepper
white sesame seeds, toasted
   (see page 9), to serve
black sesame seeds, to serve
chopped parsley leaves, to serve

1   If using dried beans, put them in a bowl, cover with water, and let soak overnight,
   then drain. Transfer to a saucepan, add 7 cups water, cover, and bring to a boil.
   Lower the heat and simmer, covered, 50 minutes to 1 hour, then drain.
2   Heat the oil in a saucepan over medium heat. Add the onion and fry, stirring,
   2 minutes. Add the garlic and stir 1 to 3 minutes until the onion is softened. Add
   the stock, bay leaves, chili flakes, and cheese rind, if using, and season with salt
   and pepper but remember the rind is salty, if using. Cover and bring to a boil. Add
   the pumpkin, lower the heat to medium, and simmer 5 to 8 minutes until tender.
3   Add the beans and heat through 3 minutes. Stir in the spinach and simmer
   1 to 2 minutes until it wilts. Discard the cheese rind, if used. Adjust the salt and
   pepper, if necessary, and serve sprinkled with sesame seeds and parsley.

241 Country-Style Bean & Vegetable Soup

PREPARATION TIME 25 minutes, plus soaking the beans overnight and making the stock
COOKING TIME 1¼ hours

1 cup dried navy beans
2 tablespoons chopped bacon
2 tablespoons sunflower oil
2 celery ribs, thinly sliced, with the
   leaves reserved
2 large garlic cloves, finely chopped
2 shallots, peeled and diced
1 carrot, peeled and diced
½ turnip, peeled and diced
5½ cups Chicken Stock (see page 11)
   or ready-made stock

1 bouquet garni made with the
   celery leaves, 1 bay leaf, and
   several parsley and thyme sprigs
   tied together
2 cups cored and chopped
   white cabbage
salt and freshly ground black pepper
finely chopped parsley leaves,
   to serve

1. Put the beans in a bowl, cover with water, and let soak overnight, then drain.
2. Heat a saucepan over medium-high heat. Add the bacon and fry, stirring, 30 seconds to 1 minute until its fat runs. Add the oil and lower the heat to medium. Stir in the celery, garlic, shallots, carrot, and turnip and fry, stirring occasionally, 5 to 8 minutes until softened but not colored.
3. Add the beans and stock, adding water, if necessary, so the vegetables are covered. Cover and bring to a boil. Skim, lower the heat, add the bouquet garni, and simmer, covered, 45 minutes.
4. Stir in the cabbage and season with salt and pepper. Cover and simmer 5 to 15 minutes until the beans are tender. Discard the bouquet garni and adjust the salt and pepper, if necessary. Serve sprinkled with parsley.

242 Nicola's Bean & Onion Soup

PREPARATION TIME 15 minutes, plus soaking the beans overnight, making the stock, and 1½ hours soaking the onions   **COOKING TIME** 1¼ hours

½ cup dried borlotti beans
3½ cups chopped onions
1 tablespoon extra-virgin olive oil,
   plus extra to serve
1 large carrot, peeled and quartered
1 celery rib, cut into large chunks

several sage sprigs, tied together
5½ cups Vegetable Stock
   (see page 12) or ready-made stock
2 bay leaves
salt and freshly ground black pepper

1. Put the beans in a bowl, cover with water, and let soak overnight, then drain.
2. Put the onions in a large bowl, cover with water, and let soak 1½ hours. Meanwhile, put the beans and enough water to generously cover in a saucepan. Cover and bring to a boil. Add the oil, carrots, celery, and sage, then lower the heat and simmer, covered, 50 minutes to 1 hour until the beans are tender. Strain the beans, discard the flavorings and set the cooking liquid aside.
3. Drain the onions and use your hands to squeeze out and discard the juices. Put the onions, stock, and bay leaves in another saucepan and season with salt and pepper. Cover and bring to a boil, then boil 5 minutes. Strain into a bowl and reserve both the onions and cooking liquid. Discard the bay leaves and return the onions and half the cooking liquid to the pan.
4. Blend the onions until smooth, then stir in enough of the remaining cooking liquid to achieve the preferred consistency. Rub the soup through a strainer for an even smoother texture, if you like. Adjust the salt and pepper, if necessary. Ladle the onion soup into bowls, spoon the beans over them and drizzle with oil. Serve with extra oil for adding at the table.

243 Winter Bean & Mushroom Soup

PREPARATION TIME 10 minutes, plus making the stock   COOKING TIME 40 minutes

1½ tablespoons olive or hemp oil
1 onion, chopped
2 garlic cloves
3½ cups trimmed and sliced
    portobello mushrooms
2½ cups Vegetable Stock
    (see page 12) or ready-made stock

1 can (15-oz.) crushed tomatoes
a pinch of sugar
2 teaspoons dried rosemary
2 cups drained and rinsed canned
    navy or cannellini beans,
salt and freshly ground black pepper
chopped parsley leaves, to serve

1   Heat the oil in a saucepan over medium heat. Add the onion and fry, stirring,
    2 minutes. Stir in the garlic and fry 1 to 3 minutes until the onions are softened.
    Add the mushrooms, season with salt, and stir 5 to 8 minutes until they give off
    their juices.
2   Stir in the stock, tomatoes, and sugar and season with salt and pepper. Cover and
    bring to a boil, then stir in the rosemary. Lower the heat and simmer, covered,
    15 minutes. Add the beans and warm through. Adjust the salt and pepper,
    if necessary, then serve sprinkled with parsley.

244 White Chili Soup

PREPARATION TIME 15 minutes, plus making the stock and cooking the chicken
COOKING TIME 20 minutes

1½ tablespoons olive oil
1 onion, chopped
2 large garlic cloves
1 green chili, seeded and chopped
1 teaspoon dried oregano
½ teaspoon dried thyme leaves
½ teaspoon ground cumin
¼ teaspoon cayenne pepper, or to taste

3¼ cups Chicken Stock (see page 11)
    or ready-made stock
2 cans (15-oz.) navy or cannellini
    beans, drained and rinsed
2 cups boneless, skinless cooked
    chicken cut into bite-size pieces
salt and freshly ground black pepper
chopped parsley leaves, to serve

1   Heat the oil in a saucepan over medium heat. Add the onion and fry, stirring,
    2 minutes. Add the garlic and chili and stir 1 to 3 minutes until the onion is softened
    but not colored. Add the oregano, thyme, cumin, and cayenne and stir 30 seconds.
    Watch closely so the spices do not burn. Add the stock and season with salt and
    pepper, then cover and bring to a boil.
2   Add the beans and chicken. Lower the heat and simmer, covered, 3 to 5 minutes
    to heat through. Adjust the salt and pepper, if necessary, then serve sprinkled
    with parsley.

245 Oat Soup with Carrot & Rutabaga

PREPARATION TIME 20 minutes, plus making the stock   COOKING TIME 45 minutes

2 tablespoons butter
1 tablespoon olive or hemp oil
2 carrots, peeled and finely diced
1 leek, halved lengthwise, sliced,
    and rinsed
1 onion, finely chopped
½ cup peeled and finely diced
    rutabaga

5½ cups Vegetable Stock
    (see page 12) or ready-made stock
½ cup fine rolled oats
1 bay leaf
⅔ cup milk
freshly grated nutmeg, to taste
salt and freshly ground black pepper
chopped parsley leaves, to serve

1   Melt the butter with the oil in a saucepan over medium heat. Add the carrots,
    leek, onion, and rutabaga and fry, stirring, 3 to 5 minutes until the vegetables are
    softened. Stir in the stock, oats, and bay leaf and season well with salt and pepper.
2   Bring to a boil, stirring, then lower the heat and simmer, covered, 25 to 30 minutes,
    stirring occasionally, until thick and the vegetables are tender. Stir in the milk,
    season with nutmeg, and reheat without boiling. Adjust the salt and pepper,
    if necessary, and serve sprinkled with parsley. If you reheat the soup, do not boil.

Green & White Bean Soup

PREPARATION TIME 20 minutes, plus soaking the beans overnight and making the stock
COOKING TIME 1½ hours

1 cup dried lima beans
2 tablespoons fruity extra-virgin olive
  oil, plus extra to serve
4 large garlic cloves, finely chopped
1 leek, thinly sliced and rinsed
1 onion, chopped
6 cups Vegetable Stock (see page 12)
  or ready-made stock
1 small handful of sage and ½ celery
  rib with its leaves, tied together

1 heel of prosciutto (see page 9;
  optional)
¼ head savoy cabbage, cored
  and shredded
½ cup chopped green beans
½ cup shelled fava beans, peeled
  if not young and tender
1 handful of baby spinach leaves
salt and freshly ground black pepper
pesto, to serve (optional)

1 Put the lima beans in a bowl, cover with water, and let soak overnight, then drain.
2 Heat the oil in a saucepan over medium heat. Stir in the garlic, leek, and onion,
  reduce the heat to low and cook, covered, 10 to 12 minutes, stirring occasionally,
  until softened but not colored. Stir in the lima beans and stock, cover, and bring
  to a boil. Skim, then lower the heat, stir in the sage and ham heel, if using,
  and simmer, covered, for 40 minutes to 1 hour until tender.
3 Remove the ham heel and set aside until cool enough to handle. Add the cabbage,
  green beans, and fava beans to the pan and simmer, uncovered, 10 to 12 minutes
  until all the beans are tender. Stir in the spinach and simmer 1 minute longer,
  or until the leaves wilt.
4 Remove the meat from the ham heel, shred it into small pieces, and set aside.
  Season the soup with salt and pepper, but remember the ham heel will have been
  salty. Serve with the ham sprinkled over the top, if used. Add a dollop of pesto
  to each portion and serve with olive oil on the side for drizzling.

247 Persian Lentil & Squash Soup

PREPARATION TIME 10 minutes, plus making the stock
COOKING TIME 45 minutes

¼ cup olive or hemp oil
1 large onion, chopped
2 large garlic cloves, crushed
1 teaspoon turmeric
6 cups Vegetable Stock (see page 12) or ready-made stock

1⅓ cups dried green lentils, rinsed
1 teaspoon cornstarch
2½ cups peeled and diced butternut squash
salt and freshly ground black pepper
shredded mint leaves, to serve

1 Heat the oil in a saucepan. Add the onion and fry, stirring, 2 minutes. Add the garlic and fry 1 to 3 minutes until the onion is softened. Stir in the turmeric, then add the stock and lentils, cover, and bring to a boil. Lower the heat and simmer 15 minutes. Meanwhile, put the cornstarch and 1 tablespoon cold water in a small bowl and mix until smooth.

2 Stir the cornstarch mixture and squash into the soup and season with salt and pepper. Cover and return to a boil, then lower the heat and simmer 12 to 15 minutes until the lentils and squash are tender and the soup thickens slightly. Adjust the salt and pepper, if necessary, and serve sprinkled with mint.

248 Lima Bean Soup with Carrots & Bacon

PREPARATION TIME 15 minutes, plus soaking the beans overnight and making the stock
COOKING TIME 1¼ hours

1 cup dried lima beans
¼ cup olive or hemp oil
several thyme sprigs, tied together
1 bay leaf
1 small carrot, grated
1 large onion, chopped
1¼ cups milk

1¾ cups Chicken Stock (see page 11) or ready-made stock, plus extra as needed
3 slices of bacon
salt and freshly ground black pepper
snipped chives, to serve

1 Put the beans in a bowl, cover with water, and let soak overnight, then drain.

2 Put the beans and water to cover generously in a large saucepan. Cover and bring to a boil, then skim. Lower the heat, add the olive oil and thyme, and simmer, covered, 35 minutes. Strain the beans, reserving the cooking liquid, and discard the thyme. Return the beans to the pan, add the bay leaf, carrot, onion, milk, and stock and season with salt and pepper. Bring to just below the boil, then lower the heat and simmer 15 to 25 minutes until the beans are tender.

3 Meanwhile, heat the broiler to high, then broil the bacon 5 minutes, turning once, or until crisp. Chop and set aside.

4 Discard the bay leaf and blend one-third of the soup until smooth. Work the mixture through a strainer back into the pan, using a spoon, then stir well. If the soup is too thick, add a little of the reserved cooking liquid. Adjust the salt and pepper, if necessary, and serve sprinkled with the bacon and chives.

249 Italian Tortellini Soup

PREPARATION TIME 5 minutes, plus making the stock   COOKING TIME 20 minutes

6 cups any homemade stock (see pages 10–13) or ready-made stock
1 pound 2 ounces fresh or dried tortellini, with your favorite filling

salt and freshly ground black pepper
freshly grated Parmesan cheese, to serve
fruity extra-virgin olive oil, to serve

1 Bring the stock to a boil in a covered saucepan over high heat. Add the pasta and season with salt and pepper. Return to a boil, then boil about 2 minutes for fresh, or 10 to 12 minutes for dried pasta, or according to the package directions, until the pasta is al dente and rises to the surface.

2 Serve sprinkled with Parmesan and with olive oil for drizzling over.

250 Pureed Kidney Bean Soup

PREPARATION TIME 15 minutes, plus soaking the beans overnight and making the stock
COOKING TIME 2½ hours

1 cup dried red kidney beans
6½ cups Vegetable Stock
  (see page 12) or ready-made stock
1 tablespoon butter
1 tablespoon olive or hemp oil
2 celery ribs, chopped
1 carrot, peeled and chopped
1 onion, chopped
4 garlic cloves, chopped

½ teaspoon ground coriander
½ teaspoon ground cumin
a pinch of cayenne pepper,
  or to taste
1 bay leaf
salt and freshly ground black pepper
Greek-style or plain yogurt, to serve
snipped chives, to serve

1   Put the beans in a bowl, cover with water, and let soak overnight, then drain.
2   Put the beans and stock in a saucepan. Cover, bring to a boil, and boil 10 minutes, then skim.
3   Meanwhile, melt the butter with the oil in another saucepan over medium heat. Add the celery, carrot, and onion and fry, stirring, 2 minutes. Add the garlic and stir 1 to 3 minutes until the onion is softened. Add the coriander, cumin, and cayenne and fry 30 seconds. Watch closely so the spices do not burn.
4   Add the stock and beans to the vegetables and add the bay leaf. Cover and return to a boil. Skim the surface again. Lower the heat and simmer 1½ to 2 hours until the beans are very tender.
5   Discard the bay leaf, then blend the soup until smooth. Season with salt and pepper and serve topped with yogurt and sprinkled with chives.

251 Fava Bean & Spinach Soup

PREPARATION TIME 20 minutes, plus overnight soaking and cooking the beans (optional) and making the stock **COOKING TIME** 30 minutes

1 cup dried fava beans or 1 can
  (15-oz.) fava beans, drained
  and rinsed
1½ tablespoons olive or hemp oil
2 shallots, chopped
2 large garlic cloves, chopped
½ to 1 tablespoon smoked paprika
2 teaspoons ground cumin

2 teaspoons ground coriander
6 cups Vegetable Stock (see page 12)
  or ready-made stock
1 can (15-oz.) crushed tomatoes
2 cups thinly sliced spinach leaves
salt and freshly ground black pepper
ground sumac, to serve
chopped cilantro leaves, to serve

1   If using dried beans, put them in a bowl, cover with water, and let soak overnight, then drain. Transfer to a saucepan and add 7 cups water. Cover and bring to a boil, lower the heat, and simmer, covered, 1 hour, then drain.
2   Heat the oil in a saucepan over medium heat. Add the shallots and fry, stirring, 2 minutes. Stir in the garlic and fry 1 to 3 minutes until the shallots are softened but not colored. Add the paprika, cumin, and coriander and stir 30 seconds. Watch closely so the spices do not burn.
3   Add the stock and tomatoes and season with salt and pepper. Cover and bring to a boil. Lower the heat and simmer 10 minutes for the flavors to blend. Meanwhile, if you have cooked dried beans, remove the thick outer skins.
4   Stir the beans and spinach into the pan and simmer 2 to 3 minutes until the beans are hot and the spinach wilts. Adjust the salt and pepper, if necessary, then serve sprinkled with sumac and cilantro.

252 The Italian Doctor's Bean & Spaghetti Soup

PREPARATION TIME 15 minutes, plus soaking the beans overnight
COOKING TIME 1½ hours

1 cup dried lima beans
1 carrot, peeled
1 celery rib, broken in half
1 onion, peeled and quartered
1 small bunch sage, tied together
¼ cup extra-virgin olive oil, plus
   extra to serve

3½ ounces spaghetti, broken into
   small pieces
salt and freshly ground black pepper
freshly grated Parmesan cheese,
   to serve

1 Put the beans in a bowl, cover with water, and let soak overnight, then drain.
2 Put the beans, carrot, celery, onion, sage, oil, and 2 quarts water in a saucepan. Cover and bring to a boil. Lower the heat and simmer 1¼ hours, stirring occasionally, until the beans are almost tender, then strain, reserving the cooking liquid. Discard the carrot, celery, and sage and blend the onion and one-third of the beans until smooth. Return the mixture to the pan and stir in the remaining beans and 6 cups of the cooking liquid. Season with salt and pepper.
3 Bring to a boil, stirring occasionally. Stir in the spaghetti and boil 8 to 10 minutes, or according to the package directions, until the pasta is al dente and the beans are tender. Stir frequently to prevent the spaghetti from sticking to the bottom of the pan. Adjust the salt and pepper, if necessary, then serve drizzled with olive oil and with cheese on the side.

253 Chickpea & Chorizo Soup

PREPARATION TIME 15 minutes, plus overnight soaking and cooking the chickpeas
(optional) and making the stock COOKING TIME 1½ hours

1 cup dried chickpeas or 1 can
   (15-oz.) chickpeas, drained
   and rinsed
1 tablespoon olive oil
3 ounces chorizo, casing removed
   and chopped
1 celery rib, finely chopped
4 large garlic cloves, finely chopped

1 red onion, finely chopped
1 can (15-oz.) crushed tomatoes
1 tablespoon tomato paste
½ teaspoon sugar
4½ cups Chicken Stock (see page 11)
   or ready-made stock
salt and freshly ground black pepper
fruity extra-virgin olive oil, to serve

1 If using dried chickpeas, put them in a bowl, cover with water, and let soak overnight, then drain. Transfer to a saucepan, add 7 cups water, cover, and bring to a boil. Lower the heat and simmer, covered, 50 minutes to 1 hour until almost tender, then drain.
2 Heat the oil in a saucepan over medium heat. Add the chorizo and fry, stirring, 2 to 3 minutes until the fat starts to run. Remove from the pan and set aside. Stir the celery, garlic, and onion into the fat remaining in the pan, reduce the heat to low, and cook, covered, 8 to 10 minutes until the onion and celery are softened. Stir in the chickpeas, tomatoes, tomato paste, and sugar.
3 Add the stock and season with salt and pepper. Cover and bring to a boil. Skim, then reduce the heat to low and simmer, covered, 10 minutes.
4 Blend half of the soup until smooth. Stir this mixture back into the soup, add the chorizo, and reheat. Adjust the salt and pepper, if necessary, and serve drizzled with fruity olive oil.

Syrian Red Lentil & Lamb Soup

PREPARATION TIME 10 minutes, plus making the stock   **COOKING TIME** 1¼ hours

5½ cups Vegetable Stock
  (see page 12) or water
1½ pounds lamb shoulder chops
1 cup split red lentils, rinsed and
  picked over
1 carrot, peeled and chopped
1 onion, peeled and finely chopped
1 teaspoon dried mint leaves
½ teaspoon ground coriander

½ teaspoon ground cumin
½ teaspoon cayenne pepper,
  or to taste
a pinch of saffron threads
salt and freshly ground black pepper
chopped cilantro or parsley leaves,
  to serve
lemon wedges, to serve
hot pepper sauce, to serve (optional)

1 Put the stock, lamb, lentils, carrot, onion, mint, coriander, cumin, cayenne, and saffron in a saucepan. Cover and bring to a boil. Reduce the heat to very low (use a heat diffuser if you have one) and simmer 1 to 1¼ hours until the lamb is tender and the lentils have fallen apart.

2 Remove the lamb and bones from the soup and set aside until cool enough to handle. Skim the soup, if necessary. Cut the meat from the bones into bite-size pieces and return to the soup. Stir well and season with salt and pepper.

3 Serve sprinkled with cilantro leaves and with lemon wedges for squeezing over and hot pepper sauce for adding at the table, if you like.

255 Mexican Bean Soup

PREPARATION TIME 15 minutes, plus overnight soaking and cooking the beans,
30 minutes soaking the chili, and making the stock   **COOKING TIME** 1 hour

½ cup dried red kidney beans
½ cup dried pinto beans
1 dried chipotle chili
1 tablespoon sunflower oil
1 onion, chopped
2 large garlic cloves,
   finely chopped
1 teaspoon ground cumin
4 cups Vegetable Stock
   (see page 12) or
   ready-made stock

1 can (15-oz.) crushed tomatoes
½ tablespoon dried oregano
a pinch of caster sugar
1½ cups frozen corn kernels
salt and freshly ground black pepper
sour cream, to serve
chopped cilantro leaves,
   to serve
tortilla chips, to serve

1   Put the kidney and pinto beans in a bowl, cover with water, and let soak overnight,
    then drain. Transfer to a saucepan and add 7 cups water. Cover, bring to a boil
    over high heat and boil 10 minutes. Lower the heat and simmer, covered, 1 hour,
    then drain.
2   Put the chipotle chili and at least 1 cup boiling water in a heatproof bowl and let
    soak 30 minutes, or until tender, then strain, reserving 1 cup of the water. Seed
    the chili, if you like, then finely chop and set aside.
3   Heat the oil in a saucepan over medium heat. Add the onion and fry, stirring,
    2 minutes. Add the garlic and fry 1 to 3 minutes until the onion is softened.
    Add the cumin and stir 30 seconds, or until it is aromatic. Watch closely
    so it does not burn. Stir in the reserved soaking liquid, beans, chili, stock, tomatoes,
    oregano, and sugar and season with salt and pepper.
4   Cover and bring to a boil, then lower the heat and simmer 40 to 50 minutes
    until the beans are tender.
5   Blend about one-third of the soup until smooth. Return this mixture to the soup,
    add the corn and boil 3 to 5 minutes until it is tender. Adjust the salt and pepper,
    if necessary, and serve topped with sour cream and cilantro and with tortilla
    chips on the side.

256 Red Lentil, Coconut & Spinach Soup

PREPARATION TIME 20 minutes, plus making the stock and seeds
COOKING TIME 55 minutes

2 tablespoons peanut
   or sunflower oil
1 large onion, chopped
1 large garlic clove, chopped
1-inch piece of gingerroot,
   peeled and grated
1 red chili, seeded and chopped
1 teaspoon ground coriander
1 teaspoon ground cumin
½ teaspoon turmeric
4½ cups Vegetable Stock
   (see page 12) or ready-made stock

½ cup split red lentils, rinsed
1 can (15-oz.) crushed tomatoes
½ teaspoon sugar
¾ cup plus 2 tablespoons
   coconut milk
2 handfuls of baby spinach leaves,
   chopped
salt and freshly ground black pepper
Spiced Seeds (see page 15), to serve
chopped cilantro leaves, to serve

1   Heat the oil in a saucepan over medium heat. Add the onion and fry, stirring,
    2 minutes. Add the garlic, ginger, and chili and stir 1 to 3 minutes until the onion
    is softened. Add the coriander, cumin, and turmeric and stir 30 seconds. Watch
    closely so the spices do not burn. Add the stock, lentils, tomatoes, and sugar.
    Cover and bring to a boil, then lower the heat and simmer 20 minutes.
2   Stir in the coconut milk and season with salt and pepper, then simmer, covered,
    10 to 20 minutes longer until the lentils are very tender. Add the spinach and
    simmer 2 to 3 minutes until it wilts. Adjust the salt and pepper, if necessary,
    and serve sprinkled with the seeds and chopped cilantro.

257 South Indian Lentil & Tomato Soup

PREPARATION TIME 15 minutes, plus making the chili bon-bon (optional)
COOKING TIME 50 minutes

6 large garlic cloves, chopped
1 long red chili, seeded and sliced
1½ tablespoons sunflower
   or peanut oil
1 large onion, finely chopped
3 tablespoons split red lentils, rinsed
2 cans (15-oz.) crushed tomatoes
1 tablespoon tomato paste

2 tablespoons tamarind paste
¼ teaspoon black mustard seeds
¼ teaspoon fenugreek seeds
4 curry leaves
a pinch of ground asafetida
salt and freshly ground black pepper
Chili Bon-Bon, to serve (optional)

1 Put the garlic and chili in a mortar and pound until a paste forms, then set aside.
2 Heat 1 tablespoon of the oil in a saucepan over medium heat. Add the onion and fry, stirring, 3 to 5 minutes until softened but not colored. Add the garlic-chili paste and stir 30 seconds, or until aromatic. Watch closely so the paste does not burn. Stir in the lentils, tomatoes, tomato paste, and 6 cups water, then cover and bring to a boil.
3 Add the tamarind paste and stir until it dissolves. Lower the heat and simmer, covered, 30 to 40 minutes until the lentils are tender. Season with salt and pepper, if necessary. Strain the soup for an even smoother texture, if you like.
4 Before serving, heat the remaining oil in a small skillet over high heat. Add the mustard seeds and stir about 30 seconds, or until they pop. Stir in the fenugreek seeds, curry leaves, and asafetida, then pour this mixture over the soup. Serve with chili bon-bon on the side for adding at the table, if you like.

258 Yellow Lentil Soup

PREPARATION TIME 15 minutes, plus making the stock   COOKING TIME 40 minutes

2 tablespoons ghee or butter
1 tablespoon peanut or sunflower oil
1 onion, finely chopped
½-inch piece of gingerroot, peeled
   and grated
6 green cardamom pods,
   lightly crushed
1 teaspoon turmeric
½ teaspoon ground coriander
½ teaspoon cumin seeds
a pinch of ground asafetida
a pinch of cayenne pepper,
   or to taste

½ cup split yellow lentils (toor dal),
   rinsed
6 cups Vegetable Stock (see page 12)
   or water
2 cilantro sprigs, leaves and stems,
   chopped, plus extra torn leaves
   to serve
lemon juice, to taste
salt and freshly ground black pepper
plain yogurt, to serve (optional)
garam masala, to serve

1 Melt the ghee with the oil in a saucepan over medium heat. Add the onion and fry, stirring occasionally, 3 to 5 minutes until softened but not colored. Add the ginger, cardamom, turmeric, coriander, cumin seeds, asafetida, and cayenne and stir 30 seconds, or until aromatic. Watch closely so the spices do not burn.
2 Add the lentils, stock, and cilantro leaves and stems. Cover and bring to a boil, then lower the heat and simmer 20 to 25 minutes until the lentils are very tender and starting to fall apart. Use a slotted spoon to fish out and discard the cardamom pods, then blend the soup to the preferred consistency. Add lemon juice and season with salt and pepper. Serve topped with yogurt and sprinkled with garam masala and cilantro leaves.

259 Sour Green Lentil Soup

PREPARATION TIME 10 minutes, plus making the stock   COOKING TIME 50 minutes

1 tablespoon peanut or sunflower oil
1 large onion, finely chopped
2 garlic cloves, finely chopped
1 teaspoon ground coriander
1 teaspoon ground cumin
¼ teaspoon chili flakes, or to taste
½ teaspoon cinnamon
5½ cups Vegetable Stock
    (see page 12) or ready-made stock

1 can (15-oz.) crushed tomatoes
½ cup dried green lentils, rinsed
2 tablespoons tamarind paste
2 tablespoons tomato paste
1 teaspoon sugar
salt and freshly ground black pepper
chopped cilantro leaves, to serve

1   Heat the oil in a saucepan over high heat. Add the onion and fry, stirring, 2 minutes.
    Add the garlic and fry 1 to 3 minutes until the onion is softened but not colored.
    Add the coriander, cumin, chili flakes, and cinnamon and stir 30 seconds. Watch
    closely so the spices do not burn.
2   Add the stock, tomatoes, lentils, tamarind paste, tomato paste, and sugar. Cover
    and bring to a boil, then lower the heat and simmer 30 to 40 minutes until
    the lentils are tender. Season with salt and pepper and serve sprinkled with
    chopped cilantro.

260 Puy Lentil & Fennel Soup

PREPARATION TIME 15 minutes, plus making the stock   COOKING TIME 40 minutes

2 tablespoons olive or hemp oil
1 celery rib, sliced
2½ cups quartered and thinly
    sliced fennel, with the
    fronds reserved
1 shallot, finely chopped
4 large garlic cloves, finely chopped
6 cups Vegetable Stock (see page 12)
    or ready-made stock

½ cup dried Puy lentils, rinsed
½ tablespoon dried dill
2 bay leaves
1 large handful of arugula leaves
salt and freshly ground black pepper
freshly grated Parmesan or pecorino
    cheese, to serve (optional)

1   Heat the oil in a saucepan over medium heat. Add the celery, fennel, and shallot
    and fry, stirring, 2 minutes. Add the garlic and fry 1 to 3 minutes until the
    vegetables are softened but not colored. Add the stock, lentils, dill, and bay leaves,
    then cover and bring to a boil. Lower the heat and simmer 20 to 30 minutes until
    the lentils are tender.
2   Discard the bay leaves and season with salt and pepper. Stir in the arugula leaves
    and simmer, uncovered, 2 to 3 minutes until they wilt. Serve with cheese for
    sprinkling over, if you like.

261 Starry Night Soup with Spinach

PREPARATION TIME 5 minutes, plus making the stock   COOKING TIME 15 minutes

6 cups any homemade stock
    (see pages 10–13)
1⅓ cups stelline, or other small
    soup pasta
a small pinch of chili flakes

2 large handfuls of baby
    spinach leaves
salt and freshly ground black pepper
fruity extra-virgin olive oil, to serve
freshly grated Parmesan cheese,
    to serve

1   Put the stock in a saucepan and season with salt and pepper. Cover and bring
    to a boil. Add the pasta and chili flakes and return to a boil, then boil 2 minutes.
2   Stir in the spinach and boil 1 to 3 minutes until the pasta is al dente. Adjust the
    salt and pepper, if necessary. Serve immediately, sprinkled with Parmesan and
    drizzled with oil.

262 Thai Chicken & Jasmine Rice Soup

PREPARATION TIME 10 minutes, plus making the chilies and garlic
COOKING TIME 30 minutes

2 cilantro sprigs, including roots,
  stems, and leaves, coarsely
  chopped, plus extra leaves to serve
½-inch piece of galangal, peeled and
  smashed in one piece
½-inch piece of gingerroot, peeled
  and smashed in one piece
1 pound 2 ounces skinned
  chicken thighs

¾ cup jasmine rice, rinsed with cold
  water and drained
1 teaspoon salt
Chilies in Vinegar (see page 15),
  to serve
Crisp-Fried Garlic (see page 15),
  to serve
fish sauce, to serve

1   Put the cilantro, galangal, ginger, and 5½ cups water in a saucepan. Cover and bring
    to a boil. Add the chicken, cover, and return to a boil. Skim, then lower the heat and
    simmer 15 to 20 minutes until the chicken is cooked through. Remove
    the chicken and set aside until cool enough to handle. Discard the cilantro stems,
    galangal, and ginger and keep the soup simmering.
2   Meanwhile, put the rice and salt in another saucepan and cover with enough water
    to come up to the first joint in your finger from the top of the rice. Bring to a boil,
    uncovered. As soon as the water boils, lower the heat and simmer, covered,
    6 to 10 minutes until the rice is tender and has absorbed most of the liquid. Turn
    off the heat, immediately stir in 4 ladlefuls of the chicken cooking liquid and let the
    rice stand, uncovered, until the soup is ready. If the rice dries out and holes appear
    on the surface, add more of the cooking liquid.
3   Cut the chicken from the bones into bite-size pieces and return it to the soup.
    Divide the rice into bowls and ladle the soup over it. Serve sprinkled with cilantro
    and with the chilies, fried garlic and fish sauce on the side.

263 Lentil & Sausage Soup

PREPARATION TIME 20 minutes, plus making the stock   COOKING TIME 55 minutes

2 ounces thickly chopped bacon
1 carrot, peeled and finely chopped
1 celery rib, finely chopped
2 shallots, finely chopped
½ leek, thinly sliced and rinsed
1 teaspoon dried thyme leaves
½ teaspoon ground cumin
a pinch of ground cloves
5½ cups Vegetable Stock (see
  page 12) or ready-made stock
1½ cups dried Puy or other
  green lentils, rinsed

1 bay leaf
2 tablespoons garlic-flavored olive oil
3 pork sausages, such as Toulouse
  or Italian sweet
1 large roasted red pepper
  in olive oil, drained and chopped
salt and freshly ground black pepper
chopped parsley leaves, to serve
balsamic or red wine vinegar,
  to serve

1   Heat a large saucepan over medium-high heat. Add the bacon and fry, stirring,
    5 to 7 minutes until it is lightly colored and starting to give off its fat. Stir in the
    carrot, celery, shallots and leek and cover. Reduce the heat to low and cook
    10 to 12 minutes until light brown. Stir in the thyme, cumin, and cloves. Add
    the stock, lentils, and bay leaf. Cover and bring to a boil. Lower the heat and
    simmer 10 minutes.
2   Meanwhile, heat the oil in a small skillet over high heat. Add the sausages and fry,
    turning occasionally, until brown all over. Transfer the sausages to the pan with
    the lentils and simmer, covered, 15 to 20 minutes until the lentils are tender and
    the sausages are cooked through. Remove the sausages and slice diagonally, then
    return to the pan, add the red pepper, and heat through. Season with salt and
    pepper, then serve sprinkled with parsley and with vinegar on the side.

Red Rice & Wild Arugula Soup

PREPARATION TIME 10 minutes, plus making the stock   **COOKING TIME** 55 minutes

6½ cups Vegetable Stock
  (see page 12) or ready-made stock
4 large garlic cloves, crushed
1 teaspoon fennel seeds
1½ tablespoons olive or hemp oil,
  plus extra to serve (optional)
2 shallots, halved lengthwise and
  thinly sliced

½ cup red rice
1 teaspoon dried thyme leaves
2 large handfuls of wild or cultivated
  arugula leaves, rinsed and torn
salt and freshly ground black pepper
French bread, to serve

1   Put the stock, garlic, and fennel seeds in a saucepan. Cover and bring to a boil, then boil slowly 10 minutes to blend the flavors. Strain the stock, discarding the garlic and seeds, and set aside.

2   Heat the oil in a saucepan over medium heat. Add the shallots and fry, stirring occasionally, 3 to 5 minutes until softened but not colored. Stir in the rice, then add the stock and thyme and season with salt and pepper. Cover and bring to a boil. Lower the heat and simmer 20 to 25 minutes, or according to the package directions, until the rice is tender but chewy.

3   Add the arugula and simmer, uncovered, 2 to 3 minutes until it wilts. Adjust the salt and pepper, if necessary, and serve with French bread.

265 Brown Lentil Soup

PREPARATION TIME 15 minutes, plus making the stock and seeds
COOKING TIME 1 hour

2 tablespoons garlic-flavored olive oil
1 carrot, diced
1 celery rib, finely chopped
1 onion, finely chopped
1 turnip, finely chopped
5½ cups Vegetable Stock
  (see page 12) or ready-made stock

1 cup dried brown lentils, rinsed
1 rosemary sprig
salt and freshly ground black pepper
Spiced Seeds (see page 15), to serve
chopped cilantro leaves, to serve

1 Heat the oil in a saucepan over medium heat. Add the carrot, celery, onion,
and turnip, reduce the heat to low, and cook 8 to 10 minutes, stirring occasionally,
until the vegetables are softened but not colored.
2 Add the stock, lentils, and rosemary. Cover and bring to a boil. Lower the heat and
simmer 35 to 40 minutes until the lentils are tender. Discard the rosemary sprig
and season with salt and pepper. Serve sprinkled with seeds and cilantro.

266 Canadian Yellow Pea Soup

PREPARATION TIME 15 minutes, plus making the stock and flavored oil
COOKING TIME 1 ½ hours

2 tablespoons olive or sunflower oil
1 carrot, peeled and very
  finely diced
1 celery rib, very finely chopped
1 onion, very finely chopped
7 cups Chicken Stock (see page 11)
  or ready-made stock

1 cup yellow split peas, rinsed
2 bay leaves
1½ cups shredded smoked ham
salt and freshly ground black pepper
1 recipe quantity Paprika & Lemon
  Oil (see page 26), to serve

1 Heat the olive oil in a large saucepan over medium heat. Stir in the carrot, celery,
and onion, reduce the heat to low and cook, covered, 8 to 10 minutes, stirring
occasionally, until softened but not colored.
2 Add the stock, split peas, and bay leaves, cover, and bring to a boil. Reduce
the heat to very low (use a heat diffuser if you have one) and simmer, stirring
occasionally, 1 ¼ to 1 ½ hours until the peas are very tender. Stir in the ham and
heat through. Season with salt and pepper, but remember the ham will probably
be salty. Discard the bay leaves. Serve drizzled with the paprika oil.

267 Split Pea & Apple Soup

PREPARATION TIME 15 minutes   COOKING TIME 2 hours

2 sweet apples, peeled, quartered,
  cored and chopped
1 tablespoon lemon juice
2 tablespoons sunflower oil
2 leeks, sliced and rinsed
1 cup green split peas, rinsed

7 cups Vegetable Stock (see page 12)
1 teaspoon ground ginger
lemon juice, to taste
½ cup heavy cream
salt and freshly ground black pepper

1 Toss the apples and lemon juice together in a bowl and set aside.
2 Heat the oil in a saucepan over medium heat. Add the leeks and fry, stirring
occasionally, 3 to 5 minutes until softened but not colored. Stir in the split peas
and stock, cover, and bring to a boil. Skim, if necessary, then lower the heat and
simmer, covered, 1 ¼ hours.
3 Add the apples and simmer, covered, 15 to 30 minutes until the split peas are very
tender. Season with salt and pepper, then blend the soup until smooth. Stir in the
ginger and add lemon juice to taste. Stir in the cream and reheat the soup,
if necessary. Adjust the salt and pepper, if necessary, and serve. If reheating this
soup, add a little extra stock, if necessary, to thin.

Split Pea & Ham Soup

PREPARATION TIME 15 minutes, plus making the flavored oil   **COOKING TIME** 2 hours

2 tablespoons sunflower oil
2 celery ribs, finely chopped
1 carrot, peeled and finely chopped
1 onion, finely chopped
1 cooked unsmoked ham bone with
  any meat that is left on it
1 cup green split peas, rinsed
2 bay leaves

½ tablespoon dried thyme leaves
2 cups diced or shredded
  cooked ham
sugar, to taste (optional)
salt and freshly ground black pepper
1 recipe quantity Crushed Mint Oil
  (see page 15), to serve

1   Heat the oil in a large saucepan over medium heat. Stir in the celery, carrot,
    and onion, reduce the heat to low, cover, and cook, stirring occasionally,
    8 to 10 minutes until softened but not colored.

2   Add the ham bone and split peas to the pan and stir in 7 cups water. Cover and
    bring to a boil. Skim, if necessary. Stir in the bay leaves and thyme, reduce the heat
    to very low (use a heat diffuser if you have one), and simmer, covered, stirring
    frequently, 1½ to 2 hours, until the split peas are very tender and have thickened
    the soup and any meat is coming away from the bone.

3   Remove the bone from the pan and set aside. When it is cool enough to handle,
    shred any meat that might have been on it. Return the meat to the soup, add the
    ham and heat through. Adjust the salt and pepper, if necessary, but remember
    the ham is salty so you might only need pepper; if the soup is too salty, stir in
    a little sugar. Serve drizzled with the mint oil.

269 Black Lentil & Cauliflower Soup

PREPARATION TIME 20 minutes, plus making the stock and preparing the tomatoes
COOKING TIME 1 ¼ hours

6½ cups Vegetable Stock
(see page 12) or ready-made stock
¾ cup split black lentils (urad dal),
rinsed
4 cilantro sprigs, leaves and stems
chopped, plus extra chopped
leaves to serve
seeds from 6 green cardamom pods,
3 cloves, 3 sliced garlic cloves,
1 bay leaf, ½ cinnamon stick, and
1 teaspoon crushed coriander
seeds, tied together in cheesecloth

½-inch piece of gingerroot,
peeled and grated
1 tablespoon peanut or sunflower oil
1 onion, finely chopped
2 garlic cloves, crushed
1 teaspoon cumin seeds
a pinch of chili flakes, or to taste
2 large tomatoes, grated (see page 9)
2 cups cauliflower florets
salt and freshly ground black pepper

1   Put the stock, lentils, cilantro, spice bundle and ginger in a saucepan. Cover and bring to a boil, then lower the heat and simmer 35 to 40 minutes until the lentils are very soft.
2   Meanwhile, heat the oil in another saucepan over medium heat. Add the onion and fry, stirring, 2 minutes. Add the garlic and fry 1 to 3 minutes until the onion is softened. Add the cumin seeds and chili flakes and stir 30 seconds, or until aromatic. Watch closely so the seeds do not burn. Stir in the tomatoes.
3   Remove two-thirds of the lentils from the soup and set aside. Discard the spice bundle. Add the tomato and onion mixture to the pan with the lentils and blend until smooth. Season with salt and pepper, then return the soup to a boil, skimming as necessary.
4   Add the cauliflower and gently boil, uncovered, 10 to 12 minutes until the florets are tender. Return the reserved lentils to the pan and heat through. Adjust the salt and pepper, if necessary, and serve sprinkled with cilantro.

270 Rice & Purple Broccoli Soup

PREPARATION TIME 10 minutes, plus making the stock   COOKING TIME 35 minutes

2 ounces chopped bacon
1 tablespoon olive oil
1 onion, finely chopped
1 garlic clove, crushed
¾ cup Arborio rice

6½ cups Chicken Stock
(see page 11) or ready-made stock
1 cup small purple or green
broccoli florets
2 sprigs fresh thyme
salt and freshly ground black pepper

1   This soup is best served just after making and not left to stand, or it will become too thick. Put the bacon in a saucepan over medium heat and fry, stirring, 3 to 5 minutes until it begins to crisp and the fat runs. Remove it from the pan and set aside. Add the oil to the fat remaining in the pan and heat. Add the onion and fry, stirring, 2 minutes. Add the garlic and fry 1 to 3 minutes until the onion is softened but not colored. Add the rice and stir 1 minute.
2   Add a ladleful of the stock and stir until it is absorbed. Stir in the remaining stock, cover, and bring to a boil, then reduce the heat to low. Add the broccoli and thyme and season with salt and pepper.
3   Simmer, uncovered, 15 to 18 minutes until the rice is tender, stirring occasionally to prevent it from sticking to the bottom of the pan. Add the bacon and discard the thyme sprigs. Adjust the salt and pepper, if necessary, and serve immediately.

271 Creamed Barley Soup

PREPARATION TIME 15 minutes, plus making the stock and toasting the seeds
COOKING TIME 50 minutes

1½ tablespoons olive or hemp oil
1 large onion, sliced
3 garlic cloves, finely chopped
½ cup pearl barley
6 cups Vegetable Stock (see page 12)
  or ready-made stock
1¼ cups peeled, seeded,
  and diced pumpkin

1 leek, sliced and rinsed
¼ cup plain yogurt (optional)
salt and freshly ground black pepper
pumpkin seeds, toasted (see page 9),
  to serve
chopped cilantro leaves, to serve

1 Heat the oil in a saucepan over medium heat. Add the onion and fry, stirring occasionally, 2 minutes. Add the garlic and fry 1 to 3 minutes until the onion is softened but not colored.
2 Stir in the barley and stock. Cover and bring to a boil. Skim the surface. Stir in the pumpkin and leek, lower the heat, and simmer, covered, 30 to 40 minutes until the barley is very tender, then season with salt and pepper. Blend half the soup for an even smoother texture, if you like.
3 Stir in the yogurt, if using, and adjust the salt and pepper, if necessary. Serve immediately, sprinkled with seeds and cilantro.

272 Egyptian Brown Lentil & Greens Soup

PREPARATION TIME 15 minutes, plus making the stock and dukkah
COOKING TIME 45 minutes

1 tablespoon garlic-flavored
  olive oil
1 onion, chopped
2 large garlic cloves,
  finely chopped
6 cups Vegetable Stock
  (see page 12) or ready-made stock
1 cup dried brown lentils, rinsed

4 cups chopped leaves from
  kale or mustard greens
1 handful of cilantro leaves,
  chopped
2 to 4 tablespoons lemon juice
salt and freshly ground black pepper
Dukkah (see page 15), to serve

1 Heat the oil in a saucepan over medium heat. Add the onion and fry, stirring, 2 minutes. Add the garlic and fry 1 to 3 minutes until the onion is softened but not colored. Add the stock and lentils, cover and bring to a boil, then lower the heat and simmer 15 minutes.
2 Add the greens, cilantro and 2 tablespoons of the lemon juice and simmer 15 to 20 minutes longer until the lentils are tender. Season with salt and pepper, adding extra lemon juice, if you like. Serve sprinkled with dukkah.

273 Greek Lentil & Garlic Soup

PREPARATION TIME 10 minutes, plus making the stock   COOKING TIME 55 minutes

2 tablespoons olive or hemp oil
8 garlic cloves, crushed
2 onions, chopped
1 can (15-oz.) crushed tomatoes
1 cup split red lentils, rinsed
4½ cups Chicken Stock (see page 11)
  or ready-made stock

1 bay leaf
1 tablespoon tomato paste
1 teaspoon sugar
salt and freshly ground black pepper
finely chopped cilantro or mint
  leaves, to serve
red wine vinegar, to serve

1 Heat the oil in a large saucepan over medium heat. Stir in the garlic and onions, reduce the heat to low, and cook, covered, 10 to 12 minutes until softened. Stir in the tomatoes, lentils, stock, bay leaf, tomato paste, and sugar. Season with pepper.
2 Cover and bring to a boil. Reduce the heat to very low (use a heat diffuser if you have one) and simmer 30 to 40 minutes until the lentils are tender, then season with salt and pepper. Serve sprinkled with cilantro and with vinegar on the side.

274 Rice & Zucchini Soup

PREPARATION TIME 15 minutes, plus making the stock and croutes
COOKING TIME 45 minutes

2 tablespoons olive or hemp oil
1 large onion, finely chopped
2½ cups zucchini cut into half-moons
6½ cups Vegetable Stock
   (see page 12) or ready-made stock
1 tablespoon tomato paste
2 garlic cloves, finely chopped
2 tablespoons chopped
   parsley leaves

1 bay leaf
½ cup long-grain white rice
salt and freshly ground black pepper
1 small handful of basil leaves,
   torn, to serve
1 recipe quantity Goat Cheese
   Croutes (see page 14), to serve

1   This soup is best made just before serving because its vibrant green color dulls
    on standing. It also thickens on standing and will need extra stock stirred in if
    reheated. Heat the oil in a saucepan over medium heat. Add the onion and fry,
    stirring occasionally, 3 minutes. Add the zucchini and fry 3 minutes until the skins
    turn bright green and the onions are softened.
2   Stir in the stock, tomato paste, garlic, parsley, and bay leaf and season with salt
    and pepper. Cover and bring to a boil, then lower the heat and simmer, covered,
    10 to 15 minutes until the zucchini are very soft. Discard the bay leaf and blend
    the soup to the preferred consistency. Stir in the rice and return the soup to a boil,
    then boil, uncovered, 10 to 15 minutes until the rice is tender, stirring frequently
    to prevent it from sticking to the bottom of the pan. Adjust the salt and pepper,
    if necessary, and serve immediately, sprinkled with basil and with cheese croutes.

275 Wild Rice & Mushroom Soup

PREPARATION TIME 15 minutes, plus 30 minutes soaking the mushrooms and making
the stock   COOKING TIME 1 hour

1 ounce dried porcini mushrooms
1 tablespoon butter
1 tablespoon olive or hemp oil
1 celery rib, finely chopped
1 onion, finely diced
3 cups trimmed and sliced portobello
   or cremini mushrooms
2¼ cups Vegetable Stock (see
   page 12) or ready-made stock

1 cup wild rice
1 tablespoon chopped tarragon
   or ½ tablespoon dried
½ tablespoon Worcestershire Sauce,
   or to taste
salt and freshly ground black pepper
2 scallions, finely chopped,
   to serve

1   Put the porcini mushrooms and 3 cups boiling water in a heatproof bowl and let
    soak 30 minutes until tender. Strain through a cheesecloth-lined strainer,
    and reserve the liquid. Squeeze the mushrooms dry and trim the stems,
    if necessary, then thinly slice the caps and stems and set aside.
2   Melt the butter with the oil in a saucepan over medium heat. Add the celery and
    onion and fry, stirring occasionally, 3 to 5 minutes until softened but not colored.
    Stir in the porcini and portobello mushrooms, season with salt, and fry, stirring
    occasionally, 5 to 8 minutes until they give off their juices. Add the stock and
    wild rice and season with pepper. Cover and bring to a boil.
3   Stir in the tarragon, lower the heat, and simmer, covered, 35 to 40 minutes
    until the rice is tender. Stir in the Worcestershire sauce and adjust the salt
    and pepper, if necessary, but the soup is unlikely to need salt. Serve sprinkled
    with the scallions.

276 Wild Mushroom Risotto Soup

PREPARATION TIME 10 minutes, plus making the stock **COOKING TIME** 1 hour

1 ounce dried porcini mushrooms
½ ounce dried morel mushrooms
5½ cups Vegetable Stock
   (see page 12) or ready-made stock,
   plus extra as needed
5 tablespoons olive oil
2 tablespoons finely chopped parsley
1 large onion, finely chopped

2 garlic cloves, very finely chopped
⅔ cup Arborio rice
¼ cup dry red wine
⅓ cup freshly grated Parmesan
   cheese, plus extra to serve
1 tablespoon butter
salt and freshly ground black pepper
basil leaves, to serve

1   Put both mushrooms and the stock in a saucepan and season lightly with salt.
Cover and bring to a boil, then lower the heat and simmer 15 minutes, or until the
mushrooms are tender. Strain through a cheesecloth-lined strainer, then set the
liquid aside to simmer in a covered saucepan over low heat. Rinse the mushrooms,
then squeeze them dry, trim the stems and thinly slice the caps and stems.

2   Heat 2 tablespoons of the oil in a skillet over medium heat. Add the mushrooms,
season lightly with salt, and stir 5 to 8 minutes until the mushrooms give off their
juices. Stir in the parsley and season with pepper, then transfer to a bowl and
set aside.

3   Heat the remaining oil in the wiped-out skillet over medium heat. Add the onion and
fry, stirring, 2 minutes. Stir in the garlic and fry 1 to 3 minutes until the onion
is softened. Add the rice and stir until the grains are coated. Add the wine and cook
2 to 4 minutes until it is absorbed, then add a ladleful of the stock and stir until
it is absorbed. Continue adding stock, ladleful by ladleful, 15 to 20 minutes, stirring,
until the rice is tender. The texture should be "soupy" and not as thick
as a conventional risotto, so stir in extra stock, if necessary.

4   Add the mushrooms, cheese, and butter and stir until the cheese melts. Adjust the
salt and pepper, if necessary, but remember the mushrooms have already been
salted and the cheese is salty. Serve sprinkled with basil and cheese.

277 Venetian Rice & Pea Soup

PREPARATION TIME 10 minutes, plus making the stock **COOKING TIME** 35 minutes

5 tablespoons butter
1 tablespoon extra-virgin olive oil,
   plus extra to serve
1 shallot, finely chopped
3 ounces pancetta, skin removed,
   if necessary, and chopped
5 tablespoons dry vermouth
   or dry white wine

1 cup Arborio rice
5½ cups Chicken Stock (see page 11)
   or ready-made stock, plus extra
   as needed
1 cup frozen peas
⅓ cup freshly grated Parmesan
   cheese, plus extra to serve
salt and freshly ground black pepper

1   Melt 4 tablespoons of the butter with the oil in a saucepan over medium heat.
Add the shallot and fry, stirring, 2 minutes. Stir in the pancetta and fry
1 to 3 minutes until the shallot is softened but not colored. Add the vermouth and
simmer 4 to 6 minutes until it almost evaporates.

2   Add the rice and stir until coated. Stir in the stock and season with salt and pepper.
Bring to a boil, stirring occasionally, then lower the heat and simmer 10 minutes,
stirring. Add the peas and stir 5 to 10 minutes until the rice is tender but not
overcooked and the peas are tender. The texture should be "soupy" and not as thick
as a conventional risotto, so stir in extra stock, if necessary. Stir in the remaining
butter and the cheese and adjust the salt and pepper, if necessary, but remember
the cheese is salty. Serve with olive oil and cheese on the side.

Mixed Grain & Red Lentil Soup

PREPARATION TIME 10 minutes, plus making the stock and preparing the tomatoes
COOKING TIME 50 minutes

1 tablespoon olive or hemp oil
1 large onion, finely chopped
2 large garlic cloves, chopped
6 cups Vegetable Stock (see page 12)
    or ready-made stock
¼ cup split red lentils, rinsed
2 tablespoons bulgur wheat
2 tablespoons long-grain white rice
3 tomatoes, grated (see page 9)

1 tablespoon dried mint, plus extra
    to serve
2 tablespoons tomato paste
½ tablespoon hot or sweet paprika,
    or to taste
½ teaspoon cayenne pepper,
    or to taste
salt and freshly ground black pepper
extra-virgin olive oil, to serve

1   Heat the oil in a saucepan over medium heat. Add the onion and fry, stirring,
    2 minutes. Add the garlic and fry 1 to 3 minutes until the onion is softened but not
    colored. Add the stock, lentils, bulgur wheat, rice, tomatoes, mint, tomato paste,
    paprika, and cayenne. Cover and bring to a boil, then lower the heat and simmer
    30 to 40 minutes until the lentils, wheat, and rice are all tender. Stir occasionally
    to prevent the grains from sticking to the bottom of the pan.
2   Blend half of the soup until smooth. Return the mixture to the pan, stir well, and
    season with salt and pepper. Serve sprinkled with mint and drizzled with olive oil.

279 Moroccan Vegetable & Couscous Soup

PREPARATION TIME 20 minutes, plus making the stock and dukkah
COOKING TIME 20 minutes

1½ tablespoons olive or hemp oil
1 red onion, chopped
2 large garlic cloves, crushed
1 teaspoon ground coriander
1 teaspoon ground cumin
1 teaspoon turmeric
2 teaspoons harissa paste, or to taste
5½ cups Vegetable Stock
   (see page 12) or ready-made stock
1½ cups peeled, seeded, and
   chopped pumpkin

1 zucchini, quartered lengthwise
   and sliced
1 red bell pepper, seeded and sliced
½ cup couscous
1 tablespoon butter
salt and freshly ground black pepper
Dukkah (see page 15), to serve
shredded cilantro leaves, to serve
hot pepper sauce, to serve

1   Heat the oil in a saucepan over medium heat. Add the onion and fry, stirring occasionally, 2 minutes. Add the garlic and fry 1 to 3 minutes until the onion is softened. Stir in the coriander, cumin, and turmeric and fry 30 seconds. Watch closely so the spices do not burn.

2   Stir in the harissa paste, then add the stock, pumpkin, zucchini, and red pepper and season with salt and pepper. Cover and bring to a boil. Lower the heat and simmer 10 to 15 minutes until all the vegetables are tender. Adjust the salt and pepper, if necessary.

3   Meanwhile, put the couscous and butter in an heatproof bowl, season with salt and pepper, and add enough boiling water to cover by 1 inch. Cover with a clean, folded dish towel and set aside 10 minutes, or according to the package directions, until the water is absorbed and the grains are tender. Pour off any excess water, if necessary, then fluff with a fork. Divide the couscous into bowls and ladle the soup over it. Sprinkle with the dukkah and cilantro leaves and serve with hot pepper sauce.

280 Mushroom & Millet Soup

PREPARATION TIME 20 minutes, plus making the stock   COOKING TIME 40 minutes

1½ tablespoons garlic-flavored
   olive oil
½ cup millet
1 leek, thinly sliced and rinsed
2 large garlic cloves, chopped
5 cups trimmed and sliced cremini
   or button mushrooms
5½ cups Beef Stock (see page 10)
   or ready-made stock

2 carrots, peeled, halved lengthwise,
   and sliced
1 bay leaf
2 teaspoons dried marjoram
1 small bunch parsley, leaves finely
   chopped and stems tied together
   and crushed
salt and freshly ground black pepper

1   Heat 1 tablespoon of the oil in a saucepan over medium heat. Add the millet and stir 1 to 2 minutes until it gives off a toasted aroma and just starts to brown. Watch closely so it does not burn. Immediately transfer it to a bowl and set aside.

2   Heat the remaining oil in the pan. Add the leek and fry, stirring occasionally, 2 minutes, then add the garlic and fry 1 to 3 minutes until the leek is softened but not colored. Add the mushrooms, season with salt, and fry, stirring occasionally, 5 to 8 minutes until the mushrooms give off their juices.

3   Return the millet to the pan. Add the stock, carrots, bay leaf, marjoram, and parsley stems and season with salt and pepper. Cover and bring to a boil, then lower the heat and simmer 15 to 20 minutes until the millet is tender. Discard the bay leaf and parsley stems and stir in the parsley leaves. Adjust the salt and pepper, if necessary, and serve.

281 Turkish Chickpea Soup

PREPARATION TIME 15 minutes, plus soaking the chickpeas overnight and making the stock **COOKING TIME** 2 hours

1 cup dried chickpeas
2 tablespoons garlic-flavored
    olive oil, plus extra to serve
1 large onion, finely chopped
2 large garlic cloves, chopped
½ teaspoon ground coriander
½ teaspoon ground cumin
a pinch of chili flakes,
    or to taste

5½ cups Vegetable Stock
    (see page 12) or ready-made stock
1 can (15-oz.) crushed tomatoes
salt and freshly ground black pepper
ground sumac, to serve
feta cheese, crumbled, to serve
chopped cilantro leaves, to serve

1 Put the chickpeas in a bowl, cover with water, and let soak overnight, then drain.
2 Heat the oil in a saucepan over medium heat. Add the onion and fry, stirring, 2 minutes. Add the garlic and stir 1 to 3 minutes until the onion is softened. Add the coriander, cumin, and chili flakes and stir 30 seconds. Watch closely so the spices do not burn.
3 Stir in the stock, tomatoes, and chickpeas, cover, and bring to a boil, then lower the heat and simmer 1½ to 2 hours, stirring occasionally and topping up with water, if necessary, until the chickpeas are very tender. Season with salt and pepper.
4 Blend about one-third of the soup until smooth. Stir this mixture back into the pan, adjust the salt and pepper, if necessary. Serve sprinkled with sumac, feta, and cilantro.

282 Hearty Barley & Mushroom Soup

PREPARATION TIME 15 minutes, plus 30 minutes soaking the mushrooms and making the stock **COOKING TIME** 1 hour

½ ounce dried porcini mushrooms
2 ounces chopped bacon
1 tablespoon olive or hemp oil,
    as needed
1 large red onion, finely chopped
2 garlic cloves, chopped
3½ cups trimmed and chopped
    portobello or cremini mushrooms

4½ cups Beef Stock (see page 10)
    or ready-made stock
¼ cup pearl barley
1 tablespoon dried oregano or sage
½ tablespoon Worcestershire sauce
salt and freshly ground black pepper
chopped parsley leaves, to serve

1 Put the porcini mushrooms in a heatproof bowl, cover with 1 cup hot water, and let soak 30 minutes until tender. Strain the mushrooms through a cheesecloth-lined strainer, and reserve the liquid. Squeeze the mushrooms dry, then trim off the bottom of the stems, chop the stems and caps, and set aside.
2 Put the bacon in a saucepan over medium heat and fry, stirring, 3 to 5 minutes until it begins to crisp and the fat runs. Remove it from the pan and set aside.
3 Add as much oil as necessary to the fat remaining in the pan to make about 1 tablespoon and heat. Add the onion and fry, stirring, 2 minutes, then add the garlic and fry 1 to 3 minutes until the onion is softened but not colored. Add the portobello mushrooms, season with salt, and stir 5 to 8 minutes until the mushrooms give off their liquid. Add the porcini mushrooms, soaking liquid, stock, barley, and oregano.
4 Cover and bring to a boil, then lower the heat and simmer 30 to 40 minutes until the barley is tender. Add the Worcestershire sauce and adjust the salt and pepper, if necessary, but remember the mushrooms have already been salted. Serve sprinkled with the reserved bacon and parsley.

283 Spelt & Pinto Bean Soup

PREPARATION TIME 15 minutes, plus overnight soaking and cooking the beans
COOKING TIME 1½ hours

½ cup dried pinto beans
1½ tablespoons olive or hemp oil,
  plus extra to serve
1 carrot, peeled and finely chopped
½ celery rib, finely chopped
½ onion, finely chopped
2 large garlic cloves, finely chopped

1 can (15-oz.) crushed tomatoes
1 small handful of thyme,
  tied together
1½ teaspoons dried sage
⅔ cup spelt
salt and freshly ground black pepper
chopped parsley leaves, to serve

1 Put the beans in a bowl, cover with water, and let soak overnight, then drain. Transfer to a saucepan and add 7 cups water. Cover and bring to a boil, then lower the heat and simmer, covered, 50 minutes to 1 hour. Drain.

2 Heat the oil in a saucepan over medium heat. Add the carrot, celery, and onion and fry, stirring occasionally, 2 minutes. Add the garlic and fry 1 to 3 minutes until the onion is softened but not colored. Stir in the beans, tomatoes, thyme, sage, and 6 cups water. Cover and bring to a boil, then lower the heat and simmer 30 minutes.

3 Add the spelt and return the soup to a boil, stirring. Lower the heat and simmer, covered, 35 to 45 minutes until the beans and spelt are tender. Discard the thyme sprigs and season with salt and pepper, if necessary. Serve sprinkled with parsley and with oil on the side for drizzling. If reheating this soup, add a little extra stock, if necessary, to thin it.

284 Quinoa Soup with Tomatoes & Broccoli

PREPARATION TIME 15 minutes, plus making the stock and gremolata and preparing the tomatoes   **COOKING TIME** 35 minutes

1 tablespoon hemp or olive oil
1 onion, finely chopped
4 large garlic cloves, very
  finely chopped
3 cups tomato puree
4 cups Vegetable Stock (see page 12)
  or ready-made stock

4 large tomatoes, peeled
  (see page 9), seeded, and chopped
¼ head broccoli, cut into small florets
¾ cup quinoa, rinsed
salt and freshly ground black pepper
1 recipe quantity Gremolata
  (see page 198), to serve

1 Heat the oil in a saucepan over medium heat. Add the onion and fry, stirring occasionally, 2 minutes. Add the garlic and fry 1 to 3 minutes until the onion is softened but not colored, then stir in the tomato puree and 2½ cups of the stock and season with salt and pepper.

2 Cover and bring to a boil, then lower the heat and simmer 10 minutes. Stir in the tomatoes and broccoli and simmer, uncovered, 10 to 15 minutes until the broccoli is tender.

3 Meanwhile, put the quinoa and remaining stock in a separate saucepan, cover, and bring to a boil. Lower the heat and simmer 15 to 20 minutes until the grains are tender and most of the liquid is absorbed. Drain.

4 Stir the quinoa into the soup and adjust the salt and pepper, if necessary. Serve topped with gremolata.

285 Buckwheat & Vegetable Soup

PREPARATION TIME 10 minutes, plus making the stock and shallots
COOKING TIME 20 minutes

6 cups Beef Stock (see page 10)
   or ready-made stock
2 cups small cauliflower florets and
   the thinly sliced stems
2 carrots, peeled and thinly sliced
1 bouquet garni made with 1 piece
   of celery rib with its leaves and
   1 rosemary sprig tied together

¼ cup buckwheat groats
salt and freshly ground black pepper
Crisp-Fried Shallots (see page 15),
   to serve
chopped parsley leaves, to serve

1   Put the stock, cauliflower stems, carrots, and bouquet garni in a saucepan and
    season with salt and pepper. Cover and bring to a boil. Add the buckwheat and
    cauliflower florets, then lower the heat and simmer, covered, 5 minutes. Remove
    the pan from the heat and let stand, covered, 2 to 3 minutes until the buckwheat
    and vegetables are tender. Discard the bouquet garni.
2   Adjust the salt and pepper, if necessary. Serve sprinkled with shallots and parsley.

286 Kasha & Tomato Soup

PREPARATION TIME 10 minutes, plus making the stock and pumpkin seeds
and preparing the tomatoes   COOKING TIME 30 minutes

1½ tablespoons olive or hemp oil
1 large onion, chopped
4 large garlic cloves, finely chopped
3 cups tomato puree
3¼ cups Vegetable Stock
   (see page 12) or ready-made stock
6 thyme sprigs, tied together

¼ cup kasha (toasted buckwheat)
2 tomatoes, grated (see page 9)
salt and freshly ground black pepper
chopped parsley leaves, to serve
Roasted Pumpkin Seeds
   (see page 15) to serve

1   Heat the oil in a saucepan over medium heat. Add the onion and fry, stirring,
    2 minutes. Add the garlic and fry 1 to 3 minutes until the onion is softened, then
    add the tomato puree, stock and thyme and season with salt and pepper. Cover
    and bring to a boil, then lower the heat and simmer 10 minutes. Stir in the kasha.
2   Simmer, covered, 5 minutes. Remove the pan from the heat, stir in the tomatoes
    and let stand, covered, 2 to 3 minutes until the kasha is tender. Discard the thyme
    and adjust the salt and pepper, if necessary. Serve sprinkled with parsley and
    seeds. If reheating this soup, add a little extra stock, if necessary, to thin.

287 Fragrant Mung Bean Soup

PREPARATION TIME 15 minutes, plus soaking the beans overnight, making the stock
and preparing the tomato   COOKING TIME 55 minutes

½ cup dried mung beans
1 tablespoon olive or hemp oil
1 large onion, finely chopped
3 large garlic cloves, finely chopped
1 teaspoon Chinese five-spice
5½ cups Vegetable Stock
   (see page 12) or ready-made stock

1 carrot, peeled and finely diced
1 large tomato, peeled (see page 9),
   seeded and diced
salt and freshly ground black pepper
shredded cilantro leaves, to serve

1   Put the beans in a bowl, cover with water, and let soak overnight, then drain.
2   Heat the oil in a saucepan over medium heat. Add the onion and fry, stirring,
    2 minutes, then add the garlic and fry 1 to 3 minutes until the onion is softened.
    Add the five-spice powder and stir 30 seconds. Watch closely so it does not burn.
    Add the beans and stock, cover, and bring to a boil, then boil 10 minutes.
3   Add the carrot and tomato, lower the heat, and simmer, covered, 25 to 30 minutes
    until the mung beans are tender. Season with salt and pepper, then serve sprinkled
    with cilantro leaves.

288 Wild Mushroom & Toasted Spelt Soup

PREPARATION TIME 15 minutes, plus 30 minutes soaking the mushrooms and making the stock **COOKING TIME** 1 hour

1 ounce dried porcini mushrooms
2 tablespoons olive or hemp oil
½ cup spelt
1 tablespoon butter
1 celery rib, finely chopped, with the leaves reserved
1 large red onion, finely chopped
4½ cups trimmed and coarsely chopped mixed wild mushrooms, such as chanterelles, horns of plenty, and oysters
2 large garlic cloves, chopped

4½ cups Beef Stock (see page 10) or ready-made stock
1 bouquet garni made with the celery leaves, 1 bay leaf, and several parsley and thyme sprigs tied together
1 large waxy potato, diced
1 small handful of dill, finely chopped
salt and freshly ground black pepper
sour cream or smetana, to serve (optional)

1 Put the porcini mushrooms and at least 1 cup boiling water in a heatproof bowl and let soak 30 minutes until tender. Strain through a cheesecloth-lined strainer and set the liquid aside. Squeeze the mushrooms and trim the stems, if necessary, then thinly slice the caps and stems and set aside.

2 Heat 1 tablespoon of the oil in a saucepan over high heat. Add the spelt and stir 2 to 3 minutes until it gives off a toasted aroma. Immediately transfer to a bowl and set aside.

3 Melt the butter with the remaining oil in the pan over medium heat. Add the celery and onion and fry, stirring, 2 minutes. Stir in the wild mushrooms and garlic, season with salt, and fry 5 to 8 minutes, stirring occasionally, until the mushrooms soften and give off their liquid.

4 Stir in the spelt and fry 2 minutes, then add the stock, bouquet garni, porcini mushrooms, and reserved soaking liquid and season with salt and pepper. Cover and bring to a boil. Lower the heat and simmer 20 minutes, then stir in the potato and simmer 15 to 20 minutes until the spelt and potato are tender. Stir in the dill and adjust the salt and pepper, if necessary. Serve with sour cream, if using.

CHAPTER 6

BIG BOWL SOUPS

A big bowl of steaming soup makes a fantastic one-pot meal, ideal when you want simple meals for friends or for eating in front of the TV. All the meat-based and vegetarian soups in this chapter contain a mix of protein and starch with plenty of vegetables, so you don't have to spend time preparing lots of side dishes. These are the recipes for easy cooking.

Restaurant favorites, such as Teriyaki Salmon Ramen and Shrimp Laksa, are here, along with slow-cooked winter warmers like Beef & Vegetable Hotpot and Winter Vegetable Soup with Quinoa. Lamb Shank & Lima Bean Soup and Borscht are two examples of soups that can be made a day in advance and reheated just before serving, for even easier entertaining when friends are coming around.

For filling vegetarian meals, try Buddha's Delight, Vegetable Jungle Curry with Noodles, and Yogurt Soup with Chickpea Dumplings. The inspiration for these soups comes from predominately vegetarian cultures, so you are guaranteed a satisfying meal in a bowl.

TERIYAKI SALMON RAMEN (SEE PAGE 187)

289 Italian Wedding Soup

PREPARATION TIME 35 minutes, plus 30 minutes chilling and making the stock
COOKING TIME 1¼ hour

7½ cups Beef Stock (see page 10)
  or ready-made stock
1 Parmesan cheese rind, about
  2 x 3 inches (see page 9)
1 prosciutto heel (see page 9)
1 bay leaf
2 tablespoons fruity extra-virgin
  olive oil, plus extra to serve
2 celery ribs, finely chopped
1 onion, finely chopped
2 garlic cloves, chopped
3½ cups chopped escarole
  or kale leaves
1½ cups chopped spinach
salt and freshly ground black pepper
freshly grated Parmesan cheese,
  to serve

VEAL MEATBALLS
½ cup dried breadcrumbs
¼ cup milk
1¾ pounds veal
5 garlic cloves, finely chopped
4 scallions, very finely chopped
3 tablespoons very finely chopped
  parsley leaves
3 tablespoons very finely
  chopped dill
¾ cup finely grated Parmesan cheese
2 eggs, beaten
olive oil, for frying

1 The meatballs can be made up to one day in advance. Put the breadcrumbs and milk in a bowl and let soak. Meanwhile, line a baking tray or two plates that will fit in your refrigerator with waxed paper. Put the veal, garlic, scallions, parsley, dill, and cheese in a large bowl, add the bread crumb mixture, and season with salt and pepper. Add the egg little by little and work it into the mixture with your fingers. Fry a small amount of the mixture to test for seasoning. With wet hands, divide the mixture into 12 equal portions, then divide each portion into 6 equal portions to make a total of 72. Roll into meatballs and put them on the baking tray. Cover with plastic wrap and chill at least 30 minutes.

2 Meanwhile, put the stock, cheese rind, ham heel, and bay leaf in a saucepan. Cover and bring to a boil, then reduce the heat to very low (use a heat diffuser if you have one) and simmer while you fry the meatballs.

3 To fry the meatballs, heat one or two large skillets over high heat until a splash of water "dances" on the surface. Add a thin layer of olive oil, lower the heat to medium, and add as many meatballs as will fit without overcrowding the pan. Fry the meatballs, turning gently, 5 to 8 minutes until golden brown. Drain on paper towels and set aside until required. (At this point they can be left to cool completely and chilled for up to 24 hours.)

4 To finish making the soup, heat the olive oil in another large saucepan over medium heat. Stir in the celery and onion, reduce the heat to low, and cook, covered, 10 to 12 minutes until softened but not colored. Add the stock, along with the cheese rind, ham heel, and bay leaf, cover, and bring to a boil. Add the escarole and spinach, lower the heat, and simmer, covered, 30 minutes.

5 Gently add the meatballs and simmer 5 minutes longer, or until warmed through. Season with salt and pepper, but remember the cheese rind and ham heel are salty.

6 Discard the cheese rind, ham heel, and bay leaf. Divide the meatballs and greens into bowls and ladle the soup over them. Serve immediately with olive oil and grated Parmesan cheese on the side.

290 Tuscan "Twice-Cooked" Vegetable & Bean Soup

PREPARATION TIME 10 minutes, plus making the minestrone a day in advance and making the croutes   COOKING TIME 55 minutes

2 garlic cloves, halved
2 recipe quantities Winter
   Minestrone (see page 142), made
   through step 3 with cavolo nero
   or savoy cabbage instead
   of white cabbage

2 recipe quantities Garlic Croutes
   (see page 14)
extra-virgin olive oil, to drizzle
1 red onion, thinly sliced

1 Heat the oven to 375°F. Rub the inside of a large ovenproof serving dish with the garlic cloves, pressing down firmly, then discard the garlic. Put half the soup in the casserole, top with enough of the croutes to cover, and drizzle with oil. Repeat the layers, then sprinkle the onion over the top and drizzle with more oil.

2 Bake, uncovered, 45 minutes to 1 hour until the onion is tender. Serve straight from the dish with any remaining croutes on the side.

291 Carl's Mulligatawny Soup

PREPARATION TIME 20 minutes, plus making the stock, rice, and chili bon-bon (optional) and overnight chilling (optional)   COOKING TIME 35 minutes

2 tablespoons butter
1 tablespoon sunflower or peanut oil
2 carrots, chopped
2 celery ribs, chopped
1 onion, chopped
2 teaspoons Madras curry powder
1 teaspoon ground coriander
a pinch of cayenne pepper (optional)
1 large sweet cooking apple, peeled,
   cored, and chopped
1 can (15-oz) crushed tomatoes
salt and freshly ground black pepper
2 cups cooked long-grain brown rice,
   hot, to serve
chopped cilantro leaves, to serve
Chili Bon-Bon (see page 15), to serve
   (optional)

LAMB STOCK
3 lamb shanks
5 bay leaves
3 garlic cloves, chopped
2 celery ribs, with their leaves,
   chopped
1 large carrot, chopped
1 onion, chopped
1 teaspoon coriander seeds, crushed
1 teaspoon black peppercorns,
   crushed

1 The stock can be made up to 2 days in advance. Put the lamb in a large saucepan and cover with water. Cover and bring to a boil. Skim, then add the bay leaves, garlic, celery, carrot, onion, coriander seeds, and peppercorns. Lower the heat to very low (use a heat diffuser if you have one) and simmer, covered, 1½ to 2 hours until the lamb is very tender and coming away from the bones. Strain the stock, set the lamb aside until cool enough to handle, and discard the rest of the flavorings. Skim the fat from the surface of the stock. (Alternatively, leave the stock to cool completely, then cover and chill overnight. The fat can then be lifted off.) Set aside 7½ cups of the stock. (Any leftovers can be frozen up to 3 months to use in other soups.) Remove the meat from the bones and shred, then cover and chill until required.

2 Melt the butter with the oil in the washed-out and dried saucepan. Add the carrots, celery, and onion and fry, stirring, 3 to 5 minutes until the onion is softened. Add the curry powder, ground coriander, and cayenne, if using, and stir 30 seconds. Watch closely so the spices do not burn. Stir in the apple, then add the reserved stock and tomatoes and season with salt and pepper. Cover and bring to a boil, then lower the heat and simmer 20 minutes.

3 Blend the soup, then add the lamb and warm through. Adjust the salt and pepper, if necessary. Serve over hot rice, sprinkled with chopped cilantro, and with chili bon-bon on the side, if you like.

292 Slow-Cooked Pork & Bean Soup

PREPARATION TIME 15 minutes, plus soaking the beans overnight and making the stock
COOKING TIME 2 hours

1¾ cups dried navy beans
7½ cups Vegetable Stock
  (see page 12) or ready-made stock
3 carrots, peeled and chopped
2 celery ribs, chopped, with the
  leaves reserved
2 large onions, chopped
1 bouquet garni made with the celery
  leaves, 2 bay leaves, and a handful
  of parsley sprigs tied together

¼ cup tomato paste
1½ tablespoons dried thyme
2¾ pounds pork belly
salt and freshly ground black pepper
chopped parsley leaves, to serve
hot pepper sauce, to serve

1   Put the beans in a bowl, cover with water, and let soak overnight, then drain.
    Transfer to a saucepan, add 6½ cups water, cover, and bring to a boil. Lower the
    heat and simmer, covered, 1 hour, then drain.
2   Meanwhile, put the stock, carrots, celery, onions, bouquet garni, tomato paste,
    thyme, and pork in a large saucepan. Cover and bring to a boil. Skim, then reduce the
    heat to low (use a heat diffuser if you have one) and simmer, covered, 30 minutes.
3   Stir in the beans and return the soup to a boil. Skim, then lower the heat and
    simmer for another 1 to 1¼ hours until the pork and beans are both very tender.
    Remove the pork from the pan and set aside until cool enough to handle. Discard
    the bouquet garni.
4   Trim and discard the rind and excess fat from the pork and shred the meat into
    bite-size pieces. Return it to the soup and reheat, if necessary. Season with salt and
    pepper and serve sprinkled with parsley and with hot pepper sauce on the side.

293 Chicken Gumbo Soup

PREPARATION TIME 20 minutes, plus making the stock and rice
COOKING TIME 1 ½ hours

¼ cup (½ stick) butter
2 tablespoons sunflower oil
¼ cup all-purpose flour
4 garlic cloves, finely chopped
1 large onion, finely chopped
1 green bell pepper,
  seeded and chopped
1 red bell pepper,
  seeded and chopped
1 celery rib, thinly sliced
6½ cups Chicken Stock (see page 11)
  or ready-made stock

2 cups chopped okra
2 bay leaves
2 tablespoons chopped parsley
1 teaspoon dried thyme leaves
2 cans (15-oz.) crushed tomatoes
½ teaspoon sugar
cayenne pepper, to taste
2¼ pounds skinless chicken thighs
salt and freshly ground black pepper
2 cups cooked long-grain rice, hot,
  to serve
hot pepper sauce, to serve

1   First, make a roux: melt the butter with the oil in a saucepan over low heat
    (use a heat diffuser if you have one). Sprinkle in the flour and cook, stirring,
    15 to 20 minutes until it turns a deep golden brown. Watch closely because
    when the roux starts to brown it will color very quickly.
2   Add the garlic, onion, bell peppers, and celery and stir 5 to 8 minutes until the
    onion is softened. Add half the stock, stirring continuously to prevent lumps from
    forming. Add the remaining stock, okra, bay leaves, parsley, thyme, tomatoes,
    and sugar and season with salt and pepper. Cover and bring to a boil, then lower
    the heat and simmer 45 minutes. The okra will make the soup glutinous.
3   Add the chicken, cover, and bring to a boil, then skim. Lower the heat and simmer
    10 to 15 minutes until the chicken is cooked through and the juices run clear when
    you cut a piece. Remove the chicken and set aside until cool enough to handle,
    then cut the meat from the bones into bite-size pieces and return it to the soup.
    Discard the bay leaves. Reheat, adjust the salt and pepper, if necessary,
    and serve with hot pepper sauce.

294 Smoky Mixed Bean & Sausage Soup

PREPARATION TIME 15 minutes, plus making the stock   COOKING TIME 1 hour

¼ cup chopped bacon
1 tablespoon sunflower or olive oil
2 onions, chopped
1 celery rib, finely chopped
2 teaspoons smoked paprika
7½ cups Beef Stock (see page 10)
   or ready-made stock
5 smoked frankfurters, cut into
   bite-size pieces
1 large carrot, peeled and sliced

1 bay leaf
1 tablespoon dried thyme leaves
2 teaspoons caraway seeds
½ teaspoon cinnamon
½ can (15-oz) pinto beans, drained
   and rinsed
1 can (15-oz.) navy or cannellini
   beans, drained and rinsed
1 tablespoon red-wine vinegar
salt and freshly ground black pepper

1   Put the bacon in a saucepan over high heat and fry, stirring, 3 to 5 minutes until
    it starts to crisp and gives off its fat. Remove it from the pan and set aside.
2   Add the oil to the pan and heat over medium heat. Add the onion and celery and
    fry, stirring, 3 to 5 minutes until the onion is softened. Add the paprika and stir
    30 seconds. Add the stock, frankfurters, carrot, bay leaf, thyme, caraway seeds,
    and cinnamon and season with salt and pepper. Cover and bring to a boil, then
    lower the heat and simmer 30 minutes.
3   Add the beans and simmer 10 minutes. Discard the bay leaf and stir in the vinegar.
    Adjust the salt and pepper and add extra vinegar, if necessary, then serve.

295 Thai Duck Soup with Noodles

PREPARATION TIME 20 minutes, plus 30 minutes marinating   COOKING TIME 1½ hours

½ duck, about 2½ pounds,
   chopped into large pieces
2 tablespoons sunflower oil,
   plus extra for frying
1 tablespoon light or sweet
   soy sauce
1 teaspoon salt, plus extra to season
4 garlic cloves, chopped
6 cilantro sprigs, including the roots
   and leaves, 4 left whole and
   2 coarsely chopped, plus 4 roots,
   left whole
5 ounces bean sprouts

2 carrots, peeled and sliced
1 celery rib, sliced
1 onion, peeled and cut in half
2 teaspoons Chinese five-spice
   powder
1 tablespoon palm sugar or light
   brown sugar
9 ounces medium-width ready-to-eat
   rice noodles
1 teaspoon sesame oil
1 teaspoon fish sauce
freshly ground black pepper

1   Put the duck in a bowl. Add the sunflower oil, soy sauce, salt, garlic, and chopped
    cilantro sprigs and rub everything together. Let marinate at room temperature
    30 minutes. Put the bean sprouts in a bowl, cover with cold water, and set aside.
2   Put the carrots, celery, onion, whole cilantro sprigs and 2 quarts water
    in a saucepan. Cover and bring to a boil, then lower the heat and simmer.
3   Heat enough oil to cover the bottom of a large wok over high heat. Add the
    five-spice powder, cilantro roots, and sugar, reduce the heat to low and stir
    30 seconds. If the spice powder looks like it is about to burn, immediately add
    a ladleful of water from the simmering pan.
4   Add the duck and marinade and fry over medium heat, turning occasionally,
    15 minutes, then transfer the duck and liquid in the wok to the simmering pan.
    Season with salt and pepper, but remember the duck is already salted. Bring
    to a boil and skim. Reduce the heat to very low (use a heat diffuser if you have one)
    and simmer, partially covered, 40 minutes to 1 hour until the duck is very tender.
5   Remove the duck and set aside. Strain the broth, return it to the pan, and keep hot.
6   Just before serving, put the noodles in a heatproof bowl and cover with boiling
    water 30 seconds. Drain and transfer to a bowl. Add the sesame oil and fish sauce
    and toss well, then set aside. Drain the bean sprouts.
7   Cut the duck into bite-size pieces, discarding the skin and bones. Divide the
    noodles, bean sprouts and duck into bowls, ladle the broth over them, and serve.

Vietnamese Beef & Noodle Soup

PREPARATION TIME 20 minutes, plus making the stock   **COOKING TIME** 20 minutes

1 small handful of bean sprouts

7½ cups Beef Stock (see page 10)

1½-inch piece of gingerroot,
   peeled and thinly sliced

4 star anise

1 cinnamon stick

seeds from 4 green cardamom pods

1 tablespoon fish sauce, or to taste

1 red bell pepper, halved, seeded,
   and very thinly sliced

1 pound medium-width
   ready-to-eat rice noodles

1 pound 5 ounces sirloin or topside,
   in one piece, very thinly sliced
   against the grain

TO SERVE

lime wedges

1 handful of mint leaves

1 handful of cilantro leaves

2 scallions, thinly sliced

thinly sliced red chilies

1   Put the bean sprouts in a bowl, cover with cold water, and set aside. Put the stock,
   ginger, star anise, cinnamon stick, cardamom seeds, and fish sauce in a large
   saucepan. Cover and bring to a boil, then lower the heat and simmer 10 minutes.
   Add the bell pepper for the final 3 minutes of simmering to soften.

2   Just before serving, use a slotted spoon to scoop the spices out of the stock and
   discard, then return the stock to a boil. Put the noodles in a heatproof bowl, cover
   with boiling water, and let soak 15 to 30 seconds to warm through. Drain and divide
   into serving bowls, then divide the beef into the bowls.

3   Drain the bean sprouts and add them to the bowls. Ladle the boiling stock and red
   peppers over and serve immediately with lime wedges and small bowls of mint,
   cilantro, scallions, and chilies on the side for adding at the table.

297 Hot & Sour Pork Soup with Noodles

PREPARATION TIME 20 minutes, plus marinating the pork and making the stock, chilies, and garlic   COOKING TIME 20 minutes

1 pound 10 ounces pork tenderloin, very thinly sliced
4 teaspoons sesame oil
2 teaspoons soy sauce
4 cilantro sprigs, leaves and stems, finely chopped
7½ cups Vegetable Stock (see page 12) or ready-made stock
6 kaffir lime leaves
3 large garlic cloves, crushed
2 lemongrass stems, thickly sliced, with outer leaves removed
3 tablespoons lime juice
3 tablespoons fish sauce

1 pound ready-to-eat rice noodles
1 teaspoon toasted sesame oil
salt and freshly ground black pepper

TO SERVE
4 scallions, thinly sliced
2 carrots, very thinly sliced
2 celery ribs, very thinly sliced
2 handfuls of baby spinach leaves
lime wedges
Chilies in Vinegar (see page 15)
Crisp-Fried Garlic (see page 15)

1   Put the pork, sesame oil, soy sauce, and cilantro in a bowl and mix well. Season with salt and pepper, mix again, and let marinate at room temperature.
2   Put the stock, lime leaves, garlic, lemongrass, lime juice, and fish sauce in a saucepan and season with salt and pepper. Cover and bring to a boil, then boil 5 minutes.
3   Meanwhile, prepare the bowls for serving. Divide the scallions, carrots, celery, and spinach into the serving bowls and set aside.
4   Uncover the stock and lower the heat to a gentle simmer. Add the noodles and simmer 30 seconds to warm through, then use tongs or chopsticks to transfer them to a large bowl. Toss with the toasted sesame oil so they don't stick together, then divide them into the bowls and set aside.
5   Add the pork to the stock and cook 3 to 5 minutes until cooked through when you cut a piece. Skim and adjust the salt and pepper, if necessary, then divide the pork into the bowls and ladle the stock over it. Serve with a lime wedge and the chilies in vinegar and fried garlic on the side.

298 Beef & Vegetable Hotpot

PREPARATION TIME 20 minutes, plus making the stock and cooking the beef
COOKING TIME 45 minutes

2 quarts Beef Stock (see page 10) or ready-made stock
1 can (15-oz.) crushed tomatoes
10 black peppercorns, lightly crushed
4 garlic cloves, chopped
2 bay leaves
2 leeks, coarsely chopped and rinsed
1 bouquet garni made with 1 piece of celery rib with its leaves, 1 bay leaf, and several parsley and thyme sprigs tied together

5 new potatoes, sliced
2 carrots, peeled and sliced
1 turnip, peeled and chopped
1 can (15-oz.) lima beans, drained and rinsed
5 cups boneless cooked beef trimmed and cut into bite-size pieces
1½ cups shredded savoy cabbage
salt and freshly ground black pepper
chopped parsley leaves, to serve

1   Put the stock, tomatoes, peppercorns, garlic, bay leaves, and leeks in a saucepan and season with salt and pepper. Cover and bring to a boil. Uncover and boil 10 to 15 minutes. Strain the stock, return it to the pan and add the bouquet garni. Add the potatoes, carrots, and turnip and season with salt and pepper. Cover and bring to a boil, then lower the heat and simmer 10 to 15 minutes until the potatoes and carrots are tender.
2   Stir in the lima beans, beef, and cabbage and simmer 5 minutes longer, or until everything is warmed through. Discard the bouquet garni. Adjust the salt and pepper, if necessary, then serve, sprinkled with parsley.

299 Beef & Tomato Soup

PREPARATION TIME 15 minutes   COOKING TIME 2¼ hours

1 bone-in beef shin, about 3 pounds
  5 ounces, with the bone cracked
  in several places (use a mallet
  to do this or ask the butcher)
1 cup trimmed and chopped
  boneless beef brisket or chuck
2 garlic cloves, halved
2 onions, unpeeled and halved
1 leek, chopped and rinsed

1 bouquet garni made with
  1 piece of celery rib with its
  leaves, 1 bay leaf, and several
  parsley and thyme sprigs tied
  together
2 cans (15-oz.) crushed tomatoes
2 tablespoons tomato paste
1 teaspoon caster sugar
salt and freshly ground black pepper
chopped parsley leaves, to serve

1   Put the beef shin and brisket, garlic, onions, leek, and bouquet garni
    in a large saucepan. Add enough water to cover the meat and season with salt and
    pepper. Cover and bring to a boil. Skim, then reduce the heat to very low
    (use a heat diffuser if you have one) and simmer, covered, 1¾ to 2 hours until the
    beef shin meat is very tender and almost falling off the bone and the brisket
    is tender.
2   Add the tomatoes, tomato paste, and sugar and simmer, uncovered, 10 minutes,
    using a spoon to break up the tomatoes. Remove the shin and brisket from the
    pan and set aside until cool enough to handle. Strain the soup into a large bowl,
    using a spoon to press through as much of the tomatoes as possible, then return
    the soup to the pan and simmer, uncovered, 5 minutes to reduce slightly. Skim
    any excess fat from the surface.
3   Remove the shin meat from the bone, then finely shred both types of beef,
    return the meat to the soup and reheat. Adjust the salt and pepper, if necessary.
    Serve sprinkled with parsley.

300 Lamb Shank & Lima Bean Soup

PREPARATION TIME 15 minutes, plus overnight soaking and cooking the beans
and making the stock and flavored oil (optional)   COOKING TIME 2½ hours

½ cups dried lima beans
3 tablespoons garlic-flavored olive oil
3 lamb shanks
2½ cups chopped fennel
2 large garlic cloves, chopped
2½ cups Beef Stock (see page 10)
  or ready-made stock
3 cups tomato puree

1 bouquet garni made with
  1 piece of celery rib with its
  leaves, 2 bay leaves, 2 rosemary
  sprigs, and several parsley and
  thyme sprigs tied together
salt and freshly ground black pepper
1 recipe quantity Paprika & Lemon
  Oil (see page 24) or extra-virgin
  olive oil, to serve

1   Put the beans in a bowl, cover with water and let soak overnight, then drain.
    Transfer to a saucepan and add 2 quarts water. Cover and bring to a boil. Lower
    the heat and simmer, covered, 1 hour, then drain.
2   Heat the oil in a saucepan over medium heat. Working in batches, if necessary,
    fry the lamb shanks until brown on both sides. Remove from the pan and set aside.
    Pour off all but 1½ tablespoons of the oil, then add the fennel and fry, stirring
    occasionally, 3 minutes. Add the garlic and fry 1 to 2 minutes until the fennel
    is softened but not colored, then return the shanks to the pan.
3   Add the stock, tomato puree, and enough water to cover the lamb shanks,
    if necessary. Cover and bring to a boil, then skim. Add the bouquet garni and
    season with salt and pepper. Lower the heat and simmer, covered, 1¼ hours.
4   Stir in the beans, cover and return to a boil. Lower the heat and simmer
    40 to 50 minutes until the lamb is tender and falling off the bones and the
    beans are tender. Remove the shanks and set aside until cool enough to handle.
5   Remove the bones, any fat and sinew from the lamb shanks, and cut the meat
    into bite-size pieces. Return it to the soup and reheat. Adjust the salt and pepper,
    if necessary, and serve drizzled with the paprika oil.

301 Borscht

PREPARATION TIME 25 minutes, plus making the stock and horseradish cream
COOKING TIME 2½ hours

2¼ pounds boneless beef brisket
    or chuck, in one piece,
7½ cups Beef Stock (see page 10)
    or ready-made stock
4 carrots, peeled and sliced
4 large tomatoes, coarsely chopped
3 celery ribs, sliced, with the
    leaves reserved
2 onions, halved and studded with
    several cloves in each half
2 tablespoons tomato paste

1 bouquet garni made with the celery
    leaves, 2 bay leaves, a small
    handful of parsley sprigs, and
    several dill sprigs tied together
a pinch of sugar
4 large cooked beets, peeled and
    coarsely grated
2 bay leaves
2 tablespoons red wine vinegar
salt and freshly ground black pepper
1 recipe quantity Horseradish & Dill
    Cream (see page 21), to serve
chopped dill, to serve

1 Put the beef, stock, carrots, tomatoes, celery, onions, tomato paste, bouquet garni, and sugar in a saucepan and season with salt and pepper. Cover and bring to a boil. Skim, then reduce the heat to very low (use a heat diffuser if you have one) and simmer, covered, 2 hours, or until the meat is tender.

2 Remove the beef from the pan and set aside until cool enough to handle. Strain the soup, pressing down to extract as much flavor as possible, then discard the flavorings and return the stock to the pan.

3 Discard any sinew from the beef, cut the meat into bite-size pieces and return it to the soup. Add the beets, bay leaves, and vinegar and simmer, covered, 15 minutes, or until the beef is very tender. Discard the bay leaves and adjust the salt and pepper, if necessary. Serve topped with the horseradish cream and sprinkled with dill.

302 Indonesian Chicken & Noodle Soup

PREPARATION TIME 25 minutes, plus making the stock, hard-boiled eggs and shallots
COOKING TIME 35 minutes

1 large handful of bean sprouts
8 shallots, 6 halved and 2 chopped
4 garlic cloves
2 tablespoons chopped gingerroot
½ tablespoon turmeric
2 tablespoons peanut oil
7½ cups Chicken Stock (see page 11)
  or ready-made stock
2¼ pounds skinless chicken thighs
6 waxy new potatoes,
  peeled and sliced
2 cups shredded white cabbage

1 lemongrass stem, halved
  and crushed, with outer
  leaves removed
¾-inch piece of galangal, peeled
  and sliced
1 bird's-eye chili, seeded and sliced
1 pound ready-to-eat vermicelli rice
  noodles
salt and freshly ground black pepper
3 hard-boiled eggs, sliced, to serve
Crisp-Fried Shallots (see page 15),
  to serve

1   Put the bean sprouts in a bowl, cover with cold water, and set aside. Pound the
    halved shallots, 2 garlic cloves, the ginger, and turmeric with a mortar and pestle,
    or use a small food processor and blend until a paste forms, then set aside.

2   Heat the oil in a stockpot over medium heat. Add the remaining shallots and fry
    2 minutes. Add the remaining garlic and fry 1 to 3 minutes longer until the shallots
    are softened. Add the shallot paste and fry 2 to 3 minutes until aromatic. Watch
    closely so it does not burn and add a spoonful of the stock, if necessary.

3   Add the stock and chicken, cover, and bring to a boil. Skim, then add the potatoes,
    cabbage, lemongrass, galangal, and chili and season with salt and pepper. Lower
    the heat and simmer, covered, 15 to 20 minutes until the chicken is cooked
    through. Discard the lemongrass and galangal. Remove the chicken from the soup
    and set aside. Shred or cut the chicken from the bones into bite-size pieces.

4   Return the chicken to the soup. Drain the bean sprouts and add them to the soup.
    Warm though, then adjust the salt and pepper, if necessary. Divide the noodles into
    bowls. Ladle the soup over and serve topped with hard-boiled eggs and shallots.

303 Chicken & Chickpea Tagine Soup

PREPARATION TIME 10 minutes, plus making the stock and toasting the almonds
COOKING TIME 40 minutes

3 tablespoons olive or hemp oil
2 large onions, finely chopped
4 large garlic cloves, crushed
1½ pounds skinless chicken thighs
7½ cups Chicken Stock (see page 11)
  or ready-made stock
a large pinch of saffron threads
1 bouquet garni made with 1 piece
  of celery rib, 1 bay leaf, and
  several cilantro, parsley, and
  thyme sprigs tied together
1½ tablespoons ground coriander

1½ tablespoons ground cumin
1½ tablespoons ground ginger
½ teaspoon harissa paste, or to taste
1 can (15-oz.) chickpeas, rinsed
1 cup ready-to-eat dried apricots
2 preserved lemons, sliced
1⅓ cups couscous
1 tablespoon butter
salt and freshly ground black pepper
toasted slivered almonds
  (see page 9), to serve

1   Heat the oil in a large saucepan over medium heat. Add the onions and fry,
    stirring, 6 minutes. Stir in the garlic and fry 1 to 2 minutes until softened.

2   Add the chicken and stock and season with salt and pepper. Cover and bring
    to a boil, then skim. Stir in the next six ingredients. Lower the heat and simmer,
    covered, 10 minutes. Stir in the chickpeas, apricots, and preserved lemons and
    simmer, covered, 10 to 15 minutes longer until the chicken is tender.

3   Meanwhile, put the couscous and butter in an heatproof bowl and season with
    salt and pepper. Add enough boiling water to cover by ½ inch and cover. Let stand
    10 minutes until the water is absorbed. Fluff with a fork.

4   Remove the chicken from the pan, cut the meat into bite-size pieces, and return
    it to the soup. Adjust the salt and pepper and add extra harissa, if necessary. Divide
    the couscous into bowls and ladle the soup over it. Serve sprinkled with almonds.

304 Chicken & Vegetable Chowder

PREPARATION TIME 25 minutes, plus making the stock, toasting the seeds, and making the croutes (optional)   **COOKING TIME** 40 minutes

2¼ pounds skinless chicken thighs
7½ cups Chicken Stock (see page 10)
   or ready-made stock
1½ cups peeled, seeded, and diced
   butternut squash
4 waxy new potatoes, sliced
2 carrots, peeled and sliced
2 celery ribs, thinly sliced, with the
   leaves reserved
2 large garlic cloves, finely chopped
1½ tablespoons dried tarragon
1 tablespoon dried oregano

2 tablespoons chopped parsley
   leaves, plus extra to serve
1 bouquet garni made with the
   celery leaves, 1 bay leaf, and
   several parsley and thyme sprigs
   tied together
2 cups broccoli florets
1 cup long-grain rice
½ cup whole milk
salt and freshly ground black pepper
Cheddar Croutes (see page 14),
   to serve (optional)

1   Put the chicken and stock in a saucepan and season with salt and pepper. Cover
    and bring to a boil. Skim, then add the squash, potatoes, carrots, celery, garlic,
    tarragon, oregano, parsley, and bouquet garni. Lower the heat and simmer,
    covered, 15 minutes. Add the broccoli and rice and return to a slow boil.
2   Cook, uncovered, 10 to 15 minutes until the chicken is cooked through and the
    juices run clear when you cut a piece. Stir occasionally to prevent the rice from
    sticking to the bottom of the pan. Remove the chicken and set aside until cool
    enough to handle. Discard the bouquet garni.
3   Cut the chicken from the bones into bite-size pieces and return it to the soup.
    Stir in the milk and heat through without boiling. Adjust the salt and pepper,
    if necessary, and serve sprinkled with parsley and with croutes on the side,
    if you like. If you reheat the soup, do not boil it.

305 Japanese Salmon Hotpot

PREPARATION TIME 20 minutes, plus making the dashi   **COOKING TIME** 30 minutes

14 ounces watercress, thick stems
   and any yellow leaves removed
10 ounces thin rice noodles
2 quarts Dashi (see page 12)
   or prepared instant dashi
4-inch piece of daikon, peeled and
   finely grated
1 red chili, seeded and thinly sliced
1 pound 10 ounces salmon fillet,
   small bones removed, and fish
   cut across the grain into
   ½-inch-thick slices

12 shiitake mushroom caps
10 ounces firm tofu, drained and cut
   into 12 cubes
7 ounces enoki mushrooms,
   stems trimmed
salt
ponzu dipping sauce, to serve

1   Bring a saucepan of lightly salted water to a boil, and bring another saucepan
    of unsalted water to a boil. Boil the watercress in the salted water just until the
    leaves wilt, which will be almost instantly. Drain and immediately rinse under cold
    running water, then drain again and set aside. Meanwhile, boil the rice noodles
    in the unsalted water 6 to 8 minutes, or according to the package directions, until
    tender. Drain and immediately rinse under cold running water and set aside.
2   Put the dashi in a saucepan, cover, and bring to just below the boil. Meanwhile,
    mix together the daikon and chili in a small bowl and set aside. Just before the
    dashi boils, reduce the heat to low, add the salmon and shiitake mushrooms and
    simmer 5 minutes, or until the salmon is cooked to your liking. One minute before
    the end of the cooking, add the tofu and enoki mushrooms and simmer until the
    enoki are tender. Season with salt.
3   Divide the noodles into bowls and top with the salmon. Use a slotted spoon to
    add the watercress, mushrooms, and tofu into the bowls. Ladle the dashi over and
    serve with small bowls of dipping sauce and the daikon and chili mixture.

306 Hot, Hot, Hot Caribbean Chicken Soup

PREPARATION TIME 25 minutes, plus making the stock and rice and overnight chilling (optional) **COOKING TIME** 45 minutes

3 tablespoons sunflower oil
1 onion, chopped
2 garlic cloves, crushed
½ teaspoon ground coriander
½ teaspoon black mustard seeds
1 Scotch bonnet chili, left whole
  or chopped, as desired
6½ cups Chicken Stock (see page 11)
  or ready-made stock
1 pound 10 ounces boneless, skinless
  pieces of chicken, such as breasts,
  drumsticks, and thighs
2 cups peeled and seeded butternut
  squash cut into bite-size pieces

3 waxy new potatoes, diced
2 bay leaves
½ eggplant, cut into bite-size pieces
1¾ cups coconut milk
½ tablespoon tamarind paste
1 mango, peeled, seeded and diced
1 papaya, peeled, seeded, and
  chopped
juice of 1 lime, plus extra lime
  wedges to serve
salt
2 cups cooked long-grain rice,
  hot, to serve

1 This soup is best made a day in advance and chilled so the excess fat can be removed. Heat the oil in a large saucepan over medium heat. Add the onion and fry, stirring occasionally, 7 minutes. Stir in the garlic and fry 1 to 3 minutes until the onion is golden brown. Add the coriander, mustard seeds, and chili and stir 30 seconds. Watch closely so the spices do not burn.

2 Add the stock, chicken, squash, potatoes, bay leaves, and eggplant and season with salt. Cover and bring to a boil. Skim, then stir in the coconut milk and tamarind paste. Lower the heat and simmer, covered, 15 to 20 minutes until the chicken is cooked through and the juices run clear when you cut a piece. Remove the chicken from the pan and set aside until cool enough to handle.

3 Skim the fat from the surface of the soup. (At this point, the soup can be left to cool completely, then covered and chilled overnight so the excess fat can be removed before serving.)

4 Add the mango, papaya, and lime juice to the pan and simmer 5 minutes. Cut the chicken into bite-size pieces and return it to the soup. Adjust the salt, if necessary, then discard the bay leaves. Serve immediately over rice and with lime wedges for squeezing over.

307 Chinese Chicken Noodle Soup

PREPARATION TIME 15 minutes, plus making the stock   COOKING TIME 20 minutes

1 small handful of bean sprouts
3 tablespoons peanut or sunflower oil
1 pound 10 ounces boneless, skinless
    chicken breasts, thinly shredded
3 cups shredded Chinese cabbage
½ cup thinly sliced canned
    bamboo shoots
8 shiitake mushroom caps, sliced
4 scallions, thinly sliced

1 teaspoon Chinese five-spice powder
1 tablespoon Chinese rice wine
1 tablespoon light soy sauce
7½ cups Chicken Stock (see page 11)
    or ready-made stock
1 pound ready-to-eat Chinese egg
    noodles
salt and freshly ground black pepper
toasted sesame oil, to serve

1   Put the bean sprouts in a bowl, cover with cold water, and set aside. Heat a wok
    over high heat. Add 2 tablespoons of the oil, then add the chicken and stir-fry
    2 to 3 minutes until it is cooked through. Remove from the wok and set aside.
2   Add the remaining oil to the wok, if necessary, and heat. Add the cabbage, bamboo
    shoots, mushrooms, scallions, and five-spice powder and stir-fry 2 to 3 minutes
    until tender. Stir in the rice wine and soy sauce, then add the stock and bring
    to a boil, uncovered. Add the chicken, noodles, and bean sprouts to the soup
    and warm through. Serve sprinkled with sesame oil.

308 Buddha's Delight

PREPARATION TIME 20 minutes, plus 30 minutes soaking the bean curd skins,
mushrooms, and lily buds and making the dashi   COOKING TIME 20 minutes

2 ounces dried bean curd skins
½ ounce dried lily buds or golden
    flower vegetable
2 ounces dried wood ear mushrooms
1 small handful of bean sprouts
3 tablespoons sunflower oil
½-inch piece of gingerroot, peeled
    and sliced
2 cups small broccoli florets
½ cup sliced canned bamboo shoots
3 ounces canned or vacuum-packed
    lotus root slices, drained and sliced
½ cup sliced canned water chestnuts
12 baby corns, halved lengthwise

2 quarts Vegetarian Dashi
    (see page 12) or prepared
    instant dashi
1 cup sliced shimeji mushrooms
8 shiitake mushroom caps, sliced
6 snow peas, very thinly sliced
2 tablespoons Chinese rice wine
1½ tablespoons light soy sauce
1 teaspoon Chinese five-spice
    powder
3 tablespoons arrowroot
5 ounces fried tofu, cubed
4 scallions, thinly sliced
2 ounces ready-to-eat thin
    rice noodles

1   Put the bean curd skins and lily buds in separate heatproof bowls, cover with
    boiling water, and let soak 30 minutes, or until tender, then drain. Thinly slice the
    bean curd skins and set aside. Tie each lily bud into a knot and set aside. Put
    the dried mushrooms and 1 cup boiling water in a heatproof bowl and let soak
    30 minutes. Strain through a cheesecloth-lined strainer into a bowl and set the
    liquid aside. Squeeze the mushrooms, cut off the stems, and slice the caps, then
    set aside. Put the bean sprouts in a bowl, cover with cold water, and set aside.
2   Heat the oil in a large wok or saucepan over high heat. Add the ginger and fry
    1 to 2 minutes until golden, then remove and discard. Add the broccoli, bamboo
    shoots, lotus roots, water chestnuts, and baby corn and stir-fry 2 minutes. Add the
    dashi and bring to a boil, then reduce the heat to low. Add the bean curd skins, all
    the mushrooms, and the snow peas. Stir in the rice wine, soy sauce, and five-spice
    powder and simmer, covered, 2 minutes.
3   Meanwhile, put the arrowroot and 3 tablespoons cold water in a small heatproof
    bowl until smooth. Stir in a ladleful of the hot liquid and mix, then stir this mixture
    into the soup and simmer 2 to 3 minutes until the soup thickens slightly. Drain
    the bean sprouts and add them to the soup with the tofu and scallions. Add the
    noodles and warm through. Serve.

309 Yogurt Soup with Chickpea Dumplings

PREPARATION TIME 15 minutes   COOKING TIME 25 minutes

3½ cups Greek-style yogurt
½ teaspoon white wine vinegar
¼ cup chickpea flour
2 to 3 tablespoons soft light
   brown sugar
1 teaspoon cayenne pepper
½ teaspoon ground asafetida
½ teaspoon cinnamon
½ tablespoon salt .
¼ cup peanut or sunflower oil, plus
   extra for deep-frying

2 teaspoons mustard seeds
10 curry leaves, or 2 teaspoons
   crumbled dried curry leaves
2 whole dried chilies
freshly ground black pepper
chopped cilantro leaves, to serve

CHICKPEA DUMPLINGS
1 cup chickpea flour
1 teaspoon salt
½ teaspoon baking soda

1   To make the dumplings, mix the chickpea flour, salt, and baking soda together and
    make a well in the middle. Add ½ to ⅔ cup cold water to the well and stir in the
    flour from the side to make a smooth batter that just falls off the tip of a spoon
    without lingering. Set aside 15 minutes.
2   Meanwhile, put the yogurt in a large bowl and beat in the vinegar until smooth.
    Mix a spoonful of the yogurt mixture into the chickpea flour, then stir chickpea flour
    into the yogurt until blended with no lumps. Stir in the sugar, cayenne, asafetida,
    cinnamon, and salt. Stir in 4½ cups water and set aside.
3   Heat the sunflower oil in a saucepan over high heat. Add the mustard seeds, curry
    leaves, and chilies and stir 30 seconds, or until the seeds pop. Slowly stir in the
    yogurt mixture and bring to a boil, stirring. Reduce the heat to very low and simmer
    15 to 20 minutes until the soup is the consistency of milk.
4   Meanwhile, fry the dumplings. Heat enough oil for deep-frying in a saucepan over
    high heat until it reaches 375°F, or until a cube of bread browns in 30 seconds.
    Line a plate with paper towels. Grease a spoon with a little oil and stir the batter.
    Working in batches, drop spoonfuls of the batter into the oil. Fry the dumplings
    60 to 90 seconds until dark golden brown. Remove and drain on the plate. Reheat
    the oil between batches, if necessary, and keep the finished dumplings warm.
5   Divide the dumplings into bowls, ladle the soup over them, and serve, sprinkled
    with cilantro leaves.

310 North African Lamb & Chickpea Soup

PREPARATION TIME 15 minutes   COOKING TIME 2¼ hours

2 tablespoons olive oil
1 pound 10 ounces boneless lamb
   shoulder, cut into 3 large chunks
2 carrots, peeled and finely chopped
6 large garlic cloves, chopped
2 large red onions, chopped
1 tablespoon ras el hanout,
   or to taste
2 cans (15-oz.) crushed tomatoes
2 tablespoons tomato paste

2 teaspoons sugar
1 handful of cilantro leaves, chopped,
   plus extra to serve
1 can (15-oz.) chickpeas, rinsed
⅔ cup split red lentils, rinsed
a large pinch of saffron threads
7 ounces fine egg pasta, broken
½ teaspoon salt, plus extra to season
freshly ground black pepper

1   Heat the oil in a saucepan over medium heat. Fry the lamb 2 to 3 minutes until
    brown on all sides. Set aside. Add the carrots, garlic, and onions to the pan, reduce
    the heat to low, and cook, covered, 10 to 12 minutes until the onions are golden
    brown. Add the ras el hanout and stir 30 seconds. Stir in the tomatoes, tomato
    paste, sugar, and cilantro. Return the lamb and its juices to the pan.
2   Add 2 quarts water and bring to a boil. Skim, then simmer, covered, 1 hour.
    Add the chickpeas and lentils and simmer 30 to 40 minutes until tender. Remove
    the lamb and set aside. Stir in the saffron, pasta, and salt and gently boil, uncovered
    and stirring, 10 to 15 minutes until the pasta is tender.
3   Remove any remaining fat or sinew from the lamb and cut the meat into bite-size
    pieces. Return it to the soup. Adjust the salt and pepper and serve sprinkled
    with cilantro.

311 Spiced Vegetable Soup with Couscous

PREPARATION TIME 25 minutes, plus making the stock   **COOKING TIME** 45 minutes

2 tablespoons olive oil
2 large onions, finely chopped
4 cloves garlic, chopped
2 tablespoons sweet or smoked
  paprika, to taste
1 teaspoon turmeric
½ teaspoon cinnamon
7½ cups Vegetable Stock
  (see page 12) or ready-made stock
3 cups peeled, seeded, and diced
  butternut squash
1 can (15-oz) crushed tomatoes

2 celery ribs, finely chopped
1 carrot, peeled and finely chopped
2 bay leaves
1 red or green jalapeño chili, seeded
  and finely chopped
1 to 2 tablespoons tahini
2 cans (15-oz.) chickpeas, drained
  and rinsed
1½ cups couscous
1 tablespoon butter
salt and freshly ground black pepper
chopped cilantro leaves, to serve

1   Heat the oil in a saucepan over medium heat. Add the onion and fry, stirring,
    2 minutes. Add the garlic and fry 1 to 3 minutes until the onion is softened. Stir
    in the paprika, turmeric, and cinnamon and fry 30 seconds. Watch closely so the
    spices do not burn. Add the stock and squash and season with salt and pepper,
    then cover and bring to a boil.
2   Add the tomatoes, celery, carrot, bay leaves, chili, and tahini. Lower the heat
    and simmer, covered, 25 to 30 minutes until the vegetables are tender. Add the
    chickpeas and warm through. Discard the bay leaves and adjust the salt and
    pepper, if necessary.
3   Meanwhile, put the couscous and butter in an heatproof bowl and season with salt
    and pepper. Add enough boiling water to cover by 1 inch and cover with a clean,
    folded dish towel. Set aside 10 minutes, or until the water is absorbed and the
    grains are tender, then fluff with a fork.
4   Divide the couscous into bowls and ladle the soup and vegetables over it. Serve
    sprinkled with cilantro.

312 Chicken-Udon Hotpot

PREPARATION TIME 10 minutes, plus making the stock   **COOKING TIME** 35 minutes

2 quarts Chicken Stock (see page 11)
  or ready-made stock
1½ pounds skinless chicken thighs
2 slices of carrot for each bowl
1 shiitake mushroom cap for
  each bowl
5 cups baby spinach leaves

3 snow peas for each bowl
1 pound fresh udon noodles
salt and freshly ground black pepper
yuzu powder or grated lemon zest,
  to serve
togarashi seasoning, to serve
  (optional)

1   Put the stock in a saucepan over high heat. Add the chicken and season with salt
    and pepper. Cover and bring to just below the boil. Skim, then lower the heat and
    simmer, covered, 15 to 20 minutes until the chicken is cooked through. Remove
    from the pan and set aside until cool enough to handle. Skim the excess fat from
    the stock, then add the carrots and shiitake mushrooms and leave to simmer.
2   Meanwhile, bring a separate saucepan of lightly salted water to a boil and cook
    the spinach 30 seconds, or until it just wilts. Transfer to a colander, using a slotted
    spoon, and immediately rinse under cold running water, then set aside. Return the
    water to a boil, add the snow peas and boil 2 to 3 minutes until just tender. Drain
    and immediately rinse under cold running water.
3   Cut the chicken from the bones into bite-size pieces. Return the stock to just below
    the boil, add the noodles and simmer 1 to 2 minutes, or according to the package
    directions, to warm through.
4   Divide the noodles and spinach into bowls and top each portion with some of the
    chicken, 3 snow peas, 2 carrot slices, and 1 shiitake mushroom. Add the stock and
    serve sprinkled with yuzu and togarashi, if you like.

313 Iraqi Chicken, Lentil & Rice Soup

PREPARATION TIME 10 minutes, plus making the stock and 1 hour soaking the rice
COOKING TIME 50 minutes

½ cup long-grain white rice
2 tablespoons olive or hemp oil
1 large onion, finely chopped
1 teaspoon ground coriander
1 teaspoon ground cumin
¼ teaspoon turmeric
7½ cups Chicken Stock (see page 11)
  or ready-made stock

2¼ pounds skinless chicken thighs
½ cup split red lentils, rinsed
salt and freshly ground black pepper
finely shredded mint leaves, to serve
finely chopped parsley leaves,
  to serve
hot pepper sauce, to serve

1   Put the rice in a bowl, cover with cold water, and let soak 1 to 2 hours, then drain and set aside.
2   Heat the oil in a saucepan over medium heat. Add the onion and fry 3 to 5 minutes until softened, then stir in the coriander, cumin, and turmeric and fry 30 seconds. Watch closely so the spices do not burn.
3   Add the stock and chicken and season with salt and pepper. Cover and bring to a boil. Skim the surface, then stir in the rice and lentils, lower the heat, and simmer, covered, 30 to 40 minutes until the lentils are tender. Remove the chicken and set aside until cool enough to handle.
4   Cut the chicken into bite-size pieces, return it to the soup, and heat through. Adjust the salt and pepper, if necessary. Serve sprinkled with mint and parsley and with hot pepper sauce on the side.

314 Danish Cabbage & Meatball Soup

PREPARATION TIME 25 minutes, plus making the stock and 30 minutes chilling
COOKING TIME 45 minutes

12 ounces finely ground veal
  or a mixture of veal and beef
12 ounces finely ground pork
1 large onion, grated
½ tablespoon dried thyme leaves
1 cup fresh white breadcrumbs
1 egg, beaten
3½ tablespoons soda water or milk
3 tablespoons butter

1 tablespoon sunflower oil, plus
  extra for frying the meatballs
5 cups finely shredded
  white cabbage
7½ cups Beef Stock (see page 10)
  or ready-made stock
salt and freshly ground black pepper
chopped parsley leaves, to serve

1   To make the meatballs, line a baking sheet or 2 plates that will fit in your refrigerator with waxed paper. Mix the ground meats together in a large bowl. Add the onion, thyme, breadcrumbs, egg, and soda water and season with salt and pepper. Mix well with wet hands. Divide the mixture into 6 equal portions, then divide each portion into 9 equal portions to make a total of 54. Roll into meatballs and put on the baking sheet. Cover with plastic wrap and chill 30 minutes. (At this point they can be chilled for up to 24 hours.)
2   Meanwhile, melt the butter with the oil in a saucepan over low heat (use a heat diffuser if you have one). Add the cabbage and cook, covered, 30 minutes, stirring occasionally, until very soft and light brown. Add the stock and season with salt and pepper. Bring to a boil, covered, then reduce the heat to very low and simmer while the meatballs are chilled and cooked.
3   When ready to fry the meatballs, heat one or two large skillets over high heat until a splash of water "dances" on the surface. Add a thin layer of oil, lower the heat to medium-low, and add as many meatballs as will fit without overcrowding the pan. Fry 5 to 8 minutes, turning gently, until golden brown. Drain on paper towels and set aside until all the meatballs are fried. (At this point they can be left to cool completely and chilled for up to 24 hours.)
4   Gently drop the meatballs into the simmering soup and warm through. Adjust the salt and pepper, if necessary, and serve sprinkled with parsley.

315 Chicken, Leek & Pancetta Risotto Soup

PREPARATION TIME 10 minutes, plus making the stock and cooking the chicken
COOKING TIME 35 minutes

3 ounces pancetta
2 tablespoons olive oil
1 leek, halved lengthwise, sliced,
    and rinsed
2 large garlic cloves, crushed
1½ cups Arborio rice
⅔ cup dry white wine

2 quarts Chicken Stock (see page 11)
    or ready-made stock, simmering,
    plus extra as needed
4 cups shredded cooked chicken
¾ cup freshly grated Parmesan
    cheese, plus extra to serve
salt and freshly ground black pepper
basil leaves, torn, to serve

1   Put the pancetta in a saucepan over medium heat and fry, stirring, 3 to 5 minutes
    until it begins to crisp and the fat runs. Remove it from the pan and set aside.
    Add the olive oil to the pan and heat. Add the leek and fry 2 minutes. Stir in the
    garlic and fry 1 to 3 minutes until the leek is softened but not colored.
2   Add the rice and stir until the grains are coated. Add the wine and cook, stirring,
    until it is absorbed. Add a ladleful of the stock and stir until it is absorbed. Continue
    adding stock this way, ladleful by ladleful, 15 to 20 minutes, stirring, until the
    rice is tender.
3   Add the chicken, cheese, and pancetta, then stir in the remaining stock and simmer
    to warm the chicken through. The texture should be "soupy" and not as thick
    as a conventional risotto, so stir in extra stock, if necessary. Season with salt and
    pepper, but remember the cheese is salty. Serve sprinkled with basil and with
    extra cheese on the side.

316 Teriyaki Salmon Ramen

PREPARATION TIME 15 minutes, plus making the dashi, stock, and seeds and at least
30 minutes marinating   COOKING TIME 20 minutes

1 pound 10 ounces salmon fillet,
    small bones removed, cut into
    serving portions
5 tablespoons teriyaki sauce
1 tablespoon sesame oil
4½ cups Dashi (see page 12)
    or prepared instant dashi
4½ cups Fish Stock (see page 11)
    or ready-made stock
2-inch piece of gingerroot, peeled
    and grated
2 large garlic cloves, finely chopped

2 long red chilies, seeded and
    thinly sliced
5 shiitake mushroom caps, sliced
¾ cup sliced pickled preserved
    bamboo shoots
4 teaspoons toasted sesame oil
1 pound ramen noodles
1 large handful of bean sprouts,
    rinsed
sesame seeds, toasted (see page 9),
    to serve
torn cilantro leaves, to serve

1   Put the salmon on a plate, add the teriyaki sauce, and rub it all over with your
    hands. Cover and chill 30 minutes to 2 hours. When ready to cook, remove the
    salmon from the refrigerator and heat a skillet over high heat until a splash of water
    "dances" on the surface. Add the sesame oil to the pan and swirl around. Add the
    salmon, skin-side down, and cook 3 minutes on each side, or until cooked to your
    liking. Remove from the pan and set aside.
2   Meanwhile, to cook the noodles, fill a large saucepan three-quarters full of water
    and bring to a boil. Ramen noodles froth up so the pan needs to be very large.
3   Put the dashi and stock in another saucepan and bring to a boil. Lower the heat
    to low, stir in the ginger, garlic, chilies, mushrooms, bamboo shoots, and half the
    toasted sesame oil. Cover and keep warm while the noodles cook.
4   Add the noodles to the boiling water and cook for 4 minutes, or according to the
    package directions. For the last minute of the cooking time, add the bean sprouts
    to the other pan to soften slightly. Drain, then divide the noodles into bowls. Divide
    the mushrooms, bamboo shoots, and bean sprouts into the bowls, then add the
    salmon pieces. Ladle the soup over and serve sprinkled with the remaining toasted
    sesame oil, sesame seeds, and cilantro.

317 Winter Vegetable Soup with Quinoa

PREPARATION TIME 20 minutes, plus making the stock and toasting the seeds
COOKING TIME 50 minutes

2 quarts Vegetable Stock
(see page 12) or ready-made stock
6 large garlic cloves, peeled and
thickly sliced
1 bouquet garni made with 1 large
piece of celery rib with its leaves,
2 bay leaves, and several parsley
and thyme sprigs tied together
a pinch of chili flakes, or to taste
2 cups peeled and chopped sweet
potatoes

1 large leek, sliced and rinsed
2 green bell peppers, cored, seeded,
and cut into bite-size pieces
2 large handfuls of kale, thick stems
removed and leaves chopped
1¾ cups quinoa, rinsed
salt and freshly ground black pepper
Chinese chives, chopped,
or scallions, chopped, to serve
pumpkin seeds, toasted (see page 9),
to serve

1 Put the stock, garlic, bouquet garni, and chili flakes in a saucepan and season with
salt and pepper. Cover and bring to a boil, then boil, partially covered, 10 minutes,
or until slightly reduced.
2 Add the sweet potatoes, cover, and return to a boil. Boil 5 minutes, then lower the
heat, add the leek and bell peppers and simmer, uncovered, 10 to 15 minutes. Stir
in the kale and simmer 3 minutes, or until tender. Discard the bouquet garni. Adjust
the salt and pepper, if necessary.
3 Meanwhile, put the quinoa and 3¼ cups water in another saucepan, cover,
and bring to a boil. Lower the heat and simmer 20 minutes, or until the grains are
tender. Drain and keep warm. Divide the quinoa into bowls, ladle the soup over,
and serve sprinkled with chives and pumpkin seeds.

318 Bouillabaisse

PREPARATION TIME 30 minutes, plus making the stock, croûtes and rouille
COOKING TIME 40 minutes

2 tablespoons olive oil
1 fennel, quartered and thinly sliced
1 leek, thinly sliced and rinsed
1 onion, chopped
4 garlic cloves, chopped
¼ cup aniseed-flavored spirit
5 cups Fish Stock (see page 11)
2¼ cups tomato puree
2 large pinches of saffron threads
12 live mussels, scrubbed, with
"beards" removed and soaked
in cold water

2 pounds mixed fish, such as sea
bass, halibut, mullet, or red mullet,
dressed, boned, trimmed
as necessary, and cut into
large chunks
1 pound large raw shrimp, shelled
and deveined
salt and freshly ground black pepper
2 recipe quantities Croutes
(see page 14), to serve
1½ recipe quantities Rouille
(see page 14), to serve

1 Heat the oil in a saucepan over medium heat. Add the fennel, leek, and onion
and fry, stirring, 2 minutes. Add the garlic and fry 1 to 3 minutes until the onion
is softened. Add the spirit and cook 2 to 4 minutes until it almost evaporates,
then add the stock, tomato puree, and saffron and season with salt and pepper.
Cover and bring to a boil. Lower the heat and simmer 10 minutes.
2 Meanwhile, calculate the cooking time for the fish at 10 minutes per 1 inch of
thickness. Discard any mussels with broken shells or open ones that do not close
when tapped. Add the mussels to the pan and cook, covered, 3 to 5 minutes,
shaking the pan frequently, until all the shells open. Remove the mussels from
the pan and set aside. Discard any closed mussels.
3 Add the fish to the pan and simmer for the calculated time until all the fish
is cooked through and flakes easily. If necessary, add the fish in stages, starting
with the thickest pieces. Three minutes before the end of the calculated cooking
time, add the shrimp and cook until they curl and turn pink. Return the mussels
in their shells to the pan and adjust the salt and pepper, if necessary. Serve with
croutes spread with rouille on the side.

319 Vegetable Jungle Curry with Noodles

PREPARATION TIME 20 minutes, plus making the stock   COOKING TIME 25 minutes

2 tablespoons sunflower oil
1 to 2 tablespoons red curry paste
1 tablespoon light brown sugar
½ tablespoon rice vinegar, to taste
7½ cups Vegetable Stock
  (see page 12) or ready-made stock
3 cups peeled, seeded, and diced
  butternut squash
4 asparagus spears, woody ends
  removed and stems and tips
  chopped and kept separate

6 kaffir lime leaves, finely shredded
2 carrots, peeled and sliced
1 red onion, quartered and sliced
2 tablespoons fish sauce, or
  to taste
2½ cups sliced white cabbage
8 cherry tomatoes
2 long red chilies, seeded
  and sliced
1 pound ready-to-eat
  udon noodles
chopped cilantro leaves, to serve

1   Heat the oil in a saucepan over high heat. Stir in the curry paste, sugar, and vinegar, then reduce the heat to low and stir-fry 2 minutes. Watch closely and stir in a little stock if the paste begins to brown. Stir in 1 cup of the stock and cook until the fat separates and the surface is shiny.
2   Add the squash, asparagus stems, lime leaves, carrots, onion, and several more ladlefuls of the stock so the vegetables are covered. Cover and bring to a boil. Lower the heat and simmer 5 minutes, then stir in the fish sauce, asparagus tips, cabbage, tomatoes, half of the sliced chilies, and the remaining stock. Simmer, covered, 5 to 10 minutes until the vegetables are tender.
3   Add the noodles to the pan and warm through. Add extra fish sauce, if you like. Divide the noodles into bowls, ladle the soup over them, and serve sprinkled with the remaining sliced chili and cilantro leaves.

320 Shrimp Laksa

PREPARATION TIME 20 minutes, plus making the stock   COOKING TIME 50 minutes

2¼ cups Fish Stock (see page 11)
  or ready-made stock
2¼ pounds raw large shrimp,
  shelled and deveined, with heads
  and shells reserved
½ teaspoon salt
1 large handful of bean sprouts
12 cilantro sprigs, leaves and stems
  coarsely chopped, plus extra
  chopped leaves to serve
5 large garlic cloves, chopped
1 bird's-eye chili, seeded (optional)
  and chopped

1 lemongrass stem, chopped,
  with outer leaves removed
1½-inch piece of gingerroot,
  peeled and chopped
2 tablespoons shrimp paste
½ teaspoon turmeric
¼ cup peanut or sunflower oil
4½ cups coconut milk
1 tablespoon fish sauce, or to taste
1 tablespoon lime juice, or to taste
9 ounces medium ready-to-eat
  rice noodles

1   Put the stock, shrimp heads and shells, and salt in a saucepan. Cover and bring to a boil, then lower the heat and simmer 10 minutes. Put the bean sprouts in a bowl, cover with cold water, and set aside.
2   Meanwhile, to make the laksa paste, put the cilantro, garlic, chili, lemongrass, ginger, shrimp paste, and turmeric in a mini food processor and blend until a paste forms. Add 3 tablespoons of the oil and blend again, then set aside.
3   Strain the stock through a cheesecloth-lined strainer and set aside. Heat the remaining oil in a large saucepan over high heat. Add the paste and stir-fry 1 to 2 minutes until fragrant. Watch closely so it doesn't burn and add a little of the simmering stock if necessary. Stir in the stock, coconut milk, fish sauce, and lime juice and bring to a boil, stirring. Cover, lower the heat, and simmer 20 minutes.
4   Add the shrimp and simmer 2 to 3 minutes until they curl and turn pink. Drain the bean sprouts and add them and the noodles to the soup and cook 30 seconds to warm through. Adjust the fish sauce and lime juice, if necessary. Serve sprinkled with cilantro.

321 Edamame & Pumpkin Soup with Jasmine Rice

PREPARATION TIME 25 minutes, plus making the rice   **COOKING TIME** 30 minutes

2 tablespoons hemp or sunflower oil
1 onion, chopped
2 carrots, peeled and sliced
3½ cups peeled, seeded, and
  chopped pumpkin
4½ cups coconut milk
1 cup frozen shelled edamame beans
4 bok choy, quartered lengthwise
salt and freshly ground black pepper
2 cups cooked Thai Jasmine Rice
  (see recipe 262), hot, to serve
chopped cilantro leaves, to serve
lime wedges, to serve

RED CHILI PASTE
5 garlic cloves, chopped
1-inch piece of gingerroot,
  peeled and chopped
2 red chilies, seeded (optional)
  and chopped
2 lemongrass stems, chopped,
  with outer leaves removed

1   Put all the ingredients for the chili paste and 2 tablespoons water in a mini food processor and process 20 to 30 seconds until a thin, coarse paste forms.

2   Heat the oil in a heavy-bottomed stockpot over high heat. Add the onion and fry, stirring occasionally, 3 to 5 minutes until softened but not colored. Add the chili paste and stir 2 to 3 minutes until the fat separates around the edge. Add the carrots, pumpkin, and 4½ cups water and season with salt and pepper. Cover and bring to a boil, then lower the heat and simmer 10 minutes.

3   Add the coconut milk, edamame, and bok choy and simmer, uncovered, 3 to 5 minutes until the edamame are tender. Adjust the salt and pepper, if necessary.

4   Divide the rice into bowls and ladle the soup over it. Serve sprinkled with chopped cilantro and with lime wedges for squeezing over.

322 Posole

PREPARATION TIME 15 minutes, plus overnight soaking and cooking the hominy
and making the stock   COOKING TIME 1¾ hours

2 cups hominy (dried corn kernels)
2 quarts Chicken Stock (see page 11)
   or ready-made stock
2¼ pounds boneless pork shoulder,
   in one piece, rind and fat removed
any available pork bones (optional;
   ask the butcher for these)
4 large garlic cloves, chopped
2 large onions, unpeeled,
   quartered, and each piece
   studded with one clove

1 tablespoon dried oregano
2 teaspoons ground cumin
2 green jalapeño chilies, seeded
   (optional), and sliced
2 tablespoons dried thyme leaves
1 teaspoon dried ancho chili powder
1 teaspoon salt, plus extra to season
freshly ground black pepper
1 handful of cilantro leaves, chopped,
   to serve

1   Put the hominy in a bowl, cover with water, and let soak overnight, then drain.
    Transfer to a saucepan and cover generously with water. Cover and bring to a boil,
    then lower the heat and simmer 4 hours. Drain and set aside.
2   Put the stock, pork, and pork bones, if using, in a saucepan. Cover and bring
    to a boil. Skim, then add the garlic, onions, oregano, and cumin. Lower the heat
    and simmer, covered, 30 minutes.
3   Add the hominy, chilies, thyme, chili powder, and salt. Cover and return to a boil,
    then lower the heat and simmer 1 to 1¼ hours longer until the meat and hominy
    are very tender. Remove the pork and set aside until cool enough to handle.
    Discard the onions and bones, if used.
4   Shred the pork, then return it to the pan. Adjust the salt and pepper, if necessary,
    and serve sprinkled with cilantro.

323 Peruvian "Breakfast" Soup— for Any Time of the Day

PREPARATION TIME 15 minutes, plus making the stock and hard-boiling the eggs
COOKING TIME 45 minutes

1 egg for each bowl
2 quarts Rich Chicken Stock
   (see page 10) or ready-made stock
6 garlic cloves, crushed
3 celery ribs, coarsely chopped
1½-inch piece of gingerroot, peeled
   and coarsely chopped
2¼ pounds skinless chicken pieces,
   such as breasts and drumsticks

2½ cups peeled and chopped
   waxy potatoes
salt and freshly ground black pepper
chopped cilantro leaves, to serve
2 roasted red peppers in olive oil,
   drained and sliced, to serve
chopped scallions, to serve

1   Put the eggs in a saucepan, add enough water to cover by 1 inch, and bring
    to a boil, then lower the heat and simmer 9 minutes. Pour off the hot water, then
    run cold water over the eggs 1 to 2 minutes to stop the cooking. Set aside until
    cool enough to handle, then peel and set aside.
2   Meanwhile, put the stock, garlic, celery, and ginger in a saucepan and season with
    salt and pepper. Cover and bring to a boil, then boil, uncovered, 10 minutes until
    slightly reduced. Discard the flavorings.
3   Add the chicken and potatoes to the pan, cover, and bring to a boil. Skim, then
    lower the heat and simmer 15 to 20 minutes until the potatoes are tender and the
    chicken is cooked through and the juices run clear when you cut a piece. Remove
    the chicken from the pan and set aside until cool enough to handle.
4   Cut the chicken from the bones into bite-size pieces and return to the stock to
    warm through. Adjust the salt and pepper, if necessary. Cut the hard-boiled eggs
    in half lengthwise and arrange on a plate. Serve the soup sprinkled with cilantro and
    with the peppers, eggs, and scallions on the side for adding a the table.

CHAPTER 7

CHILLED SOUPS

The sweet and savory soups in this chapter are the key to

staying cool in the kitchen when the temperatures are high.

These recipes include many vegetarian and vegan soups,

as well as a good selection of super-healthy raw soups,

such as Raw Emerald Soup, Green Cucumber & Chili Soup,

and Big Red Raw Soup.

From sunny Spain, Gazpacho and White Garlic and Almond

Soup are ideal for summer entertaining, as is Bloody Mary Party

Soup. And if rain clouds threaten your catering plans, don't

worry: soups like Vichyssoise, Fennel & Apple Soup, and

Sweet Buttermilk Dessert Soup do double duty as hot soups.

The important thing to remember with all the recipes in this

chapter is to taste and adjust the salt and pepper, if necessary,

before serving. Chilling soups dulls the flavors and what

previously tasted fresh and exciting might need more

seasoning after a couple hours in the refrigerator. Most soups

also thicken as they chill and will require a little extra liquid

stirred in before serving.

ICED TOMATO & ORANGE SOUP WITH GOAT MILK YOGURT SORBET (SEE PAGE 203)

324 Vichyssoise

PREPARATION TIME 15 minutes, plus making the stock, cooling and at least
2 hours chilling   COOKING TIME 40 minutes

¼ cup (½ stick) butter
6 cups chopped and rinsed leeks
1 onion, sliced
4½ cups Vegetable Stock
   (see page 12) or ready-made stock,
   plus extra as needed

2 cups peeled and chopped
   russet potatoes
1 cup light cream
salt and ground white pepper
snipped chives, to serve

1   Melt the butter in a saucepan over medium heat. Add the leeks and onion, reduce
    the heat to low, and cook, covered, 8 to 10 minutes until softened but not colored.
    Add the stock and potatoes and season with salt and white pepper. Cover and
    bring to a boil, then reduce the heat to very low (use a heat diffuser if you have
    one) and simmer 20 to 25 minutes until the vegetables are very tender.
2   Blend the soup until smooth, then work it through a strainer into a large bowl,
    rubbing back and forth with a spoon and scraping the bottom of the strainer.
    Set aside to cool completely, then cover and chill at least 2 hours.
3   When ready to serve, stir in the cream and a little extra stock if the soup is too
    thick. Adjust the salt and pepper, if necessary, and serve sprinkled with chives.

325 Consommé & Vegetable Soup

PREPARATION TIME 15 minutes, plus making the consommé, preparing the tomato,
cooling, and at least 2 hours chilling

1 carrot, peeled and grated
1 zucchini, peeled and grated
1 tomato, peeled (see page 9),
   seeded, and finely diced
2 tablespoons finely snipped chives
2 tablespoons finely chopped
   parsley leaves

1 recipe quantity Beef or Chicken
   Consommé (see page 13)
   or 5½ cups canned beef or chicken
   consommé, at room temperature
salt and freshly ground black pepper
dry sherry, to serve
1 pomegranate, to serve (optional)

1   Put the carrot, zucchini, tomato, chives, parsley, and consommé in a bowl, stir well,
    and season very lightly with salt and pepper. Cover and chill at least 2 hours.
    The consommé will lightly gel while chilling.
2   When ready to serve, put 1 teaspoon dry sherry in each bowl, then ladle in the
    soup. If you want to garnish with pomegranate seeds, bash the pomegranate
    with a wooden spoon, then cut it in half. Hold one half over one of the bowls
    and tap the top with the spoon so the seeds fall over the soup, then remove
    any white pith, if necessary. Repeat to sprinkle the remaining bowls with seeds,
    then serve.

326 Cherry Tomato & Consommé Soup

PREPARATION TIME 10 minutes, plus making the consommé, flavored oil, and croutes
and at least 2 hours chilling

1 recipe quantity Chicken Consommé
   (see page 13), at room temperature
6 cups seeded and chopped cherry
   tomatoes
4 scallions, finely chopped
2 tablespoons tomato paste

a pinch of sugar
salt and freshly ground black pepper
1 recipe quantity Crushed Mint Oil
   (see page 15), to serve
1 recipe quantity Goat Cheese
   Croutes (see page 14), to serve

1   Put the consommé, tomatoes, scallions, tomato paste, and sugar in a blender and
    season with salt and pepper. Blend the soup until smooth, then work it through
    a nylon strainer into a bowl, using a large spoon. Cover and chill at least 2 hours.
2   When ready to serve, stir well and adjust the salt and pepper, if necessary. Serve
    drizzled with the oil and with croutes on the side, if you like.

327 Fennel & Apple Soup

PREPARATION TIME 10 minutes, plus making the stock and seeds, cooling and at least
2 hours chilling **COOKING TIME** 40 minutes

1½ sweet cooking apples, peeled,
   cored and chopped
1 tablespoon lemon juice
1½ tablespoons olive or hemp oil
2 cups sliced fennel, with the fronds
   reserved
1 leek, thinly sliced and rinsed
¼ cup dry vermouth

5½ cups Vegetable Stock
   (see page 12) or ready-made stock,
   plus extra as needed
apple juice, as needed (optional)
salt and freshly ground black pepper
Crunchy Mixed Seeds (see page 15),
   to serve

1   Toss the apple and lemon juice together in a bowl and set aside.
2   Heat the oil in a saucepan over medium heat. Stir in the fennel and leek and fry
   2 minutes. Reduce the heat to low and cook, covered, 8 to 10 minutes until
   softened but not colored. Stir in the vermouth and cook 2 to 4 minutes until
   it evaporates, then add the stock and season with salt and pepper. Cover and bring
   to a boil. Lower the heat and simmer 5 minutes.
3   Add the apples and simmer 8 to 10 minutes until they are falling apart. Stir in the
   fennel fronds, then blend the soup until smooth and work it through a strainer into
   a bowl, rubbing back and forth with a spoon and scraping the bottom of the
   strainer. Set aside to cool completely.
4   Cover and chill at least 2 hours. When ready to serve, stir well and add a little extra
   stock or apple juice if the soup is too thick. Adjust the salt and pepper, if necessary,
   and serve sprinkled with the seeds. This soup also tastes good served hot. After
   blending, adjust the salt and pepper, if necessary, and serve.

328 Curried Chicken Soup

PREPARATION TIME 20 minutes, plus making the stock and almonds, cooling and
at least 2 hours chilling **COOKING TIME** 40 minutes

1½ tablespoons sunflower oil
2 celery ribs, thinly sliced
2 leeks, white parts only, halved
   lengthwise, thinly sliced and rinsed
1 large onion, finely chopped
1½ teaspoons Madras curry powder
4½ cups Rich Chicken Stock
   (see page 10) or ready-made stock,
   plus extra as needed

14 ounces skinless chicken pieces,
   such as drumsticks and thighs
2 cups peeled and chopped
   russet potatoes
1 cooking apple
1 cup light cream
salt and freshly ground black pepper
toasted slivered almonds
   (see page 9), to serve

1   Heat the oil in a saucepan over medium heat and add the celery, leeks, and onion.
   Cover, reduce the heat to low, and cook, stirring occasionally, 8 to 10 minutes until
   the onion is softened. Add the curry powder and stir 30 seconds. Watch closely
   so it does not burn.
2   Add the stock, chicken, and potatoes and season with salt and pepper. Cover and
   bring to a boil. Skim, then lower the heat and simmer, covered, 15 to 20 minutes
   until the chicken is cooked through and the juices run clear when you cut a piece.
   Remove the chicken and set aside to cool completely. Blend the soup until smooth
   and set aside to cool completely.
3   Cut the chicken from the bones into bite-size pieces and return it to the soup.
   Cover and chill at least 2 hours.
4   Just before serving, stir a little extra stock into the soup if it is too thick. Peel, core,
   and finely chop the apple, then stir it and the cream into the soup. Adjust the salt
   and pepper, if necessary, and serve sprinkled with toasted almonds.

329 Beet Soup

PREPARATION TIME 10 minutes, plus making the consommé, cooling, and at least 4 hours chilling **COOKING TIME** 30 minutes

1 recipe quantity Beef Consommé (see page 13) or 5½ cups canned consommé, plus extra as needed
4½ cups peeled and grated beets
1 onion, halved

2 tablespoons lemon juice, or to taste
1 tablespoon light brown sugar, or to taste
salt and freshly ground black pepper
chopped dill, to serve

1 Put the consommé, beets, and onion in a saucepan and season with salt and pepper. Cover, and bring to a boil. Lower the heat and simmer 20 minutes, then let cool completely. Once cooled, cover and chill at least 4 hours.

2 When ready to serve, discard the onion halves. Stir in the lemon juice and sugar and add a little extra consommé if the soup is too thick. Adjust the salt and pepper, if necessary, and serve sprinkled with dill.

330 Carrot & Orange Soup

PREPARATION TIME 15 minutes, plus making the stock, cooling and at least 2 hours chilling **COOKING TIME** 45 minutes

1½ tablespoons olive or hemp oil
2¼ cups peeled and chopped carrots
1 leek, chopped and rinsed
1 large red onion, chopped
4 cups Vegetable Stock (see page 12) or ready-made stock
¼ cup orange juice, plus extra as needed

1 large garlic clove, crushed
1 teaspoon sugar
finely grated zest of 1 orange
a pinch of cayenne pepper
salt and freshly ground black pepper

1 Heat the oil in a saucepan over medium heat. Add the carrots, leek, and onion, cover, and reduce the heat to low. Cook 10 to 12 minutes, stirring occasionally, until the vegetables are softened but not colored. Add the stock, orange juice, garlic, sugar, orange zest, and cayenne pepper and season with salt and pepper. Cover and bring to a boil, then lower the heat and simmer 20 to 25 minutes until the carrots are very tender.

2 Blend the soup until smooth, then work it through a strainer into a bowl, rubbing back and forth with a spoon and scraping the bottom of the strainer. Set aside to cool completely, then cover and chill at least 2 hours.

3 When ready to serve, stir well and add a little extra orange juice if the soup is too thick. Adjust the salt and pepper, if necessary, and serve.

331 Creamy Zucchini Soup

PREPARATION TIME 15 minutes, plus making the stock, cooling and at least 2 hours chilling **COOKING TIME** 20 minutes

4¼ cups Vegetable Stock (see page 12) or ready-made stock, plus extra as needed
2½ cups sliced zucchini
1 onion, chopped

¾ cup soft garlic-and-herb cream cheese
salt and ground white pepper
2 tablespoons finely chopped parsley leaves, to serve

1 Put the stock, zucchini, and onion in a saucepan. Season with salt and white pepper, cover, and bring to a boil. Lower the heat and simmer 8 to 10 minutes until the zucchini are very tender, then blend until smooth.

2 Put the cheese in a small bowl, add several spoonfuls of the soup and beat until smooth. Add this mixture to the soup, stirring until well blended. Set aside and let cool completely, then cover and chill at least 2 hours.

3 When ready to serve, add a little extra stock if the soup is too thick. Adjust the salt and pepper, if necessary, and serve sprinkled with parsley.

332 Zucchini & Basil Soup

PREPARATION TIME 15 minutes, plus making the stock, flavored oil, and croutes (optional), cooling, and at least 2 hours chilling   **COOKING TIME** 30 minutes

5½ cups Vegetable Stock
   (see page 12) or ready-made stock,
   plus extra as needed
4 garlic cloves, cut in half
1 can (15-oz.) crushed tomatoes
½ teaspoon sugar
1 large handful of basil leaves
2 tablespoons garlic-flavored olive oil

1 onion, finely chopped
5½ cups zucchini cut into
   half-moon slices
salt and freshly ground black pepper
1 recipe quantity Crushed Basil Oil
   (see page 15), to serve
Goat Cheese Croutes (see page 14),
   to serve (optional)

1   Put the stock, garlic, tomatoes, sugar, and basil in a saucepan and season with salt and pepper. Cover and bring to a boil, then boil 10 minutes.

2   Meanwhile, heat the garlic oil in another saucepan over medium heat. Add the onion and fry, stirring, 2 minutes. Add the zucchini and fry 2 to 3 minutes until the skins turn bright green and the onion is softened.

3   Strain the stock into a large heatproof bowl, pressing down on the flavorings to extract as much flavor as possible, then discard them. Return the stock to the pan, add the zucchini, and return to a boil. Reduce the heat to low and simmer, uncovered, 5 to 8 minutes until the zucchini are tender. Set aside to cool completely, then cover and chill at least 2 hours.

4   When ready to serve, stir well and add a little extra stock if the soup is too thick. Adjust the salt and pepper, if necessary, and serve drizzled with basil oil and with croutes on the side, if you like. This soup also tastes good served hot. When the zucchini are tender, adjust the salt and pepper, if necessary, and serve.

333 Curried Zucchini Soup

PREPARATION TIME 15 minutes, plus making the stock, cooling, and at least 2 hours chilling   **COOKING TIME** 25 minutes

1½ tablespoons sunflower oil
6 scallions, chopped
1 large garlic clove, crushed
5½ cups chopped zucchini
2 teaspoons mild curry powder
1¾ cups Vegetable Stock
   (see page 12) or ready-made
   stock, plus extra as needed

¾ cup Greek-style yogurt
salt and freshly ground black pepper
torn or chopped cilantro or mint
   leaves, to serve
mini poppadoms, fried, to serve
   (optional)

1   Heat the oil in a saucepan over medium heat. Add the scallions and garlic and fry, stirring, 3 minutes, or until the scallions are softened but not colored. Add the zucchini and fry, stirring, 2 to 3 minutes until the skins turn bright green. Add the curry powder and stir 30 seconds. Watch closely so it does not burn.

2   Add the stock and season with salt and pepper. Cover and bring to a boil, then lower the heat and simmer 8 to 10 minutes until the zucchini are tender. Blend until smooth, then transfer to a heatproof bowl and set aside to cool completely. Once cool, stir in the yogurt, then cover and chill at least 2 hours.

3   When ready to serve, stir well and add a little extra stock if the soup is too thick. Adjust the salt and pepper, if necessary, and serve sprinkled with cilantro and with mini poppadoms on the side, if you like.

334 Chargrilled Yellow Pepper Soup

PREPARATION TIME 25 minutes, plus making the stock and chargrilled peppers, cooling and at least 2 hours chilling   **COOKING TIME** 25 minutes

3 tablespoons garlic-flavored olive
   oil, plus extra to serve
1 onion, finely chopped
5 large yellow bell peppers,
   chargrilled (see page 9), peeled,
   seeded, and chopped
1 small carrot, peeled and sliced
1 potato, peeled and chopped

4½ cups Vegetable Stock
   (see page 12), plus extra as needed
salt and ground white pepper

GREMOLATA
finely grated zest of 1 lemon
1 garlic clove, very finely chopped
3 tablespoons finely chopped
   parsley leaves

1   Heat the oil in a saucepan over medium heat. Add the onion and fry, stirring occasionally, 3 to 5 minutes until softened but not colored. Stir in the peppers, carrot, and potato, season with salt and white pepper, and fry, stirring occasionally, 5 minutes. Add the stock, cover, and bring to a boil. Lower the heat and simmer 5 to 10 minutes until the vegetables are very tender.

2   Blend the soup until smooth, then work it through a strainer into a bowl, rubbing back and forth with a spoon and scraping the bottom of the strainer. Set aside to cool completely, then cover and chill at least 2 hours.

3   Shortly before serving, mix together all the ingredients for the gremolata in a bowl. (This is best made just before serving, although it will retain its fresh flavor for several hours, if you want to make it in advance.) Stir the soup well and add a little extra stock if it is too thick. Adjust the salt and pepper, if necessary, and serve sprinkled with the gremolata and drizzled with garlic oil.

335 Spanish White Garlic & Almond Soup

PREPARATION TIME 15 minutes, plus at least 2 hours freezing the grapes and chilling the water   **COOKING TIME** 10 minutes

1 small bunch of seedless
   white grapes, to serve
8 large garlic cloves,
   peeled but left whole
9 ounces day-old country-style
   bread, crusts removed

4 to 6 tablespoons sherry vinegar
2½ cups very finely ground
   blanched almonds
½ cup extra-virgin olive oil,
   plus extra to serve
salt and ground white pepper

1   At least 2 hours before serving, put the grapes in the freezer and put a jug with 5½ cups water in the refrigerator to chill. If your refrigerator is large enough, chill the serving bowls as well.

2   Put the garlic cloves in a small saucepan and cover with water. Cover and bring to a boil, then strain into a bowl and set the garlic aside. Tear the bread into a large bowl, sprinkle with the garlic-flavored water, and set aside 10 to 12 minutes until softened, then use your hands to squeeze any water from the bread.

3   Blend the bread with the garlic, ¼ cup of the vinegar, ground almonds, and oil to form a thick pastelike mixture. Season with salt and white pepper. Slowly add the chilled water and continue blending to achieve the preferred consistency. Adjust the salt and pepper and add the remaining sherry vinegar, if you like. At this point, the soup can be served as it is, or covered and chilled until required.

4   When ready to serve, stir well and add extra chilled water if the soup is too thick. Serve with the frozen grapes acting as ice cubes and drizzle with oil.

336 No-Cook Cucumber & Horseradish Soup

PREPARATION TIME 10 minutes, plus making the stock and croutons and at least
2 hours chilling

1 cup Vegetable Stock (see page 12)
  or ready-made stock
4 scallions, chopped
1¼ pounds cucumbers,
  peeled and seeded

1 cup sour cream
1 tablespoon grated horseradish
salt and ground white pepper
1 recipe quantity Dill Croutons
  (see page 14), to serve

1 Put the stock and scallions in a blender and blend. Add the cucumbers, sour cream,
  and horseradish and blend again. Season with salt and white pepper.
2 Cover and chill at least 2 hours. When ready to serve, stir well because the soup
  will have separated. Adjust the salt and pepper, if necessary. Serve sprinkled
  with croutons.

337 Cucumber & Yogurt Soup with Mint

PREPARATION TIME 15 minutes, plus making the stock, cooling, and at least
2 hours chilling   COOKING TIME 30 minutes

2½ cups Vegetable Stock
  (see page 12) or ready-made stock
1 shallot, finely chopped
3 cups peeled, seeded, and
  chopped cucumber
2 tablespoons mint leaves, plus
  extra, finely shredded, to serve

1¾ cups Greek-style yogurt
scant 1 cup buttermilk, plus extra
  as needed
finely grated zest of 1 lemon
a pinch of cayenne pepper
salt and ground white pepper
chopped pistachio nuts, to serve

1 Put the stock and shallot in a saucepan. Cover and bring to a boil, then boil for
  10 minutes. Lower the heat, add the cucumber and simmer, covered, 10 minutes,
  then add the mint and blend until smooth.
2 Transfer the soup to a bowl and set aside to cool completely. Once cool, stir in
  the yogurt, buttermilk, lemon zest, and cayenne pepper and season with salt and
  white pepper.
3 Cover and chill at least 2 hours. When ready to serve, stir well and add a little extra
  buttermilk if the soup is too thick. Adjust the salt and pepper, if necessary, and
  serve sprinkled with mint and pistachio nuts.

338 Yellow Tomato Soup

PREPARATION TIME 15 minutes, plus cooling and at least 2 hours chilling and making
the flavored oil   COOKING TIME 30 minutes

1½ tablespoons olive or hemp oil
1 yellow pepper, seeded and
  chopped
1 shallot, chopped
3½ cups chopped yellow tomatoes
4 cups Vegetable Stock (see page 12)
  or ready-made stock, plus extra
  as needed

½ teaspoon sugar
salt and ground white pepper
1 recipe quantity Crushed Basil
  or Mint Oil (see page 15), to serve
crumbled feta cheese, to serve

1 Heat the oil in a saucepan over medium heat. Add the pepper and shallot and fry,
  stirring, 3 to 5 minutes until the shallot is softened. Add the tomatoes and cook
  5 minutes. Add the stock and sugar and season with salt and pepper. Cover and
  bring to a boil, then lower the heat and simmer 10 minutes. Blend the soup.
2 Work the soup through a strainer into a bowl, rubbing back and forth with a spoon.
  Set aside to cool completely, then cover and chill at least 2 hours.
3 When ready to serve, stir well and add a little extra stock if the soup is too thick.
  Adjust the salt and pepper, if necessary, and serve drizzled with herb oil and
  sprinkled with cheese.

339 Bloody Mary Party Soup

PREPARATION TIME 15 minutes, plus making the stock, cooling, and at least 2 hours chilling
COOKING TIME 30 minutes   **MAKES** 14 x scant ½ cup servings or 4 to 6 conventional servings

1 tablespoon chili-flavored olive oil
¾ cup peeled and diced carrot
1 celery rib, finely chopped,
   plus extra celery ribs with
   leaves to serve
1 onion, finely chopped
3 cups tomato puree, plus extra
   as needed

4¼ cups Vegetable Stock
   (see page 12) or ready-made stock,
   plus extra as needed
⅔ cup vodka
a pinch of chili flakes, or to taste
lemon juice, to taste
salt and freshly ground black pepper
sweet sherry, to serve
celery salt, to serve
celery seeds, to serve

1   Heat the oil in a saucepan over medium heat. Stir in the carrot, celery, and onion,
    reduce the heat to low, and cook, covered, 8 to 10 minutes, stirring occasionally,
    until softened. Stir in the tomato puree, stock, vodka, and chili flakes and season
    with salt and pepper. Cover and bring to a boil, then lower the heat and simmer
    10 minutes. Add lemon juice to taste, then blend until smooth.
2   Strain the soup through a strainer into a large bowl, rubbing back and forth with
    a spoon and scraping the bottom of the strainer. Set aside to cool completely,
    then cover and chill at least 2 hours.
3   When ready to serve, stir the soup and add a little extra tomato puree or stock
    if it is too thick. Adjust the salt and pepper, if necessary. Put ½ teaspoon sweet
    sherry in fourteen small or four to six regular mugs or glasses. Add the soup,
    sprinkle with celery salt and celery seeds, and add celery ribs to
    act as stirrers, if you like, and serve.

340 Minted Pea Soup

PREPARATION TIME 15 minutes, plus making the stock, cooling, and at least 2 hours chilling   **COOKING TIME** 30 minutes

1½ tablespoons olive or hemp oil, plus extra to serve
4 scallions, finely chopped, plus extra, thinly sliced on the diagonal, to serve
1 russet potato, peeled and finely chopped

4 cups Vegetable Stock (see page 12) or ready-made stock, plus extra as needed
4 cups frozen peas
1 small bunch mint leaves, about 1 ounce, plus small leaves to serve
salt and freshly ground black pepper

1   Heat the oil in a saucepan over medium heat. Add the scallions and fry, stirring, 3 to 5 minutes until softened but not colored. Stir in the potato, add the stock, and season with salt and pepper. Cover and bring to a boil, then lower the heat and simmer 10 to 12 minutes until the potato is tender.
2   Add the peas and mint, return to a boil, uncovered, then simmer 3 to 5 minutes until the peas are tender.
3   Blend the soup. For a smoother texture, work it through a strainer, if you like, rubbing back and forth with a spoon and scraping the bottom of the strainer to remove the pea skins. Let cool completely, then cover and chill at least 2 hours.
4   When ready to serve, stir well and add extra stock if the soup is too thick. Adjust the salt and pepper, if necessary. Serve sprinkled with scallions and mint leaves and drizzled with a little olive oil.

341 Edamame & Pea Soup with Crushed Basil Oil

PREPARATION TIME 10 minutes, plus making the stock and flavored oil, cooling, and at least 2 hours chilling   **COOKING TIME** 15 minutes

¾ cup frozen shelled edamame beans
2 cups Vegetable Stock (see page 12) or ready-made stock
finely grated zest of 1 lemon
a pinch of chili flakes, or to taste
2⅔ cups frozen peas

1¾ cups rice milk or almond milk, plus extra as needed
½ tablespoon lemon juice, plus extra to taste
salt and freshly ground black pepper
1 recipe quantity Crushed Basil Oil (see page 15), to serve
flaxseed, lightly crushed, to serve

1   Bring a covered saucepan of salted water to a boil. Add the edamame and boil, uncovered, 5 minutes, or until tender. Drain and immediately rinse under cold running water. Set aside.
2   Meanwhile, put the stock, lemon zest, and chili flakes in another saucepan and season with salt and pepper. Cover and bring to a boil. Add the peas, lower the heat, and simmer, uncovered, 3 to 5 minutes until tender, then stir in the rice milk.
3   Blend two-thirds of the pea mixture to the preferred consistency. Rub the mixture through a strainer for an even smoother texture, if you like. Return the mixture to the pan, stir in the edamame and lemon juice, and set the soup aside to cool completely, then cover and chill at least 2 hours.
4   When ready to serve, add a little extra milk if the soup is too thick. Stir well and adjust the salt and pepper and add extra lemon juice, if necessary. Serve drizzled with basil oil and sprinkled with flaxseed.

342 Gazpacho

PREPARATION TIME 20 minutes, plus preparing the tomatoes, at least 2 hours chilling, and making the croutons

6 large tomatoes, peeled
(see page 9), seeded and chopped
2 red bell peppers,
seeded and chopped
2 large garlic cloves,
coarsely chopped
3 cups peeled, seeded,
and chopped cucumbers
¼ cup extra-virgin olive oil,
plus extra to serve
tomato juice (optional)
sherry vinegar, to taste
salt and freshly ground black pepper

TO SERVE
1 recipe quantity Garlic Croutons
(see page 14)
2 scallions, thinly sliced
1 large green bell pepper,
seeded and finely diced
1 large red bell pepper,
seeded and finely diced
½ cucumber, peeled,
seeded, and finely diced
ice cubes (optional)

1 Blend the tomatoes, bell peppers, garlic, cucumber, and oil to the preferred consistency. Depending on how juicy the tomatoes were, it might be necessary to stir in a little tomato juice to give the soup a more liquid texture. Strain the soup for an even smoother texture, if you like.

2 Season with salt and pepper, add sherry vinegar, and blend again. Cover and chill at least 2 hours.

3 When ready to serve, stir well. Adjust the salt and pepper and add more vinegar, if necessary. Serve with an ice cube added to each portion, if you like, and with the croutons, scallions, peppers, and cucumber on the side.

343 Chilled Tomato & Yogurt Soup

PREPARATION TIME 15 minutes, plus making the stock and seeds, preparing the tomatoes, cooling, and at least 2 hours chilling **COOKING TIME** 30 minutes

1½ tablespoon fruity extra-virgin
olive oil
1 red onion, finely chopped
2 large garlic cloves, chopped
1 teaspoon dried thyme or mint
½ teaspoon cinnamon
2¼ cups Vegetable Stock
(see page 12) or ready-made stock,
plus extra as needed
5 tomatoes, grated (see page 9)

2 sun-dried tomatoes in oil,
drained and chopped
a pinch of sugar
2½ cups Greek-style yogurt
salt and freshly ground black pepper
oil from the sun-dried tomatoes
or extra-virgin olive oil, to serve
Toasted Pumpkin Seeds (see page 9),
to serve
chopped cilantro leaves, to serve

1 Heat the oil in a saucepan over medium heat. Add the onion and fry, stirring, 2 minutes. Add the garlic and fry, stirring, 1 to 3 minutes until the onion is softened but not colored. Add the thyme and cinnamon and stir 30 seconds, or until aromatic. Watch closely so they do not burn.

2 Add the stock, tomatoes, sun-dried tomatoes, and sugar and season with salt and pepper. Cover and bring to a boil. Lower the heat and simmer 10 to 15 minutes until the onions are very tender.

3 Blend the soup until smooth, then stir in the yogurt. Set aside to cool completely, then cover and chill at least 2 hours.

4 When ready to serve, stir well and a little extra stock if the soup is too thick. Adjust the salt and pepper, if necessary, and serve drizzled with oil and sprinkled with seeds and cilantro.

344 Iced Tomato & Orange Soup with Goat Milk Yogurt Sorbet

PREPARATION TIME 5 minutes, plus making, cooling and at least 2 hours chilling the soup and 2 hours freezing the sorbet   COOKING TIME 10 minutes

1 recipe quantity Slow-Cooked
   Tomato & Orange Soup
   (see page 40), chilled at least
   2 hours
orange juice (optional)
salt and freshly ground black pepper
   (optional)
very finely chopped parsley, to serve

GOAT MILK YOGURT SORBET
1 cup plus 2 tablespoons goat
   milk yogurt
scant 1 cup sugar
1 tablespoon lemon juice

1   To make the sorbet, combine the yogurt, sugar, lemon juice, and ¾ cup water
    in a saucepan over medium heat and stir until the sugar dissolves. Bring to a boil,
    then boil, without stirring, 5 minutes. Brush down the side of the pan with a wet
    pastry brush, if the mixture splashes the sides, but do not stir.
2   Pour the mixture into a shallow, heatproof bowl and set aside to cool completely.
    Churn the sorbet in an ice-cream maker, following the manufacturer's directions,
    then transfer to a freezerproof bowl and freeze until required. Alternatively, put the
    mixture in the freezer and freeze 2 hours. Use an electric mixer or fork to beat the
    semifrozen mixture, then return it to the freezer. Repeat two more times, then
    return the sorbet to the freezer until required.
3   Remove the sorbet from the freezer 10 minutes before serving. When ready
    to serve, stir the soup well and add extra orange juice, if you like. Adjust the salt
    and pepper, if necessary, and serve immediately with 1 scoop of sorbet per portion,
    sprinkled with parsley. Any leftover sorbet can be kept frozen up to 3 months.

345 Big Red Raw Soup

PREPARATION TIME 15 minutes, plus preparing the tomatoes, making the seeds, and at least 2 hours chilling

2¾ pounds tomatoes, peeled
   (see page 9), seeded, and chopped
2½ cups peeled and chopped carrots
2 red bell peppers,
   seeded and chopped
½ cup Vegetable Stock (see page 12),
   or ready-made stock,
   plus extra as needed

tomato juice (optional)
2 teaspoons sugar
finely grated zest of 2 oranges
salt
1 tablespoon Greek-style yogurt
   for each bowl, whisked, to serve
Crunchy Mixed Seeds (see page 15),
   to serve

1   Put the tomatoes, carrots, peppers, and stock in a blender or food processor and
    blend until smooth. Working in batches, strain through a nylon strainer, rubbing
    back and forth with a spoon and scraping the bottom of the strainer. Depending
    on how juicy the tomatoes are, you might have to add tomato juice to make the
    soup up to 5½ cups, or to thin it to the preferred consistency.
2   Stir in the sugar and orange zest and season with salt. Cover and chill at least 2 hours.
3   When ready to serve, stir well and add a little orange or tomato juice if the soup
    is too thick. Adjust the salt, if necessary, and serve with a swirl of yogurt and
    sprinkled with seeds.

346 Raw Emerald Soup with Crushed Basil Oil

PREPARATION TIME 10 minutes, plus making the flavored oil and stock and 2 hours chilling

3 avocados
2 tablespoons lime juice, or to taste
1 teaspoon olive or hemp oil
14 ounces baby spinach leaves
3½ cups Vegetable Stock
   (see page 12) or ready-made
   stock, plus extra as needed

3 garlic cloves, crushed
salt and ground white pepper
1 recipe quantity Crushed Basil Oil
   (see page 15), to serve

1   Cut the avocados in half, remove the seeds, and use a spoon to scoop the flesh into a blender. Add the lime juice, oil, spinach, stock, and garlic and season with salt and white pepper, then blend until smooth. Cover with plastic wrap directly resting on the surface of the soup and chill 2 hours.
2   When ready to serve, stir well and adjust the salt and pepper, if necessary. Serve drizzled with basil oil.

347 Fresh Red Detox Soup

PREPARATION TIME 15 minutes, plus at least 2 hours chilling and making the seeds

3½ cups carrot juice
2 celery ribs, chopped
1 small cooked beet,
   peeled and chopped
1½ cups seeded and chopped
   cucumbers

½ fennel bulb, chopped
½ teaspoon celery seeds
orange juice, to taste
Crunchy Mixed Seeds (see page 15),
   to serve

1   Blend the carrot juice, celery, beet, cucumber, fennel, and celery seed to the preferred consistency. Rub the soup through a strainer for an even smoother texture, and to remove the fibers from the vegetables, if you like. Cover and chill at least 2 hours.
2   When ready to serve, stir in the orange juice. Serve sprinkled with seeds.

348 Green Cucumber & Chili Soup

PREPARATION TIME 15 minutes, plus 30 minutes standing, making the croutes and at least 2 hours chilling

1 large cucumber, seeded and
   coarsely chopped
½ teaspoon salt, plus extra to season
4¼ cups Vegetable Stock
   (see page 12) or ready-made stock
6 scallions, chopped
1 handful of cilantro leaves,
   plus extra to serve
5 tablespoons extra-virgin olive oil,
   plus extra to serve

1 green serrano chili, seeded
   (optional) and chopped
1 teaspoon ground cumin
1 tablespoon Chinese rice vinegar,
   or to taste
freshly ground black pepper
flaxseed, lightly crushed, to serve
Goat Cheese Croutes (see page 14),
   to serve

1   Put the cucumber in a strainer, sprinkle with the salt, and let drain 30 minutes, then rinse under cold running water and squeeze dry.
2   Put the cucumber, stock, scallions, cilantro, oil, chili, cumin, and vinegar in a blender and blend until well mixed and finely chopped but not pureed. Season with salt and pepper. Transfer to a bowl, cover, and chill at least 2 hours.
3   When ready to serve, stir the soup well because it will have separated. Adjust the salt and pepper, if necessary, and add extra oil or vinegar, if you like. Serve sprinkled with cilantro and flaxseed and drizzled with olive oil, and with croutes on the side.

349 Fennel & Red Pepper Soups

PREPARATION TIME 25 minutes, plus making the stock, cooling, and at least
2 hours chilling   **COOKING TIME** 40 minutes

¼ cup olive oil
2 onions, very finely chopped
2 bulbs fennel, finely chopped, with
   the fronds reserved and chopped
½ cup Vegetable Stock (see page 12)
   or ready-made stock
2 tablespoons lemon juice

1 teaspoon aniseed-flavored spirit,
   such as Pernod
2 large red bell peppers, seeded and
   diced
a pinch of cayenne pepper
1 tablespoon crème fraîche
salt and ground white pepper

1   Heat the oil in a saucepan over medium heat. Add the onions and fry, stirring
    occasionally, 3 to 5 minutes until softened. Remove half the onions and set aside.

2   To make the fennel soup, add the fennel to the onion in the pan and cook, stirring,
    5 minutes. Add half the stock, the lemon juice, spirit, and enough water to cover.
    Season with salt and white pepper. Cover and bring to a boil, then lower the heat
    and simmer 12 to 15 minutes until the fennel is very tender. Blend until smooth,
    then work the soup through a strainer into a bowl. Stir in the crème fraîche and set
    aside to cool completely, then cover and chill at least 2 hours.

3   Meanwhile, make the red pepper soup. Put the remaining onion in a saucepan and
    reheat. Add the bell peppers and cook, stirring, 5 minutes. Add the remaining stock,
    cayenne pepper, enough water to cover, and season with salt. Cover and bring
    to a boil, then lower the heat and simmer 12 to 15 minutes until the red peppers
    are very tender. Blend until smooth. Work the soup through a strainer into a bowl.
    Set aside to cool completely, then cover and chill at least 2 hours.

4   To serve, stir each soup and adjust the salt and pepper, if necessary. Filling one soup
    bowl at a time, put the fennel soup in half the bowl, then add the red pepper soup to
    the other half and use the tip of a knife to swirl decoratively. Alternatively, put a metal
    ring in the middle and fill it with the fennel soup. Spoon the red pepper soup around
    the outside of the ring, then carefully lift the ring. In any case, always pour the fennel
    soup first because it is thicker and will remain in position. Sprinkle with the fennel
    fronds and serve.

350 Avocado & Coconut Soup

PREPARATION TIME 15 minutes, plus making the stock and seeds, cooling, and at least
2 hours chilling   COOKING TIME 15 minutes

1 pound 2 ounces avocados
1½ tablespoons lime juice, or to taste
1½ tablespoons olive or hemp oil
1 leek, sliced and rinsed
3¾ cups Chicken Stock (see page 11)
   or ready-made stock
finely grated zest of 1 lime

2 tablespoons chopped
   cilantro leaves
⅔ cup coconut milk
salt and ground white pepper
Spiced Seeds (see page 15), to serve
toasted coconut flakes, to serve
lime wedges, to serve

1   Peel and remove the seeds from the avocados, chop the flesh, and toss it in a bowl
    with 1 tablespoon of the lime juice, then set aside.
2   Heat the oil in a saucepan over medium heat. Add the leek and fry, stirring,
    3 to 5 minutes until softened. Add the stock, avocados, remaining lime juice,
    and lime zest and season with salt and white pepper. Cover and bring to a boil,
    then simmer 2 to 3 minutes until the avocado is tender. Stir in the cilantro leaves
    and blend the soup until smooth. Transfer to a bowl and set aside to cool, then
    cover and chill at least 2 hours.
3   When ready to serve, stir in the coconut milk and adjust the salt and pepper,
    if necessary, and add extra lime juice, if you like. Serve sprinkled with the seeds
    and coconut flakes, and with lime wedges for squeezing over.

351 Mexican Corn & Pepper Soup

PREPARATION TIME 15 minutes, plus making the stock, cooling, and at least
2 hours chilling   COOKING TIME 1¼ hours

6 cups Vegetable Stock (see page 12)
   or ready-made stock,
2 cups fresh corn kernels, cobs
   reserved and cut in half
2 yellow bell peppers
1 large garlic bulb
1 hot or mild chili, to taste
¼ cup olive oil, plus extra as needed
1 red onion, finely chopped

1 celery rib, thinly sliced
1 teaspoon ground coriander
1 teaspoon ground cumin
salt and freshly ground black pepper
Mexican queso fresco or feta cheese,
   drained and crumbled, to serve
tortilla chips, to serve
lime wedges, to serve

1   Preheat the oven to 425°F. Put the stock and corn cobs into a saucepan and season
    with salt. Cover and bring to a boil, then reduce the heat to very low (use a heat
    diffuser if you have one) and simmer, covered, 45 minutes.
2   Meanwhile, rub the bell peppers, garlic, and chili with oil. Put the peppers on the
    oven rack and roast 20 minutes. Add the chili and garlic and roast 20 to 25 minutes
    until all are lightly charred and the garlic is soft.
3   Transfer the peppers and chili to a bowl, cover, and let cool, then peel, seed, and
    chop the peppers. Seed the chili, scrape the flesh from the skin, and set aside.
    Reserve any juices that accumulate in the bowl. When cool enough to handle,
    separate the garlic into cloves and squeeze the flesh onto a plate.
4   Bring a saucepan of salted water to a boil. Meanwhile, heat the oil in a saucepan
    over medium heat. Add the onion and celery and fry, stirring, 3 to 5 minutes until
    softened. Add the coriander and cumin and stir 30 seconds.
5   Add the peppers, garlic, and chili flesh to the onion mixture, then stir in half the
    corn kernels, the stock with the corn cobs, and any reserved juices from the chilies.
    Cover and bring to a boil, then lower the heat and simmer 5 to 7 minutes until the
    kernels are tender. Meanwhile, put the remaining corn kernels in the pan of boiling
    water and boil 3 to 5 minutes until tender, then drain and set aside.
6   Discard the corn cobs from the large pan and blend the soup until smooth. Add the
    drained corn kernels and season with salt and pepper. Transfer to a bowl and set
    aside to cool completely, then cover and chill at least 2 hours.
7   When ready to serve, stir well and add stock if the soup is too thick. Adjust the salt
    and pepper, if necessary, and serve sprinkled with cheese and with tortilla chips
    on the side and lime wedges for squeezing over.

352 Jeweled Cucumber & Walnut Soup

PREPARATION TIME 15 minutes, plus making the stock, toasting the walnuts,
30 minutes standing, and at least 2 hours chilling

2 cups grated cucumber
½ teaspoon salt, plus extra to season
2½ cups Greek-style yogurt, plus
   extra as needed
2½ cups Vegetable Stock
   (see page 12) or ready-made stock
2 garlic cloves, crushed

¾ cup walnut halves, very lightly
   toasted (see page 9) and chopped
2 tablespoons finely chopped mint
   leaves, plus extra to serve
freshly ground white pepper
pomegranate syrup, to serve
walnut oil, to serve
1 pomegranate, to serve

1   Put the cucumber in a strainer, sprinkle with the salt, and let drain 30 minutes, then
rinse under cold running water and pat dry. Transfer the cucumber to a bowl and stir
in the stock, yogurt, garlic, walnuts, and mint. Season with salt and white pepper,
then cover and chill at least 2 hours.

2   When ready to serve, stir well and add a little extra yogurt if the soup is too thick.
Adjust the salt and pepper, if necessary, and divide into bowls. Sprinkle with mint and
drizzle with pomegranate syrup and walnut oil. Bash the pomegranate with a wooden
spoon, then cut it in half. Hold one half over one of the bowls and tap the top with the
spoon so the seeds fall over the soup. Remove any white pith, if necessary. Repeat
to sprinkle the remaining bowls with pomegranate seeds, then serve.

353 Lebanese Cucumber Soup

PREPARATION TIME 15 minutes, plus 30 minutes standing, making the stock and shrimp and at least 2 hours chilling

2½ cups seeded and diced cucumber
½ teaspoon salt, plus extra to season
1 egg
2 large garlic cloves, one halved and
  one crushed in one piece
⅔ cup Greek yogurt
2½ cups tomato juice, plus extra
  as needed
2½ cups Vegetable Stock
  (see page 12) or ready-made stock

freshly ground black pepper
12 shelled and deveined cooked
  shrimp, cut in half lengthwise,
  to serve
chopped dill, to serve
extra-virgin olive oil, to serve
  (optional)
hot pepper sauce, to serve (optional)

1   Put the cucumber in a strainer, sprinkle with the salt, and let drain 30 minutes, then rinse under cold running water and pat dry.
2   Meanwhile, put the egg in a saucepan, cover with 1 inch water, and bring to a boil, then lower the heat and simmer 9 minutes. Pour off the hot water, then run cold water over the egg 1 to 2 minutes to stop the cooking. Set aside until cool enough to handle, then peel.
3   Rub the garlic halves over the inside of the bowl you are going to make the soup in, pressing down very firmly to extract as much flavor as possible, then discard. Put the yogurt in the bowl and slowly whisk in the tomato juice until evenly blended, then add the stock and season with salt and pepper. Add the cucumber and crushed garlic, then cover and chill at least 2 hours.
4   When ready to serve, stir well and adjust the salt and pepper, if necessary. Stir in a little extra tomato juice if the soup is too thick and discard the crushed garlic. Dice the hard-boiled egg. Divide the shrimp into bowls and ladle the soup over them. Sprinkle with the hard-boiled egg and dill and serve with oil and hot pepper sauce on the side, if you like.

354 Lemon & Saffron Soup

PREPARATION TIME 10 minutes, plus making the stock, cooling, and at least 2 hours chilling
COOKING TIME 45 minutes

1 large lemon, well scrubbed
2 tablespoons butter
2 tablespoons all-purpose flour
a large pinch of saffron threads
4½ cups Vegetable Stock
  (see page 12) or ready-made stock,
  plus extra as needed

⅔ cup crème fraîche or sour cream
salt and ground white pepper
finely shredded mint leaves, to serve
goji berries (optional), to serve

1   Put the lemon in a small saucepan and cover generously with water. Cover, bring to a boil and boil 5 minutes, then drain. Repeat this process three more times. After the fourth time, cut the lemon in half in a soup bowl to capture all the juices and set aside.
2   Melt the butter in a large saucepan over medium heat. Sprinkle in the flour, add the saffron, and stir 2 minutes. Remove the pan from the heat and slowly pour in the stock, stirring continuously to prevent lumps from forming. Stir in the crème fraîche, then return the soup to the heat and bring to a boil, stirring. Boil 2 minutes, then remove from the heat and set aside.
3   Use the tip of a knife to remove the seeds from the lemon halves, then chop each half, including the skins. Add the lemon and any accumulated juices to the soup and blend until smooth. Season with salt and white pepper. Set aside to cool completely, then cover and chill at least 2 hours.
4   When ready to serve, add a little extra stock if the soup is too thick and stir well. Adjust the salt and pepper, if necessary, and serve sprinkled with mint leaves and goji berries, if you like. This soup is also good served hot, sprinkled with mint leaves and chopped pistachio nuts.

355 Arugula Soup with Smoked Salmon

PREPARATION TIME 25 minutes, plus making the stock and flavored oil, cooling and at least 2 hours chilling   COOKING TIME 35 minutes

1 tablespoon olive or hemp oil
1½ cups chopped fennel
4 scallions, chopped
4½ cups Chicken Stock (see page 11), plus extra as needed
1 ounce arugula, leaves and stems separated, with the stems tied together and crushed

salt and freshly ground black pepper
2 ounces smoked salmon, shredded, to serve
1 recipe quantity Crushed Mint or Basil Oil (see page 15), to serve

1   Heat the oil in a saucepan over medium heat. Add the fennel and fry, stirring, 5 minutes. Add the scallions and fry 1 to 2 minutes until softened, then add the stock and season with salt and pepper. Cover and bring to a boil. Lower the heat and simmer 15 to 20 minutes until the fennel is very tender. Add the arugula leaves and stems and simmer 1 minute, or until the leaves wilt.

2   Discard the stems and blend the soup until smooth, then work it through a strainer. Let cool completely, then cover and chill at least 2 hours.

3   When ready to serve, add extra stock if the soup is too thick. Stir and adjust the salt and pepper, if necessary. Serve topped with smoked salmon and drizzled with the mint oil.

356 Peach & Orange Buttermilk Soup

PREPARATION TIME 15 minutes, plus toasting the almonds and at least 2 hours chilling

5 cups peeled, pitted, and chopped peaches
2¼ cups buttermilk, plus extra as needed
⅔ cup orange juice
1 teaspoon honey, or to taste

½ teaspoon almond extract
a small pinch of salt
lemon juice, to taste (optional)
toasted slivered almonds (see page 9), to serve

1   Put the peaches, buttermilk, orange juice, honey, almond extract, and salt in a blender and blend until smooth. Add lemon juice, if necessary.

2   Cover and chill at least 2 hours. When ready to serve, add extra buttermilk if the soup is too thick. Stir well, then adjust the salt and add extra honey or lemon juice, if necessary. Serve sprinkled with toasted almonds.

357 Spiced Fruit Salad Soup

PREPARATION TIME 20 minutes, plus at least 1 hour infusing, cooling, and at least 2 hours chilling   COOKING TIME 10 minutes

2¼ cups pomegranate juice
2¼ cups orange juice
2 tablespoons lime juice
finely grated zest of 1 lime
2 star anise
1 cinnamon stick
1 thin slice of gingerroot, crushed
1½ cups seeded and diced cucumber

1½ cups finely diced pineapple
1 mango, peeled and finely diced
1 crisp apple, halved, cored, and diced
2 tablespoons finely chopped mint leaves
1 pomegranate, to serve

1   Pour all the juices into a saucepan, cover, and bring to a boil. Remove from the heat, add the zest, star anise, cinnamon stick, and ginger and let stand, covered, at least 1 hour for the flavors to blend.

2   Transfer the mixture to a bowl and let cool completely. Add the cucumber, pineapple, mango, apple and mint leaves. Stir well, cover, and chill at least 2 hours.

3   When ready to serve, stir well. Discard the spices and divide the soup into bowls. Decorate with pomegranate seeds (see recipe 352), then serve.

358 Sweet Buttermilk Dessert Soup

PREPARATION TIME 20 minutes, plus toasting the almonds, 30 minutes soaking, cooling and at least 2 hours chilling   **COOKING TIME** 7 minutes

½ cup golden raisins
2 tablespoons light or dark rum
¼ cup rice flour
5½ cups buttermilk
1 cinnamon stick
2 egg yolks
2 tablespoons sugar, or to taste
finely grated zest of 1 orange,
 plus extra to serve

⅔ cup heavy cream, lightly whipped
salt
finely grated zest of 1 lemon, to serve
finely grated zest of 1 lime, to serve
toasted slivered almonds
 (see page 9), to serve

1 Put the golden raisins in a bowl, cover with the rum, and let soak 30 minutes until soft, then drain.
2 Put the rice flour in a saucepan and slowly add the buttermilk, stirring to prevent lumps from forming. Add the golden raisins and cinnamon stick and season lightly with salt. Heat over low heat, stirring, 5 to 7 minutes until thicker. Remove from the heat, discard the cinnamon stick, and set the soup aside.
3 In a large bowl, beat the egg yolks and sugar, using an electric mixer, until thick and pale and the mixture holds a "ribbon" on the surface when the beaters lifted. Slowly beat in the soup, then add extra sugar or salt, if you like. Set aside to cool completely, then stir in the orange zest, cover, and chill at least 2 hours.
4 When ready to serve, stir well. Stir in the whipped cream and serve sprinkled with citrus zests and almonds.

359 Refreshing Honeydew Melon Soup

PREPARATION TIME 15 minutes, plus at least 2 hours chilling

6 cups peeled, seeded,
 and diced cucumbers
1 honeydew melon, 2¼ pounds,
 peeled, seeded, and diced
1 large celery rib, strings removed,
 if necessary, and sliced
4 scallions, white parts only,
 finely chopped

1 cup Greek-style yogurt
white wine vinegar, to taste
3 tablespoons shredded mint leaves,
 plus extra to serve
salt and ground white pepper

1 Put the cucumbers, melon, celery, scallions, yogurt, vinegar, and mint in a large bowl or blender. Season with white pepper and mix well. Blend until smooth, then season with salt and extra pepper, if necessary. Cover and chill at least 2 hours.
2 When ready to serve, stir well and adjust the salt and pepper, if necessary, and add extra vinegar, if you like. Serve sprinkled with mint leaves.

360 Strawberry Soup with Orange Sorbet

PREPARATION TIME 15 minutes, plus at least 1 hour standing and at least 2 hours chilling

3¼ pounds strawberries, hulled
1 cup sugar, plus extra as needed
orange juice (optional)
orange sorbet, to serve

freshly ground black pepper, to serve
finely grated orange zest, to serve
balsamic vinegar, to serve

1 Stir the strawberries and sugar together in a large nonreactive bowl and leave to stand at least 1 hour until the juices run, then blend until smooth. Strain the liquid through a strainer into a bowl, rubbing back and forth with a spoon. Cover and chill at least 2 hours.
2 When ready to serve, stir well. Add extra sugar and stir in a little orange juice, if necessary, and divide into bowls. Put 1 scoop of sorbet in each one and sprinkle with pepper and orange zest. Serve immediately, with balsamic vinegar on the side.

361 Green Tea Soup with Coconut Jelly

PREPARATION TIME 15 minutes, plus chilling the coconut jelly, cooling and at least 2 hours chilling   **COOKING TIME** 15 minutes

2 tablespoons matcha
  (green tea powder)
5½ cups whole milk
1 tablespoon sugar, or to taste
finely grated lime zest, to serve

COCONUT JELLY
1 cup coconut milk
1 heaping tablespoon agar agar
  flakes
1 tablespoon sugar

1   To make the coconut jelly, rinse the inside of a shallow, heatproof 4½- x 3½-inch dish (or use a small ice cube tray), then pour the water out, but do not dry it, and set aside. Put the coconut milk, agar agar flakes, and sugar in a saucepan. Bring to a simmer over low heat, without stirring. Once it is simmering, stir occasionally 3 to 5 minutes until the agar agar flakes dissolve completely— put some of the mixture in a clean spoon and look closely for any specks of agar agar. Pour the mixture into the prepared dish and set aside to cool completely. Cover and chill to set while you make the soup. You can speed up the cooling process by resting the dish inside a larger dish filled with cold water.

2   To make the soup, mix the matcha and a little of the milk together in a small bowl to make a thin paste, then stir the mixture into the rinsed-out saucepan, along with the remaining milk and the sugar. Bring to just below the boil and stir until the sugar dissolves, then immediately remove the pan from the heat and pour the soup into a heatproof bowl. Set aside to cool completely, then cover and chill at least 2 hours.

3   When ready to serve, run the tip of a round-bladed knife around the edges of the coconut jelly, then invert it onto a plate, shake well, and remove the dish. Cut the jelly into bite-size pieces. Stir the soup and add extra sugar, if you like. Serve topped with the coconut jelly and sprinkled with lime zest.

362 Hungarian Cherry Soup

PREPARATION TIME 15 minutes, plus toasting the almonds, cooling and at least 2 hours chilling **COOKING TIME** 20 minutes

2 pounds fresh cherries, pitted
1 cup rosé or dry red wine
1 tablespoon light brown sugar
1 cinnamon stick
pared zest of 1 large lemon, all bitter
    white pith removed
¾ cup Greek yogurt, smetana,
    or sour cream

1 teaspoon almond extract
lemon juice, to taste (optional)
salt
2 tablespoons cherry brandy
    or kirsch (optional)
toasted slivered almonds
    (see page 9), to serve

1   Put the cherries, wine, sugar, cinnamon stick, lemon zest, and scant 1 cup water in a saucepan and stir to dissolve the sugar. Cover and bring to just below the boil, then lower the heat and simmer 10 to 12 minutes until the cherries are very tender.

2   Discard the cinnamon stick and lemon zest and blend the soup until smooth. Stir in the yogurt, almond extract, and lemon juice and season lightly with salt. Transfer to a bowl and set aside to cool completely, then cover and chill at least 2 hours.

3   When ready to serve, stir in the brandy, if using. Adjust the salt and add extra lemon juice, if necessary, then serve sprinkled with almond flakes, either as a dessert soup or, as in Hungary, as a first course.

363 Cantaloupe "Gazpacho"

PREPARATION TIME 15 minutes, plus at least 2 hours chilling

1 cantaloupe, about 2¼ pounds,
   peeled, seeded, and
   coarsely chopped
1½ cups peeled, seeded,
   and chopped cucumbers
1 cup Greek-style yogurt

sherry or balsamic vinegar, to taste
salt and ground white pepper
2 ounces prosciutto or Serrano ham,
   very thinly sliced, to serve
scallions, white parts only, finely
   chopped, to serve

1   Put the cantaloupe, cucumber, and yogurt in a blender and blend until smooth.
    Season with salt and white pepper, then cover and chill at least 2 hours.
2   When ready to serve, stir well, add the vinegar, and adjust the salt and pepper,
    if necessary. Serve sprinkled with ham and scallions.

364 Adzuki Bean Soup with Orange Sorbet

PREPARATION TIME 5 minutes, plus overnight soaking, cooling, and at least
2 hours chilling   COOKING TIME 1½ hours

1 cup dried adzuki beans
6-inch piece of dried kombu
2½ tablespoons sugar, or to taste

orange sorbet, to serve
finely grated orange zest, to serve
cinnamon, to serve

1   Put the adzuki beans and kombu in a large saucepan and cover generously with
    water. Cover and bring to a boil. Boil 10 minutes, then skim and lower the heat
    to very low (use a heat diffuser if you have one). Simmer, covered, 1 to 1¼ hours
    until the beans are soft enough to mash against the side of the pan. Strain, discard
    the kombu, and reserve the cooking liquid.
2   Put the beans, sugar, and 2¼ cups of the reserved cooking liquid in a bowl and stir
    until the sugar dissolves. Blend until smooth, then work the mixture through
    a strainer into a bowl, rubbing back and forth with a spoon and scraping the bottom
    of the strainer. Slowly stir in enough of the reserved cooking liquid to achieve the
    preferred consistency. Set the rest of the cooking liquid aside. Leave the soup
    to cool completely, then cover and chill at least 2 hours.
3   About 5 minutes before serving, remove the sorbet from the freezer. When ready
    to serve, stir a little of the reserved liquid into the soup if it is too thick and adjust
    the sugar, if necessary. Divide into bowls, put one scoop of sorbet in each one and
    serve immediately, sprinkled with orange zest and cinnamon.

365 Watermelon & Strawberry Soup

PREPARATION TIME 20 minutes, plus making the stock, cooling, and at least
2 hours chilling   COOKING TIME 15 minutes

½ tablespoon sunflower oil
½ onion, chopped
10 ounces strawberries, hulled and
   coarsely chopped
½ cup Vegetable Stock (see page 12)
   or ready-made stock
a pinch of salt, or to taste

3 pounds watermelon, rind removed,
   seeded, and chopped
½ tablespoon orange juice,
   or to taste (optional)
feta cheese, crumbled, to serve
very thinly shredded mint leaves,
   to serve

1   Heat the oil in a saucepan over medium heat. Add the onion and fry, stirring,
    3 to 5 minutes until softened but not colored. Add the strawberries, stock, and salt
    and bring to a boil, then lower the heat and simmer 3 to 4 minutes, stirring, until
    the strawberries are soft. Remove from the heat and stir in the watermelon and the
    orange juice if the berries aren't at the height of their summer flavor.
2   Blend the soup until smooth, then work it through a strainer into a bowl, rubbing
    back and forth with a spoon and scraping the bottom of the strainer. Let cool
    completely, then cover and chill at least 2 hours.
3   When ready to serve, stir well. Adjust the salt and add extra orange juice,
    if necessary. Serve sprinkled with feta cheese and mint leaves.

Index

almonds
  Spanish white garlic & almond soup
    198
  alphabet soup 143
anchovies
  broccoli, orecchiette & anchovy
    soup 138
  whiting & anchovy soup 126
apples
  beet & apple soup 21
  fennel & apple soup 195
  spiced pumpkin & apple soup 58
  split pea & apple soup 158
arame & tofu soup 47
artichoke soup with red pepper swirl 18
asparagus
  asparagus and pea soup 21
  crab & asparagus soup 116
arugula
  arugula soup with smoked salmon
    209
  red rice & wild arugula soup 157
  zucchini & arugula soup with croutes
    54
avocados
  avocado & coconut soup 206
  Mexican poultry & avocado broth 107
  raw emerald soup with crushed basil
    oil 204

bacon
  bacon & corn soup 78
  lima bean soup with carrots & bacon
    149
  onion, tomato & chicken soup 110
barley
  chicken & barley soup 104
  creamed barley soup 164
  game & barley broth 84
  hearty barley & mushroom soup 166
  oxtail soup with barley 85
basil
  edamame & pea soup with crushed
    basil oil 203
  mussel & basil soup 127
  raw emerald soup with crushed basil
    oil 204
  zucchini & basil soup 197
beans. See also edamame beans
  adzuki bean soup with orange sorbet
    213
  Basque-style cabbage & bean soup 23
  black-eye pea & rice soup 144
  borlotti bean & fennel soup 144
  corn & bean broth 59
  country-style bean & vegetable
    soup 146
  Cuban black bean soup 143
  fava bean & spinach soup 150
  fragrant mung bean soup 168
  green & white bean soup 148
  halloween soup 145
  Italian doctor's bean & spaghetti
    soup 151
  lamb shank & lima bean soup 178
  lima bean soup with carrots & bacon
    149
  Mexican bean soup 153
  Nicola's bean & onion soup 146
  pureed kidney bean soup 150
  roast lamb & bean soup 75
  sausage, fennel & bean soup 82
  slow-cooked pork & bean soup 174
  smoky mixed bean & sausage soup
    175
  spelt & pinto bean soup 167
  Thai green curry chicken & bean
    soup 101
  Tuscan "twice-cooked" vegetable &
    bean soup 173
  two-bean soup 19
  winter bean & mushroom soup 147
beef
  beef & bulgur wheat soup 66
  beef & celery root soup 66
  beef & coconut soup with pea
    eggplants 67
  beef & tomato soup 178
  beef & vegetable hotpot 177
  beef & wild rice soup 69
  beef consommé 13
  beef consommé with porcini
    mushrooms 67
  beef soup with mushrooms & peas 65
  beef stock 10
  Chinese beef & greens soup 67
  curried beef & potato soup 62
  hearty beef & stout soup 63
  Mrs. Schultz's beef & vegetable
    soup 68
  quick Tex-Mex chili soup 62
  stuffed-pepper-in-a-bowl soup 62

Thai beef & cabbage soup 65
Vietnamese beef & noodle soup 176
beets
  beet & apple soup 21
  beet soup 196
  borscht 179
  vegetarian borscht 21
Belgian endive
  ham & cheese Belgian endive soup 80
bok choy
  Chinese beef & greens soup 67
bouillabaisse 188
Brazilian fish soup 123
bread
  breakfast tea soup 56
  Italian bread & tomato soup 32
  thick cabbage & bread soup 24
broccoli
  broccoli & parsley soup 22
  broccoli & spinach soup 23
  broccoli, orecchiette & anchovy
    soup 138
  chicken & purple broccoli soup 99
  quinoa soup with tomatoes & broccoli
    167
  rice & purple broccoli soup 160
Brussels sprouts
  creamy Brussels sprouts soup 23
buckwheat
  buckwheat & vegetable soup 168
  kasha & tomato soup 168
Buddha's delight 183
bulgur wheat
  beef & bulgur wheat soup 66
  mixed grain & lentil soup 161
buttermilk
  peach & orange buttermilk soup 209
  sweet buttermilk dessert soup 210
butternut squash
  butternut squash & chestnut soup 56
  curried lamb & squash soup 74
  Persian lentil & squash soup 149
  roasted squash & tomato soup 57

cabbage
  Basque-style cabbage & bean soup 23
  cabbage & sauerkraut soup 24
  cabbage soup 132
  Danish cabbage & meatball soup 186
  Portuguese caldo verde 79
  shiitake & Chinese cabbage soup 46
  smoked sausage & red cabbage
    soup 81
  Thai beef & cabbage soup 65
  thick cabbage & sour bread soup 24
Caribbean callaloo 129
Carl's mulligatawny soup 173
carrots
  Bloody Mary party soup 202
  carrot & cilantro soup 27
  carrot & orange soup 196
  carrot & parsnip soup 25
  carrot & roasted pepper soup 25
  fresh red detox soup 204
  golden carrot & sesame soup 26
  lima bean soup with carrots & bacon
    149
  oat soup with carrot & rutabaga 147
  Parmesan broth with peas & carrots
    25
cauliflower
  black lentil & cauliflower soup 160
  cauliflower & cheese soup 27
  curried cauliflower & potato soup 28
  roasted cauliflower & pepper soup 28
cavolo nero
  very garlicky pasta & cavolo nero
    soup 143
celery root
  beef & celery root soup 66
  celery root & pear soup 28
  celery & celery root soup 33
  fennel & celery root soup 30
celery
  celery & celery root soup 33
  smoked ham & celery chowder 81
cheese
  cauliflower & cheese soup 27
  ham & cheese chicory soup 80
  Parmesan broth with peas & carrots
    25
  pea green soup with ham & blue
    cheese 80
  Welsh leek & parsley soup with
    rarebit "soldiers" 48
  zucchini & dolcelatte soup 31
cherries
  Hungarian cherry soup 212
chestnuts
  butternut squash & chestnut soup 56
  chorizo & chestnut chowder 80
  rich orange-scented chestnut soup 49

venison & chestnut soup 82
chicken
  African-style chicken & vegetable
    soup 94
  chicken & Asian mushroom soup 101
  chicken & barley soup 104
  chicken & chickpea soup 93
  chicken & chickpea tagine soup 180
  chicken & corn soup 100
  chicken & leek broth 107
  chicken & parsley dumpling soup 106
  chicken & pumpkin broth 99
  chicken & purple broccoli soup 99
  chicken & spring vegetable soup 101
  chicken & vegetable chowder 181
  chicken, fennel & saffron soup 89
  chicken gumbo soup 174
  chicken, leek & pancetta risotto
    soup 187
  chicken, leek & tarragon soup 99
  chicken liver & sweet onion soup 105
  chicken mulligatawny soup 103
  chicken noodle soup 88
  chicken, pepper & rice soup 94
  chicken soup with matzo balls 89
  chicken stock 11
  chicken-udon hotpot 185
  Chinese chicken noodle soup 183
  Colombian chicken & corn soup 102
  cream of chicken soup with tarragon
    & lemon 98
  creamy chicken & mushroom soup 96
  curried chicken & tomato soup 92
  curried chicken soup 195
  hot, hot, hot Caribbean chicken
    soup 182
  Indonesian chicken & noodle soup
    180
  Iraqi chicken, lentil & rice soup 186
  Japanese-style curried chicken
    soup 91
  Malay-style chicken soup 91
  Mexican chicken noodle soup 88
  Mexican poultry & avocado broth 107
  Mexican-style chicken soup 93
  Middle Eastern-spiced chicken & rice
    soup 96
  Peruvian "breakfast" soup—for any
    time of the day 191
  Provençal-style chicken soup 92
  rich chicken stock 10
  roast chicken soup 104
  Scottish cock-a-leekie 90
  Sunday night chicken & ham soup 102
  sweet-and-sour chicken soup 97
  Thai chicken & jasmine rice soup 156
  Thai green curry chicken & bean
    soup 101
  Thai red curry chicken soup 95
  "velvet" chicken & edamame soup 97
  zucchini & pea chicken soup 102
chickpeas
  chicken & chickpea soup 93
  chicken & chickpea tagine soup 180
  chickpea & chorizo soup 151
  chickpea & pasta soup 138
  North African lamb & chickpea soup
    184
  spiced lamb & chickpea soup 72
  spicy vegetable soup with couscous
    185
  Turkish chickpea soup 166
  yogurt soup with chickpea dumplings
    184
chili
  creamy peanut & chili soup 49
  green cucumber & chili soup 204
  mackerel in chili-lime broth 119
  Tex-Mex chili soup 62
  white chili soup 147
chorizo
  chickpea & chorizo soup 151
  chorizo & chestnut chowder 80
cilantro
  carrot & cilantro soup 27
  tilapia & cilantro soup 134
  yogurt & cilantro soup 58
clams
  Manhattan clam chowder 114
  New England clam chowder 114
coconut
  avocado & coconut soup 206
  beef & coconut soup with pea
    eggplants 67
  curried spinach & coconut soup 54
  green tea soup with coconut jelly 211
  mushroom & coconut soup 46
  red lentil, coconut & spinach soup 153
  Thai meatball & coconut soup 77
consommé & vegetable soup 194
corn
  bacon & corn soup 78

chicken & corn soup 100
Colombian chicken & corn soup 102
corn & bean broth 59
cream of corn soup 51
Mexican corn & pepper soup 206
okra & corn soup 50
plantain & corn soup 49
couscous
  cardamom-scented lamb soup with
    couscous 74
  Moroccan vegetable & couscous
    soup 165
  spicy vegetable soup with couscous
    185
crab
  Caribbean callaloo 129
  crab & asparagus soup 116
  rich crab soup with dill croutons 117
  spicy tomato & crab soup 115
croutes 14
croutons 14
cucumber
  cucumber & yogurt soup with mint
    199
  fresh red detox soup 204
  green cucumber & chili soup 204
  jeweled cucumber & walnut soup
    207
  Lebanese cucumber soup 208
  no-cook cucumber & horseradish
    soup 199

dashi 12
duck
  duck in ginger broth 110
  Jerusalem artichoke soup with duck
    confit 111
  Thai duck soup with noodles 175

edamame beans
  edamame & mushroom soup 43
  edamame & pea soup with crushed
    basil oil 203
  edamame & pumpkin soup with
    jasmine rice 190
  "velvet" chicken & edamame soup 97
eel
  smoked eel & kale soup 115
eggplants
  beef & coconut soup with pea
    eggplants 67
  eggplant & mushroom soup 19
  Egyptian eggplant & tomato soup 20
eggs
  Chinese egg-drop soup 105
  egg butterballs 55
  Greek lemon & egg soup with orzo
    105
  roasted pepper, garlic & egg soup 106
  Roman egg soup 107

fall farmers' market soup 35
fava bean & spinach soup 150
fennel
  borlotti bean & fennel soup 144
  chicken, fennel & saffron soup 89
  fennel & apple soup 195
  fennel & celery root soup 30
  fennel & red pepper soups 205
  mackerel & fennel soup 119
  Mediterranean fennel soup 29
  Puy lentil & fennel soup 155
  sausage, fennel & bean soup 82
finishing touches 15
fish stock 11

game & barley broth 84
garlic
  forager's nettle & wild garlic soup 48
  goji berry & garlic flu buster 108
  Greek lentil & garlic soup 161
  roasted garlic & tomato soup 40
  roasted pepper, garlic & egg soup 106
  soothing lemon thyme & garlic
    broth 104
  Spanish white garlic & almond soup
    198
  Swiss chard & garlic broth 58
  very garlicky pasta & cavolo nero
    soup 143
gazpacho 200
German liver dumpling soup 83
goji berry & garlic flu buster 108
green tea noodle soup 139
green tea soup with coconut jelly 211

haddock
  haddock chowder with spinach 122
  North Sea haddock & pea soup 124
  Scottish cullen skink 118
  smoked haddock & sweet potato
    chowder 118

haggis soup 83
hake & mixed herb soup 123
halibut
  spiced halibut & sweet potato soup
    135
ham
  ham & cheese chicory soup 80
  ham & pepper soup 78
  pea green soup with ham & blue
    cheese 80
  smoked ham & celery chowder 81
  split pea & ham soup 159
  Sunday night chicken & ham soup 102
hoki soup with pesto 125

Italian wedding soup 172

Jerusalem artichoke soup with duck
  confit 111

kale
  curried potato & kale soup 39
  lamb meatball & kale soup 73
  Portuguese caldo verde 79
  smoked eel & kale soup 115

lamb
  cardamom-scented lamb soup with
    couscous 74
  curried lamb & squash soup 74
  lamb meatball & kale soup 73
  lamb shank & lima bean soup 178
  lamb vindaloo soup 71
  North African lamb & chickpea soup
    184
  roast lamb & bean soup 75
  Scotch broth 71
  spiced lamb & chickpea soup 72
  spring lamb soup 73
  Syrian red lentil & lamb soup 152
  Welsh mountain lamb & leek soup 70
  winter lamb & onion soup 72
leeks
  chicken & leek broth 107
  chicken, leek & pancetta risotto
    soup 187
  chicken, leek & tarragon soup 99
  leek & sweet potato soup 38
  Scottish cock-a-leekie 90
  Vichyssoise 194
  Welsh leek & parsley soup with
    rarebit "soldiers" 48
  Welsh mountain lamb & leek soup 70
legumes 8
lemons
  cream of chicken soup with tarragon
    & lemon 98
  Greek lemon & egg soup with orzo
    105
  lemon & saffron soup 208
lentils
  black lentil & cauliflower soup 160
  brown lentil soup 158
  Egyptian brown lentil & greens
    soup 161
  Greek lentil & garlic soup 161
  Iraqi chicken, lentil & rice soup 186
  lentil & sausage soup 156
  mixed grain & red lentil soup 161
  Persian lentil & squash soup 149
  Puy lentil & fennel soup 155
  red lentil, coconut & spinach soup 153
  roast pheasant & lentil soup 84
  rosemary-scented pea & lentil
    soup 59
  sour green lentil soup 155
  South Indian lentil & tomato soup 154
  Syrian red lentil & lamb soup 152
  yellow lentil soup 154

mackerel
  mackerel & fennel soup 119
  mackerel & shiitake miso soup 125
  mackerel in chili-lime broth 119
Mediterranean minestrone 142
melon
  cantaloupe "gazpacho" 213
  refreshing honeydew melon soup 210
miso
  mackerel & shiitake miso soup 125 203
  mushroom miso soup 44 52
  wakame miso soup 44 52
monkfish
  golden monkfish soup 128
mung beans
  spinach & mung bean soup 54
mushrooms
  beef consommé with porcini
    mushrooms 67
  beef soup with mushrooms & peas 65
  cream of mushroom soup 45
  chicken & Asian mushroom soup 101

creamy chicken & mushroom soup 96
edamame & mushroom soup 43
eggplant & mushroom soup 19
hearty barley & mushroom soup 166
mackerel & shiitake miso soup 125
mixed mushroom broth 46
mushroom & coconut soup 46
mushroom & millet soup 165
mushroom miso soup 44
pork, mushroom & snow pea soup 76
pork, mushroom & tofu soup 76
shiitake & Chinese cabbage soup 46
wild mushroom & toasted spelt
  soup 169
wild mushroom risotto soup 163
wild rice & mushroom soup 162
winter bean & mushroom soup 147
mussels
  mussel & basil soup 127
  saffron-scented mussel soup 127

nettles
  forager's nettle & wild garlic soup 48
New England seafood chowder 121
noodles
  buckwheat noodle soup with nori 141
  chicken-udon hotpot 185
  Chinese chicken noodle soup 183
  green tea noodle soup 139
  hot & sour pork soup with noodles
    177
  Indonesian chicken & noodle soup
    180
  teriyaki salmon ramen 187
  Thai duck soup with noodles 175
  vegetable jungle curry with noodles
    189
  Vietnamese beef & noodle soup 176

oat soup with carrot & rutabaga 147
okra & corn soup 50
onions
  chicken liver & sweet onion soup 105
  French onion soup 64
  Nicola's bean & onion soup 146
  onion & mustard soup 51
  onion, tomato & chicken soup 110
  winter lamb & onion soup 72
oranges
  adzuki bean soup with orange sorbet
    213
  carrot & orange soup 196
  iced tomato & orange soup with goat
    milk yogurt sorbet 201
  parsnip & orange soup 52
  peach & orange buttermilk soup 209
  rich orange-scented chestnut soup 49
  rich pepper & orange soup 53
  slow-cooked tomato & orange
    soup 40
  strawberry soup with orange sorbet
    210
orzo
  Greek lemon & egg soup with orzo
    105
  orzo primavera soup 140
  shrimp & orzo soup 130
  turkey & orzo soup 109
osso buco soup with gremolata 69
oxtail soup with barley 85
oysters
  Irish oyster soup 129
  oyster & salmon soup 130

pancetta
  chicken, leek & pancetta risotto
    soup 187
parsley
  broccoli & parsley soup 22
  chicken & parsley dumpling soup 106
  parsley dumplings 13
  Welsh leek & parsley soup with
    rarebit "soldiers" 48
parsnips
  carrot & parsnip soup 25
  curried parsnip soup 52
  parsnip & orange soup 52
pasta. See also Orzo
  alphabet pasta 143
  broccoli, orecchiette & anchovy
    soup 138
  chickpea & pasta soup 138
  Italian doctor's bean & spaghetti
    soup 151
  Italian tortellini soup 149
  pasta & potato soup 141
  starry night soup with spinach 155
  very garlicky pasta & cavolo nero
    soup 143
peach & orange buttermilk soup 209
peanuts
  creamy peanut & chili soup 49

peas
  Annie's herbed peas-in-a-pod soup 18
  asparagus and pea soup 21
  beef soup with mushrooms & peas 65
  Canadian yellow pea soup 158
  edamame & pea soup with crushed
    basil oil 203
  minted pea soup 203
  North Sea haddock & pea soup 124
  Parmesan broth with peas & carrots
    25
  pea green soup with ham & blue
    cheese 80
  rosemary-scented pea & lentil
    soup 59
  split pea & apple soup 158
  split pea & ham soup 159
  Venetian rice & pea soup 163
  zucchini & pea chicken soup 102
peppers
  carrot & roasted pepper soup 25
  chargrilled pepper & sun-dried tomato
    soup 42
  chargrilled yellow pepper soup 198
  chicken, pepper & rice soup 94
  fennel & red pepper soups 205
  ham & pepper soup 78
  Mexican corn & pepper soup 206
  red-hot pepper soup 52
  rich pepper & orange soup 53
  roasted cauliflower & pepper soup 28
  roasted pepper, garlic & egg soup 106
  stuffed-pepper-in-a-bowl soup 62
Peruvian "breakfast" soup—for any
  time of the day 191
pheasant
  roast pheasant & lentil soup 84
plantain & corn soup 49
pollock quenelle soup 126
pork
  Bangkok pork & shrimp soup 77
  hot & sour pork soup with noodles
    177
  pork, mushroom & snow pea soup
    76
  pork, mushroom & tofu soup 76
  slow-cooked pork & bean soup 174
  Thai meatball & coconut soup 77
Portuguese caldo verde 79
posole 191
potatoes
  Amish potato soup with rivvels 59
  curried beef & potato soup 62
  curried cauliflower & potato soup 28
  curried potato & kale soup 39
  pasta & potato soup 141
  Portuguese caldo verde 79
  potato & mixed vegetable soup 39
  Scottish cullen skink 118
  Vichyssoise 194
pumpkin
  chicken & pumpkin broth 99
  edamame & pumpkin soup with
    jasmine rice 190
  spiced pumpkin & apple soup 58
  Thai-style pumpkin soup 56
  pumpkin seed pesto 33
pureeing and sieving soups 6

quinoa
  quinoa soup with tomatoes & broccoli
    167
  winter vegetable soup with quinoa
    188

red mullet
  Aegean red mullet soup 120
red wine soup 63
rice
  beef & wild rice soup 69
  black-eye pea & rice soup 144
  chicken, leek & pancetta risotto
    soup 187
  chicken, pepper & rice soup 94
  edamame & pumpkin soup with
    jasmine rice 190
  Iraqi chicken, lentil & rice soup 186
  Middle Eastern-spiced chicken & rice
    soup 96
  red rice & wild arugula soup 157
  rice & zucchini soup 162
  rice & purple broccoli soup 160
  Thai chicken & jasmine rice soup 156
  turkey & rice soup 109
  turkey meatball & rice soup 109
  Venetian rice & pea soup 163
  wild mushroom risotto soup 163
  wild rice & mushroom soup 162
rouille 14
rutabagas
  oat soup with carrot & rutabaga 147

salmon
  arugula soup with smoked salmon
    209

Japanese salmon hotpot 181
oyster & salmon soup 130
Scandinavian salmon & shrimp soup
  135
Scottish poached salmon & cabbage
  soup 132
teriyaki salmon ramen 187
salt cod soup 115
sauerkraut
  cabbage & sauerkraut soup 24
sausages
  lentil & sausage soup 156
  sausage, fennel & bean soup 82
  smoked sausage & red cabbage
    soup 81
  smoky mixed bean & sausage soup
    175
scallops
  elegant Japanese scallop soup 134
  lightly spiced scallop & spinach
    soup 134
  Vietnamese-style scallop & shrimp
    soup 132
Scotch broth 71
shellfish chowder with herbs 117
shrimp
  Bangkok pork & shrimp soup 77
  shrimp & orzo soup 130
  shrimp ball soup 131
  shrimp bisque 122
  shrimp laksa 189
  Scandinavian salmon & shrimp
    soup 135
  Thai hot-and-sour soup with shrimp
    132
  Vietnamese-style scallop & shrimp
    soup 132
soupe de poissons 121
spelt
  spelt & pinto bean soup 167
  wild mushroom & toasted spelt
    soup 169
spiced fruit salad soup 209
spicy vegetable soup with couscous
  185
spinach
  broccoli & spinach soup 23
  curried spinach & coconut soup 54
  fava bean & spinach soup 150
  haddock chowder with spinach 122
  lightly spiced scallop & spinach
    soup 134
  raw emerald soup with crushed basil
    oil 204
  red lentil, coconut & spinach soup
    153
  spinach & buttermilk soup 53
  spinach & mung bean soup 54
  spring spinach & sorrel soup with egg
    butterballs 55
  starry night soup with spinach 155
spring farmers' market soup 36
squid
  hot-and-sour squid soup 129
stock 7–8
  beef stock 10
  chicken stock 11
  dashi 12
  fish stock 11
  game stock 11
  rich chicken stock 10
  turkey stock 11
  vegetable stock 12
  vegetarian dashi 12
strawberries
  strawberry soup with orange sorbet
    210
  watermelon & strawberry soup 213
summer farmers' market soup 35
sunshine winter soup 34
sweet potatoes
  leek & sweet potato soup 38
  smoked haddock & sweet potato
    chowder 118
  spiced halibut & sweet potato soup
    135
  twice-cooked sweet potato soup 37
Swiss chard & garlic broth 58
swordfish
  Mediterranean swordfish soup 125

tarragon
  chicken, leek & tarragon soup 99
  cream of chicken soup with tarragon
    & lemon 98
Thai wonton soup 139
thyme
  tomato & thyme soup with polenta
    dumplings 41
tilapia & cilantro soup 134
tofu
  arame & tofu soup 47
  hot & sour vegetable soup with
    tofu 44
  pork, mushroom & tofu soup 76

tomatoes
  beef & tomato soup 178
  big red raw soup 201
  Bloody Mary party soup 202
  chargrilled pepper & sun-dried tomato
    soup 42
  cherry tomato & consommé soup 194
  chilled tomato & yogurt soup 200
  curried chicken & tomato soup 92
  Egyptian eggplant & tomato soup 20
  hot tomato & yogurt soup 43
  iced tomato & orange soup with goat
    milk yogurt sorbet 201
  Italian bread & tomato soup 32
  kasha & tomato soup 168
  onion, tomato & chicken soup 110
  quinoa soup with tomatoes & broccoli
    167
  roasted garlic & tomato soup 40
  roasted squash & tomato soup 57
  slow-cooked tomato & orange
    soup 40
  South Indian lentil & tomato soup 154
  spicy tomato & crab soup 115
  summer tomato soup with noodles 42
  tomato & thyme soup with polenta
    dumplings 41
  yellow tomato soup 199
trout
  cream of smoked trout soup 133
tuna escabeche soup 128
turkey
  Mexican poultry & avocado broth 107
  turkey & orzo soup 109   177
  turkey & rice soup 109   177
  turkey meatball & rice soup 109 177
Tuscan "cooked water" soup 45

veal
  Danish cabbage & meatball soup 186
  Italian wedding soup 172
  osso buco soup with gremolata 69
vegetable soups
  buckwheat & vegetable soup 168
  fall farmers' market soup 35
  gazpacho 200
  hot & sour vegetable soup with
    tofu 44
  Moroccan vegetable & couscous
    soup 165
  no-fat vegetable pot 39
  potato & mixed vegetable soup 39
  roasted Mediterranean vegetable
    soup 30
  Scandinavian vegetable soup 32
  spring farmers' market soup 36
  summer farmers' market soup 35
  sunshine winter soup 34
  Tuscan 'cooked water' soup 45
  Tuscan 'twice-cooked' vegetable &
    bean soup 173
  vegetable "spaghetti" soup 27
  vegetable chowder 31
  vegetable jungle curry with noodles
    189
  winter farmers' market soup 36
  winter potage 33
  winter vegetable soup with quinoa
    188
vegetable stock 12
venison & chestnut soup 82
Vichyssoise 194

wakame miso soup 44
walnuts
  jeweled cucumber & walnut soup 207
watercress soup 53
watermelon & strawberry soup 213
white fish soup 119
whiting & anchovy soup 126
winter farmers' market soup 36
winter minestrone 142
winter potage 33

yogurt
  chilled tomato & yogurt soup 200
  cucumber & yogurt soup with mint
    199
  Gujarati yogurt soup 37
  hot tomato & yogurt soup 43
  iced tomato & orange soup with goat
    milk yogurt sorbet 201
  yogurt & cilantro soup 58
  yogurt soup with chickpea dumplings
    184

zucchini
  zucchini & basil soup 197
  zucchini & Dolcelatte soup 31
  zucchini & arugula soup with croutes
    54
  creamy zucchini soup 196
  curried zucchini soup 197
  rice & zucchini soup 162
  zucchini & pea chicken soup 102